AMERICAN WAYS

A Brief History of American Cultures

AMERICAN
WAYS

■

A Brief History of American Cultures

BENJAMIN G. RADER

University of Nebraska at Lincoln

HARCOURT COLLEGE PUBLISHERS

Fort Worth   Philadelphia   San Diego   New York   Orlando   Austin   San Antonio
Toronto   Montreal   London   Sydney   Tokyo

PUBLISHER	Earl McPeek
EXECUTIVE EDITOR	David Tatom
MARKET STRATEGIST	Steve Drummond
PROJECT EDITOR	Elizabeth Cruce Alvarez
ART DIRECTOR	David A. Day
PRODUCTION MANAGER	Christopher Wilkins

Cover images by PhotoDisc®

ISBN: 0-15-503689-0

Library of Congress Catalog Card Number: 00-102488

Address for Domestic Orders: Harcourt College Publishers, 6277 Sea Harbor Drive, Orlando, FL 32887-6777. 800-782-4479

Address for International Orders: International Customer Service, Harcourt, Inc., 6277 Sea Harbor Drive, Orlando, FL 32887-6777. 407-345-3800. (fax) 407-345-4060. (e-mail) hbintl@harcourtbrace.com

Address for Editorial Correspondence: Harcourt College Publishers, 301 Commerce Street, Suite 3700, Fort Worth, TX 76102.

Web Site Address: http://www.harcourtcollege.com

Printed in the United States of America

0 1 2 3 4 5 6 7 8 9 066 9 8 7 6 5 4 3 2 1

Harcourt College Publishers

INTRODUCTION

In the older neighborhoods of countless American towns and cities today, one can observe refurbished gingerbread houses with turrets, cupolas, and extended verandas. Built in the nineteenth or early twentieth centuries, these houses serve as vivid monuments of a past age. They convey to our time a message of white, Protestant, middle-class respectability; of stern, bearded fathers; of sweet, caring mothers; of obedient, well-mannered children; of the saying of grace before meals; of sumptuous Sunday family dinners; and, above all else, of familiar routines. It was these routines, recalled Henry Seidel Canby when describing his family life in the Wilmington, Delaware, of the 1890s, "that inspired confidence in a patterned universe," a confidence that Canby found sorely wanting in the twentieth century.

It is the ways of the American past, such as those represented by the middle-class Victorian families in their gingerbread houses, that are the subject of *American Ways: A Brief History of American Cultures*. Rather than recounting the horrors and heroics of wars, pivotal presidential elections, or stunning technological breakthroughs, this book looks beneath the surface of American history. It examines those fundamental customs, beliefs, values, and practices that are, or have been, characteristic of Americans or of various groups of Americans. In particular, *American Ways* looks at religious, social (including class, gender, race, and ethnicity), family, work, and leisure ways. Frequently such ways are related to one another. Together, they comprise what may be described as a culture.

The recurring tensions between the individual, with her or his interests on the one side, and community, with ties and obligations that exist beyond the self on the other, constitute the major theme of this book. While individualism has long been at the very core of American culture, it always has been caged in by widely agreed-upon constraints. For example, the founders of the republic loudly proclaimed the principles of individual freedom, but at the same time they insisted that a virtuous citizenry—a citizenry that exercised self-restraint—was essential to the new republic's survival. Similarly, each of the nation's major religious communities defended individual freedom, but they invariably justified such freedom only within the limits imposed by obligations to God, the community, and a divinely ordained system of personal morality. Hence, the pursuit of material welfare, for example, never exempted an individual from obeying the Ten Commandments. In addition, the unequal rights and obligations embedded in the nation's social ways long limited the individual freedom of women, African Americans, Native Americans, and working-class people.

The growing acceptance of modern ways in the nineteenth and twentieth centuries weakened each of these traditional constraints on the individual. Cultural pluralism challenged the inequalities built into the nation's social ways, secularization eroded support for religion as a source of transcendental moral authority, and a consumer-centered economy encouraged Americans to abandon the middle-class Victorian emphasis on self-control. The 1960s revolution in rights and the dismissal of many forms of traditional cultural authority, when combined with the continuing imperatives of consumer capitalism, gave even freer reign to the individual. Americans increasingly came to identify individualism with individuality, or what was said to be the expression of one's authentic, inner self.

American Ways also explores the historical relationships of American ways to political, social, and economic forces. For example, the War for Independence and the Industrial Revolution triggered significant departures from traditional ways. In turn, the adoption of new ways affected social, economic, and political history. For example, the ethos of self-control adopted by the middle class in the nineteenth century helped to create a more efficient workforce, one that expedited industrialization, while the spirit of self-fulfillment in the twentieth century encouraged the development of a mass-consumption society.

In addition, this book represents one way—certainly not the only one— of generalizing about the history of American cultures. It begins with a prologue that examines the Ways of the First Americans. It then proceeds to The Regional Ways of Early America, The Ways of the New Republic, Middle-Class Ways, and finishes with Modern Ways.

While there were at least a dozen identifiable regional cultures in early American history, The Regional Ways of Early America focuses on the striking contrasts between the North and the South. Central to Northern ways was religion. In the North, both the Puritan New Englanders and the Delaware Valley Quakers sought to build special religious communities. In the more secular South, the life of the Tidewater planters revolved around hierarchical ways. African slaves, those at the bottom of the hierarchical pyramid, built a culture of their own. And away from the Tidewater, in the vast backcountry, settlers from mostly North Britain established a third major variant of Southern culture. Aspects of these regional ways persist to a striking degree to this day. For example, Southerners and New Englanders are likely to take decidedly different positions on women's rights, gun control, and capital punishment.

As the title of part two suggests, The Ways of the New Republic shifts from a regional to a national focus. During the Revolutionary era of the late eighteenth and early nineteenth centuries, Americans took the first giant steps toward replacing the hierarchical ways of monarchy with the more egalitarian ways of a republic. They sought to create a community comprised of an unselfish citizenry who would choose as their leaders those with superior morality and talents. But their dreams for the most part went unrealized. The idea of equality enunciated in the Declaration of Independence and the flinging open of the doors of economic opportunity for ordinary white men led instead to the United States becoming a white man's democracy and a people especially dedicated to commerce and to personal gain. To the utter astonishment of the nation's deistically inclined founders, the United States also became the world's foremost example of an evangelical republic.

These developments helped to usher in the supremacy of another set of ways, Middle-Class Ways (sometimes also described as Victorian or bourgeois). Mostly Protestant in faith, materially ambitious, and concerned with the consequences flowing from the destruction of traditional social ties, the middle class gave special attention to self-control. In constructing its own set of ways, the middle class even emptied the other groups of some of their vitality. By appropriating from the working class the value of work, from the aristocracy the value of genteel refinement, and from evangelical Protestants the value of personal morality and high moral purpose, the middle class claimed (and to a substantial extent gained) the cultural leadership of the entire nation. Yet, as powerful as middle-class culture was, it never achieved a complete hegemony over American life. In the nineteenth century and beyond, the great regional chasm between North and South remained in place, race continued to divide Americans, and the Industrial Revolution widened the cleavage between middle- and working-class cultures. Finally, the arrival of millions of immigrants from Europe, Canada, Mexico, and Asia added yet another challenge to middle-class cultural supremacy.

The fifth and final set of ways, Modern Ways, refers to a culture with which we are familiar today. Beginning in the late nineteenth century and continuing through the twentieth century, large numbers of Americans retreated from the Victorian ways of the nineteenth century. The rise of an economy revolving around mass consumption and leisure encouraged greater self-indulgence and secular (nonreligious) values, even within the ranks of the middle class itself. But not without conflict. Many Americans clung to the older ways, and even those who most fully embraced modern ways experienced agonizing doubts. Throughout much of the twentieth century, adherents of modern ways have clashed with supporters of older ways. Furthermore, a new tide of immigrants in the last four decades of the twentieth century added to the nation's cultural diversity.

These are in brief the major sets of ways examined in this book. The divisions between them are not meant to be hard and fast. To this day, aspects of earlier cultures obviously remain important. Strong echoes of earlier cultures may still be heard in the nation's speech dialects, in its regional patterns of life, in its political behavior, in its religious practices, and even in its family life. Furthermore, each of the cultures was evolutionary rather than discrete, each enveloped and expanded upon earlier ones. Hence, the beginning of one culture closely resembled the end of the preceding one. Indeed, a central point of this book is that the legacy of earlier ways remains a key determinant of our ways today. It is for this reason that many modern Americans find comfort in viewing and living in the Victorian houses that still stand in our midst. They recognize, even if only half-consciously, what Abraham Lincoln once described so eloquently as the "mystic chords of memory."

A Brief Note to the Reader

This book has been shaped by my conviction that there is a special need for a work presenting the broad outlines of the history of American ways. Knowledge of this history is, I believe, essential to understanding more fully the world about us. It will assist you, the reader, in comprehending what you read in the serious press, what you encounter in major literary and scientific texts, what you see in museums, and what you see and hear on television. In short, by reading this book, you will gain a familiarity with the key cultural paradigms that shape much of the discourse in contemporary life.

To achieve this aim, *American Ways* seeks to provide a coherent narrative of the major changes and continuities in the history of American culture. Coherence arises principally from a focus on the tension between the contradictory impulses toward individualism and toward community that run throughout the course of American history. *American Ways* may also be thought of as a road map. You will not find here a discussion of every road, only the major highways into the American past. Without such a guide, none of us can travel far in our quest for understanding what the past has to teach us.

Acknowledgments

Direct contributions to the completion of this book came from a wide variety of sources. In particular, the questions, papers, and comments of literally dozens of students helped to form the contents and organization of this book. From the outset, Drake Bush offered invaluable direction and support. For their substantial contributions to rendering the manuscript into final shape, my thanks go to executive editor David Tatom, photo researcher Judy Mason, project editor Elizabeth Alvarez, copy editor Steven B. Baker, art director David A. Day, and production manager Christopher Wilkins. Reviewers Robert Becker, Louisiana State University; Bruce J. Dierenfield, Canisius College; Van Beck Hall, University of Pittsburgh; and Elizabeth Van Beek, San Jose State University, read and proffered advice on one or more chapters, as did Jessica Coope, Heather Furnas, Thomas Jundt, Wendy Katz, Dane Kennedy, Timothy Mahoney, Christin Mamiya, Susan Miller, Charlene Porsild, Kenneth Winkle, and Sharon Wood. Most (though not all) of their suggestions have found their way into the final draft. Several of these individuals are also associated with the Nineteenth Century Studies Group of the University of Nebraska–Lincoln, an interdisciplinary scholarly community that provided me with warm encouragement and intellectual stimulation. A Faculty Development Leave awarded by the University of Nebraska in the spring semester of 1998 allowed me to devote my full time to writing. Few if any librarians equal the skill and helpfulness of Gretchen Holten Poppler; I am once again in her debt. Anne Rader, Ken Gatter, Alex Gatter, Steve Rader, Lisa Rader, and Ariella Rader extended the kind of support that can come only from one's family. And words are inadequate to describe the contributions of Barbara Koch Rader, not only to this book but to my life more generally.

CONTENTS

AMERICAN WAYS

A Brief History of American Cultures

PROLOGUE—
THE WAYS OF THE FIRST AMERICANS

The Western Hemisphere has long been a land of multiple cultures. While there is no evidence of the existence in either South or North America of pre-human hominids, thousands of years ago peoples from Asia (and perhaps other continents as well) began to arrive in the Americas. Confronted with novel circumstances and with diversity in their own ranks, these first Americans slowly altered their traditional ways. By the time Christopher Columbus happened by chance upon the Caribbean Islands in 1492, the native peoples had established hundreds of separate cultures. Each had its own language or dialect, its own history, and its own set of ways.

Beginning some nine thousand years ago an "agricultural revolution" transformed the lives of many of the first Americans. It was then that the native inhabitants of south-central Mexico began to plant an ancestor of maize, later to be called corn. In time, they experimented with other kinds of seeds: beans, squash, cotton, potatoes, tomatoes, tobacco, and peanuts. Except in the coldest and driest places and in some of the sea coastal areas, cultivated crops, in particular maize, came to provide an increasingly vital part of the native people's food supply. The agricultural revolution encouraged population growth, the construction of villages, and the emergence of more complex economies. Agricultural economies were the most complete in Mexico, Central America, and Peru. When the Spaniards reached these places, they found elaborate irrigation systems, multistory buildings, stone temples, and cities as large as Paris or London.

REGIONAL WAYS

Region provides an important key to understanding native cultures. Along the Northwest Coast and the Columbia River Plateau, for example, the indigenes depended for their livelihood on an abundance of salmon and other fish as well as forests teeming with game and edible plants. Families in the Northwest lived in large communal houses made of cedar planks. Potlatches, ceremonies in which superiors gave away food, blankets, and other possessions to inferiors, strengthened the bonds of community. The region was also

FIGURE P.1	CULTURAL REGIONS OF NATIVE PEOPLES IN NORTH AMERICA ABOUT 1500

Regions provide a valuable clue to understanding the ways of the native peoples. Nonetheless, each region also contained dozens of distinctive cultures.

SOURCE: Adapted from Mary Kupiec Cayton, Elliot J. Gorn, Peter W. Williams, eds., *Encyclopedia of American Social History*, Vol. I (New York: Charles Scribner's Sons, 1994), p. 19.

known for its craftsmen who carved distinctive religious masks and memorial poles with images of supernatural beings.

In the Southwest—the region extending from southern Colorado, Utah, and southeastern California through Arizona, New Mexico, and western Texas, and into northwestern Mexico—aridity was the central fact of life. Summer rains there averaged only 10 to 20 inches annually; indeed, much of the area was so dry, bereft of rivers for irrigation, or mountainous that cultivation was impossible. Despite parched lands, ancestors of the present-day Hopi, Zuni, and Pueblo began farming in the Southwest at least two thousand years before the Spanish arrived there in the sixteenth century. The native Americans dug hundreds of miles of irrigation canals to carry precious water to corn, squash, bean, cotton, and sunflower fields.

One group of Southwestern peoples, the Pueblos, are well-known for their villages. (Pueblo villages are today the oldest continuously inhabited communities in the United States.) Living in the close quarters of stacked, interconnected apartments, the Pueblos imposed a strict communal code of behavior on their members. Enforcement rested with matrilineal (female-related) clans. Despite its scale and complexity, Pueblo society was roughly egalitarian; a council of religious elders drawn from the various clans ruled each village. Religious ceremonies naturally focused on rainmaking. Singing, chanting, dancing, and impersonating ancestral spirits accompanied public ceremonies. Other occupants of the Southwest lived in the mountains and deserts where they hunted and foraged for food in small bands. In quest of food, they also frequently raided the Pueblo villages.

Agriculture was equally important to Indian life of the Southeast, a region extending along the Gulf and Atlantic Coasts and into the Appalachian highlands. Ample rainfall, short winters, long summers, and fertile soils made farming much easier than in the Southwest. Abundant wildlife supplemented diets of farm produce. This mixture of farming, fishing, and hunting permitted support of a far larger population in the Southeast than in the Southwest. Nearly all of the inhabitants lived in villages ranging from twenty or so dwellings to larger towns of several thousand people.

Southeastern native ways owed extensive debts to older cultures. For several centuries prior to the arrival of Europeans, mound-building agricultural societies thrived in the Mississippi and Ohio river valleys. They built hundreds of huge ceremonial earthworks, some of them seventy feet high, sculptured in the shape of gigantic serpents, birds, and humans. Believing that the natives were incapable of executing such spectacular projects, the Europeans initially reasoned that the mounds were the artifacts of ancient European cultures, perhaps of the Lost Tribes of Israel referred to in the Bible. Although the Mississippian mound-building societies declined long before the coming of the Europeans, their ways continued to influence Indian cultures in the vast mid-continent region.

Like their Mississippi mound-building ancestors, the peoples of the Southeast organized themselves into confederacies of farming communities. In these societies, the chiefs, who usually claimed to have special spiritual

powers, enjoyed unbridled authority over their people. At the apex of Natchez society in Louisiana, for example, stood the Great Sun, a supreme chief
who was also the high priest and brother to a heavenly counterpart. His residence on a great ceremonial mound in the midst of the capital city elevated
his status. When out among his people, he was carried on a litter, an entourage of servants and wives sweeping clean the path before him. Unlike the
Pueblos, Natchez society was highly stratified. Below the Great Sun was the
war chief, the "Tattooed Serpent," who was the Sun's younger brother, and in
descending order, the nobles, the Honored Men, and the Stinkards (the ordinary people).

Like the agricultural peoples of Europe, harvests and other seasonal turning points frequently served as occasions for religious-centered festivals.
Clans from surrounding villages came together to celebrate harvest festivals,
a time of expressing gratitude for nature's abundance and starting life anew.
In preparation for the festival, the people cleaned their homes and villages
and purified themselves by imbibing the "black drink," a beverage that induced heavenly visions. They put out old fires and ignited new ones. They
danced and competed in games of chance. In playing lacrosse, the name
given by the French to a stick-and-ball game, groups of both men and women
engaged in a far more vigorous sport. Versions of lacrosse were popular in
several other North American Indian cultures.

The Woodlands Indians of the Northeast confronted a varied topography
of coastal plains and mountains. Along the coast and the river bottoms where
the growing season was long enough, populations were denser than in the
more rugged and colder areas. Most of the Woodlands peoples followed a
seasonal cycle of life. During the summer months, they lived in semiperma-
nent villages that contained houses made of poles and bark. Women tended
the fields that surrounded each village; when the soil had been depleted, the
group moved to another place, burned the underbrush, girdled the trees, and
planted crops in the cleared spaces. Villages frequently dispersed in the fall
and winter when the men took up fishing and hunting and the women gathered wild fruits and root crops.

Two great language stocks, the Iroquoian and the Algonquian, were predominant in the Northeast. The Algonquians, who were scattered along the
northeastern coast and extended westward into the Ohio and Mississippi
river valleys, were patrilineal, lived in small villages, and tended to organize
themselves into autonomous bands. Located in upstate New York, northern
Ohio, and Ontario, the five tribes comprising the legendary Iroquois confederacy lived in agricultural villages of three thousand or more people each.
Several families typically resided in longhouses, structures often sixty feet or
more in length that were divided into apartments with a communal space for
cooking, child care, and socializing.

In Iroquoian society, men and women occupied separate spheres. While
the men hunted, fished, and fought, the women handled household chores
and farmed. The importance of farming to the livelihood of the Iroquois elevated the status of women. When a man married, he moved from his female-

headed family to one governed by the matriarch of his wife's family. Divorce might consist simply of the wife setting her husband's possessions outside the door of their longhouse. As in other matrilineal societies, the families traced their origins through the female side, and clan matriarchs chose the men who would serve as judges and members of tribal councils. Several kinship groups related on their mother's side frequently comprised a clan. In times of special crises, clans might come together and form loose confederacies.

While it is illuminating to think about native American cultures regionally, it can also be quite misleading. In the first place, a regional analysis tends to neglect interactions among Indian cultures. Few indigenous societies existed in isolation. They overlapped and interacted with one another in highly complex ways.

One of these ways was trade. Almost everywhere Indian societies carried on trade with one another. Evidence suggests the existence of a centuries-long active trade between peoples living in the Southwest and in the Mississippi Valley with those in Mexico. Christopher Columbus encountered one such trading party. Manned by twenty-five men, their large canoe was loaded with cotton blankets, wooden swords, ornaments, and cocoa beans. Some groups such as the Anasazi peoples, who lived in the Chaco Canyon in the Southwest from the first to the tenth centuries, built elaborate road systems. Designed to carry traffic by foot, more than four hundred miles of their roads have been mapped. Trade networks not only entailed the exchanges of goods but ideas as well. Thus Indians in one area learned about the ways of peoples from other locales. From other peoples they might learn new techniques for procuring food and new medicinal uses of plants.

Neither should native cultures be conceived in static terms. Pre-Columbian Indians, like Europeans, experienced frequent and sometimes startling changes in their lives. Changing climatic conditions, years of plenty and years of drought, and the introduction of new foods could quickly alter the fundamental conditions of life. Even more common in effecting change were incursions from other groups. Ever-shifting migrations, often accompanied by warfare, introduced new ways and modified old ones.

SHARED WAYS

While the ways of the native peoples were neither static nor uniform, their cultures nevertheless possessed some important similarities. Religion, a set of beliefs and practices central to nearly all cultures, was one. Unlike the Europeans, whose beliefs sprang from the authority of written scriptures as well as a large body of supplementary religious literature and a highly organized clergy, native societies based their religious beliefs on oral transmission, dreams, and artificially altered states of consciousness. And instead of belief in a single sovereign god who ruled over all, most Indian groups believed in a world of ubiquitous spirits. The wildflowers in the forest, the glistening white sand on the beaches, the mule deer, the sun, the moon, and even the wind—all possessed spirits. A world suffused by both the material and the spiritual provided a unified conception of all that existed; all things were alive and in some sense related to one another. Humans, for example, had animal ancestors and living animals were in effect relatives of humans. This view made such mysteries as life, death, and suffering more tolerable and comprehensible.

The first Americans looked upon nature differently than the typical Europeans. "Subdue the earth," commanded God according to the first book of the Bible, "and have dominion over every living thing that moves on the earth." Contrary to a romanticized version of the relationship between Indians and nature, Indians, too, were willing to alter their environments in order to increase their food and comfort. As farmers, they cultivated and irrigated the soil. By regularly burning the forests and thereby increasing the grassland acreage, the Eastern Woodlands societies encouraged the growth of the local deer population.

Yet, to the first Americans, ignoring the residual spirits in nature could be perilous. Some groups believed that the unnecessary slaughter of wild animals could result in their spirits wreaking untold disasters upon those responsible for the outrage. To protect themselves from adverse effects of animal spirits, hunting frequently entailed explicitly spiritual rules. Among the Micmac, for example, the moose and the beaver, indispensable to their survival, received a carefully prescribed treatment after having been killed. Fearing that the spirits of the killed animals would inform the living animals of their fates and therefore elude future hunters, the Micmacs never gave the bones of the dead animals to their dogs or threw them into the rivers.

The importance of the spiritual world extended to sacred places, to pilgrimages, and to ceremonial games. Games accompanied fertility rites, healing services, burials, and efforts to control one's enemies. Elaborate rituals denoted the spiritual dimensions of play. Before a contest of stickball among the Cherokees, for example, they abstained from sexual intercourse for a month and refrained from eating rabbit for fear of becoming timid. The night before the game, they built a huge campfire and danced through the night to the rhythms of drums, chants, and rattles. Shamans said prayers, painted the athlete's bodies, and smoked pipes—less to ensure victory than to enhance the spirituality of the games.

Meshing the spiritual and the material world together also shaped the native American view of property. Both the private ownership of land and the transformation of the land's resources into individual wealth were alien to native ways. Rather than setting aside land for the exclusive use of individuals or specific families, Indian societies offered its resources to all group members. The communal control of land meant that each member had rights to its harvests, just as all enjoyed the bounty of the hunt. Indian societies, unlike their European counterparts, had no almshouses and rarely a class of the distinctly poor. Families seldom hoarded maize or beans when any member of the group faced starvation or famine. "A whole village must be without corn before any individual can be obliged to endure starvation," wrote a Jesuit priest about the Iroquois.

The indigenous peoples placed a high value on gift giving. Reciprocity in gift giving and the roughly equal distribution of wealth in many Indian societies encouraged the placement of group welfare ahead of individual interest. Native societies had no legislation nor an elaborate police and judicial system for the maintenance of order. Instead, public disapproval, ridicule, shunning, or—most drastically—expulsion curbed dangerous and unacceptable behavior.

The ease with which captive whites converted to the ways of the native peoples should give pause to anyone who believes in the intrinsic superiority of European or Euro-American cultures. During the colonial wars between the English and the French (wars in which both sides employed Indian allies), the native peoples sometimes took white captives into their families. When the opportunity arose to return, captives frequently refused to go back to their white families. Even when captives were convinced to come back, as Benjamin Franklin reported, "in a short time they become disgusted with our manner of life and the care and pains that are necessary to support it, and take the first opportunity of escaping again to the woods, from whence there is no reclaiming them." These "white" Indians obviously preferred the strong sense of community, integrity, and generosity of native American ways over the more individualistic and competitive ways of European cultures.

"THE DARK AGES" OF INDIAN HISTORY

The sixteenth through the nineteenth centuries have been described as "the dark ages" of Indian history. Not only did the arrival of large numbers of Europeans in the sixteenth and seventeenth centuries eventually result in a loss of tribal independence, but the European conquest of the Americas set in motion a chain of other catastrophes for the indigenous peoples.

Within only a few decades, European-carried diseases killed millions of the first Americans. Europeans, located between Asia and Africa and therefore exposed to many of the world's most deadly diseases by traders and migrants, had built up effective immunities to a wide range of contagious diseases. But the continentally isolated Indians had no such protection. They were utterly defenseless against smallpox, measles, and many other deadly infections. In some cases diseases wiped out entire tribal cultures.

The toll of disease on the survivors was also heavy. As they stood by helplessly, unknown diseases struck down their families and friends. "Those that are left," wrote a New England Pilgrim in 1622, "have their courage abated, and their countenance is dejected." Smallpox pocked the faces of many, leaving some so despondent that they killed themselves. The loss of family

members and leaders rent gaping holes in the social fabric of many native societies. Given the inexplicable and horrible devastation, the survivors could
no longer rely confidently on the collective memory and wisdom of their
elders to guide them. The massive deaths weakened Indian confidence in
traditional religious beliefs; religious leaders could no longer command the
same respect that they had once enjoyed, leaving the native peoples more
vulnerable to the religious blandishments of the invading Europeans.

While diseases literally struck down millions, no uniform set of relationships unfolded between the European colonial powers and the Indians. Both
Spain and France frequently incorporated native peoples into their colonial
societies. Indeed, Indians comprised large majorities of the population in
many parts of New Spain and in New France. Furthermore, a disproportionate number of males emigrated from France and Spain to the Americas, a fact
that eventually resulted in substantial numbers of peoples of mixed Indian,
European, and African ancestry.

English colonial societies, on the other hand, were more likely to exist sep-
arately from the native peoples. Unlike the Spanish and the French, the English tended to transplant entire societies to the Western Hemisphere. Hence,
in the English colonies the sex ratio was nearly equal, a fact that made sexual
unions between the English and the indigenous peoples less frequent than in
New France and New Spain. Finally, again unlike the French and the Spanish, in sheer numbers the English settlers quickly overtook and shortly overwhelmed the local Indian populations.

Only a tiny fraction of the native Americans who once lived on the Atlantic Slope side of the Continental Divide managed to survive the English invasion. As one native explained to the Maryland assembly in 1666: "Your hogs
& cattle injure us, you come too near us to live & drive us from place to place.
We can fly no farther; let us know where to live & how to be secured for the
future from the hogs & cattle." Often living alone in a largely alien world, a
few eked out an existence on the margins of colonial English society where
they might engage in occasional and unskilled work as wage laborers. In scattered, isolated pockets, a few (such as the Seneca in upstate New York and the
Narragansetts in New England) even retained their tribal identities and small
allotments of land. They survive to this day. Others moved across the Appalachian Mountains where they, by joining with stragglers from other tribal
units, sometimes formed new Indian societies.

During the eighteenth century, in the vast region between the Appalachian
Mountains and the Mississippi River, the native peoples occupied what
historians have sometimes described as "a middle ground," a position between the contesting European powers. Here, large, independent tribes and
confederacies, altogether comprising several hundred thousand peoples,
employed their strategic location and their military power to play off one
European nation against the other. But, with the defeat of France by Great
Britain in 1763 and the creation of the United States as an independent republic in 1776, such a strategy lost much of its effectiveness.

CONCLUSION

The Americas, when first encountered by the Europeans in the last decade of the fifteenth century, already contained millions of people and hundreds of distinctive native cultures. Rather than hunting, these first Americans usually relied on farming or a combination of farming, hunting, fishing, and gathering for their livelihoods. Rather than living in isolation, distinct native American peoples effected many overlapping and complex interactions through trade, migrations, and warfare. The invasion of the Europeans soon altered and in some cases obliterated the native peoples and their ways. Yet, given the brutal and concerted assault upon them and their ways, the indigenous peoples also exhibited a remarkable resilience. To this day, native Americans have been able to preserve and perpetuate—often, to be sure, in attenuated forms—many of their traditional ways.

The Regional Ways
of Early America, 1600–1800

Northern Ways

A wave of excitement swept through the ranks of the passengers aboard the good ship *Arbella*. The year was 1630, and these people, called Puritans, were on their way to plant a new colony in the North American "wilderness." John Winthrop, their leader and the first governor of the Massachusetts Bay Colony, rose to speak. A hush fell over the passengers. Theirs was a momentous enterprise, Winthrop said. God had chosen them as "instruments for a sacred historical design." They were to build "a city upon a hill" that would serve as a shining example to people everywhere. As a place truly committed to the execution of God's will, community welfare would precede the interests of individuals. "We must delight in each other, make others conditions our own, rejoice together, mourn together, labor and suffer together," said Winthrop, "always having before our eyes our community. . . ."

And so it was that one of the English colonies on the North American mainland, that of Massachusetts Bay, inaugurated an awe-inspiring *community-building enterprise*. Others followed. Indeed, all of New England became a region marked by peoples with a special dedication to community. So did Pennsylvania, New Jersey, and Delaware, though in these colonies the Quakers sought to set up communities of a different sort than those that were planted by the New England Puritans. While neither the Quakers nor the Puritans fully realized their ambitious dreams, nothing distinguished their enterprises from others more than their community-building ways. In principle and frequently in practice, both sets of colonies placed an extraordinarily high value on the creation of strong communities.

NEW ENGLAND'S COMMUNITY-BUILDING WAYS

Consistent with John Winthrop's admonition that the settlers "must delight in each other, make others conditions our own, rejoice together, mourn together, labor and suffer together," everywhere and in all aspects of life the New Englanders sought to foster ties to one another. While for the most part not breaking radically with familiar patterns of life brought with them from England, the Puritans, unlike many English people of the day, did place religious beliefs and practices at the center of their community-building ways. Their understanding of scripture guided every aspect of their community life. From the Bible, they developed a complex set of "covenants," or today what we might call contracts or understandings. These covenants ensured that no individual stood alone. They bound each and every person—to God, to the church, to the family, and to the community.

THE ORIGINS OF THE PURITANS

Comprehending the origins of both the Puritans' and the Quakers' community-building ways requires us to step back in time, to more than a hundred years earlier, when in 1517 Martin Luther nailed ninty-five theses or statements to the church door in the tiny German village of Wittenberg. Luther was a loyal Catholic friar, but he protested that he could find no biblical justification for the sale by the church of indulgences or pardons. By buying indulgences, the church permitted guilty persons to obtain relief from their sins without doing penance.

In time, Luther's hatred of indulgences led him to an even more startling conclusion, one that ultimately subverted the authority of the church itself. According to Catholic doctrine, God had not only founded the church but had given it the authority (through the Pope) to interpret the Bible. In short, only through the church could humans obtain salvation; the church held the keys to the gates of heaven.

On the contrary, said Luther. Based upon his careful reading of the Bible, Luther decided that simple individual faith was the *only* requirement for salvation. "Salvation by faith" meant that ordinary laypeople must come to terms with God directly. Ultimately no priest nor minister could aid them; neither could good works, penance, or partaking of the sacraments prevent them from spending an everlasting life in hell. Luther's bold position launched the Protestant Reformation.

Among the leaders of the Reformation was John Calvin, a French Protestant who was to exercise a particularly large influence on the community-building ways of the Puritans. In his *Institutes of the Christian Religion* (1536), Calvin insisted on the absolute sovereignty of God, predestination, the total depravity of humans, and the choice by God of only a limited number of persons for eternal life. But, rather than acquiesce to fate, as Americans today might be inclined to do, Calvin's followers were energized by his ideas. They saw themselves as literally God's warriors against all evil.

At Geneva (today in Switzerland), Calvin and other "reform" Protestants, as Calvin's followers were sometimes called, established a theocratic community, one in which God was to rule through the ministers and the civil magistrates. The city's leaders insisted upon personal austerity, public fasting, evening curfews, and intensive religious instruction. They prohibited dancing, card playing, heavy drinking, and fashionable dressing. In common with state authorities elsewhere (whether Catholic or Protestant), the Geneva reformers burned religious dissenters at the stake. While serving, in the words of Calvin, as "the most perfect school of Christ" since the days of the apostles, religious refugees from France, England, Spain, Scotland, and elsewhere flocked to Geneva. Geneva became an inspiration for reform Protestants everywhere. French Huguenots, Scottish Presbyterians, and Puritans in England (and later in New England) tried to emulate the strenuous piety that Calvin and his followers displayed in Geneva. (See Figure 1.1.)

At first, Calvin's ideas and his remarkable Geneva experiment had little if any impact in England. Neither earthshaking theological issues nor a demand for more Christlike daily lives among the English people propelled that nation into the Protestant Reformation. Instead, it was the monarch Henry VIII who brought the Reformation to the island kingdom. When the Pope refused to grant him a divorce, Henry VIII in 1534 severed the ancient ties between his nation and Rome. While declaring the monarch henceforth the head of the Church of England (also commonly called the Anglican Church), the king had no intention of otherwise altering traditional Catholic practices. In the Anglican Church, sacraments and penances remained in place, and the priests retained great powers. Yet the king's actions in rejecting Rome inadvertently opened the door to centuries of religious strife.

Indeed, Henry VIII's death in 1553 set in motion a train of events that in the end brought an enormous Calvinistic influence to England and subsequently to that nation's colonies as well. When Henry's daughter Mary became queen of England in 1553, she, following the religion of her mother, reestablished Roman Catholicism as England's official state religion. She had 273 Protestant leaders put to death. Others, known as the "Marian exiles," fled the country. Several of the fugitives made their way to Geneva where they imbibed the heady religious brew offered up by the Calvinists. Upon Mary's death in 1558, the new monarch, Henry's Protestant daughter, Elizabeth, sought a middle way between the traditional Catholic practices of the Church of England and the demands of the reform Protestants. The "Elizabethan Compromise" kept in place the ages-old rituals, the power of the priests, and the church hierarchy while accepting the central Protestant tenet that salvation could be obtained only by personal faith.

But an outspoken minority, the reform Protestants, especially the excited exiles who had recently returned from Calvin's Geneva, rejected Elizabeth's compromise. They wanted all of England to become another Geneva. Religious practices not expressly provided for in the Bible should be ended, they announced. This meant the abolition of the episcopal hierarchy and the formal rituals of the Church of England. They insisted on a personal conversion experience, the importance of private devotional practices, Bible reading, and listening to sermons. Because of their insistence on purifying the Anglican Church and on living more austere personal lives, these reformed Protestants or Calvinists became known as the Puritans.

After the death of Elizabeth in 1603, religious conflict in England escalated. Her successor, James I, hated the Puritans, and the Puritans reciprocated his animosity. One small group of dissenters, known in folklore as the Pilgrims, gave up on reforming the Church of England altogether; they formed

| FIGURE 1.1 | THE SPREAD OF CALVINISM IN SIXTEENTH-CENTURY EUROPE |

The ideas of John Calvin and his remarkable experiment in Geneva eventually exercised an enormous influence in Scotland, England, and the English colonies in North America.

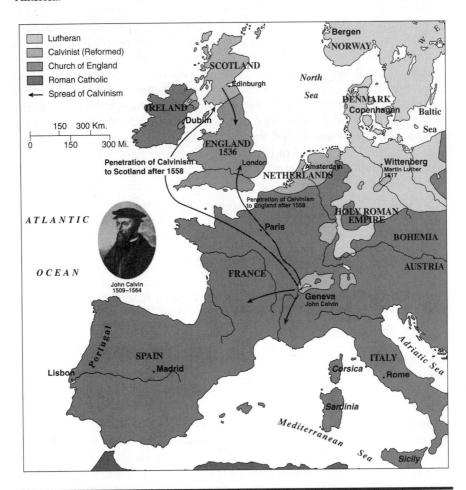

SOURCE: Adapted from John P. Mackay et al., *A History of Western Society*, 4th ed., Vol. II (Boston: Houghton Mifflin, 1991), p. 446.

a separate church, left England, and eventually founded the Plymouth Colony in 1620. When Charles I came to the throne in 1625, religious dissension ratcheted up another notch. Charles's archbishop, William Laud, aggressively persecuted the Puritans. Growing religious oppression and economic hardships, plus dreams of building a more godly community, triggered the "Great Migration," the emigration of more than twenty thousand Puritans to the Massachusetts Bay Colony between 1629 and 1640. In short order, these settlers overwhelmed the tiny Plymouth colony of the Pilgrims, both in sheer numbers and in influence.

Except for settlers in Rhode Island, the Puritans who came during the Great Migration shaped much of the subsequent history of New England. Until late in the seventeenth century, when imperial authorities in England began to exercise more direct control over their North American colonies, the Puritans were virtually free of external authority. No substantial numbers of new peoples entered New England either. It was not until nearly two hundred years later that thousands of Irish began to flood into the region. In the meantime, the progeny of the first settlers multiplied rapidly. As their offspring moved westward across the northern half of the nation, they carried with them, albeit it in modified forms, the ways of the first New England Puritans. Later generations sometimes called them "Yankees."

TIES BEYOND THE SELF

The community-building ways of the New England Puritans began with the key relationship of one's self to God. To the Puritans, establishing a satisfactory tie to God was no easy matter. They believed that Adam, the first human, had broken the "covenant of works" with God. By eating the Forbidden Fruit in the Garden of Eden, Adam had sinned against God, thereupon passing on to all his descendants "original sin." Hence, unable on their own to lead perfect lives, no humans deserved eternal life. But God, in his infinite mercy, offered a new covenant to Abraham's progeny and, with the coming of Christ, to all of humanity. To fulfill the terms of the new "covenant of grace," God sent his only son to earth as a sacrificial redeemer. God thereby bequeathed Christ's purity to all of those who possessed the faith to accept him as the redeemer. They would be rewarded with eternal life. Paradoxically, at least to most twentieth-century people, God also bestowed or withheld faith to humans. Ultimately, without the assistance of God, individual humans were helpless, for they could not obtain faith from the church nor exclusively from their own efforts.

Not surprisingly, those who believed that they were among the select few, the limited numbers whom God had selected or "elected" for salvation, conceived of themselves as a special or a chosen people. This fact alone served as a powerful social adhesive. The elect further strengthened ties to one another by allowing only those who had testified that they had experienced God's gift of grace—a conversion experience that gave one the sense that they had been elected—to become members of the church. (In most regions of Europe, everyone, simply by virtue of their birth, became a member of a state-established church.) Rejecting the religious hierarchy of both the Church of England and the Catholic Church, the Puritans also believed that each congregation (local church) should govern itself. Consequently, in time, the heirs of the American Puritans would become known as Congregationalists.

Puritan Meetinghouse. The stark interior of this 1790 Congregational meetinghouse in Townshend, Vermont, stands in sharp contrast with the Roman Catholic and Anglican church buildings of the day. Fearful that religious icons might distract the congregation from focusing its attention on God and foster the worship of false idols, the Puritans banned all stained-glass windows, crosses, and statuary.

The Puritan style of worship was startlingly simple. Fearing that the playing of musical instruments in church services might conjure up nonreligious feelings and that it smacked too much of Catholic and Anglican practices, the early Puritan services permitted only the chanting of psalms. In contrast to the neoclassical picture-postcard churches found in New England villages today, the seventeenth century Puritans met in plain, unadorned, and unheated rectangular structures that they called "meetinghouses." To have called them "churches" would have been too Catholic and too Anglican for the Puritans. For the same reason, no statues, crosses, stained-glass windows, or other traditional Christian symbols adorned their churches. To remind themselves of the awful fate that awaited the damned, in their graveyards near their meetinghouses they carved images of skulls into the tombstones of the dead.

Regardless of whether they had received the gift of grace or not, the requirement that every town resident attend Sunday services strengthened the bonds of community. Worshipers heard two sermons—one in the morning and another in the afternoon—each of them about two hours in duration. The ministers preached in the "plain style," one that could be easily comprehended by their listeners. Many congregants took notes on the sermons that they heard. Nearly everyone gave great weight to the opinions of their ministers. Even though ministers could not hold public office (hence the colony was not technically a theocracy), before making important decisions public officials frequently sought ministerial advice.

Consistent with their hostility to everything deemed "popish" and their insistence on ridding their religious practices of everything that might distract the worshiper from God's awesome glory, the Puritans sought to wipe out ages-old celebrations of Christmas, Easter, and other holy days as well as saints' days and Sunday merriments. These special days, the Puritans believed, were too frequently given over to drink, excessive eating, and the release of uninhibited feelings. Like observant Jews, the Puritans set aside a weekly "Sabbath." From sundown on Saturday to sundown on Sunday, they forbade work, recreation, travel, idle conversation, sexual intercourse, and even "unnecessary and unreasonable walking in the streets and fields." In 1656, for instance, a Captain Kemble of Boston had to sit in the stocks for two hours for "lewd and unseemly conduct." After having been at sea for three years, the indiscreet captain had publicly kissed his wife on the Sabbath.

Beliefs and practices associated with hierarchy also helped to tie the New England settlers together. Like nearly all peoples of their day, the Puritans took the existence of a hierarchical social order for granted. "God Almighty," declared John Winthrop, "hath so disposed of the condition of mankind [that] some must be rich, some poor, some high and eminent in power and dignity; others mean [inferior] and in subjection." Rigid deference governed relationships between the social ranks. The ordinary people rarely challenged the right of "gentlemen," such as Winthrop, to make decisions on behalf of the entire community. All inferiors saluted gentlemen by doffing their hats or curtsying and addressing them as "Mister" and their wives as "Mistress." Proper salutations to the yeomen or the middling ranks included the terms "Goodman" or "Goodwife." The upper ranks addressed everyone else—that is, the servants, the slaves, and the ordinary people—by their first names. Unlike today, conspicuous evidence of social hierarchy was on daily display. Laws specifically forbade "men and women of mean condition, educations, and callings" from wearing "the garb of gentlemen." But higher rank in New England, as in England, carried with it more responsibilities. Richer and better-born men were expected to assume heavier burdens than the ordinary people in caring for the weak and in all other ways promoting the community's welfare.

Recognizing that a homogenous population could strengthen their ties to one another and to God, the New England settlers tried to exclude those whom they believed might endanger them and their experiment. While a hierarchical order provided a connective tissue across the boundaries of social rank, the New Englanders consciously resisted a complete duplication of England's complex system of ranks. Few came to the colonies from the very top, and those who did shortly departed. Few migrated from the bottom either. Puritan leaders actively discouraged servants and ordinary laborers

Village Green, Concord, Massachusetts, 1830s. This nineteenth-century woodcut reflects the seventeenth-century origins of Concord. In order to build stronger communities and facilitate the worship of God, the New Englanders favored compact settlements.

from entering the colony. This truncated version of England's ranking system helped to reduce potential antagonisms within New England's communities. They also turned away prospective settlers who seemed to be lacking in proper moral character or whose beliefs might jeopardize the stability of their communities. Although both Roger Williams and Anne Hutchinson were widely recognized for their saintly lives, their challenges to the authority of the Massachusetts Bay Colony's religious and political leaders led to their expulsion. Likewise, Quakers who ventured into the colony were sent away, flogged, or hanged. As late as 1718, Boston authorities ordered several hundred newly arrived Scots-Irish immigrants to move on to the frontier.

A policy of encouraging settlement in towns rather than allowing settlers to scatter about the countryside was also designed to strengthen the bonds of community. Colonial officials granted congregations blocs of land upon which they were expected to found towns. Members of the congregation itself decided how the land was to be distributed; those of higher social rank usually obtained more than those below them. Each family typically received a small home plot in the town near the church where they built a house and additional land outside the town for farming. The village held some land in common; hence the "commons" or "village green" that survives in much-abbreviated forms in some New England villages to this day. Each town had a meetinghouse, a school, and stocks and pillories for the punishment of transgressors.

While in time more and more people began to scatter across the countryside, these early agricultural villages offered a density of daily life that fostered cultural continuity and ties beyond the self. Not only was it possible for everyone to attend religious meetings with ease and regularity, but residents had more frequent face-to-face encounters with one another. They could more easily monitor one another's personal behavior. Swift and frequently harsh justice awaited those who violated the town's behavioral standards, standards derived mainly from the Old Testament of the Bible and the English practices of the day. Always fearful of jeopardizing their membership in the community, town residents carefully watched their own behavior. Not unexpectedly, rates of homicide, rape, and other crimes against a person were extraordinarily low.

The New Englanders had no reluctance about employing governments to promote the general welfare of their religiously centered communities. Believing that the state had been ordained by God, they thought it appropriate for governments to carefully regulate all aspects of life. Regulation included the economy. To protect the community's welfare, the General Court, the lawmaking body of the Massachusetts Bay Colony, attempted to prohibit excessive interest rates and impose a "just price" on commodities and wages. So it was, for example, that in 1639 the town of Boston convicted Edward Palmer of overcharging for a set of stocks that he had built. Fittingly, as punishment, the town magistrates ordered Palmer to be the first to sit in the newly made stocks.

RELATIONS WITH NATIVE AMERICANS

Both a presumption of the superiority of their own ways and the wish to build strong communities guided Puritan relationships with the local Native Americans. According to the Massachusetts Bay Company's charter, the "principal end" of their settlement was to convert "the natives to the knowledge and obedience of the only true God and Savior of mankind." Given the Puritan belief that God alone elected individuals for salvation, this proviso, which was probably intended mainly to please English authorities, was not taken very seriously. The amount of missionary effort devoted by the Puritans to the Indians paled beside that of the Spanish Franciscans and the French Jesuits. Yet a few ministers did heed the call; one, John Eliot, was especially prominent. He went so far as to learn Algonquian, a major Indian language of the region. Due to the work of Eliot and a few other missionaries, by the last quarter of the seventeenth century several hundred Native American converts had relocated in fourteen English-style villages called "praying towns."

Yet, the New Englanders made little or no effort to integrate the indigenous peoples into their communities. When smallpox struck the region in 1633, leaving in its wake thousands of dead natives, the white settlers interpreted

the epidemic as an act of God designed to give them more room for settlement. By cultivating the "unused" lands of the Indians, the Puritan settlers
reasoned that they could fulfill the biblical commandment to "be fruitful, and
multiply, and replenish the earth, and subdue it." When the Native Americans resisted incursions onto their lands, the New Englanders did not hesitate to use force against them.

The late seventeenth century witnessed a series of fierce Anglo-Indian
struggles along the entire Atlantic Coast. King Philip's War, fought in 1675
and 1676 in New England, left some four thousand Algonquians and two
thousand English colonists dead and dozens of Indian and English towns in
smoking ruins. Bent upon establishing their ascendancy over a vast trading
area, the Iroquois assisted the English in subduing the Algonquians. The New
England colonists even attacked and killed Christian Indians in the praying
towns. (A few survived, and several thousand of their descendants live in
New England today.) After victory, the Massachusetts settlers exhibited the
bloody head of Metacom, the Algonquian rebel leader, on a pole as an example to other would-be insurrectionists and sold many of Metacom's followers (including his wife and son) as slaves to the West Indies. While King
Philip's War ended serious Indian resistance to European colonization in
New England, it failed to resolve such questions as the sovereignty of the
indigenous peoples, the legitimacy of colonial land claims, and colonial fears
of Europeans "degenerating" into the "savage" ways of the Indians. Furthermore, according to historian Jill Lapore, the war encouraged the New England colonists to retain their traditional ways while cultivating a distinctive
identity, one that was neither Indian nor European.

WAYS OF MARRIAGE AND THE FAMILY

The family was, as one New England minister aptly put it, "the root whence
church and commonwealth cometh." In sharp contrast to the early Chesapeake Bay settlers in the South, nearly all of the New Englanders arrived in
North America as members of established families. Adult New Englanders
married in record numbers (for their day), had record numbers of children,
and because of a more healthful climate, lived longer than their Chesapeake
counterparts. Exceptionally long life expectancies kept alive traditions and
memories that deepened family connections and a sense of community.

A family covenant, the Puritans believed, included a complex set of mutual responsibilities between husbands and wives, parents and children, and
masters and servants. To ensure that families functioned properly, public
officials regularly inspected them. Laws also compelled everyone, including
the unmarried, to live in a family. Upon discovering in 1672 that John Littleale
of Haverhill was living by himself, "whereby he is subject to much sin and in-
iquity, which ordinarily are the companions and consequences of a solitary
life," the Essex County Court, in a typical decision for this kind of case, ordered Littleale to "settle himself in some orderly family in town, and be subject to the orderly rules of family government."

Young men and women themselves usually initiated courtship, though ideally they always considered the opinions of others before proposing marriage. Reflecting the influence of reform Protestantism, the Puritans rejected marriage as a religious sacrament; they considered marriage a civil contract rather than an eternal bonding of a man and a woman that had been ordained by God (the Catholic and the Anglican position). While husbands were in theory patriarchs, the marriage covenant carried with it an elaborate set of mutual obligations. Cruelty, desertion, and adultery could even result in divorce, though in practice divorce in New England was rare.

In some respects, the Puritans modified prevailing attitudes and practices of the day toward women. True, as a general proposition, the Puritans believed that women should be subordinate to men. Woman's descent from Eve made her more vulnerable both to irrationality and to sin than man. Anne Bradstreet, a devout Puritan, expressed the prevailing view of women's inferiority this way:

> Let Greeks be Greeks, and women what they are,
> Men have precedency and still excel,
> It is but vain, unjustly to wage war;
> Men can do best, and women know it well.

Yet the Puritans considered women and men to be spiritual equals, a premise that had important implications for the treatment of women then and later on. Law and custom required that husbands treat their wives with both decency and respect. Driven by powerful religious imperatives, including the command to love and nurture one another, many Puritans worked diligently at achieving harmonious marriages.

Men frequently expressed warm and sometimes even a jealous admiration for the degree of piety and virtue that they observed among the colony's women. The greater spirituality among women, Cotton Mather, a prominent Puritan minister, concluded, was due to their subordinate status and the pain that they experienced during childbirth. Many men testified that their mothers, wives, and other female relatives had exercised a more positive influence on their lives than their fathers or other male relatives. The respect earned by Puritan women for their moral stature not only provided them with a more meaningful existence but left an important heritage for later generations of New England women.

Like other dimensions of their lives, religion guided the sex ways of New Englanders. Contrary to popular mythology, the Puritans were not sexual ascetics; they found no biblical justification for the value placed on chastity by the Roman Catholic Church. After all, they said, the Bible had commanded humans to multiply. In private correspondence and diaries, there is even evidence that they believed sex could strengthen the marriage covenant. Neither did the Puritans discuss sexuality with the excruciating indirection that is commonly associated with nineteenth-century Victorian America.

Yet the Puritans were certainly not proponents of a modern sexuality. When considering sexuality, they invariably tied it to reproduction. Hence, they savagely punished adultery, premarital intercourse, bestiality, and sodomy. Such violations of community standards could result in incarceration, public whippings, fines, disfranchisement, even execution, or a combination of these. The results of repression were impressive. Rates of prenuptial pregnancy and bastardy in seventeenth-century New England were far below those of the Chesapeake settlers in the South or in most regions of Britain.

Neither were the Puritans advocates of permissive child-rearing practices. Quite the contrary. Consistent with their interpretation of Adam's fall from grace, they believed that newborns were predisposed to do evil. Thus, parents should strive to "break the wills" of their children. While extending love and affection, both fathers and mothers, with the active assistance of community members, simultaneously set about systematically destroying all manifestations of a spirit of autonomy in their children. Indeed, in order to keep from becoming too attached to their children and hence weakening their capacity to break the child's will, Puritans frequently "put out" their children to other families. At a tender age, sometimes as young as four or five but usually nine or ten, the child became a member of another family where they might learn a trade and experience the discipline of adults uncontaminated by deep emotional attachments to them. That early New England parents were able to resist the tearful entreaties of their young children (as revealed in diaries) to return home after having been put out to another family reflected the depth of parental commitment to their child-rearing ways.

The Life of the Mind

Since a knowledge of the Bible was deemed essential to understanding the terms of the covenants and lay persons were expected to be keen listeners to sermons, the New Englanders valued education far more than other peoples of their day. As early as 1642, the Bay colony ordered that all children should receive instruction in reading from their parents, and in 1647 the "Old Deluder [Satan] Law" required that all towns of fifty families or more hire a teacher. Although these laws were not rigorously enforced, the results were extraordinarily high literacy rates. By 1760, some 80 percent of the males and perhaps 65 percent of the females could read and write, a literacy rate far higher than in the other English colonies or in England itself.

New England led all other English colonies in the founding of colleges. "Dreading to leave an illiterate ministry to posterity when our present ministers shall lie in dust," the Massachusetts settlers established Harvard College in 1636. Religious controversy led to the founding of Yale in 1701, and later the Great Awakening religious revivals spawned the establishment of Brown by Baptists in 1764 and Dartmouth as a Congregationalist school in 1769. Other colleges—Amherst, Bowdoin, Williams, Bates, and Colby—soon followed. Later, in the nineteenth century, descendants of New Englanders founded a set of colleges across the region north of the Ohio River. New Englanders were also at the forefront of the great public education movement of the nineteenth century.

No region of the nation has been more important to the history of American literature than New England. Not only did New Englanders and their descendants furnish most of America's literary giants prior to the mid-twentieth century, but Puritanism (though frequently misunderstood and confused with Victorianism) has furnished a theme for much of American literature. While New England nurtured strong traditions in literature and philosophy, the region was less hospitable toward music and the arts. Identifying liturgy, music, and the decorative arts with the Church of England and the Roman Catholic Church, the Puritans and their descendants were suspicious of any art forms that might distract them from their earthly and spiritual duties.

INTERNAL STRAINS IN NEW ENGLAND'S WAYS

As we have seen, to execute God's will more effectively and to build strong communities, the New England Puritans sought to establish and nurture an extensive set of ties beyond the self. Yet within New England ways themselves lurked profound dangers—dangers that could unravel their best-laid plans. One potential difficulty lay in their political ways. While the Puritans strenuously disavowed all forms of government except a dictatorship of God's elect, at the same time the idea of a civil covenant between the governed and their governors contained implications that could and did in time lead to more democratic political practices. Other potential difficulties arose from their theology. While the Puritans never equated salvation with the accumulation of wealth, their idea that all were called by God to pursue both worldly and spiritual callings could and did encourage the pursuit of personal gain at the expense of one's other, more important obligations. Finally, the belief that each individual must come to terms with God personally could and sometimes did encourage religious unorthodoxy.

INTERNAL RELIGIOUS STRIFE

The instances of Anne Hutchinson and Roger Williams demonstrated the intrinsic problems in imposing religious uniformity while at the same time arguing that each individual alone was ultimately responsible for establishing her or his relationship with God. From his arrival in 1631, Roger Williams, a saintlike minister with a keen mind, refused to accept what he considered to be compromises by the Massachusetts Bay authorities with God's intents. From his pulpit in Salem, he questioned the mingling of state and church. State power should not extend to matters of conscience and religion, said Williams. He also condemned the colony for its treatment of the Indians and the churches for their failure to completely separate themselves from the Church of England. Banished in 1636, Williams made his way to Rhode Island where he set up a new colony that completely separated church and state and permitted liberty of conscience in religious matters.

In the so-called Antinomian controversy, Anne Hutchinson divided the Puritan community over what today seems an abstruse theological issue. A loyal Calvinist, she believed that election to salvation was an arbitrary act of God; thus individual moral conduct had nothing whatever to do with whether one went to hell or heaven. Rejecting the necessity of good works and insisting that salvation consisted of a direct infusion of the Holy Spirit into the soul, she threatened the colony's tranquility. Although the Puritan leaders agreed with her basic premise that God alone conferred salvation, they saw Hutchinson as an extremist, especially in rejecting good works as a sign of salvation.

Fearful of the ramifications of Hutchinson's position for the stability of the community and resentful of a woman engaging in such a conspicuous public role, in 1637 the General Court brought her to trial. The civil authorities called upon the ministers to unveil her heresies. Hutchinson defended herself with wit and brilliance, but, unfortunately for her defense, she did blurt out that her knowledge of God sprang from "an immediate revelation," one totally free of the Bible and the church. Since the Puritans believed that all direct revelation from God had ceased with the Bible, to them Hutchinson's assertion constituted heresy. The General Court banished her from the colony. She went to Rhode Island, which was rapidly becoming a refuge for Puritans who insisted on disagreeing with the authorities in Massachusetts Bay.

The banishment of Hutchinson and Williams did not end internal religious strains. Authorities found it difficult to sustain the zeal and orthodoxy of the first settlers. When the children and the grandchildren of the original "elect" failed to experience evidence of a conversion, an association of ministers in 1662 approved a "Halfway Covenant" that allowed baptized children of the elect to have their own children baptized. Such a compromise fell far short of the traditional requirement for church membership; potential members no longer had to be able to relate a personal reception of grace. By the end of the seventeenth century, many New England churches were rejecting entirely the idea of limiting church membership to those who could testify to a conversion experience.

In the final decade of the seventeenth century, the Puritans also lost their monopoly on New England's religious polity. In 1691 England forced on the Bay Colony a new charter that provided for religious toleration. No longer could Quakers and Baptists be banned from the colony. Soon Boston even hosted an unreformed Church of England.

The issue of witchcraft also divided New England communities. The witchcraft hysteria in 1692 (mainly in Salem) revealed the widespread persistence of beliefs in sorcery, magic, and other forms of the occult. Puritans tried to explain "wonders" or the "unnatural" in religious terms. Believing that God had discontinued direct revelation to humans with the death of the apostles, the Puritans nevertheless interpreted the unexpected or unusual as possible clues or signs of "God's remarkable Providences in the world." They saw such events as doors or windows mysteriously flying open or shut, dishes rattling on the table, or a child falling through the ice and drowning while skating on a local pond as signs from God. For nothing, they believed, was due to chance; everything—every event, large and small—had a larger, divine meaning.

Some wonders, such as the magic emanating from the Devil through witches, threatened to usurp God's power. New Englanders, like most seventeenth-century Europeans and Americans, believed that people could and did make agreements with Satan. In exchange for their souls, Satan would give them the power of black magic. The Puritans also took seriously the biblical injunction: "Thou shall not suffer a witch to live." During the witchcraft hysteria they executed thirty-five people for practicing witchcraft.

Belief in the occult was not limited to Puritans nor always interpreted in religious terms. Indeed, nearly all people of the day (as well as an astounding number of Americans today) believed in some forms of the occult. In eighteenth-century colonial America, almanacs in particular served as a popular source of astrological and occult information. Typically selling more copies than the Bible, millions of Americans turned to them for guides about when to plant and when to harvest and for clues to their future.

Despite the internal divisions, religious convictions continued long after the seventeenth century to occupy a central place in New England communities. Great religious revivals in the eighteenth and early nineteenth centuries, subsequently labeled by historians as "great awakenings," provided the region with massive transfusions of new spiritual energy. In Massachusetts, the Congregational Church was not "disestablished" (severed from the state) completely until 1833. In addition, Puritanism in Old and New England gave birth to a multitude of new sects. Apart from the Congregationalists, they included Presbyterians, Baptists, and Unitarians. In the early nineteenth century such new bodies as the Latter-day Saints and the Christian Scientists also drew their first followers mainly from Puritan descendants.

New England's Political Ways

The first settlers in New England had no intentions of establishing democracies. Indeed, John Winthrop once described democracy as "the meanest and worst of all forms of government." Instead of a political system that responded to the interests of ordinary people, the Puritans insisted that governments should be instruments for the execution of God's will. Both the governed and the governors should be bound by a "civil covenant," an agreement that spelled out their respective duties. "It is evident by the light of nature that all civil relations are founded in covenant," declared a prominent Boston minister, John Cotton.

New Englanders conceived of liberty in terms of freedom to accept God's commandments rather than in terms of individual rights to do as one wishes. "Tolerance stinks in God's nostrils," the Puritan minister Nathaniel Ward announced. Freedom meant giving up a life of sin and embracing the teachings of Christ. "Where the spirit of the Lord is," declares the New Testament, "there is liberty." In a speech to the General Court in 1645, Governor John Winthrop distinguished between two kinds of liberty: "natural" and "civil." In nature, plants, animals, and humans had the freedom to do as they wished—"to do evil as well as good," said Winthrop. Civil liberty, on the other hand, arose from the "covenant between God and man." It was the freedom to do only what God commanded, to do "that only which is good, just and honest." Civil liberty implied self-control. To the Puritans, an absence of self-control amounted to a state of unfreedom or slavery. In other words, such individuals were slaves to their impulses or to the wiles of the Devil.

In order to execute the civil covenant more effectively, communities and individuals might enjoy special "liberties," or what we might today call privileges. For example, a "gentleman" was granted exemption from a public whipping "unless his crime be very shameful, and his course of life vicious and profligate." The Massachusetts Body of Liberties in 1641 gave every free man "liberty to come to any public court, council or town meeting" and participate in its proceedings. But, unlike modern conceptions of liberty, Puritan ideas of freedom simultaneously permitted detailed restraints upon individual behavior. Anyone "who shall exceed the bounds of moderation" in speech or any other behavior could be punished severely.

Yet, while the goal of the Puritans was a government designed to execute God's will, the idea of a civil covenant included the possibility of placing limits on governmental power. What if those in charge of the state violated the terms of the civil covenant? To determine whether governors (including the monarchs themselves) had been guilty of failing to discharge their obligations, one needed only to refer to the Bible. For scriptures were a higher form of law than that formulated by the churches, the king, or any other public officials. Hence, the English Puritans turned to the scriptures to justify their rebellion against Charles I in the English Civil War of the 1640s. More than a century later, in 1750, Jonathan Mayhew, a New England minister, resorted to the same source when he delivered a famed sermon against unlimited submission to royal authority. He thereby justified the Puritan rejection of Charles I while anticipating an argument for the American Revolution that began in 1775.

The inclination by the Puritans to conceive of all social relationships in terms of covenants also encouraged the adoption of written constitutions. The charters granted to the New England colonies by the monarchs offered one kind of written agreement that limited the discretionary power of both the monarch and the settlers. In addition, the colonists drew up their own written compacts. These included the Mayflower Compact of the Plymouth Colony (1620), Connecticut's Fundamental Orders (1638), and the Massachusetts Body of Liberties (1641). Unlike the English, who relied upon a body of unwritten precedents for their constitution, the Puritans helped establish an American tradition of insistence upon written constitutions. These documents spelled out laws of a fundamental character, that is, laws considered superior to ordinary statute law.

The Puritan Work Ethic

Next to religious unorthodoxy, the gravest danger to community solidarity arose from the temptations of the secular world. Ministers advised their flocks that they must live in this world and that they must work diligently while here, *but* at the same time they were always to subordinate material rewards and worldly pleasures to the welfare of the community and to the glorification of God. Under such circumstances, restraining worldly or secular impulses was difficult, even for an exceptionally pious people.

The idea of "callings," which was central to Puritan conceptions of work and time, tended to draw attention to and to foster worldly success. Though seeking material gain for its own sake was completely forbidden, the Puritans believed that God commanded all humans to commit themselves unsparingly to both the pursuit of their worldly vocations and to living a godly life. Time was sacred, given by God to humans for the execution of his will. In order to ensure that they had not spent any time idly, conscientious Puritans examined themselves daily. "Abhor . . . one hour of idleness as you would be ashamed of one hour of drunkenness," a Puritan admonished his son. Such an acute time-consciousness and dedication to one's callings encouraged an unintended consequence—the accumulation of material wealth by individuals.

In time, efforts to curb the impulse toward personal gain weakened. Early in the colony's history (in 1639), in a much-cited case, a Massachusetts court convicted Robert Keayne, a Boston merchant, of "extortion," fined him, and required that he make a public confession of his errors to the church. Keayne, according to the court, had charged an "excessive" price for nails. But such heavy-handed supervision of the merchants was short-lived. Well before the end of the seventeenth century, popular resentment made enforcement of wage and price regulations impossible. By the middle of the eighteenth century, Boston-born (but not ardently religious) Benjamin Franklin was exhorting young tradesmen to "Remember that TIME is money," and in *Poor Richard,* published in 1733 he wrote: "Idleness is the greatest prodigality." Horrified by the discovery that Parisians slept until midday and wasted money by burning candles far into the night, Franklin invented what would become known as daylight saving time.

The importance attached by Protestantism, especially in its Anglo-American Puritan form, to time and hard work led to the formulation of the Weber thesis. In the twentieth century, German sociologist Max Weber concluded that the Puritan work ethic (sometimes also described as the Protestant ethic or simply as the work ethic) encouraged a "this-worldly asceticism"—that is a habit of self-denial, frugality, and dedication to work that had promoted the growth of modern capitalism. Yet, even the time-obsessed, hard-bargaining, stereotypical Yankee merchant, who later may have come closer to representing the region than the first Puritans, never completely rejected the ideal of subordinating personal economic interest to the welfare of the community. Furthermore, later day New Englanders never endorsed the principle that the pursuit of wealth exempted the individual from such moral or religious obligations as obeying the Ten Commandments.

THE DIVERSE WAYS OF THE MIDDLE COLONIES

Regions represent only one way of looking at colonial Anglo-American cultures. Another is *ethnoreligious*. Indeed, the antecedents of modern America's multiculturalism originated in the remarkable ethnic and religious diversity of the English colonies. Unlike New Spain and New France, the English colonies eventually admitted a bewildering variety of Protestants plus a few Catholics and Jews. Growing numbers of non-English ethnics also made their homes in the English colonies. According to the first federal census of the United States, taken in 1790, slightly less than half of the population originated in England; nearly 20 percent were African; about 15 percent were Scots, Scots-Irish, and Irish; and 7 percent were German. (See Figure 1.2.)

The degree of religious and ethnic diversity in the colonies differed sharply by region. Settled almost entirely by English Puritans, the New England colonies, as we have seen, remained a homogeneous region until well into the nineteenth century. On the other hand, by the middle of the eighteenth century, the coastal South had become a biracial society comprised mainly of those of English and African origins. The Middle Atlantic colonies of New York, New Jersey, Delaware, and Pennsylvania featured yet another ethnoreligious pattern. These colonies contained an assortment of Europeans of varying religious persuasions. Finally, mostly north Britons (northern English, Scots, and Scots-Irish) settled in the backcountry, a sprawling area that included much of Appalachia.

Ethnic and religious heterogeneity arose in part from the English mode of colonization. Spain and France permitted only their own subjects who were loyal to the Catholic faith to leave the homeland for their colonies. France, for example, refused to allow thousands of Protestant Huguenots to emigrate to Canada. New Englanders likewise practiced exclusion; they welcomed only English Puritans, but the other English colonies in North America opened their doors to a variety of ethnoreligious groups. As early as the 1680s William Penn received permission from the English crown to recruit religious dissenters from Great Britain as well as colonists from France, Holland, and the German principalities. Anxious to profit from selling or renting land, other colonial proprietors and joint stock companies soon followed suit. They too began sending agents to scour the European continent in quest of potential settlers.

NEW YORK'S HETEROGENEITY

Entirely different motives drove the Duke of York and William Penn, the two most important promoters of settlement in the Middle Colonies. The duke hoped to enhance his family fortunes in New York while Penn sought to

FIGURE I.2	DISTRIBUTION OF EUROPEAN AND AFRICAN IMMIGRANTS IN THE NORTHERN COLONIES ABOUT 1775

While New England was settled by predominately English immigrants, the middle colonies of New York, Pennsylvania, and New Jersey contained large numbers of non-English peoples.

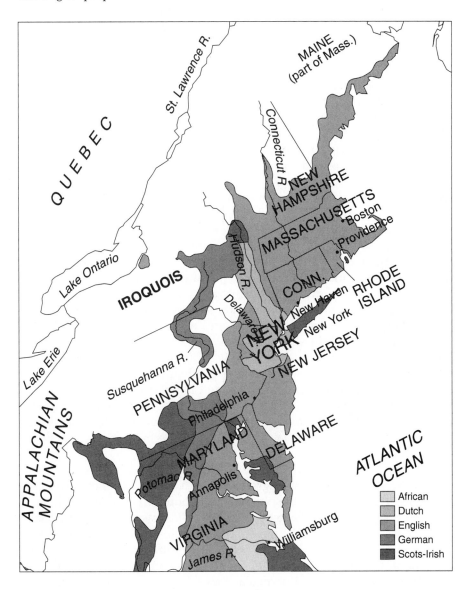

SOURCE: Adapted from Robert A. Divine et al., *America: Past and Present*, 4th ed. (New York: HarperCollins, 1995), p. 103.

create a sanctuary for persecuted Quakers in New Jersey, Pennsylvania, and Delaware. Yet, the results in one important respect were the same: Each colony attracted a heterogeneous population.

New York's heterogeneity began with the Dutch who quickly displaced most of the local indigenous Native American population. Establishing a trading post at New Amsterdam (New York City) on Manhattan Island in 1624, the colony soon attracted an astonishing hodgepodge of European and African peoples. In 1643, Isaac Jogues, a visiting French Jesuit priest, claimed, perhaps with some exaggeration, that there were eighteen languages spoken on the streets of the small port city. The city included (among others) Dutch, English, Germans, Swedes, Finns, and Africans. When the Portuguese seized Brazil from the Dutch in 1654, a portion of that colony's Jewish population migrated to New Amsterdam as well.

Heterogeneity continued to characterize the region after the establishment of English hegemony in 1664. The Duke of York, the new proprietor, allowed the Dutch to remain in the colony, to retain their property, and to practice their religion (Dutch Reformed Calvinism). Soon outnumbered by the English, many of the Dutch diluted their distinctive ways by eventually intermarrying with other ethnic groups. Other Dutch colonists planted settlements in the river valleys of New Jersey as well as in the Hudson and Mohawk River Valleys of upstate New York. Until at least the nineteenth century, their religion, their compact settlements, and their native language bound most of the Dutch into tight ethnic enclaves. In these isolated ethnic communities, the Dutch managed to retain many of their traditional ways for a century or more.

While attracting a diverse ethnic population, New York City also became something of a haven for a wide spectrum of religious dissenters. In 1686 Governor Thomas Dongan complained that the Anglicans had to compete not only with Dutch Calvinists, French Huguenots, and Quakers but also with "Singing Quakers, Ranting Quakers; Sabbatarians; antisabbatarians; some Anabaptists; some Independents; some Jews; in short all sorts of opinions there are some." Dongan did not even attempt to classify the religious beliefs of the Africans, who by the middle of the eighteenth century comprised nearly a third of the city's population. Nor did he anticipate the later arrival of substantial numbers of Germans, Scots, and Scots-Irish to the region.

After the Act of Union, which created Great Britain in 1707–8, tens of thousands of Scots and Scots-Irish migrated mostly to the backcountry (see Chapter 2), but substantial numbers scattered throughout Britain's North American colonies. Some were merchants from around Glasgow who were especially prominent in the Chesapeake region. Others were royal officials; several of the colonial governors hailed from Scotland. A third group were educators and tutors. They played prominent roles in promoting the ideas of the Enlightenment in America. In particular they introduced to the colonists the ideas of two major Scottish thinkers—Thomas Hutchinson, a moral philosopher, and Adam Smith, a political economist.

New York's ethnoreligious pluralism had mixed results. Ethnoreligious conflicts regularly erupted and spilled over into the political arena; even among British settlers, Anglicans, Congregationalist Puritans, and Scottish Presbyterians frequently assailed one another. Yet New York's diversity gave the city a special vibrancy; it daily displayed an amazing assortment of European and African ways. No other colonial city equaled New York in the abundance of its pageantry or the range of its pastimes. Unlike Boston or Philadelphia, New Yorkers enthusiastically patronized the theater, horse racing, cockfighting, and animal baiting. Given its origins, perhaps it is not surprising that New York would one day become a special American city, one marked not only by cosmopolitanism and ethnic heterogeneity but as a national center of intellectual and artistic life as well.

THE QUAKER PLAN

Some fifty years after the Great Migration to Massachusetts Bay, William Penn (between 1674 and 1715) launched a decidedly different kind of experiment in the Delaware River Valley. Penn and his fellow Quakers sought to build religiously centered communities in Pennsylvania, West Jersey, and Delaware. But, unlike the New Englanders, the Quakers flung their doors open to all comers. They abhorred persecution by the state for religious beliefs and they spurned hierarchy as a foundation of social order. Unlike any place else in Christendom, their "Holy Commonwealth" was to rest on the biblical Golden Rule: "Do unto others as you would wish them to do unto you." Such a radical plan horrified Puritans and Anglicans alike and it sent shudders through the ranks of ruling hierarchies everywhere.

As with the Puritans, the Quaker plan originated in England. The religious turmoil following in the wake of the English Civil War (1642–46) splintered Protestantism in all directions. Apart from Congregationalists, Presbyterians, and Baptists, a host of other sects sprang into existence. Among them was a group founded by George Fox. They called themselves the Society of Friends, though they were better known as the Quakers since they sometimes literally trembled in the presence of God's spirit. Rather than the Bible or clerical authority, the Quakers relied upon the promptings of the Holy Spirit for most of their beliefs and actions. Dedicated missionaries, Quaker women and men fanned out over England, the European continent, and the American colonies in pursuit of converts.

After the restoration of the monarchy and the reestablishment of the Church of England in 1660, the Friends paid an extraordinarily high price for their unorthodoxy and their missionary zeal. For refusal to take oaths and pay tithes (among other offenses) authorities imprisoned the Quakers, sometimes tortured and maimed them, and frequently seized their property. Between 1661 and 1685, some 450 Friends died on behalf of their faith.

Fortunately for the Quakers, their devout leader, William Penn, was a close friend of King Charles II. The son of a distinguished admiral (a non-Quaker), Penn was wealthy, learned, and at home in the royal court. In 1681 Charles II granted Penn an immense tract of land between New York and Maryland. Immigrants, many of whom were Quakers, soon poured into the Delaware Valley, the eastern part of the tract. Mostly of modest means, they arrived as families rather than as individual settlers. By 1750, the Friends had become the third largest religious group in the English colonies. In sheer totals, only the Congregationalists (Puritans) and the Anglicans (adherents to the Church of England) outnumbered them.

Quaker beliefs and practices departed sharply from both the Anglicans and the Puritans. Theologically, the Friends supplanted the awesome and sometimes wrathful deity of John Calvin with a God of love, one whose benevolence reached out and harmonized everything in the universe. Each soul, they believed, possessed at least intermittently the presence of the divine light or the "inner spirit" in sufficient power to lead each to salvation. Christ died not for the few, but for the many. Belief in the inward presence of Christ reduced the importance of scripture, elevated the position of ordinary laypeople, and led to the startling conclusion that a formal clergy was unnecessary.

Proper worship to the Quakers was decidedly simple. They rejected ostentatious church buildings, an official clergy, a standard liturgy, or formal sermons. Quaker "meetings" began in complete silence, a time in which women, men, and children sought to cast away all human thoughts and desires. Only after having cleansed their minds of the presence of this world, the Quakers believed, could humans be filled with divine agency and guided by the Holy Spirit. While complete silence could occupy an entire Quaker worship service, usually after a period of silence, one by one, men, women, and children—moved by an elevated state of spirituality—rose and spoke or prayed. A time of silence might then return until one member, usually an elder, stood up and shook hands with another. Everyone then quietly departed for their homes.

The Friends challenged Christian orthodoxy in other respects. In an age when nearly all religious groups systematically persecuted those with whom they disagreed, the Friends championed liberty of religious conscience. No one in the Quaker colonies had to pay taxes to support a church nor did the Quakers penalize anyone for having religious beliefs different from their own. Unlike the Puritans, the Quakers executed no one for witchcraft. The Quakers, however, extended full religious liberty only to believers. To exercise voting rights and serve in government, one had to be a professing Christian. Finally, the Quakers were pacifist. Consistent with the Golden Rule, they advised anyone who had been wronged to turn the other cheek.

THE QUAKER CHALLENGE TO HIERARCHIES

No group spawned by the Protestant Reformation offered more resistance to social hierarchies than the Quakers. "Woe unto you that are called *Lords, Ladies, Knights, Gentlemen,* and *Gentlewoman* . . . ," English Quaker James Parnell warned in 1655, "Woe unto you . . . who are called *Mister* and *Sir* and *Mistress.* . . . Because . . . by fraud, deceit and oppression . . . you are exalted above your fellow-creatures, and grind the faces of the poore." While other Quakers were less strident in their condemnations of the upper strata, even the high-born William Penn hated social distinctions based on "blood" and "birth." All should be judged by what they do, or have done, said Penn, not by their birth. Only those who had exhibited extraordinary virtue should receive special acknowledgment from other mortals.

The Quakers repudiated the social etiquette required by deference to rank. Upon meeting superiors, Quakers frequently refused to bow, curtsey, or doff their hats, or use such titles as "sir," "mister," or "your grace" in the case of dukes or lords. Instead of obeisance to the elaborate formalities of the day that signified rank, Quakers insisted on the simple act of extending a handshake to all and addressing everyone as "Friend." They addressed all others as "thee" or "thou" rather than the more formal "you." For adherence to their equalitarian practices, Quakers in England and in the non-Quaker colonies paid dearly. But imprisonment and whippings failed to alter their egalitarian behavior; indeed, punishment seemed only to strengthen their resolve.

That the Quakers almost made a fetish out of plain speech and dress also defied prevailing social conventions. As emblems of Adam's fall from grace, the Friends concluded that clothes were badges of shame and potential incitements to envy and lust. Consequently, they rejected superfluous buttons, belts, sashes, and the wearing of fine cloths. Other colonial Americans became admirers of the simplicity and egalitarianism of their dress, including Benjamin Franklin, a non-Quaker who fled from Boston to Philadelphia while still a youngster. When Americans rejected monarchy during the Revolutionary era, simpler "republican" dress, influenced in part by the Quakers, grew in popularity and later spread westward into the American midlands.

Ordinary free men (those free of enslavement or indentureship to others) enjoyed far more political power in the Quaker colonies than they did elsewhere. Penn's constitution for West Jersey, for example, provided that legislative power would be vested in an assembly chosen annually by nearly all of the free males in the colony. The free men also chose the justices of the peace and local officeholders. All settlers were guaranteed freedom of religion and the right to trial by jury. "We put the power in the people," Penn explained to the other trustees of the colony. Men of property and power responded to Penn's position with horror. To place the power to govern in the hands of ordinary men, they believed, would lead inevitably to anarchy and tyranny.

The Friends came closer than any other major group of their day to endorsing the idea of equality between the sexes. Although the Quakers normally expected women to defer to men in marriage, they had a saying: "In souls there is no sex." Not only were women and men equal spiritually, but the Quakers believed that the Inner Spirit manifested itself apart from its human source. For that reason the Spirit might speak through women and even children for that matter. While the apostle Paul had written "suffer not a woman to preach," female Friends spoke in religious services and served as missionaries.

Despite their startling unorthodoxy in beliefs and practices, the Quakers built extraordinarily stable societies. At the center of their colony was the town of Philadelphia. Laying out the streets of the "green country town" in a gridiron pattern and allowing ample spaces for parks, Philadelphia was the

Quaker Couple. The Quakers were ardent proponents of leading a simple life and practicing the Bible's Golden Rule. Unlike most peoples of their day, they rejected all forms of social hierarchy.

first "planned city" in English North America. At the time of the American Revolution, the City of Brotherly Love was "the second city of the British Empire," smaller only than London in the English-speaking world. As the basic foundation of their social order, the Quakers tried to practice the Golden Rule. Doing unto others as you would have them do unto you required severe self-restraint.

Restraint included sexual behavior. The Quakers drew a sharp distinction between love and lust. Even a married man should "not go into her [his wife] but for propagation," explained a Quaker. Similarly, they advised against taking sensual delight in eating. "Eat to live, not live to eat," was a Quaker aphorism. The Quakers carefully monitored one another's behavior. Monthly public meetings regularly examined charges of individual misbehavior. If, after a visit from a committee of overseers personal reform failed, the guilty person could be disowned or in essence shunned. Unlike colonists in the South, the Quakers were intolerant of violence against and the sexual exploitation of social inferiors. They punished offenses against persons more swiftly and harshly than those against property.

THE QUAKERS AND NON-QUAKERS

Few if any dominant groups in history have been more tolerant or generous than the Friends to minorities. Unlike all other major groups of English settlers of their day, the Quakers even questioned the institution of African slavery. While the first generation of settlers had been troubled by slavery's inconsistency with the Golden Rule, they had not prohibited it and many Quakers purchased slaves, including William Penn himself.

But within a decade of settlement, sentiment against slavery began to grow. In 1696, the Philadelphia annual meeting advised Quakers "not to encourage the bringing in of any more Negroes" to the colony, and in 1712 the Pennsylvania assembly passed a prohibitive duty on the importation of slaves only to have it disallowed by the English crown. Finally, in 1758, the Philadelphia meeting unanimously went on record against slavery in any form; by this time only a few Quakers still owned slaves. Nor were Quakers oblivious to the plight of newly manumitted slaves; they frequently aided ex-slaves in making the transition to freedom.

Likewise, Quakers treated Native Americans more humanely than other European groups. Even before his arrival, William Penn tried to reassure the Delaware chiefs. "The king of the Country where I live, hath given me a great Province," he wrote, "but I desire to enjoy it with your Love and Consent, that we may always live together as Neighbors and friends." In this astonishing statement, Penn dissociated himself from the entire history of European colonization and the prevailing attitudes towards Indians. Penn insisted that lands had to be purchased from the local Indians before they could be conveyed to Europeans and he considered agreements reached with the Native Americans as forever binding.

When compared to other Indian-European relationships, the peaceful coexistence established between the Quakers and the Indians is quite remarkable. In fact, the reputation of the Quakers for fairness and pacifism so impressed Native American groups that they began viewing Pennsylvania as something of a sanctuary from ravaging Europeans elsewhere. But, unfortunately for the Indians, the Quaker policy of welcoming everyone to the colony eventually attracted thousands of non-Quaker European immigrants to

Pennsylvania. Hungry for land and without the scruples of the Friends, the newcomers soon began pushing the Indians out of the way, and by the middle of the eighteenth century their actions jeopardized the peaceful co-existence of the two peoples in the Delaware Valley.

The Quakers not only dealt with Native Americans and African slaves more humanely than other colonists; they also welcomed peoples of different national origins and religious persuasions to live in their colonies on terms of near equality. As an effective promoter of colonization, William Penn had no peer. He flooded Protestant Europe with promotional tracts printed in several languages. In the eighteenth century, families from the Rhine Valley, Switzerland, Ulster (Northern Ireland), Scotland, and England poured into the colony. Before the end of the eighteenth century, the Quakers found themselves outnumbered by non-Quakers.

Non-Quakers were not the only challenge to Quaker efforts to build a holy commonwealth based on the Golden Rule. Factionalism within Quaker ranks became a more formidable problem than William Penn anticipated. Relentless persecution had bound the Quakers together in England, but once relieved of external threats for their beliefs by settling in the Delaware Valley, internal bickering became more common. Why, asked William Penn, were his settlers "so brutish, so susceptible to scurvy quarrels?"

Eventually material success became an equally serious threat to the Quaker's holy community. No group, not even the Puritans, seemed to embody more fully Max Weber's version of the Protestant work ethic than the Quakers. To them, time was sacred, extended by God to humans for the performance of worldly and spiritual callings. Furthermore, putting material ahead of spiritual values was as much an anathema to the Quakers as it was to the Puritans. Hence, the Quakers, like the early Puritans, were not modern capitalists. They never endorsed the accumulation of wealth as a worthy end in itself.

Yet hard work and personal austerity tended to encourage worldly success and, in time, the subordination of religious and community values to individual and secular values. Quaker spirituality declined and the lust for wealth and luxurious living increased. Both in symbol and practice, Philadelphia became, in the words of a Quaker historian, more of a "countinghouse" than a "meetinghouse." In time, many prosperous Quakers rebelled against the austere demands of their predecessors. Some of the richest and most powerful even renounced Quakerism and joined the less severe Anglican Church.

THE WAYS OF THE PENNSYLVANIA DUTCH (GERMANS)

Next to Africans, German migrants were the largest non-English speaking group of colonists. Between 1683 and the end of the American Revolution in 1783, some 120,000 Germans streamed into the English colonies. Confusing *Deutsch* (meaning German) with *Dutch* (a person from Holland), the English mistakenly called these new settlers—some of whom were in fact Dutch— the Pennsylvania Dutch.

Nearly all were Protestants. Holding views roughly similar to the Quakers, one German-speaking group of Protestants, the pietistic dissenters, fled the Rhine Valley in order to escape the religious persecution of Lutheran, Calvinistic, and Catholic princes. One of these sects, the Mennonites, along with a few German Quakers, founded Germantown, Pennsylvania, in 1684. Groups of sectarians continued to arrive in the eighteenth century, but by then a growing majority of German migrants came from the established Lutheran and Reformed (Calvinistic) Churches. The Lutheran and Reformed churches were quite unlike the Quakers.

Economic opportunity rather than religious freedom brought the Lutherans and the Reformed Protestants to Pennsylvania. After the expense of a six-week trip or so down the Rhine and then across the Atlantic, many arrived penniless. To pay for their transatlantic voyage, perhaps half to two-thirds of them sold themselves into servitude for a period of four years or more. Most became farmers in eastern Pennsylvania, though later many wandered into the Appalachian backcountry. The Germans acquired a reputation for industriousness, skill, and frugality. It was reputed that they cared more for their land and livestock than for their own comfort.

Reflecting their Protestant southwest German village culture, the Pennsylvania Germans placed a high value on their faith and their homes. Nearly all arrived as families; some families even came from the same German village. More patriarchal than either the New Englanders or the Quakers, the Germans assigned rigidly defined roles to each sex. Women's lives revolved around marriage and the family while men occupied the public sphere and assumed the main responsibility for the family's livelihood. As with the English colonists, belief in the occult supplemented Christian beliefs. Traditional witchcraft and hexing, along with incantations to protect home, barns, and persons against curses, long survived in German-American communities.

The German immigrants constructed distinctive ethnic enclaves or subcommunities within the Delaware Valley Quaker settlements. Religion was a central component of these enclaves. At first there were few ministers among the early immigrants, but soon pietists, Calvinists, and Lutherans all sent missionaries. The growth of institutional religion fostered the use of the German language and laid the groundwork for an ethnic school system. By 1775 Reformed churches had sixty-three schools and Lutherans had as many as forty-three. A growing German press also nourished ethnic consciousness. The German press included newspapers—some thirty-eight were published between 1732 and 1800—along with almanacs, political tracts, and religious books.

With the virtual discontinuation of immigration to America in the Revolutionary era, acculturation and assimilation of Germans proceeded rapidly in both the cities and the frontier regions. Many anglicized their names and intermarried with non-Germans. Urban German churches even substituted English for German in their services. Consequently, until the coming of a massive new wave of German immigrants after 1820, strong ethnic enclaves existed only in rural Pennsylvania.

Conclusion

While the religious superstructure of the Delaware Valley colonies eventually weakened and devout Quakers increasingly turned inward, the Friends sought and to a substantial degree implemented a remarkable social experiment. It included a generous recognition of human rights, a tolerance for religious and ethnic diversity, and the absence of a hereditary social hierarchy. Such beliefs and practices pointed toward the nation's future. Beginning with the Revolutionary era and continuing through the "rights revolution" of the late twentieth century, the legacy of the Friends offered a vision of a more generous and a more tolerant society.

Important aspects of New England's ways have also persisted. Such major upheavals as the American Revolution, the Industrial Revolution, massive immigration, and urbanization failed to totally obliterate them. Throughout American history, New England and the states settled mainly by New Englanders have tended to vote as a bloc in national elections. Even to this day, these states have measurably lower per capita homicide rates, higher educational achievements, higher per capita local taxes, and support such causes as women's rights with more fervor than the nation's other major regions. To a remarkable degree, the New Englanders and their descendants have acted in conformity with John Winthrop's 1630 admonition of "always having before our eyes our community."

2

SOUTHERN WAYS

That the North and South developed strikingly different regional cultures seems in some respects quite puzzling. After all, both sets of colonies were extensions of the same European nation—England or Great Britain as the larger entity of England, Scotland, Wales, and Ireland became known in the eighteenth century. The English people founded both the southern and northern colonies at roughly the same time, the colonists spoke the same language, both sets of colonists were overwhelmingly Protestants, and both paid fealty to the same monarch. Yet, when northerners crossed over the Mason-Dixon line separating Pennsylvania from Maryland, it seemed to them almost as if they were entering another country. Southerners had the same feelings when they crossed over into the North. In particular, observers found that in the more secular South individuals were for the most part freer of community controls than they were in the more religious North. (See Figure 2.1.)

Nonetheless, as in the North, it is misleading to think of the colonial South as a single, monolithic culture. By 1750 the South contained three major subsidiary cultures as well as a variety of lesser subcultures. One of the major cultures revolved around the plantation gentry. In the Tidewater region along the Atlantic Coast, the "Great Planters" forged a tightly knit set of hierarchical ways. In the same region, African American slaves, upon whose shoulders the Great Planters' way of life came to rest, constructed an important culture of their own. And away from the Tidewater, in the backcountry, peoples from mostly North Britain developed a third distinctive culture. The ways of these three groups—the backcountry settlers, the African Americans, and the plantation gentry—taken together and interacting with one another long shaped the main contours of Southern life (and, in adumbrated forms, continue to this day).

THE WAYS OF THE PLANTATION GENTRY

Unlike the New England Puritans or the Delaware Valley Quakers, none of the would-be settlers in the southern Tidewater set out to establish religiously centered communities. Dreams of quick, dazzling profits, similar to those realized by the Spanish conquistadors, drove the starry-eyed merchants who planted the first permanent English settlement at Jamestown, Virginia, in

| FIGURE 2.1 | DISTRIBUTION OF EUROPEAN AND AFRICAN IMMIGRANTS IN THE SOUTHERN COLONIES ABOUT 1775 |

Between 1700 and 1775 large numbers of non-English settlers (especially Africans and Scots-Irish) arrived in the southern colonies of British North America.

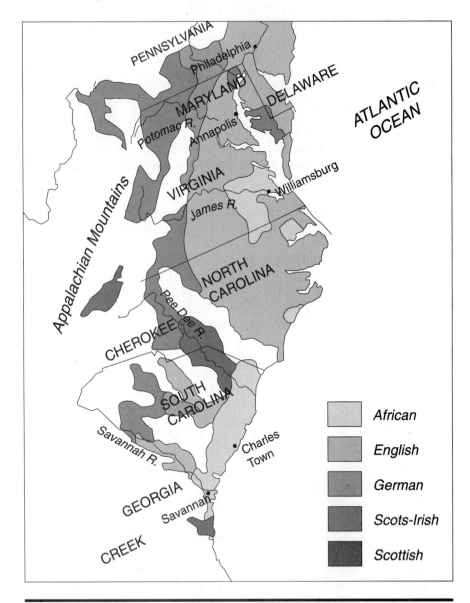

SOURCE: Adapted from Robert A. Divine et al., *America: Past and Present*, 4th ed. (New York: HarperCollins, 1995), p. 103.

1607. But nothing worked out according to plan. Eventual survival of the desperate colony came from a completely unexpected source—tobacco. In the early years of the seventeenth century, everyone—or so it seemed—joined in the mad scramble to profit from what King James I had contemptuously referred to as that "stinking weed." The settlers fanned out around the Chesapeake Bay and up its vast network of navigable streams. Social order was essentially nonexistent. "For how is it possible to govern a people so dispersed," mourned George Sandys to his brother early in the seventeenth century.

Yet, despite startlingly high mortality rates, a scattered population, shattered families, and rampant individualism, life in the Chesapeake gradually took on a less contingent character. While continuing to live on isolated farms, larger family and neighborhood networks slowly formed. By the 1640s, Virginians were laying out new parishes "at a remarkable and prolific pace." Soon churches, albeit spatially far-flung compared to Old England or New England, sprang up throughout the Chesapeake region. Political institutions also acquired additional powers. By the 1660s, the Chesapeake leaders could visualize the possibility of forming a society much like the one they had left behind in England.

While neither the Virginia, Maryland, nor later colonists elsewhere in the South were able to construct exact duplicates of English society, they did eventually reproduce one critically important similarity. That was a *hierarchical* social order. At its base was a huge laboring class (first comprised of indentured servants and later of African slaves); above them came the artisans and the small farmers; and, finally, at the top the Great Planters, a permanent elite of the plantation gentry. In Virginia, the gentry became known as the First Families of Virginia (FFV). For more than two centuries, the First Families, like the southern elites elsewhere, dominated their society. That four of the nation's first five presidents descended from Virginia's plantation gentry provides visible evidence that the FFV's powers and influence extended far beyond the boundaries of their own colony.

ESTABLISHING CLAIMS TO GENTRY STATUS

During the late seventeenth and in the eighteenth century, everywhere and in all things, the Great Planters worked to establish their claims to gentry status. They built elaborate plantation houses, wore the latest finery, engaged in conspicuous leisure, reared their children in the ways of the English upper classes, and sought official acknowledgment of their high status by obtaining from Herald's College in London an officially recognized family coat of arms.

To give weight to their presumed origins among distinguished English families, the Great Planters nourished the "Cavalier myth," the idea that their ancestors had been dashing Cavaliers (Royalists) who had fought valiantly on the side of King Charles I against the Puritans during the English Civil War. For one generation after another, stories of the English Civil War of the 1640s and 1650s seared their memories and bonded them together. Believing that their ancestors had been victimized by the Puritans, the planters

A Great House of the Southern Gentry. Great Houses, such as that in this nineteenth-century lithograph of a colonial Maryland manor house, served as monuments to the power and status of the Tidewater gentry. Notice the cooking and servant quarters on each side of the manor house.

ardently supported the crown (at least until the Revolutionary era), the aristocracy, and the Anglican Church. Only a hierarchical order, they believed, could prevent such horrors from recurring.

But nothing offered more tangible proof of their high status than the possession of a great estate or manor. Men such as Charles Carroll of Maryland and Robert "King" Carter and William Byrd of Virginia counted their acres by the thousands and their slaves by the hundreds. Modeled on English architectural styles, they built "great houses." Typical was George Washington's home. To transform Mount Vernon into a structure befitting his soaring social aspirations, Washington added a second story and extra wings on each side of the building. Outbuildings for cooking and servants surrounded the great houses. Upon approaching the mansion, visitors were greeted by a large formal garden. In order to make their grounds look more like the gardens of the English country gentry, the Great Planters reshaped the contours of the land and ruthlessly pruned or ripped out native trees and shrubs.

The Great Planters gave equal care to the interiors of their houses. Inside, visitors encountered expensive paneling, elaborate plasterwork, and marble fireplaces. A central passage or "summer hall" typically ran from the front to the back of the building. The hall and high ceilings kept the house cooler during the hot and humid summers of the South. No single room was more important in providing evidence of gentry status than the parlor; this expensively decorated room was designed for entertaining guests with music, card games, dancing, and sometimes billiard playing.

Consumption, dress, and entertainment—all offered opportunities to display high status. The southern gentry entertained one another and visitors far more lavishly than did the upper classes in the North. Even to complete strangers, they rarely closed their doors. They kept well-stocked cellars of port and Madeira wines that had been imported from Europe. They ate on porcelain dishes and with genuine silver, including forks, which were rapidly becoming eating implements that signified high social position. Slaves in livery attended the family and their guests. The planters worried about keeping up with the latest London styles. George Washington once complained to his London agent that "instead of getting things good and fashionable . . . we often have articles sent to us that cou[l]d only have been us[e]d by our forefathers in the days of yore." Dressed in fragile and delicate fabrics, articles of clothing confirmed distinctions between gentlemen and plebeians: silk stockings versus wool socks, tight-fitting brightly colored breeches versus loose-fitting grey trousers, and hats versus caps. Until late in the eighteenth century, the Virginia elite continued to wear swords, a privilege reserved to the gentry.

The Great Planters took far more delight in the sensual than did the devout Puritans or Quakers. Not only did they imbibe freely of fine wines, but they savored roast beef and wild game. They developed a distinctive regional style of cooking that included strong seasonings and the frying, simmering, and roasting of meats. The southern gentry ate far more food than settlers elsewhere; they seized every opportunity to schedule great feasts at which they regularly stuffed themselves with food and drink. Sexuality was also less inhibited in gentry culture. Both husbands and wives seemed to enjoy what William Byrd described in his secret diary as "flourishes" or "rogerings." Byrd himself, along with many of the other gentry males, apparently exercised little restraint in employing their superior power and rank to sexually exploit social inferiors.

Unlike in New England, where learning and literacy were promoted so that ordinary lay persons could read the Bible and religious tracts, the Great Planters employed learning on behalf of hierarchy. Commissioning private tutors to educate their children, nearly all of the males and most of the females in gentry society could read and write. But the gentry actively discouraged literacy among those in the lower ranks. "I thank God there are no free schools [in Virginia] nor printing . . . for learning has brought disobedience, and heresy, and sects into the world, and printing has divulged [publicized] them" explained Governor William Berkeley of Virginia. "God keep us from both!"

Certain sports separated the gentry from the lower social ranks. In Britain, only kings and noblemen enjoyed the privilege of stalking the stag and chasing foxes; likewise in colonial Virginia, only the gentry, accompanied by much pomp and ceremony, hunted deer and chased foxes. When the indigenous gray foxes proved too elusive, Virginians imported less wily red foxes from England. No pastimes ignited the passions of the southern gentry more than gambling and horse racing, pursuits reserved by custom and law to gentlemen. When in 1674 James Bullocke, a common tailor, had the temerity to enter his mare in a race against a horse owned by Dr. Matthew Slader, a "gentleman," the county court fined Bullocke two hundred pounds of tobacco and asserted the principle that horse racing was "a sport for gentlemen only."

As was the case throughout the Western world, ways of time and work helped to define a southern gentlemen. A gentleman by definition never worked or, at the least, never worked with his hands. "It would derogate greatly from his character," reported a colonial Virginian, "to learn a trade; or to put his hand to any servile employment." The gentry tried to give the impression that they had the freedom to ignore the restraints of work and time. Rather than using every spare moment to glorify God or in the pursuit of a worldly calling, a gentleman might conspicuously flaunt his contempt for time by getting up late in the morning and deliberately "killing time" by engaging in frivolous pastimes.

Yet aping the English upper ranks presented the gentry with practical difficulties. While England's rural elites relied upon agricultural rents for their incomes—sources that frequently did not require their detailed attention—the gentry's welfare in America usually rested on successful entrepreneurship. To succeed in tobacco, rice, or commerce required long hours of devotion to business. For a planter, careful decisions regarding planting, harvesting, sales, purchases, and management of a subservient work force could and frequently did make the difference between success or failure. Too much time spent at the gaming tables, at the racetracks, or in entertaining could spell disaster for the American gentry. While they might try to disguise their daily routines, the more materially successful planters were usually in fact hardworking entrepreneurs.

THE PLANTATION GENTRY'S FAMILY WAYS

The hierarchical ways of the Great Planters included a patriarchal family. William Byrd, who kept an extensive diary that detailed the life of the gentry, thought of himself as an Old Testament biblical patriarch. "Like one of the Patriarchs, I have my flocks and my herds, my bondsmen & bond women and every sort of trade amongst my own servants so that I live in a kind of Independence of every one but Providence." As with Byrd, the planter-patriarch's family included not only blood relatives of varying degrees, but servants, slaves, and even temporary lodgers. In principle, his authority and protection extended to all of them. All family members deferred to him and addressed him as "Sir" or as "Worthy Sir." Upon meeting him, all lesser men doffed their hats and all women curtsied.

Considerations of piety, love, or mutual compatibility—major desiderata in New England—had little to do with the selection of a marriage partner in planter society. Rather than taking into account romantic infatuations or the likelihood of love developing later in marriage, family patriarchs carefully calculated how a prospective union would affect the family's power and fortunes. A patriarch left nothing to chance; he tried to arrange the marriages of those under his roof so that the unions would strengthen rather than jeopardize the family's position in the colony's hierarchy. Normally members of the Church of England, the gentry conceived of marriage as an indissoluble union consummated in heaven rather than as a covenant between mere mortals. Hence, divorce was technically an impossibility.

As suggested by the practice of arranged marriages and by the gentry's religious views of marriage, concerns with the preservation of hierarchy also influenced Chesapeake gender ways. Anxiety about the perpetuation of blood lines and family status helps to explain why women were punished far more severely than men for extramarital sex and bastardy. A discussion at a Virginia planter's table reported by Philip Fithian, a northern-born tutor, reflected the inferior status of women in planter society. The issue, according to the astonished Fithian, was whether women had souls!

Gentry society prepared girls for lives of subordination and domesticity. Each woman's primary purpose in life was her husband's welfare and happiness—not her own. As Benedict Calvert explained to George Washington in 1773, he and his wife had brought up their daughter "in such a manner, as to ensure the happiness of her future husband." Future wives sought to acquire the arts and skills associated with domesticity, including cooking and sewing; even more important, they spent countless hours at becoming adept at sociability. This meant learning to play a musical instrument, dancing, dressing and grooming properly, polite conversation, and the careful management of bodily motions.

Gentry society prepared boys for lives of mastery and leadership. Unlike New England, "bending" rather than the destruction of the will was the major objective of gentry child-rearing practices. Indeed, gentry parents, concerned about preserving and nurturing their children's autonomous wills, indulged and even encouraged childhood boisterousness, impetuosity, and expressions of rage. But, as their children grew older, parents simultaneously urged them to develop self-restraint. Consequently, boys (as well as girls) spent countless hours learning the social graces and the formal rules of proper conduct for "gentlemen" and "ladies." Internalizing the rituals of self-restraint by the gentry helped to perpetuate the South's hierarchical order.

Nonetheless, an inclination to individual violence was far more common in the Tidewater South than in New England or in the Delaware Valley. The growth in the institution of slavery encouraged violence or the threat of its use, for white youths regularly witnessed the use of physical force against slaves. Throughout the Tidewater region, both the Great Planters and white yeomen farmers extolled reckless courage and physical prowess, though the gentry preferred more genteel forms of boxing and the ritualistic duel to the rough and tumble brawling common to whites lower in the southern social ranks.

The domination and power of the Great Planters rested on more than the cultivation of a hierarchical lifestyle. In time, marriages created vast networks of cousins; these bonds strengthened gentry power. Comprising less than 10 percent of the population in mid-eighteenth century Virginia, the gentry not only owned most of the servants and nearly all the slaves in the colony but they held more than a third of the colony's land as well. They monopolized the colony's public offices. Self-perpetuating oligarchies of planters controlled the local parish churches and the county courts; in turn the county oligarchies dominated the colony-wide legislature, the House of Burgesses. The voters, who were limited to white property-holding males, rarely had a choice of candidates other than from among the ranks of the gentry. Aspirations to move up the social ladder and concerns about race led the white majority to emulate the gentry's lifestyle and acquiesce to gentry rule. As the American Revolution (1775–83) approached and the number of slaves proliferated, the South's social relations became even more hierarchical, patriarchal, and race conscious.

COLONIAL AMERICA'S HIERARCHICAL WAYS

In the eighteenth century, hierarchy became an increasingly important feature of all the colonies, not just those of the Tidewater South. In addition to the plantation gentry, large landholders in other regions, especially in the Hudson, Connecticut, and Delaware River Valleys, as well as the more prosperous merchants in colonial towns called themselves "gentlemen" and claimed gentry status. City merchants built magnificent homes, retained servants (or slaves), entertained generously, and often became part of the entourage of the royal governor.

Although regional ways circumscribed and pushed their behaviors in certain directions, the gentry in all the colonies shared a broadly common culture. That common culture included religion. Normally loyal supporters of the crown and strong believers in hierarchical arrangements in all things, the Church of England became the gentry's religion of choice. From the outset of settlement, Anglicanism was the established religion of most of the South and in New York. Even in Puritan New England and Quaker Pennsylvania, the Anglicans eventually built churches, churches that appealed in particular to the upper ranks in these colonies.

Although Anglican churches frequently included varying degrees of Puritan sentiment and practice, they required no conversion experience of members and they placed a far heavier emphasis upon rituals than did the Puritans. The Book of Common Prayer, adopted by the English church after its break with Rome, prescribed the services and the administration of the sacraments. As with Roman Catholicism, prayers and liturgy rather than sermons were at the heart of Sunday services. Anglican churches even encouraged music as part of the worship service; when they could afford it, they purchased organs. Less concerned than the Puritans about coming to terms with God personally and directly, the Anglicans also tended to be less demanding and more forgiving of human frailties. As a consequence, most of the gentry worried far less than the Puritans about the fate of their souls. They were supremely confident that God would award them with salvation just as he had rewarded them with material abundance and social standing.

Civility and virtuosity were also signs of gentry status everywhere—not just the Tidewater South. The colonial gentry sometimes sent their sons to England so that they could be exposed to refined learning and gain polish. For example, a Virginia father urged his son in England to work hard at learning the ability to converse, for this "will preserve you in the same class and rank among mankind." Ideally, a gentleman acquired the ability to read and quote from the ancient Greeks and the Romans; he also learned how to sing, dance, and perhaps play a musical instrument.

His knowledge and skills were not exclusively a matter of ornamentation or an ability to provide entertainment. Seeking a broad, Renaissance-like knowledge of the universe, a gentleman might collect fossils, flora, fauna, coins, and relics; he might travel widely; and he might pursue drawing, gardening, and architecture. The value placed on curiosity and virtuosity by the gentry (along with many of the clergy who were also normally in the ranks of the gentry) were immensely important in encouraging colonial intellectual life. These groups participated to a far larger degree than might be expected in the Enlightenment, the great intellectual awakening of the eighteenth-century Western world.

The hierarchical conception of society rested upon an age-old belief that there was a divinely ordained scale of being (sometimes called the Great Chain of Being). For example, in the world of nature, all regularities of nature, or natural laws, arose from God, who was at the apex of the chain or hierarchy. Under God were the angels and below them were humans, God's special creation. At the next level were animals, below them plants, and at the bottom of the chain were minerals. Subtly tiered ranks of being and function reflected God's glory and sense of order. In a society devoted to God, explained Jonathan Edwards, a learned New England minister, all have "their appointed office, place and station, according to their several capacities and talents, and everyone keeps his place, and continues in his proper business."

AFRICAN AMERICAN WAYS

Africans involuntarily joined Europeans and Native Americans in the Western Hemisphere. Upon discovery that the Americas offered an abundant opportunity to grow staple crops—sugar, coffee, tobacco, rice, and later on cotton—for market but a shortage of labor for their exploitation, European landholders first tried to recruit additional workers from the native population and their homelands. When these sources proved insufficient, they turned to Africa. Before the trade in human bondage ended in the middle of the nineteenth century, European traders had brought some twelve million Africans to the Americas, a number exceeding the total European migration to the Western Hemisphere for the same time frame. Of the twelve million or so, however, only some 5 percent reached the shores of what became the United States; the remainder were taken mostly to Brazil and the West Indies. Yet, because of high death rates among the slaves in Latin America and high birth rates among North American slaves, by the third decade of the nineteenth century, the United States had the largest slave population in the world.

The degree to which the African slaves transplanted their traditional ways to the mainland of Britain's North American colonies has occasioned heated debate among scholars. Put in the simplest form, some have argued that slavery quickly obliterated African customs and that they were replaced by the more dominant English colonial culture, whereas others have insisted that the slaves were remarkably successful in preserving their African heritage. In any case, this simple dichotomy is misleading. There was not a single, monolithic African nor English culture. The Africans brought with them a great assortment of ways, many of which they adapted to fit their new circumstances. The slaves quickly learned to communicate through the creation of a common language of their own devising, they created their own families, they eventually developed their own variety of Christianity, and in time they acquired a heightened sense of racial separateness or consciousness. The result was the creation of a new and distinctive culture, one that was neither English nor African. Instead, it can appropriately be labeled African American.

AFRICAN CULTURES

Any analysis of the origins of African American cultural identity must begin with African ways. Generalizations about the ways that Africans brought to the Western Hemisphere are treacherous. Few written sources exist and those that do are usually deeply biased by European frames of reference. Difficulties in comprehension are compounded by the fact of cultural diversity. Africa hosted a plethora of cultures. No common language (such as Latin in Europe) or religion provided sources of cultural unity for the vast continent.

West Africa (called "Guinea" by the slave traders), the coastal region extending from Senegambia in the north to Angola in the south, provided most of the Africans exported to the Americas. Great rain forests, in places more than six hundred miles wide, straddled the equator and extended along the West African seaboard northward and westward. Tropical savannas or grasslands, with a far greater range of temperatures and rainfall, fringed the rain forests on both the north and the south sides. Containing dozens of ethnic groups, languages, and customs, this region supported a variety of sedentary farming populations and an assortment of artisans. For thousands of years,

West African artisans had cast iron and bronze housewares, tools, and weapons, and the farmers had cultivated sorghum, rice, fruits, and vegetables.

West Africans tended to organize themselves into large families or kinship networks. These stretched across households, hence tying diverse peoples together. In a marriage system known as polygyny, a man frequently took more than one wife. Because of taboos surrounding sexual relations, women usually had fewer children than their European counterparts. Many women enjoyed a higher status as well. Descent was usually patrilineal, though some families were matrilineal. Some areas supported larger political entities that may be described as kingdoms or states. Complex feudal-like obligations connected families to these states.

Except in the northern reaches of the savanna that were influenced by Islam, West Africans practiced traditional religions. Each religion usually had a close association with a particular place, a creation myth, a myth of humans falling from a perfect world, a priestly class, and a rich set of rituals. A pervasive world of spirits connected everything—land, material objects, ancestors, and living persons. No person stood alone; all were members of a clan that comprised both the living and the dead. Everyone lived in a close relationship with ancestors, spirits, and gods. Since natural objects possessed spirits, they could be mediums or even ancestors; therefore should be revered and placated. Priests and witch doctors served as intermediaries, and they often held special powers to cure diseases and punish enemies as well.

Kinship and wealth ways shaped the institution of African slavery. Rather than by the acquisition of money or land, African kinship societies increased their wealth and strength by adding new members to their group. The extended family's numbers could be increased through marriage (with the added bonus of children) and the involuntary servitude of war captives. Since women performed most of the agricultural labor in Africa and could serve as wives or concubines, they were usually more valued than male slaves.

African slavery differed in key respects from American slavery. In Africa, slaves tended to serve in more diverse roles; they might become wives, concubines, household servants, agricultural workers, or victims of ritual sacrifice. Skin color did not distinguish them from their masters nor serve as a mark of degradation. As members of the immediate households of their masters, they, and especially their descendants, might lose their marginal status and gradually become full-fledged members of the family or clan. Slaves could, and frequently did, marry and own property; they might even own slaves themselves. Slaves destined for the Americas, on the other hand, lost nearly everything—their loved ones, their possessions, and their familiar surroundings.

The slave trade entailed collaboration between European and African traders. Launching massive attacks on inland villages, the African traders acquired most of their booty as prisoners of war, though many were also simply kidnapped. The local rulers and traders then sold their captives to European traders. Encountering Europeans for the first time, many of the slaves feared that they might be killed and eaten by the strange-looking white men.

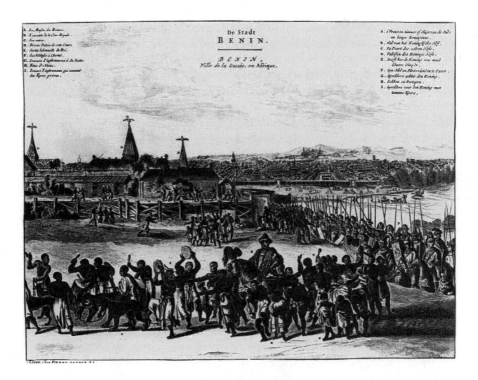

Benin, a Slave-Trading Center in West Africa. Involuntarily joining Native Americans and Europeans in the Western Hemisphere, African slaves brought with them yet another set of cultures. In time, the slaves in British North America developed and perpetuated distinctive African American cultures.

Upon boarding ship, the slave traders frequently stripped their charges— men, women, and children—of all their clothing, an act that, while justified by the slave traders as "indispensable" for "securing cleanliness and health" during the long voyage to the Americas, assaulted the dignity of their captives. Crammed into the holds of ships without adequate food, sanitation, or exercise, perhaps one in five died while on the "Middle Passage" across the Atlantic. Most perished from sickness while others refused to eat and starved to death; still others died when they jumped overboard or were killed while attempting to foment a revolt. One observer described a disembarking group of slaves who had just completed the Middle Passage as "walking skeletons covered over with a piece of tanned leather."

FORGING AN AFRICAN AMERICAN IDENTITY

Apart from the diversity of African ways brought to the Americas, conditions peculiar to the British mainland colonies also helped to shape distinctive African American ways. Traditional ways endured most successfully in the colonial areas in which African slaves comprised an overwhelming majority of the population. Such was the case in many parts of the West Indies and Brazil; in these places even today the persistence of African ways is more pronounced than they are anywhere in the United States.

In the British colonies of the North American mainland, on the other hand, many of the slaves lived among a sea of whites. Their dispersal and density varied enormously; a Boston or Philadelphia merchant might possess a single household servant and a small Virginia planter a half dozen slaves. Isolation under such circumstances made marriage, the retention of traditional ways, or the creation of a separate cultural identity difficult if not impossible. In other places, black numbers were much larger. By 1750 blacks outnumbered whites two to one in the rice-growing lowlands of South Carolina. Of Virginia's nearly three hundred thousand people in 1750, there were only fifty thousand more whites than blacks.

The experience of slaves on the mainland differed in another important respect from those toiling on the sugar plantations of the West Indies and Brazil. In Latin America, harsh working conditions and an unbalanced sex ratio resulted in the number of slave deaths consistently exceeding births. To maintain a constant labor supply, the sugar planters relied upon large transfusions of African imports. The new imports regularly reintroduced and reinforced traditional African ways. On the North American mainland, on the other hand, where the sex ratio was far more equal and conditions were healthier, the slave population grew rapidly by natural increase. By the time of the American Revolution (1775–83), only about one-fifth of the slaves in the mainland were African born; the figure fell to less than 1 percent by 1860. As it became more and more "creole" (American born), the slave population grew increasingly distant from its African roots. Without large and continuous arrivals of fresh imports from Africa to influence them, creole blacks set their own cultural course.

The institution and experience of slavery itself encouraged a sense of black separateness. Initially, Africans in Virginia received treatment that differed little from white indentured servants. Indeed, the two groups were not only subject to the same laws, but they also frequently worked together, played together, and sometimes slept and ran away together. One black, Anthony Johnson, was a servant in 1625, but by 1650 he was a free man who owned land on Virginia's Eastern Shore as well as either slaves or indentured servants. Historians Timothy Breen and Stephen Innes have found that, in Northampton County, Virginia, between 1664 and 1677, at least 13 (out of 101) blacks became free landholders. Apparently they had purchased their freedom.

But the uncertain status of Virginia blacks began to change in the 1660s. As the relative number of Africans rose abruptly in the last half of the seventeenth century, a spate of laws in Virginia and subsequently in the other colonies set black slavery clearly apart from white indentured servitude. As a complex response to racial stereotypes, the protection of property in labor, and fears by whites of the growing number of blacks, these laws required that slaves and their progeny would serve for life, severely circumscribed the rights of both slaves and free blacks, and discouraged manumission. By the middle of the eighteenth century, black slavery was firmly institutionalized, both in the southern and the northern colonies.

The enslavement of Africans in a dominant white society heightened a sense of racial consciousness. While in Africa, "blacks" had not conceived of themselves in racial terms; rather, they had identified themselves as members of clans, ethnic groups, and nations. Racial enslavement in a European overseas colony, however, made it impossible to ignore race. Europeans were (or could become) free while nearly all Africans were in perpetual bondage. In America, "blacks" and "slaves" shortly became nearly synonymous terms. Given the institution of racial slavery, common African origins necessarily became a major source of identity for African Americans.

The existence of separate slave quarters also fostered distinctive African American ways. On larger plantations, white masters usually avoided the cabins and quarters of their slaves. This allowed slaves to communicate with one another, develop family networks, and devise their own religious practices with a minimum of white control. The importance of slave quarters to black culture depended mainly on the number of its occupants. In the late colonial era, half the slaves on tobacco plantations resided in units of twenty or more slaves while half the slaves in the low country of South Carolina and Georgia lived in plantations with a hundred or more slaves. The larger the number of slaves on a plantation, the more likely it was that they could shape their own separate culture.

AFRICAN AMERICAN WAYS

Within the emerging African American culture, some African ways survived more successfully than others. Language illustrates the complex process of cultural survival and adaptation. Upon arrival in the colonies, most slaves found themselves amidst a babel of incomprehensible tongues. Required to obey white overseers, they quickly had to learn some English. English words and phrases joined African ones to form an intermediate pidgin language. On the sea islands of Georgia and South Carolina, regions with dense black populations, pidgin evolved into distinct Gullah and Geeche dialects, dialects that persisted into the twentieth century. By the nineteenth century, in the South as a whole, a distinctively black English emerged. A common language, first in the form of pidgin and later as black English, strengthened the bonds among those of African descent.

Music and dance survived the ordeal of the Middle Passage more successfully than perhaps any other aspect of African culture. Unlike language, success in the retention of musical ways arose in large part from a common African musical heritage. Whites also saw slave music as either harmless or even helpful in increasing productivity and contentedness among slaves. As in Africa, complex rhythmic structures, improvisation, a strong beat, and antiphonal call and response patterns pervaded the music of slaves as well as their descendants. The banjo (originating in Africa), the fiddle (borrowed from Europeans), and drums and tambourines (of both European and African origins) were favorite instruments. Slaves chopped weeds and thinned tobacco (and later, cotton) plants to the measured cadence of chants. In the evenings, music enlivened life in the slave quarters, and on Sundays, music comprised an integral part of black Christianity.

Black music exercised a considerable and an abiding influence on southern white society as well. Black musicians quickly became a conspicuous presence at planters' balls where they imparted versions of their own music and dance. "Towards the close of an evening when the company [of whites] are pretty well tired with country dances," reported Philip Fithian in the middle of the eighteenth century, "it is usual to dance jiggs: a practice originally borrowed, I am informed from the Negroes." Conversely, blacks sometimes entertained themselves by mocking the music and manners of their masters and mistresses. Few if any aspects of slave culture united African Americans more effectively than music.

Despite the handicaps imposed by slavery, the family was a central component of African American culture as well. Slave codes did not provide for legal marriages, children or spouses could be sold at any time, and masters deprived slave fathers of some of their traditional authority over families. Sexual predation of slave women by white masters further weakened the black family. Since African customs permitted premarital sexual relations, premarital pregnancies among the slaves were relatively common. In most cases, when a slave woman became pregnant, she and the father married. In a ceremony witnessed by fellow slaves, the man might present the wife with a small and inexpensive present.

Planters usually encouraged slaves to "marry" and have children. After all, additional slave children might enrich the planter, and the formation of families might stabilize life in the slave quarters. Though marriage between slaves from different plantations was common, most children were born into two-parent families. While slave women frequently worked in the fields, gender roles were not merged. Within the strictures of slavery, males (as in Africa and in English white society) remained dominant.

While slavery prevented the re-creation of the intricately structured kinship groups of West Africa, slaves from different African societies shared a belief in the importance of kinship. By the middle of the eighteenth century, slaves increasingly identified themselves with an extended genealogical network of parents, siblings, grandparents, aunts and uncles, nephews and nieces, and first and second cousins. In the absence of biological relatives, slaves frequently created fictive relatives. Parents encouraged their children to express respect for older, unrelated men and women by addressing them as "uncle" or "auntie," while age-mates might be called "brother" or "sister." A larger network of relatives not only provided a sense of identity but eased some of the pain arising from slavery and the separation from one's immediate family.

Neither did Africans transport intact their religious practices to North America. Religious specialists or ritualists, religious language, and ritual paraphernalia—all were necessarily left behind or so severely uprooted that traditional ways could not be fully retained. Yet before the American Revolution an overwhelming majority of black southerners practiced some form of African religion that fused the natural and the spiritual worlds. Expressive in form, religious worship included shouting and swaying in rhythm with the beat of drums or other instruments. Traditional burial ceremonies, called the "ring shout" in America, entailed a ritualistic dance around the body of the deceased. Such a religious rite, the slaves believed, helped to achieve unions with ancestors and the gods.

African Americans remained largely outside the influence of Christianity until the last three decades of the eighteenth century. Fearful that the baptism of slaves might lead them to demand their freedom, slave masters discouraged conversion. Neither did the Church of England, the religion of their masters, appeal effectively to slaves. Not only did they find Anglicanism too liturgical and inexpressive, but the church's priests required lengthy religious instruction and arduous preparation before one could join the church.

On the other hand, the evangelical (revivalistic) white denominations, which began to make large inroads in the South during the Great Awakening of the middle decades of the eighteenth century, enjoyed far more success among blacks. At first the white Baptist and Methodist preachers welcomed slaves into their midst and even questioned the legitimacy of slavery as an institution. No need to await lengthy religious training, the white exhorters said: One could be saved at once.

Black preaching, with its heavy reliance upon the vernacular and its call-and-response interaction with the audience, exploded out of the climate established by the passionate Methodist and Baptist exhorters. But growing discrimination from the white evangelicals and the successes of the black preachers gave rise at the end of the eighteenth century to the rapid growth of separate black churches. Led by their own preachers, nourished on biblical stories of a promised land of freedom, and inspired by hymns (spirituals) of sorrow and joy, independent black churches forged their own kind of Christianity. Their form of evangelical Christianity came to serve as the core of a distinctive African American identity. It helped to keep white masters at arm's length, sustain communications among blacks, and serve as an agency promoting human dignity, freedom, and equality.

The mere presence of millions of Africans affected English culture as well; indeed, it encouraged in dozens of subtle ways what may be called an "Africanization" of the South. For example, slaves introduced African culinary arts to English kitchens, including barbecues, black-eyed peas, and fried chicken as well as the use of more sharp spices. Combining African, French, and Indian dishes, Louisiana's gumbos and jambalayas remain today America's most distinctive regional cuisine. Many African words, including the most universally used word in the world, *okay*, passed into English, and some linguists believe that the southern "drawl" is mainly a product of African intonations.

To recapitulate: Africans faced unique difficulties in transplanting their ways to the Americas. Among the obstacles were the diversity of the ways that the Africans brought with them, their minority status, and, above all, the institution of slavery. However, these same circumstances, plus the "creolization" of the British mainland's black population, fostered the creation of a distinctive African American culture.

BACKCOUNTRY WAYS

In the backcountry, a region that included not only Appalachia but in the nineteenth century extended into the Mississippi and Ohio river valleys, another distinctive set of ways developed. The violent traditions of its mostly North Briton settlers and the dangerous environment of the region in which they settled came together to shape the backcountry's cultural uniqueness. Unlike New England or the Southern Tidewater, backcountry ways embodied neither the vision of a holy commonwealth nor a stable hierarchical order. Instead, a warriorlike *individualism* was its most distinguishing characteristic.

FROM NORTH BRITAIN TO THE AMERICAN BACKCOUNTRY

To comprehend the origins of backcountry individualism, we must turn back to the British borderlands, the region from which the settlers came. The borderlands refer to the southern parts of Scotland, the northern counties of England, and to Ireland and Ulster (north Ireland). Ulster was the home of the Scots-Irish (in America they were sometimes simply called the "Irish"), who had been transplanted to Ireland from Scotland by the English during the seventeenth century.

Nothing marked borderlands history as much as protracted warfare. For some seven hundred years the area had been repeatedly victimized by the invading armies of the Scottish and English monarchs. Not only did the borderlanders suffer death, pillage, and rape from invading armies, but the accompanying chaos enhanced opportunities for criminals, encouraged lawlessness, and bred mistrust. Since legal institutions could not be counted on for rendering order or justice, the borderland people acquired a profound suspicion of authority. To protect themselves and their families, they turned to their own private resources—to themselves and their families (or clans) rather than to public officials. Hence, long before their arrival in America, coping with centuries of warfare and tumult had fostered a fervent individualism among the borderland peoples.

Beginning in the seventeenth century, the borderlands underwent a profound transformation. The warring kingdoms of Scotland and England finally became one. The process began in 1603 when Scotland's James VI inherited the English throne (as James I) and culminated in the Act of Union in 1706–7, an act that formally created Great Britain. Sending some borderlanders to the gallows and forcibly relocating others in north Ireland, the new government set about brutally pacifying the region.

In particular, the Scots-Irish developed a burning hatred of everything English. They resented their Anglo-Irish landlords; usually absentees, the great landholders not only monopolized land ownership but charged exorbitant rents. Neither did the Scots-Irish, as nonconformist Presbyterians, take pleasure in paying taxes to support the established Anglican Church. As Presbyterians, they could not hold public offices or even legally marry in Presbyterian ceremonies. Suffering from oppression, high rents, and periodic famine between 1717 and 1775, thousands from the borderlands fled to America. The exodus eventually totaled more than a quarter million people, making it one of the largest folk migrations in history.

Although north Britons found their way into every American colony (especially the backcountry portions), most arrived first in Philadelphia. As early as 1730, a Pennsylvania official complained that the borderlanders brought with them their "audacious and disorderly manner." Encouraged by Quaker officials to move on, they pushed westward from Philadelphia into the Great Appalachian Valley in south-central Pennsylvania. From this point, the immigrant stream turned southward, following the natural thoroughfare of the Great Valley. By 1760 settlers occupied the central part of the Great Valley and began moving across to the western side of the Continental Divide.

Their experiences in north Britain had prepared them well for the harsh realities of the American backcountry. Although the weather was moderate, water abundant, and trees in plentiful supply, coping successfully with their new environment required an extraordinary toughness. Life itself was precarious. Many, perhaps most, of the first settlers had no legal title to the lands they occupied; they were squatters, who simply hacked out a clearing, planted a few acres of corn, let their hogs and cattle (if they had any) run wild, and supplemented their diet by hunting and fishing. Bourbon, a whisky made of corn rather than barley (the grain from which Scotch whisky was made back in the British borderlands), became a staple of American backcountry life. The self-sufficiency and physical isolation of the backcountry settlers nourished their already deep-seated individualism.

In quest of better opportunities or more security, the backcountry people relocated with startling frequency. Appropriate for their migratory habits and the uncertainties of their lives, they built small and impermanent log cabins rather than more enduring structures of stone or brick. Even today, the popularity of mobile homes and prefabricated houses throughout the southern highlands suggests the continuation of that region's impermanent and migratory ways.

Warfare with the Native Americans also fostered backcountry individualism. As the cutting edge of the eighteenth-century Anglo-American invasion of regions occupied by Indians, the former borderlands peoples once again found themselves in a war-racked land. Instead of warmly welcoming the newcomers as occupants of their lands, the Shawnees in Ohio, the Iroquois confederation in the north, and the Cherokees in the south—among other tribal units—offered a fierce resistance to the invaders. Between 1755 and 1815 fighting between the two peoples was almost continuous.

Backcountry Log Cabin. Log cabins reflected the contingent character of backcountry life. In the backcountry, the violent traditions of its mostly Scots-Irish settlers and the dangerous environment in which they settled encouraged individualistic, warrior-like ways.

Backcountry pleas to the seaboard colonists for help went mostly for naught. The backcountry settlers more often than not had to fight the Indians, the French, or later (during the Revolution) the British alone. The Indian wars gave rise to monumental legends of backcountry heroism. Both Daniel Boone and Lewis Wetzel achieved epic fame as Indian fighters. A reputation for Indian fighting skills even helped to propel Andrew Jackson (the first president of Scottish descent) into the White House.

THEIR WARRIOR WAYS

In sum, the experiences of the north Britons in the American backcountry reinforced their traditional warrior ways. Even their prayers, hymns, and sermons abounded with military metaphors. They visualized themselves as Christian warriors rather than as messengers of peace. Guided by their experiences in Britain, they distrusted clerical authority and reserved a special contempt for both Anglican and Catholic priests. Mostly of Presbyterian (and hence Calvinistic) origins, they split into numerous warring sects. Emotionally wrenching revivals regularly blazed through the backcountry, the original home of American camp meetings. By the middle of the nineteenth century, endemic revivalism had made the Baptists and the Methodists the dominant backcountry religious denominations.

The settlers supplemented their militant Christianity with beliefs in magic and the occult. While belief in the occult was present among all colonial groups, it was especially attractive to those afflicted with the insecurities and uncertainties of backcountry life. Witches, they believed, were everywhere and could, if not placated, wreak havoc with human welfare. Astrology, the belief that the stars and the planets affect earthly events, guided such important decisions as when to plant, to castrate farm animals, and to harvest. By resorting to a bountiful arsenal of magical folk cures, many forms of illness could be relieved. No sensible backcountry settler would dig a well without first employing a well diviner. Holding a special divining rod (a stick with a forked limb) in his hand, the diviner would walk over the land until a magical force pulled the limb downward. A well dug at that spot, the backcountry people believed, would offer an abundance of fresh water with a minimum of physical exertion.

Boys received training as potential warriors while girls learned how to be mothers and supporters of their fighting men. Rather than breaking (as with the Puritans) or bending (as with the Chesapeake colonists) the will, backcountry parents were exceptionally permissive; they sought to foster self-assertion, particularly among their male offspring. A later observer wrote of the southern highlands that "for three centuries . . . parents often look on it as evidence of spirit and smartness to see their children rudely insulting the quiet and often humble citizens of the country." Such indulgence had the effect of encouraging individual autonomy—of producing men who were quick-tempered and who jealously resisted external controls. Female children, on the other hand, were trained to be self-denying.

Rituals of warfare accompanied males throughout their lives. The games of boys revolved around contests for dominion—wrestling, running, tripping, and hitting one another with their fists. At a tender age each male child received his own miniature weapons—a pocket knife (an instrument to this day that many southern highlands males carry to their graves), a hatchet or axe, a bow, and perhaps even a real gun. Long after physical threats to their families had subsided, the adult males continued to act out warrior roles. They hunted not simply to put meat on the table or for sport but as a ritual of warfare.

Popular backcountry sports included wrestling, "rough and tumble" fighting, and various forms of mock warfare. No rules restrained rough and tumble fighting; combatants bit, scratched, kicked, and gouged out eyes. While the incidence of gouging was exaggerated by travelers' accounts and folklore, a South Carolina backcountry judge recalled: "Before God . . . I never saw such a thing before in the world. There is a plaintiff with an eye out! A juror with an eye out! And two witnesses with an eye out!"

Other backcountry pastimes prepared competitors for warfare in less brutal ways. Carnival-like festivities surrounded competitions in running and jumping as well as throwing axes and spears. Above all, the backcountry settlers admired shooting skills. They acquired an enduring reputation for their feats of marksmanship. The precise shooting of the "hunters from

Kentucky" reputedly accounted for American success against the British at the Battle of New Orleans in 1815.

"Where the warrior ethic is strong," writes David Hackett Fischer in his provocative study of regional colonial cultures, "the work ethic grows weak." Nothing impressed travelers in the backcountry more than the general prevalence of indolence, in particular the laziness of the men. In part, this perception grew out of the visitors' misunderstanding of the seasonal nature of farming, herding, and hunting. Planting season, for example, might require long hours of arduous labor. But once the seeds had been put in the ground, farmers might enjoy a period in which they were free to fish, hunt, or relax. The perception of backcountry sloth also arose from the gender division of work. Unlike other regional cultures, backcountry women not only managed the household, but they also frequently worked in the fields, did the gardening, and cared for the farm animals. Unlike the Puritans or the Quakers, neither men nor women experienced guilt from the way that they used time.

Neither did a warrior ethos encourage education. The southern highlands had the lowest level of formal schooling of any major region of British North America. Probably less than 10 percent of the white children were enrolled in school at any one time. In the nineteenth century, years of formal education increased in the backcountry but, until late in the twentieth century, it remained lower than elsewhere in the United States. While the backcountry was relatively impoverished in its education and its written literature, it enjoyed a rich oral culture. Backcountry peoples esteemed much more those who could tell gripping folk tales, sing ballads, and display feats of memory than those who could read well, spell correctly, or speak grammatically.

The backcountry was more open to sensuality than the other major white cultures of British America. Unlike Puritan New Englanders, Quaker Pennsylvanians, or even Anglican Virginians, backcountry people spoke freely and openly about sex. "How would the polite people of London stare, to see the females (many very pretty)," wrote Charles Woodmason, an Anglican missionary in the region. "The young women have a most uncommon practice, which I cannot break them of. They draw their shift as tight as possible round their breasts, and slender waists . . . and draw their petticoat close to their hips to show the fineness of their limbs." Woodmason added that, in the privacy of their own homes, "nakedness is counted as nothing." In 1767, Woodmason estimated that 94 percent of the backcountry brides for whom he conducted marriage ceremonies were pregnant on their wedding day. Until at least the nineteenth century, when the backcountry received a massive infusion of evangelical Protestantism, its sexual ways were far earthier and less restrained than the other major regional cultures.

THE BACKCOUNTRY'S WAYS OF ORDER

While there were gaping inequalities of wealth in the backcountry, the settlers firmly rejected hierarchical ways. Even the huge underclass of poor whites, who soon comprised a permanent majority of the region's population, insisted that it be treated with the same respect as everyone else. Visitors of upper rank repeatedly complained about the insolence and lack of deference that had been accorded to them by ordinary people in the backcountry. Even the poor refused to defer to anyone. Rich and poor wore similar clothing, addressed one another by first names, and worked, ate, played, and fought together on the same footing. The popular expression "One man is as good as another" summed up backwoods egalitarianism.

Rather than social class, the region's politics revolved around personalities and personal loyalties. Historian Charles Lee has described that style as a "macocracy," or "rule by the race of Macs," that is, by those of Scottish descent. Stories told by his mother of oppression in the British borderlands influenced Andrew Jackson's approach to politics. Reflecting the contingent character of life in both the British borderlands and the American backcountry, Jackson and other backcountry voters were suspicious of politicians and the authority exercised by governments. Rather than selecting candidates on the basis of their rank or where they stood on particular issues, they voted for those men in whom they had the highest personal trust.

Distrust of governments frequently led backcountry settlers to take justice into their own hands. The people practiced retributive justice; "every man should be a sheriff on his own hearth," proclaimed a North Carolina proverb. When wronged, a man or his family was expected to punish the wrongdoer themselves. Such a conception of justice encouraged vigilantism, the rendering of justice by self-appointed ad hoc individuals or groups rather than the state.

Retributive justice contributed to a climate of pervasive violence. In particular, families engaged in protracted and violent feuds. The legendary feud between the Hatfields and McCoys in West Virginia rested in part on fact. Even in our own time, no region has a higher tolerance for violence than the former colonial backcountry. The homicide rates in the southern highlands and the southwestern states, a region with large numbers of people whose ancestors came from the backcountry, are a third larger than the national average. Only a few of the nation's ghettos equal or exceed the per capita homicide rates of the southern highlands and the southwestern states.

The colonial backcountry settlers displayed their personal autonomy in countless other ways. The people favored a minimal government, one that exercised little control over their personal lives. Today in per capita terms the regions comprised mainly of those of backcountry origins usually continue to pay the lowest local taxes, and local governments spend the least of any region in the nation. While intolerant of others, the backcountry people prized their own liberties and were quick to defend them, even by force if necessary. Today the divorce rate in states comprised predominately of those of backcountry origins is nearly 50 percent above the national average. The presence today along Appalachian and Ozark highways of endless retail outlets, walls of signs, and countless junked cars also reflects the stubborn persistence of the region's individualistic ways.

Yet the backcountry was not without a moral order. The order sprang primarily from religion and from clan and kin. As in the British borderlands, clans—groups of related families who lived near one another and who were conscious of their own identities—were a formidable presence. The clans not only imposed an order within their own ranks but they frequently disciplined the community at large as well. Take pregnancies out of wedlock for instance. While prenuptial pregnancies were higher in the backcountry than in any of the other white regional cultures, the responsible male was expected to marry the pregnant female. Indeed, if he sought to escape responsibility for his act, he would face the retribution of the woman's extended family. In the nineteenth century, with the startling successes of revivals in the region, evangelical Christianity also became a major force in controlling backcountry behavior.

CONCLUSION

Settlers later carried southern ways south and westward. That backcountry peoples took their ways with them as they moved into the northern parts of Georgia, Alabama, Mississippi, and Louisiana, and into Kentucky, Tennessee, and Arkansas, as well as the southern parts of Ohio, Indiana, Illinois, and Missouri. The plantation gentry's ways tended to prevail in what became known as the Deep South, the lowlands of Alabama, Mississippi, Louisiana, and East Texas. There, as well as in the coastal plain extending from Maryland southward to Georgia, hierarchy, patriarchy, and race—the Deep South's major cultural matrix—exhibited a remarkable persistence. It was in the Deep South, too, that a distinctive African American culture developed.

While regional, racial, and ethnic cultures are essential to understanding early American history, their importance should not be exaggerated. The colonists also shared striking similarities. With the important exception of pockets of Germans in Pennsylvania, the Dutch in New York, and Native Americans, the overwhelming majority of the residents of all regions spoke English. Nearly all were Protestant—and by and large Protestants of a particular sort. Versions of Reformed (Calvinistic) Protestantism reigned supreme in both New England and the backcountry and even influenced Anglican and Quaker practices.

Though less tangible than their religious persuasions, the settlers also enjoyed a broadly common political culture. It included fealty to the English monarch and belief in the principle of miniparliaments or assemblies (legislative bodies) in which the colonists themselves were represented. The colonists jealously guarded their common English "liberties" as well. Broadly shared ways among the colonists were a necessary precondition for the mighty upheaval that lay ahead—the American Revolution.

II

THE WAYS OF THE NEW REPUBLIC, 1760–1860

3

REPUBLICAN WAYS

Few if any periods of American history have equaled the significance of the Revolutionary era. Between 1760 and 1820, a collection of two million colonists scattered along a narrow strip of the Atlantic Coast became a vast continental republic of nearly ten million people. In 1760, its residents were for the most part loyal monarchical subjects. They rarely challenged the hierarchical order in which they lived. But, then, over the next sixty years, the old order gave way. Americans first rejected monarchy, a far more daring step then than it seems to us today. They then created the formal political institutions—the executive, legislative, and judicial bodies of the state and national governments—that endure to this day. Equally significant, in America the gentry-dominated hierarchy (at least outside the Deep South) lost much of its vicelike grip on social relationships. Fawning and deference by the lower ranks to superiors could no longer be taken for granted. By 1820, the nation had witnessed a startling elevation of the position and power of ordinary white men. That common men enjoyed such stature struck the entire Western world with utter amazement.

But the importance of the Revolution for the history of American ways extends far beyond these momentous developments. As Dr. Benjamin Rush, the distinguished Philadelphia physician, observed in 1786, the replacement of the British monarchy with a new political system was only "the first act of the great drama." The next act should be, Rush insisted, "to effect a revolution in our principles, opinions, and manners so as to accommodate them to the forms of government we have adopted." In short, while some revolutionaries were interested only in rejecting Britain's political hegemony and establishing their individual rights, Rush and many others sought far more than this. They urged that Americans adopt a new *republican* society and culture, one that would complement and bolster the nation's new political system. Without a monarchy to hold society together any longer, republican ways should aim at creating a virtuous citizenry. Unless citizens in a republic were willing to subordinate their selfish and individualistic impulses to the common good of the community, Benjamin Rush predicted, they would devour "each other like beasts of prey."

In the end, their vision of the new republic went unrealized. While never completely renounced nor lacking in influence, the republican ideal of a public-spirited community clashed with the reality of an aggressive individualism. Rather than discouraging a scramble for individual wealth, the equality among citizens touted by the Revolution's gentry and clerical leadership nourished rising expectations on the part of ordinary white men. Rather than a republican community of self-sacrificing citizens, the Revolution culminated in a more materialistic and individualistic society. In the nineteenth century, many Americans even began to identify the pursuit of individual wealth as a major building block for their society.

THE ESTABLISHMENT OF A REPUBLICAN POLITICAL SYSTEM

At first, the main impetus behind the American Revolution had almost nothing to do with challenges to existing hierarchical and patriarchal arrangements. Indeed, virtually no one gave any thought to the possibility of enhancing the power or position of ordinary white men. For that matter, neither did they initially give any consideration to the possibility of rejecting the British monarchy. But during the crisis leading up to the Revolution (1763–76) and during the Revolution itself (1775–83), America's gentry and clerical leadership soon found themselves in the awkward position of asking the common people for assistance in resisting what they described as British "tyranny."

Then, as the ordinary people joined the protest as rioters, petitioners, and eventually as soldiers, the revolutionary movement developed a momentum that its elite leadership could no longer contain. The conceptions of liberty that were so movingly expressed in dozens of resistance pamphlets soon became much more than mere abstractions. No longer were they the exclusive concern of such towering gentry theorists as John Adams and Thomas Jefferson. The idea of arguing and fighting on behalf of liberties now moved the common people as well. Once they had taken up the cause of resistance and revolution as their own, the traditional social bonds (including hierarchy and patriarchy) that revolved around monarchy suddenly became far more vulnerable. The revolt then entailed more than simply a colonial rebellion against Great Britain. It became a movement that would potentially destroy the ties that held much of colonial society together.

THE BONDS OF MONARCHY, HIERARCHY, AND PATRIARCHY

In the eighteenth-century world of monarchies, each and every person, regardless of rank, owed a personal fealty to the king or the queen. The monarch resembled a patriarch whose subjects were in essence his or her children. Just as having common parents ties siblings to one another, a shared allegiance to the monarch connected every subject to every other subject in the realm. Great pomp and ceremony, both in Great Britain and in the colonies, bolstered royal authority. Government officials displayed royal arms and emblems on public buildings, scheduled celebrations of the king's birthday, and always acted in the name of the king or the queen. Furthermore, the Church of England was the monarch's church. With its elaborate ceremonies and close ties to the monarchy, the Anglican Church strengthened royal authority.

From the king at the top to the bonded servants and slaves at the bottom, society in both England and the colonies was also organized into a hierarchy of social ranks. Each rank had varying degrees of freedom and servility. In principle, no one was really independent or unattached; all were tied to a position within the hierarchy. Unlike modern society, few individuals were, at least in theory, free of an extensive set of obligations and responsibilities that extended beyond themselves. The emotional satisfaction of knowing that one belonged and counted for something in the hierarchy helped to offset dissatisfactions arising from inequalities in rank.

While the colonists were without the elaborate and sophisticated degrees of social rank found in the Mother Country, one great horizontal division, that between the ordinary people (the plebeian or common people) and the extraordinary people (the patricians or gentry) separated colonial Americans. Eighteenth-century colonists believed that the patricians and the plebeians differed in far more ways than dress, speech, pastimes, special political privileges, titles, and wealth. The gentry frequently assumed that the ordinary people had simple wants and minds. They sometimes regarded them as little better than mere animals. George Washington once described the common people as "the grazing multitude." Even John Adams early in his life referred to them as "the common herd of mankind" and observed that they had no understanding of "learning, eloquence, and genius."

In all matters affecting the welfare of the community, the ordinary people were expected to defer to the judgement of their superiors. And usually they did. Vividly illustrative of the power of deference was the response of a group of ordinary Virginians to their gentry leadership during the revolutionary crises of the early 1770s. "You [our gentry leaders] assert that there is a fixed intention to invade our rights and privileges. We own [admit] that we do not see this [intention on the part of the British authorities] clearly, but since you assure us that it is so, we believe the fact . . . [Therefore] we confide in you, and are ready to support you in every measure you shall think proper to adopt." In short, these Virginians, like most of the common people of the day, expected their gentry representative to act according to his own best wisdom, not theirs.

Patriarchy represented yet another vital link in the hierarchical web of colonial social connections. While the biblical fifth commandment requires only that one "honor thy father and mother," the Anglican prayer book of 1549 expanded that commandment to read: "to honor and obey the king and all that are put in authority under him: to submit myself to all my governors, teachers, spiritual pastors and masters: to order myself lowly and reverently to all my betters." Like the monarchs, the gentry conceived of their subordinates as their children. Whether slaves, indentured servants, or apprentices, all servants lived under a strict and sometimes brutal patriarchal authority. Both slaves and indentured servants could be bought and sold and were subject to corporal punishment. Together these bonded groups comprised more than half of the male population in colonial America. Although differing in its application according to region, patriarchy also characterized colonial families. Everyone within the household was dependent on and owed fealty to the father or master. In law (though not always in practice) women rarely enjoyed a position different than that of children or servants. They subordinated themselves completely to their husbands, fathers, or masters.

THE LIMITS OF HIERARCHY IN COLONIAL AMERICA

As important as the intricate ties of monarchy, hierarchy, and patriarchy were to colonial society and culture, they were never as strong in fact as they were in principle. Many colonists happily paid homage to the gentry and the monarch while opposing their acts or the acts of the king's officials. For example, colonial legislative assemblies, which were made up almost exclusively of the gentry, frequently found themselves at odds with the royal governors, who were the king's primary representatives in the colonies.

In most places, as we have previously observed, colonial America's hierarchy was not so entrenched nor so elaborate as that of England's. The colonies had at best a truncated version of England's social structure. No hereditary lords who lived off the rents from their immense estates existed at the top of American society. The merchants and large landholders who comprised the American gentry were never as wealthy as their English counterparts. While they aped the ways of the English upper classes, the American gentry, as we have seen, were far more likely to engage in active business— for example, managing a slave work force or a mercantile house—than their English counterparts.

Neither was there a great mass of destitute people at the bottom of colonial society. In the middle of the eighteenth century, two-thirds (compared to one-fifth in England) of the white families in the colonies owned land. This meant that far fewer families in America than in England were economically dependent on those above them in the social order. Well before the American Revolution, a rapidly expanding economy and population growth increased the difficulties of distinguishing gentlemen from commoners. After all, "in a country like this, where property is so equably divided," explained an eighteenth-century colonial, "every one will be disposed to rival his neighbor in goodness of dress, sumptuousness of furniture, etc."

Allegiances to monarchy and hierarchy were far stronger in some regions and among certain groups of colonists than they were among others. The Great Planters of the Tidewater South, the wealthier urban merchants, and the adherents of the Church of England were far more likely to endorse a full-blown monarchial system than were the New England Congregationalists, the Pennsylvania Quakers, or the backcountry people. In particular, the backcountry Scottish settlers harbored deep animosities toward the English, their church, and their monarchy. That the English forces referred to George Washington's Continental Army as a "Presbyterian Army" not only echoed the alignments of the earlier border wars between Scotland and England but reflected the enthusiasm with which most of those of Scottish origins embraced the American Revolution.

In the middle decades of the eighteenth century, a specific historical episode—the Great Awakening—also weakened the traditional bonds of authority. In this spectacular religious uprising that spread throughout colonial America, evangelical preachers delivered impassioned extemporaneous sermons aimed directly at the ordinary people. Those who failed to experience a searing emotional transformation (a spiritual rebirth or conversion), the evangelists declared, were doomed to an eternal life of agony, fire, and torment. Unlike Roman Catholics or Anglicans, the evangelicals had absolutely no tolerance for sin or human frailties. Insisting on purity in individual behavior, they tended to transform all social and personal conflicts into moral issues—into unambiguous issues of right and wrong. Hostile to compromise and driven by unrelenting zeal, they repeatedly launched crusades against the evils of the secular world.

The Great Awakening indirectly challenged the world of hierarchies and patriarchies. The confrontation began with the clergy itself; revival converts frequently refused to defer to the established clergy. Rather than ministers who delivered scholarly discourses, they embraced those who could stir the emotions. The evangelicals challenged the dominion of the older, established churches as well. The New England Congregationalists and Presbyterian churches frequently split into "old lights" (those who opposed revivals) and "new lights" (supporters of revivals).

In Virginia, in particular, the Great Awakening unsettled the traditional authority of the gentry. Defections from the Anglican Church came in droves as New Light Presbyterians, Baptists, and finally Methodists made new converts who came mostly from the ranks of the ordinary people. Taking literally the biblical promise that the last shall be first, the revivalists ignited a process that in the next century culminated in the massive conversion of slaves to Christianity. In general, the Great Awakening marked the beginning of a new era in southern history, one in which Anglicanism eventually gave way to evangelical Protestantism as the dominant religious persuasion in that region.

The inflammatory rhetoric of the revivalists terrified the gentry everywhere, for the evangelical communities renounced the elite's fopperies and luxurious living and rejected the gentry's preoccupations with rank. New Englander Charles Chauncy warned that the revivalists intended to "destroy all property, to make all things common, wives as well as goods." Such a statement was preposterous, but it reflected the hysteria generated by the Awakening among the gentry.

The Great Awakening drew out more fully the implications of the individualistic logic of the Protestant Reformation. Revivalistic clergymen urged the ordinary people, including poor whites, women, and African slaves, to turn inward to themselves to find the right relationship with God, even though "your Neighbors growl against you, and reproach you." With the Great Awakening, religious attachments no longer came from the top down, but rested increasingly upon the people themselves and their individual decisions. Religion could no longer be counted on as a bulwark of the status quo, as an agency invariably promoting deference and obedience to hierarchy and monarchy.

REJECTING MONARCHY

Moreover, Protestantism in a more general sense contributed directly to the eventual American rejection of the British monarchy. To Protestants, the Pope was the Antichrist (the incarnation of the Devil on earth). In the colonial era, the recurring wars between Protestant England and Catholic France had regularly reinforced a general Protestant terror of everything associated with Catholicism. Many of the revolutionaries were also dissenting Protestants. As dissenters from the Church of England, they frequently saw little difference between the Anglican and Roman Catholic churches. To the dissenters, both Anglicans and Catholics practiced false religions and both fostered corrupt and tyrannical alliances between church and state.

To the dissenters, proposals by the English government for planting an Anglican bishopric in North America, which presumably would have greatly strengthened the Anglican church in the colonies, and the passage of the Quebec Act in 1774, which provided for continuing toleration and tax support for the Catholic Church in Canada, offered irrefutable proof of a continuing church-state tyranny. It may have taken some mental gymnastics, but dissenting preachers, in the apt words of George Mardsen, were able to put "Protestant England in the columns of the Pope." To them, the Quebec Act and the proposal for a North American bishop betrayed the principles of the Protestant Reformation.

Furthermore, the belief by the colonists that they were members of a larger community of "freeborn" Englishmen contributed to their eventual rejection of monarchy. Unlike the subjects of the absolute monarchies on the European continent, the colonists, along with other English subjects, believed that the authority of the monarchy was limited by an unwritten constitution. Unlike our written constitution of 1787, the English constitution was unwritten; it consisted of custom and tradition. In addition, each English subject, again unlike the residents on the European continent, enjoyed a set of rights (such as a trial by a jury of his or her peers) that were enshrined in common law.

Between 1763 and 1776, actions by the British government triggered a growing suspicion among the North American colonists that the king and Parliament were engaged in an elaborate conspiracy to take away their traditional liberties as freeborn Englishmen. As early as 1765, when Parliament passed the Stamp Act, which was designed to raise revenues from the colonies without the consent of their legislative assemblies, John Adams concluded that there was "a direct and formal design on foot, to enslave America." Hundreds of colonial pamphlets and newspaper essays echoed the same theme. The colonists frequently greeted the British acts "to enslave" them with mock funerals to liberty. In carefully orchestrated spectacles, they would carry a coffin to a graveyard where, at the last moment, its occupant miraculously revived. The assembled crowd would then cheer and retreat to a tavern to celebrate liberty's continuing good health.

The BOSTONIAN'S Paying the EXCISE-MAN, or TARRING & FEATHERING

"The Bostonian Paying the Excise-Man" by Philip Dawe, 1774. This is a drawing that mocks British efforts to collect taxes from colonial Americans. Ordinary people, not just the gentry, joined the revolutionary movement as rioters, as petitioners, and, in time, as soldiers. They, along with John Adams, believed that the Parliamentary measures adopted between 1765 and 1776 represented "a direct and formal design on foot [by the British], to enslave America." Such conspiratorial thinking eventually led the colonists to reject monarchy entirely and in 1776 to establish a new republic.

Yet no one enunciated an argument for a complete rejection of the monarchical system until Thomas Paine wrote *Common Sense,* published in January of 1776. In this best-selling pamphlet, Paine, who had recently arrived in Philadelphia from England, stripped England's limited monarchy of its historical and theological foundations. As recent events made manifest, wrote Paine, England's "so much boasted Constitution" had utterly failed to prevent the king's tyranny. By rejecting monarchy, establishing a republic (a nonmonarchical system), and continuing to serve as an "asylum for the persecuted lovers of civil and religious liberty from *every part* of Europe," America was at the dawn of a new age in world history. "We have it in our power to begin the world over again," Paine wrote, "the birthday of a new world is at hand."

THE DECLARATION OF INDEPENDENCE

In July of 1776, the Second Continental Congress decided to declare American independence. A young Virginia planter and lawyer, Thomas Jefferson, known as a graceful writer, was largely responsible for drafting the Declaration of Independence. Jefferson included in the document a long list of specific abuses that he attributed to King George III and his ministers. These offenses were of sufficient magnitude, Jefferson said, (in words reminiscent of Englishman John Locke's defense of the Glorious Revolution of 1688) to warrant separation from Great Britain.

But nothing in the Declaration of Independence had as much significance in terms of elevating the position of ordinary people as Jefferson's assertion that "all men are created equal." Apparently Jefferson believed that human equality rested on two premises. From his reading of the moral philosophy of Francis Hutchinson, a Scot, Jefferson concluded that each individual, regardless of his or her differences physically and mentally, possessed a "moral sense." The universal possession of a moral sense—an innate capacity to determine right from wrong—made humans equals. This moral faculty distinguished them from other species in the animal kingdom.

Jefferson's second premise flowed from his understanding of nature. To Jefferson, consistent with other eighteenth-century Enlightenment thinkers, nature embodied God's intent. Every plant and animal had been placed on earth by "Nature's God" to fulfill a divine purpose. The Creator's purpose for each member of the individual human species was, according to Jefferson, "the pursuit of happiness." Hence, the Creator extended to all humans liberties or opportunities to seek their individual happiness. Unreasonable government infringements on these liberties, such as those promulgated by Britain's ministers, thwarted nature's plan. In such circumstances, Jefferson reasoned, the overthrow of that government was justified.

While God intended that all humans pursue their individual happiness and that they all enjoy liberties for doing so, Jefferson surely did *not* mean the results would be equality of wealth or privilege. Jefferson and the other gentry generally saw suffrage, for example, as a privilege rather than a right. The privilege of voting should be extended only to property holders or other taxpaying "free men"—those who had "a stake in society"—not to women, slaves, apprentices, or indentured servants.

Neither did they see the principle of equality as a complete rejection of hierarchical authority. Most of the revolutionary leadership believed that the great majority of the population could most effectively seek their happiness by subordinating themselves to their "superiors." But, the Revolution's leaders did hope to reconstruct hierarchy on a new and more solid foundation. Deference in the future should be extended only to those men who were exceptionally talented and virtuous, what Jefferson called a "natural aristocracy" rather than one based on superior birth.

Yet, whatever reservations Jefferson and his contemporaries had about the concept of equality, the promise *implicit* in the phrase "all men are created equal" was the single most radical and powerful idea unleashed by the Revolution. Once invoked, the idea of equality developed a relentless momentum of its own. During the Revolutionary era itself, both African Americans and women called attention to the apparent discrepancy between the Declaration and their own condition, and soon ordinary white men began to employ the axiom of equality on behalf of an expanded suffrage. No other principle proved so corrosive to the chains of traditional hierarchy.

In both the nineteenth and twentieth centuries, the Declaration's postulate of equality energized campaigns for human rights. Herman Melville called it "the great God absolute! The center and circumference of all democracy!" That "all men are created equal," Abraham Lincoln said, is "a standard maxim for free society which should be familiar to all and revered by all; constantly looked to, constantly labored for, and even though never perfectly attained, constantly approximated." Within a few decades of independence, the principle of equality helped make the United States the most egalitarian nation in the world, a position it retains today if equality is understood in terms of individual rights and opportunities rather than the distribution of wealth.

The Declaration gave impetus to a more general assault in the Revolutionary era on hierarchical social bonds. Not only did it explicitly reject the English monarchy but it posited the idea that societies need not be the products of custom or tradition. Instead, societies and governments could arise from the people themselves. The conception of states (or nations) springing from contracts between individual people rather than resting on hierarchy, patriarchy, or custom encouraged a preoccupation with individual liberties or freedoms rather than one concerned first and foremost with the interests of the community.

As a document that encouraged Americans to think of themselves as free from traditional constraints, the Declaration was a manifesto of individualism. During the nineteenth century, individualism became an even more dominant social philosophy. Until the twentieth century, this individualism was sometimes also called "liberalism" or "classical liberalism." It should not, however, be confused with the modern use of "liberalism" in American politics which usually entails the idea of employing governments more extensively as a tool to promote the general welfare.

SHORING UP THE FOUNDATIONS OF HIERARCHY

The Declaration of Independence and the constitution-making process that followed on both the state and national levels entailed far more than repudiations of the British monarchy. The Revolution also triggered challenges to the American gentry's power and authority. During the Revolution, impressive numbers of ordinary people mobbed British authorities, banded together in revolutionary committees, and attacked pomp in government. Fortunately for the position and power of the gentry, the actions of the common people were often guided by the gentry themselves, mob lawlessness was usually short-lived, and potential animosity toward hierarchy sometimes subsided when the leaders of the common people themselves climbed into positions of leadership.

But rather than electing those who had comprised the colonial gentry (those assumed to be the natural aristocrats or gentlemen) to public office, common white men showed inclinations to select men from their own ranks as their political leaders. According to a Boston newspaper, state legislative halls were now unfortunately being filled with "blustering ignorant men" rather than "men of sense and property." These newly elected officials cared little for abstract notions of a higher or a common good; instead, they were intent on serving the narrow interests of their constituents. They consistently supported lower taxes, a minimal role for government, and inflationary policies (achieved by the states issuing more paper money) that would relieve debtors.

To the gentry everywhere, the ordinary people, drunk with their newfound power, threatened to replace British tyranny with a new form of oppression. The majority acting through their representatives had replaced the monarchy as potential despots.

While the inability of the national government to regulate commerce precipitated the call for the Constitutional Convention of 1787, fear of a diminution of hierarchical authority was equally responsible for the contents of the final document. Specifically, the Constitution set out to strengthen the powers of the national government while curbing the democratic "excesses" of the states (and hence the collective power of ordinary men). The Constitution denied the states the power to print paper money, impair contractual obligations, or place taxes on imports or exports.

Rather than ordinary men, the Constitution's framers sought to ensure the selection of "natural aristocrats"—of selfless gentlemen of broad visions and superior talents—for government services. The government created by the Constitution, James Madison wrote in *The Federalist* No. 10, should "extract from the mass of Society the purest and noblest characters which it contains." Consistent with their hopes of choosing the best men, men who could exercise judgments separate from the narrow, specific interests of their constituencies, the Constitution provided for the *indirect* selection of the president as well as the senators and the judges in the court system. Of all the federal officials, only members of the House of Representatives were to be elected directly by the people. To check the unbridled power of majorities, the Constitution also provided for an intricate division of powers between the executive, legislative, and judicial branches. The Constitution promised to the American gentry, in the words of historian Robert Shalhope, "a last hope to preserve the republican ideal of a government in the hands of the 'worthy' rather than the 'licentious.'"

George Mason, a Virginia planter who opposed the Constitution, predicted that the new government would "commence as a moderate Aristocracy," but would evolve into either an "oppressive Aristocracy" or a "Monarchy." Mason's prognostication proved partly correct; initially the gentry elite did control the new national government created by the Constitution. Virginia planter George Washington was elected president, and Washington's secretary of the treasury, Alexander Hamilton, sought through his ambitious financial programs to strengthen hierarchy by tying the wealthier classes to the new national government. Critics accused the Federalists (as the supporters of Hamilton were known) with trying to reestablish a monarchy and with opposition to the revolution that was raging in France. They are the sort, said Abraham Bishop of Connecticut, "who wish [that] congress shall be opened with a speech from the throne to my Lords and Gentlemen."

But Hamilton's efforts to reverse the erosion of gentry power spawned opposition in the South from the rural gentry who were committed to the idea of a freehold farming nation and in the North by egalitarian social forces. They combined to form the Republican party, and with the election of that party's candidate, Thomas Jefferson, to the presidency in 1800, efforts to contain the democratic impulses unleashed by the Revolution took another decided setback. However, the final symbolic defeat of traditional hierarchy on the national level awaited Andrew Jackson's election to the presidency in 1828.

VISIONS OF A NEW REPUBLIC

As Benjamin Rush noted, the American Revolution entailed far more than the establishment of republican political ways. From the mid-1770s and on into the 1780s, idealistic hopes filled the sermons and writings of prominent Americans. *Republicanism*, while never defined precisely or explicated fully, summed up these revolutionary aspirations. For the dissatisfied in Europe and America alike, republicanism offered a compelling alternative to the monarchical order. Since republicanism called for a major overhaul of American society and culture, it added a powerful moral—indeed, even a utopian—imperative to the American Revolution.

In particular, the proponents of republican ways believed that the destruction of the older chains of monarchy required a new set of social ties. While fear, coercion, superstition, patronage, and corruption held together monarchies and traditional hierarchies, republican social adhesives required benevolence, earned respect, and a sincere fondness between the ordinary citizens and their leaders. The people should obey their republican leaders out of "love and not fear," wrote John Adams. Generosity, genuine esteem, and authentic affection should link husbands and wives, parents and children, masters and servants, and the rulers and the ruled. The successful establishment of these new republican ties required an extraordinarily enlightened and virtuous citizenry.

RELIGION

In his *Dissertation on the Feudal and Canon Law* (1765), which was written in response to the Stamp Act crisis, John Adams brought together both secular and religious sources of the republican vision of a new society. Like other children of the eighteenth-century Enlightenment, Adams paid homage to "the great examples of Greece and Rome," whose simple republican societies, Adams wrote, had yielded a wondrous array of historians, statesmen, orators, poets, and philosophers. Adams deplored the Middle Ages, a period in which he said that the monarchs and the "Romish clergy" had formed a "wicked confederacy." That evil union of church and state, Adams concluded, condemned "the common people" to "servile dependence."

Then came the Protestant Reformation, which to Adams and most other Americans, represented a fundamental turning point in human history. Beginning with the Reformation, "knowledge gradually spread in Europe" and "ecclesiastical and civil tyranny" declined proportionately. Adams took even larger liberties with an accurate rendering of the past when he argued that America had been settled by peoples who championed religious and political liberty. (Remember that, with the striking exception of the Quakers, all major colonial groups sought at best religious freedom *only* for themselves. Puritan minister Nathaniel Ward had said that "tolerance stinks in God's nostrils.") American settlement, Adams concluded, was nothing less than "the opening of a grand scene and design in Providence for the illumination of the ignorant, and the emancipation of the slavish part of mankind all over the earth."

While Adams's understanding of the past can be faulted, his connection of dreams of a new republic with religion had merit. The social plan of the eighteenth-century republicans was in some respects a secularized (more worldly) version of the aspirations of the first New England settlers. From the outset, Governor John Winthrop insisted that God had called the Massachusetts Bay settlers to plant a "Model of Christian Charity" in America, one that would serve as a blueprint for the entire world. The New England Puritans had envisioned an organic society in which individuals subordinated their personal interests to the whole and to the glorification of God. The early Puritans also tried to employ all of their social institutions—their families, towns, and churches—on behalf of building a stronger and more moral community.

Millennialism, which arose from a biblical prediction that a thousand-year kingdom of Christ on earth would precede the final judgment, encouraged religiously inclined Americans everywhere to strive for a more moral society. As early as 1702, Cotton Mather, a Boston minister, concluded that God might have chosen America for the Millennium; perhaps Boston would become the New Jerusalem. Later, during the Great Awakening, Jonathan Edwards, America's most distinguished theologian, again speculated that the Millennium, "the most glorious renovation of the world," was taking place in America. Edwards and other revivalists interpreted the Great Awakening itself as evidence of God having chosen America for the Millennium.

Clergymen saw in the American Revolution and republicanism not only millennial possibilities but heaven-sent opportunities to cleanse America of sin. From the outset of the Revolution, the clergy tried to put aside their doctrinal differences in order to mount a common crusade against evil. The very "success or failure of your exertions in the cause of virtue," they were told, would determine the fate of the republican experiment. Confronted with such an awesome task, religious groups responded to the call for promoting virtue with a stridency and a zeal that frequently far surpassed the efforts of the Revolution's more secular-oriented leaders.

THE ENLIGHTENMENT

The eighteenth-century Enlightenment also informed the republican vision. The fundamental source and inspiration for the Enlightenment had come from the Scientific Revolution of the seventeenth century. In *Principia*, published in 1687, Isaac Newton, an Englishman, set forth mathematical laws explaining motion and physical mechanics. The key to Newton's laws was his theory of universal gravitation. Every physical body in the universe, Newton said, attracts every other body in precise, measurable ways. Newton's formulations offered the vision of a universe governed by predictable, natural laws. Night followed day not because of God's whim but because of explicable natural laws. Contemporaries imagined the universe as a giant machine, analogous to a ticking clock. God might be a great watchmaker who had created the universe and then put it in motion to operate by the laws of nature. Given the Newtonian model of an orderly universe, it was now possible to imagine a society and a political system based upon principles arising from the laws of nature.

At the same time that Western Europeans embraced revolutionary scientific ideas, they formulated new theories for obtaining knowledge. Francis Bacon, René Descartes, and John Locke contributed most directly to the acceptance of the scientific or empirical method. While Newton practiced the empirical method, Bacon became its publicist. Bacon rejected speculation in favor of gathering masses of evidence, which, he believed, would (almost self-evidently) reveal natural laws. Descartes, on the other hand, started with the mind rather than what exists outside the mind. The quest for knowledge, he concluded, should begin with such self-evident propositions as human existence itself.

John Locke in his *Essay Concerning Human Understanding* (1690) rejected Descartes's view that humans are born with basic ideas and ways of thinking.

Locke insisted that at birth the human mind was like a blank tablet; thus all ideas arose from experience (from the five senses of seeing, hearing, feeling, smelling, and tasting), which filled the tablet with data. Upon receipt of such data, the mind then could organize the experience into patterns, which represented knowledge. Modern empiricism employs both the approach of Locke and of Descartes. Experiments begin with imaginative hypotheses (constructs of the mind) that are experimentally (or factually) verified by resorting to experience. Given the acceptance of Locke's analysis of how knowledge was acquired, historian Gordon Wood has written, "everything suddenly seemed possible." Now humans had it within their capacities to mold, in accordance with the laws of nature, their own world.

The Enlightenment was not limited to Europe. Better-educated Americans, including both ministers and the gentry, participated in the great intellectual upheaval. Indeed, nearly every prominent person in the Revolutionary era was familiar with Newtonian physics and Locke's theory of knowledge. Aided by newspapers, books, pamphlets, and correspondence, these Americans kept abreast of the latest currents of European thinking. In turn, Americans made significant contributions to the European Enlightenment. European intellectuals avidly read such American political documents as the Declaration of Independence (1776), the new state constitutions arising from the Revolution, the United States Constitution (1787), and *The Federalist Papers* (1788).

Americans also contributed to eighteenth-century scientific knowledge. The curiosity of Europeans about the Western Hemisphere encouraged Americans, most of whom were self-taught, to prepare extensive reports on plants, animals, temperatures, and Indian lore. Specimens of nature collected by Americans assisted the Swedish naturalist Carl Linnaeus in completing his famous biological classification scheme, and Isaac Newton used observations of a comet in 1676 by Thomas Brattle of Harvard to illustrate how the orbits of comets are fixed by gravitational force. Benjamin Franklin won international renown for his work on electricity. Franklin not only reported the results of his experiments but, by positing the idea of positive and negative charges, offered a major hypothesis about the fundamental nature of electricity. In particular, the practical applications of scientific knowledge attracted Americans. Benjamin Franklin again led the way; his ideas ranged from the invention of bifocal glasses and an improved stove to calculating a more direct way to navigate the North Atlantic Ocean. On both sides of the Atlantic, the growing faith in science and human reason encouraged social and cultural experimentation.

CLASSICAL ANTIQUITY

While on both sides of the Atlantic the growing faith in science and human reason encouraged social and cultural experimentation, the revolutionary generation also conceived of their endeavors in terms of their understanding of the ancient world of Greece and Rome. Nearly all the colonial gentry had

Charles Willson Peale, The Artist in His Museum, 1822. Hale and hearty at eighty-one years of age, one of the nation's most prominent painters lifts a curtain in his Philadelphia museum to reveal to us the marvels of nature. Contemplation of nature's order, wrote Peale in 1800, could inspire the American people "to aspire to the moral perfections" of God, "the great author of all things." In short, the displays in his museum would "influence public opinion [so] that republicanism will be highly promoted."

studied Latin and Greek; they read and reread such ancients as Homer, Virgil, Cicero, and Tacitus. From these and other ancient writers, they established lifelong friendships with the classical heroes of their childhood. Reading the classics left them with the firm conviction that liberty always rested on precarious foundations. Consequently, during the events leading to the American Revolution, they repeatedly recalled horror stories from the ancients to the effect that even the smallest concessions to tyranny would lead down a slippery slope to complete and abject slavery.

The revolutionary leadership hoped to embody in America the best of the ancient world. "I us'd to regret not being thrown into the World in the glorious third and fourth century of the Romans," said General Charles Lee shortly after the Revolution began, but now it seemed to Lee and his fellow revolutionaries that the long-held dreams of classical republicanism were about to be realized for the first time—not in Europe but rather in America. As models of the good society, the revolutionaries turned back to the Greek city-states of the fifth and fourth centuries B.C. and the Roman republic from the sixth century B.C. to the first century A.D. For a time—or so it seemed to the American revolutionaries—these nations had enjoyed a golden age. The arts flowered as never before, the construction of magnificent public buildings bore mute testimony to the vitality of republicanism, and a remarkably virtuous citizenry chose heroic, self-sacrificing men as their leaders. While each of these ancient republics eventually succumbed to tyranny, they furnished the American revolutionaries with a vivid and concrete vision of what their own republic might become.

Nearly every revolutionary leader fantasized about becoming a modern Cato, a Cincinnatus, a Cassius, or a Cicero. Joseph Warren even donned a Roman toga while delivering a Boston Massacre oration in 1775. Nothing fired their zeal for assuming ancient personas more than Joseph Addison's popular play *Cato* (1713). Addison, an Englishman, based his play on the life of Cato the Younger and Julius Caesar. Filled with declamations on virtue, the play revolved around Cato's willingness to make the supreme sacrifice, to relinquish his life on behalf of his beloved republic. Having seen the play performed many times, no revolutionary tried to model his life upon Cato more completely than George Washington. "Washington was Cato turned Virginia country gentleman," concluded his biographer James Thomas Flexner. To be successful, many revolutionaries believed that the American republic required the leadership of would-be Catos.

The American revolutionaries also admired ancient philosophy. In particular, the more secular-inclined gentry found in Stoicism a philosophy of special relevancy to their situation. With origins in ancient Greece and triumphant later in Rome, the Stoics had been the first to place natural law at the center of their philosophy. The possession of reason allowed humans to live agreeably with nature, the Stoics said. Since all men partook of reason and all nature operated according to law, the Stoics concluded that universal law should govern all humans. The Stoics also attributed a special value to virtue. Cicero, a Stoic and probably the favorite classical author of Americans, defined virtue as "reason perfected." To have lived a virtuous life, a life of self-control, was far more important than any other human achievement. Without self-control men were mere slaves. They were, as Seneca (one of the ancients once wrote), the slaves to sex, to money, and/or to ambition.

THE AMERICAN EXPERIENCE

When contemplating alternatives to societies revolving around monarchies, the American experience itself loomed large in republican thinking. By the middle of the eighteenth century, well before the American Revolution, American character and culture had acquired a special place in the minds and imaginations of enlightened thinkers throughout the Western world. To many of Europe's intellectuals, American society seemed in important respects to already embody Enlightenment and republican principles. At its most basic, they thought, America society was far less artificial, corrupt, cruel, and decadent than Europe.

The image of American purity and simplicity arose in part from the way the educated classes understood American history. To cope more successfully with the rigors of America, some speculated that the white settlers had adopted the simpler ways of the Native Americans. The European promoters of American colonization had reinforced the image of American simplicity and innocence. They had repeatedly described America as a rudimentary and benign place in which there was an abundance of land and little need for government.

British America was without Europe's haughty aristocrats and arrogant priests. Instead, simple farmers, servants, ambitious artisans, Quakers, and Puritans settled and lived there. "Every man thinks and acts for himself in a country where there is an equal distribution of property," wrote an anonymous American to a London newspaper in 1774. While the letter writer certainly exaggerated (modern studies indicate that the top 10 percent of the wealth holders in 1774 possessed about half of colonial America's net worth), property was far more equally distributed in America than in Europe.

No American group enjoyed a higher stature among enlightened Europeans than the Quakers. Once considered exotic fanatics, by the middle of the eighteenth century Quaker advocacy of toleration, pacifism, and simplicity, as well as their respect for human rights, had won the enthusiastic endorsement of many Enlightenment thinkers. The civic virtues embodied in Pennsylvania's Quaker society had actually fulfilled some Enlightenment dreams. "William Penn might glory," wrote the French philosopher Voltaire, "in having brought down upon the earth the so much boasted golden age, which in all probability never existed but in Pennsylvania."

To European and American thinkers alike, no individual incarnated American simplicity and virtue more fully than Benjamin Franklin, a Pennsylvania resident but a non-Quaker of Boston origins. His life story, which he told in his famous *Autobiography,* seemed to embody perfectly the ideals of the Enlightenment. Allegedly rising from lowly origins, unsophisticated, and guileless, Franklin equaled or out-achieved many of his far more cosmopolitan contemporaries in Europe. Franklin's astonishing accomplishments in science, letters, and statecraft seemed to offer concrete proof that genius could arise in a simple, provincial society. Franklin not only personified the best of America ways for Europeans but also shaped the conception that Americans had of themselves. They too thought of America as a land comprised of countless lesser versions of Benjamin Franklin.

CREATING A REPUBLICAN SOCIAL ORDER

Like the aspirations of other great revolutions, republican dreams for a new set of American ways fell short of complete fulfillment. True, the American revolutionaries replaced the monarchical with a republican political system, but as we have seen, the new republican governments were not exactly what the clerical and gentry leadership of the revolution had hoped to implement. The same was true of their efforts to create a republican social order. The goal of a virtuous citizenry dedicated to the common good frequently clashed with the republican emphasis on equality and individual liberties. Even to this day, the opposing impulses of freedom and community that arose in the Revolutionary era have never been fully reconciled.

REPUBLICAN SOCIAL WAYS

Consistent with their dreams of a new republic, fervent republicans tried to root out everywhere and in all things the more obvious vestiges of monarchy. But it was not easy to instantly identify and drop the older ways. Even such a dedicated patriot as George Washington had to be reminded of the republican antipathy toward presumptions of social superiority. In 1783, Washington and officers with whom he had served during the Revolution formed the Society of the Cincinnatus. Although the intent of the group was merely to keep old friendships alive, howls of protest greeted the revelation that membership in the society was to pass from father to eldest son. Aedanus Burke, a South Carolina legislator, warned that the society planned to create "an hereditary peerage [which would] undermine the Constitution and destroy civil liberty." An embarrassed Washington quickly called for the abolition of the hereditary membership provision in the society's bylaws. The crisis then subsided.

Republicanism included hostility to wearing imported finery and even the use of refined speech, both of which were associated with monarchy and aristocracy. Once independence had been declared, Benjamin Franklin and other prominent patriots promptly disposed of their periwigs. The public ridiculed judges for wearing wigs. All citizens now claimed for themselves the titles of "Mr." or "Mrs.," appellations once reserved to the gentry. Many ordinary citizens joined the Quakers in refusing to doff their hats to anyone. In assessing the influence of republicanism in Philadelphia, Benjamin Rush declared in 1805 that "wigs have generally been laid aside. . . . Tight dresses are uncommon, and stays are unknown among our women." (Rush did lament, however, the continuing exposure of and/or flimsy coverings of women's "breasts and limbs.") Even the diet of republican Philadelphians, according to Rush, underwent a healthy "revolution." Philadelphians now drank less alcohol and ate less meat and ice cream than they had during the monarchy.

Throughout the Revolutionary era and long afterwards, republicans worried that inequalities in wealth imperiled their experiment. Unlike monarchies, which rested on vast discrepancies between the wealth of the ordinary people and that of the aristocracy, a republic, they believed, could survive and prosper only when wealth was distributed widely among the citizenry. "A *general and tolerably equal distribution of landed property is the whole basis of national freedom,*" wrote Noah Webster in 1787. It was, Webster added, "the very *soul of a republic.*" In republics, unlike the prevailing practices in monarchies, all persons should receive "the fruits of their own labor." Though republicans never defined precisely what they meant by *fruits of their own labor* (did it include, for example, the profits from the buying and selling of merchants?), they agreed that a general equality of wealth was essential to the existence of a healthy republic.

Glaring inequalities in wealth, the republicans believed, usually arose from acts of governments rather than from the dynamics of the marketplace. Such fears led the states to abolish such feudalistic practices as primogeniture and entail. These laws allowed a landholder to pass his property to his eldest son with the requirement that it never be divided, sold, or given away. While historians have long believed that repealing primogeniture and entail had little practical effect on the distribution of wealth or the existence of hierarchy in America, recently Holly Brewer has persuasively argued that Thomas Jefferson was essentially correct when he argued that their repeal would end "ancient and future aristocracy" and lay "a foundation . . . for a government [that was] truly republican." Furthermore, repeal offered the satisfaction of visibly removing two conspicuous traces of hereditary hierarchy from the state laws of the new nation.

The states reexamined another link in the hierarchical/monarchical order—the close association of church and state. "That all men have a natural and unalienable right to worship Almighty God according to the dictates of their consciences" became one of the rallying cries of the Revolution. While severing ties with the established Church of England, most of the states retained a kind of multiple establishment in which a variety of religious groups could receive tax support. Led by Jefferson, who enjoyed the trust of growing numbers of Presbyterians and Baptists, Virginia took the unprecedented step of completely separating church and state in 1786. Soon other southern states followed, but in New England, churches continued to receive tax support until as late as the 1830s. The First Amendment to the federal Constitution of 1787 was initially understood as prohibiting only the national Congress from making laws affecting religion.

While the Anglican Church (after the Revolution renamed the Protestant Episcopal Church in America) suffered from both disestablishment and its association with Britain during the Revolution, the American revolutionaries, unlike later revolutionaries, rarely launched general attacks on religion. True, most of the Revolution's most renowned leaders were not orthodox Christians. Indeed, many of them embraced the French Enlightenment notion of deism. They viewed God as a great architect, a "first cause," who created a universe that operated according to predictable, mechanical-like natural laws. Even Puritan-born John Adams believed that ascribing divinity to Jesus was "an awful blasphemy." So certain was Thomas Jefferson that he could distinguish the true words of Jesus from the biblical ones—"they stood out like diamonds in a dunghill," he said—that he wrote his own version of the New Testament, one that was shorn of all claims to Jesus's divinity.

Yet the deistic-inclined founders of the republic found valuable allies against Britain among the dissenting Protestants. The Revolution enjoyed widespread clerical support, in particular among dissenting Protestants but among the sparse Catholic population as well. Sharing a dislike of the church-state tie in Britain, American Catholics, dissenting Protestants, and those like the secular-minded Thomas Jefferson joined together in their enthusiasm for republicanism.

But republicanism was not simply a matter of rejecting the visible vestiges of monarchy and hereditary hierarchy. Infected with the optimism of the Enlightenment, the revolutionary leadership also hoped to create a society that would reduce suffering while increasing pleasure. Altering the ratio of pain to pleasure in human existence, they believed, could be accomplished in large part by expelling ignorance, driving back the forces of tyranny, and increasing the understanding of nature.

Consistent with the belief that republican governments should be more benevolent and humane than monarchies, Thomas Jefferson, among others, drew up plans for softening the harsh penal codes of the colonial era. Pennsylvania led the way by dropping the death penalty for all crimes except murder, and substituting imprisonment for brutal whippings and mutilations. By isolating the offenders from the public and from one another, the penal reformers hoped that the penitentiary would become "a school of reformation." By 1805, New York, New Jersey, Connecticut, and Massachusetts had followed Pennsylvania in building penitentiaries based on the practice of solitary confinement.

The more radical of the republicans also demanded legal reform. "A system of laws of our own, dictated by the genuine principles of Republicanism and made easy to be understood to every individual in the community" should, a republican wrote, replace the complexities and mysteries of common law. Common law, which based its authority on precedent, too often favored the elite rather than the ordinary people. The profession of law itself came under assault. "Any person of common abilities," wrote Boston's Benjamin Austin, "can easily distinguish between right and wrong."

REPUBLICAN MOTHERHOOD

The revolutionary experience and republican principles also spawned a reconsideration of patriarchy in all its forms. Just as hierarchy—especially hereditary hierarchy—came under assault, writers on both sides of the Atlantic reexamined the traditional connections between husbands and wives, parents and children, and masters and servants.

As early as 1776, Abigail Adams, in a private letter to her husband John, observed that while "you are proclaiming peace and good will to men, emancipating all nations, you insist upon retaining an absolute power over all wives." Although John consulted with and respected Abigail's opinions on most matters, he brushed aside her request for a reconsideration of the powers that husbands exercised over wives by quipping that in practice husbands "have only the name of masters" and that it was in fact husbands rather than wives who were "the subjects."

Far less compromising was a widely read Englishwoman, Mary Wollstonecraft, who championed complete female equality. Influenced by her reading

Women's Rights Petition, 1792, from The Lady's Magazine and Repository of Entertaining Knowledge. Employing a classical motif, this lithograph shows a group of women petitioning Columbia, a goddess representing America, for the "Rights of Women." Liberty and equality, two of the most prominent watchwords of the Revolutionary era, led both women and African Americans to demand freedom from traditional forms of oppression.

of Wollstonecraft, Judith Sargent Murray from Massachusetts emerged as America's first avowed feminist. Women "should be taught to depend on their own efforts, for the procurement of an establishment in life," Murray wrote. Murray insisted that women enjoyed mental capacities equal to men. It was therefore in the interest of the new republic to extend equal educational opportunities to women. Murray even envisioned "our young women form-ing a new era in female history."

Murray was overly optimistic. Although during the war women had fre-quently found themselves assuming a new array of responsibilities, including the operation of family businesses and farms, their autonomy and authority was soon lost once the war ended. Divorce remained difficult to obtain, though the number of divorces increased, particularly in New England where women had always enjoyed a more equal status than in the other regions. Freedom in making marriage choices and educational opportunities for women also expanded, especially in New England and Pennsylvania, where several female academies were founded. In New Jersey until 1807, when the state legislature rewrote a provision of its constitution that allowed "all free inhabitants" owning a specific amount of property to vote, white widows and unmarried women could even vote.

While the Revolution fell far short of implementing female equality, it en-couraged the acceptance of the idea of "republican motherhood." Republican motherhood represented a first, albeit ambiguous, step in recognizing an en-larged role for women in civic affairs, for the revolutionaries charged the republican mother with the civic responsibility of rearing virtuous, liberty-loving sons. In short, while remaining a second-class citizen, the republican mother was to transform the home into a nursery for the future guardians of the republic. The new role of republican motherhood rested on and fostered the assumption that women possessed unique moral sensibilities as well as special powers to shape the character of men. Such constructions of gender differences grew increasingly popular in the nineteenth century.

ANTISLAVERY

The quest to republicanize American society and challenges to patriarchy also led to a reexamination of the institution of chattel slavery. Except for Quakers (and presumably slaves themselves), the colonists had taken slavery for granted; they assumed that it was part of a natural social hierarchy. Re-publican citizenship, on the other hand, brought into question the legitimacy of slavery as well as other forms of servitude and bondage.

That white Americans were championing equality and natural rights while keeping several hundred thousand blacks in slavery raised in glaring relief a discrepancy between republican ideals and social practices. "*Slavery is inconsistent with the genius of republicanism,*" Luther Martin told the Mary-land state legislature in 1788. "[Slavery] has a tendency to *destroy* those *prin-ciples* on which [a republic] is *supported,* as it *lessens the sense* of the *equal rights of mankind,* and habituates us to *tyranny* and *oppression.*" Jefferson, a slave-holder himself, privately conceded that "one hour of [slavery] is fraught with more misery, than ages of that which [the colonists] rose in rebellion to op-pose." The enslaved also quickly seized upon the apparent incompatibility of slavery with republican ideology. In 1779, a group of blacks in Connecticut, for example, asked members of the state assembly "whether it is consistent with present claims of the United States, to hold so many thousands, of the race of Adam, our common father, in perpetual slavery?"

The revolutionaries sought in various ways to deal with the contradictions between republican theory and practice. Early in the Revolutionary War, six states abolished the slave trade, and antislavery societies sprang into existence, even as far south as Virginia. During the war, the Second Continental Congress, the northern states, and Maryland gave freedom to slaves who enlisted in their army units. Between 1782 and 1790 Virginia planters voluntarily freed ten thousand blacks. Congress in 1785 forbade slavery in the Northwest Territory between the Appalachians and the Mississippi River but, at the same time, permitted the extension of slavery into the territories south of the Ohio River. Many hoped that the provision in the Constitution of 1787 that permitted Congress to end the slave trade in twenty years (1808) would lead to the gradual end of the institution.

In the North, where the number of slaves was smaller and the institution less important economically, slavery gradually withered away, but without great revolutionary fervor, fanfare, or much concern for the fate of the newly freed blacks. Vermont specifically prohibited slavery in its new constitution of 1777, and in 1780 Pennsylvania passed a law providing for gradual emancipation. In other northern states the courts struck blows at the foundations of slavery. By 1805 major steps had been taken in all of the states from Pennsylvania northward to end slavery.

Yet everywhere calls for freedom and equality for those of African origins confronted the harsh realities of specific economic interests and traditional ways. Even in the states that outlawed slavery, free blacks suffered from systematic discrimination. They lived as pariahs on the margins of society. They could rarely vote or serve on juries; neither did they have equal access to education nor equal employment opportunities. The invention of the cotton gin in 1793 vastly increased the economic incentives for maintaining slavery in the uplands of the South and at least in the short run foreclosed the possibility of ending slavery in that region.

Moreover, many white Americans were able to reconcile republican ideology with slavery. Republicans took it for granted that natural rights included the right to hold private property. Many reasoned that slavery was simply a form of property. A 1780 Virginia law, for instance, rewarded Revolutionary war veterans with three hundred acres of land *and* a slave. The defenders of slavery also called upon the ancients. The republics of antiquity had slavery; Aristotle himself had flatly declared that "slavery is natural." As it had in the ancient world, slavery helped make it possible for gentry like Jefferson to pursue lives dedicated to public service and to the arts and the sciences.

Others reasoned that a republic's very survival required an economically self-sufficient citizenry. Emancipating the slaves was likely to create, on the other hand, a huge dependent class. Jefferson, along with many others, worried that a growing dependent class of former slaves (as well as non-property-holding white city dwellers) would endanger the entire republican experiment. "Freedom and dependence," wrote James Wilson, were "opposite and irreconcilable terms." Not until the 1830s, when a small band of evangelical Protestants mounted a new antislavery offensive, was the incompatibility between republican principles and slavery again seriously reexamined.

THE NURTURE OF "HABITUAL VIRTUE"

As an ideology, republicanism stressed the need for public virtue, which, above all else, meant a willingness on the part of the population to sacrifice their personal interests on behalf of the community. Understood in classical terms, virtue was less a matter of personal morality than of public morality. Although private virtues such as prudence, frugality, and temperance were important to personal happiness and the creation of a healthy republic, public virtue entailed the subordination of personal interests and desires to the public interest. In its classic formulation, virtue could be severe and demanding. For example, ancient Spartans turned over everything—their lives and their fortunes—to their beloved city-state. Nothing symbolized dedication to the welfare of the community more to the Spartans than their returning dead soldiers carried on the shields that they had taken to war. In the end most of the American revolutionaries found Spartan virtue too exacting; they defined virtue in more generous terms, in terms of practicing and nurturing the "natural affections" that tied humans to one another. The main task in a republican society was, as Samuel Stanhope Smith, the soon-to-be-elected president of Princeton, described it, to cultivate among the people "habitual virtue."

THE PLASTICITY OF HUMAN NATURE

Entertaining even the possibility of making virtue a personal habit required a belief in the plasticity of human nature. In particular, it challenged the Calvinistic notion that humans had inherited Adam's predisposition to sin. In place of an immutable set of propensities to act in evil ways, many revolutionaries posited the idea that human behavior was to a large extent the product of the environment working on the five senses. "All the differences we perceive . . . in respect to virtue and vice, knowledge and ignorance," Benjamin Rush concluded, "may be accounted for from climate, country, degrees of civilization, forms of government, or accidental causes." Sometimes people did behave wickedly, but the blame arose from corrupting institutions (like monarchies) rather than inherited inclinations.

Yet few if any of the gentry revolutionaries were total environmentalists. All individuals, they concluded, possessed a moral instinct or sense that guided them in responding to the environment's bombardment of the senses. As Jefferson put it, "the Creator would indeed have been a bungling artist, had he intended man for a social animal, without planting in him social dispositions." The moral instinct, or what widely read Scottish philosophers called common sense, was an inborn gyroscope that kept humans from acting merely on blind impulses.

By the careful management of human experiences, all of the senses, including above all the moral sense, could be shaped and refined. "Habitual virtue" could be encouraged, in the words of Samuel Stanhope Smith, "by recalling the lost images of virtue [from the past]; contemplating them, and using them as motives of action, they overcome those of vice again and again . . . until after repeated struggles, and many foils, they at length acquire habitual superiority." Indeed, "it was possible," exclaimed Benjamin Rush, "to convert men into republican machines."

For many of the more optimistic revolutionaries nothing was of greater importance in nurturing a virtuous citizenry than early education. Education should have as its objective the creation of a new kind of person—an autonomous republican *citizen* rather than a dependent monarchial *subject*. This could be accomplished, according to Samuel Harrison Smith, cowinner of the American Philosophical Society's prize for an essay on the sort of education appropriate to a republic, by requiring educational works "defining correctly political, moral, and religious duty." Only if teachers could instill such duties in their students would "the radical ideas we have already established" be adequate to secure "the virtue and happiness of the United States."

Thomas Jefferson put the case for publicly supported education more concretely. Only universal tax-supported "free" education could ensure the intelligent participation of the ordinary people in the political system. Furthermore, since the lawmakers in a republic must be chosen "without regard to wealth, birth, or other accidental condition," all citizens should be educated. A public educational system would open up careers to men of talent and virtue while helping ensure the selection of natural aristocrats to public office. Nonetheless, while nearly everyone seemed to embrace in principle Jefferson's idea that a self-governing people needed at least an elementary education, until the nineteenth century publicly supported education made little headway in the new republic.

Public celebrations and rituals could also be employed to promote habitual virtue. Even John Adams, who was more pessimistic about the potentialities of elevating the general level of virtue than most of the revolutionaries, advocated the scheduling of grand public occasions. In a letter to his wife, Abigail, on July 3, 1776, he wrote that American independence "ought to be solemnized with pomp and parade, with shows, games, sports, guns, bells, bonfires and illuminations from one end of this continent to the other from this time forward forever more." Speeches, orations, and sermons, even paintings, poetry, sculptures, and architecture—these and much more could encourage habitual virtue among the people.

The drive to mold a virtuous citizenry included a special enthusiasm for examples and lessons that could be drawn from classical antiquity. By consulting "the history of Athens and Rome," Samuel Adams declared in 1785, "we should find that so long as they continued their frugality and simplicity of manners, they shone with superlative glory, but no sooner were effeminate refinements introduced amongst them, than they visibly fell . . . and became feeble and timid, dependent, slavish and false."

To evoke the lessons of the ancients, the revolutionaries turned to antiquity for names: College towns became Athenses and Ithacas; slaves became Catos and Cassiuses; horses became Ciceroes and Brutuses, and government terminology became senators and capitols. The revolutionaries signed their polemical essays with classical pseudonyms. Eager to cast the Constitution and its supporters in monarchical terms, its opponents called themselves "Cato," after Cato the Younger, a leading foe of Julius Caesar, while the authors of *The Federalist Papers* dubbed themselves as "Publius," after Publius Valerius who had established republican government in Rome in 509 B.C.

The relics of their classical dreams remain with us even today—in political symbols like the goddess Liberty, in Latin mottoes, in songs like "Hail Columbia," and of course in countless buildings based on ancient Greek and Roman models. An examination of the dollar bill vividly reveals the survival of antiquity's influence on the new republic. On one side of the bill, the Great Seal of the United States, adopted by Congress in 1782, includes the phrase *novus ordo seclorum* ("new order of the ages") and the dignified Roman numerals MDCCLXXVI (1776). Likewise, the scrolls and leaf work designs on the bill are Roman in origin.

REPUBLICAN ART

Revolutionaries also sought to employ the fine arts—music, painting, drama, literature, and architecture—on behalf of the cultivation of habitual virtue. Unshackling the tyranny of monarchy would, many believed, unleash a great artistic outpouring in America, one that would equal or surpass anything preceding it in the history of the Western world. In part such a vision of American potentialities arose from an ages-old belief that civilization and culture had inevitably traveled westward, from the Near East to Greece, from Greece to Rome, from Rome to Western Europe, and presently to America. In addition, the revolutionaries linked artistic achievements to freedom. Just as America was destined to become the world's bastion of political liberty, it was fated, they thought, to become the Western world's new Athens.

Yet, despite a remarkable record and the enthusiasm for the possibilities of the arts in the new republic, the revolutionaries approached the beaux arts with excruciating caution. New England Puritans and Pennsylvania Quakers had always been suspicious of the arts; they suspected that the arts diverted people from more important spiritual duties. And, moreover, had not Plato as early as the fourth century B.C. warned of the dangers of poets and artists for republics? By inciting the passions rather than reason, artists undermined public morality, Plato had written. John Adams concurred: "The more elegance, the less virtue, in all times and countries," he wrote in a letter from France to his wife in 1778. "I have no doubt," he continued, "that the pencil of Peter Paul Rubens [a Flemish painter of nudes] has contributed to strengthen the doctrines of papal supremacy, and to lead the minds of hundreds of thousands, more deeply into the shade of bigotry and superstition." Indeed, rather than advancing habitual virtue, a blossoming of the fine arts might result in the very opposite. The arts might encourage a love of material possessions, sensual pleasures, and personal indolence. For many republican theorists, in particular those with Calvinistic origins, ancient Sparta, with its reputation for self-restraint and its hostility to the arts, was a far better historical model for Americans to emulate than was ancient Athens.

Classical art, with its taut rationality, seemed to offer at least a partial solution to republican suspicions of artists and their work. Drawing upon what was later dubbed as neoclassicism, an artistic movement that swept through Europe in the latter half of the eighteenth century, American artists sought to emulate the forms of classical antiquity. Such art, while not daring in the originality of its form, could become a means of uplifting the public's taste and refinement. It could aid in the campaign to foster virtue and allegiance to the new republic while avoiding the vices of overrefinement and luxury associated with monarchies.

John Trumbull, for example, hoped to ennoble the glories of the American Revolution by offering grand, neoclassical paintings to the public. While acknowledging that art "as it is generally practiced, is frivolous, little use to society," Trumbull tried in his *The Death of General Warren at the Battle of Bunker Hill, 17, June, 1775* (1786) to present his version of ideal republican leadership. Nonetheless, Trumbull's paintings received a cool public reception. He even had trouble persuading Congress to pay for his huge commemorative scenes of the Revolution that he painted in the Capitol's rotunda. Charles Willson Peale obtained equally mixed public responses to his portfolio of Revolutionary heroes, a project from which he hoped to profit while performing a civic service. In addition, Peale established in Philadelphia a natural history museum. Public contemplation of nature's order in the museum, Peale wrote, could teach people "to aspire to the moral perfections of the great author of all things." In short, it would "influence public opinion [so] that republicanism will be highly promoted."

Revolutionary artists sometimes countered republican suspicions of their work by engaging in a form of dissimulation. For example, theater advertisements justified performances of Shakespeare's *Othello* by claiming that the play depicted "the evil effects of jealousy, and other bad passions, and proving that happiness can only spring from the pursuit of virtue." Contrary to a common charge that the theater promoted licentiousness, idleness, and countless other vices, defenders of a bill to license a theater in Philadelphia in 1788 asserted that the theater encouraged "the general refinement of manners, and the polish of society." "Nothing can be more favorable to the growth of the virtues" than the theater, its Philadelphia defenders concluded. Defenses of the theater as a school of virtue by no means altered the views of the more suspicious republicans. While a somewhat more favorable climate for the theater developed in the postwar era, profound suspicions of the theater and the other arts remained long afterward.

No tangible survival of the Revolutionary era exceeds architecture as evidence of the use of neoclassical art to promote public spiritedness. Referring to architecture as "an art that shows so much," Thomas Jefferson was almost single-handedly responsible for making Greek and Roman revival architecture the official style of public buildings in the new republic. In his design of public buildings and in his private residence (Monticello), Jefferson repeatedly turned to classical motifs. That a monumental city like Washington, D.C., with its vast scale, its inspiring public buildings, its wide boulevards, and its splendid parks, could have been planned and begun in the midst of a swampy wilderness was an extraordinary tribute to the neoclassical dreams of the Revolutionary leaders.

The revolutionary generation embraced neoclassical architecture not only for its hoped-for influence in shaping the morals and values of the populace, but also because its symmetry, simplicity, and rationality—all principles, they thought, more suitable to a republic than a monarchy—paralleled the Enlightenment view of nature. Finally, the construction of such buildings, having won the approval of the Western world for a millennia, conferred a special dignity and legitimacy on the new republic. Yet the neoclassical age that shaped Washington, D.C., inspired the Great Seal, and left the nation with a set of ancient place-names was a brief one. Soon few Americans could

Rotunda of the University of Virginia at Charlottesville, 1822–1826. In his design for a new university, Thomas Jefferson rejected the religious and monarchal styles of Oxford and Cambridge universities in England. When considering an appropriate architecture for the new republic, Jefferson, like most of the nation's founders, looked to models provided by the ancient Greeks and Romans.

translate the meanings of the Latin mottoes or understand the purposes behind their great public buildings.

By the end of the Revolution, agonizing dilemmas and divisive tensions characterized the arts. Some artists espoused an organic and hierarchical republicanism while others praised the egalitarian and individualistic side of the Revolution. Whatever position they took, it became increasingly evident that even the beaux arts, the highest forms of artistic expression, would be in the end shaped by the ordinary people. Rather than the artists as the enlightened few fashioning the behavior of the many, the ordinary people would ultimately determine which books would be read, which if any plays would be performed, and which paintings would be sold.

CONCLUSION

The concern for cultivating an unselfish devotion to the community among the ordinary people helped shape American ways in the Revolutionary era and long afterwards. Every major reform movement in American history has been inspired at least in part by this republican ideal. It encouraged a preoccupation with education that eventually resulted in the nation's compulsory public school system. It helped lead to the abolition of slavery, and it inspired an expanded social role for women. It resulted in a rage for the classical world—the popularity of Latin mottoes, classical architecture, and the use of classical names for towns, streets, and political institutions. It infused the arts with a larger civic purpose and stimulated interest in science and technology—in particular the possibilities of employing reason, invention, and experimentation to alleviating some of the burdens of human existence.

Yet the Revolution and republican ideology brought unintended consequences. America never became a Christian Sparta nor a modern Athens. No sooner had the Revolution commenced than ardent republicans began to worry about excessive dissipation and extravagance. Rather than acquiescing to the leadership of a natural aristocracy, ordinary men increasingly selected leaders whom they thought would represent their particular interests. Rather than acquiescing to the needs of the community, they were encouraged by the revolutionary principles of natural rights and equality to pursue individual welfare. In short, the revolutionary era ushered in the creation of a vast, sprawling democratic republic in which the celebration of commerce and self-interest at least equaled esteem for the community and for nonmaterial values.

4

OPENING THE DOORS OF OPPORTUNITY

In the wake of the American Revolution, Americans dropped their neoclassical blueprints for a new republic. To be sure, in the first half of the nineteenth century educated people continued to learn Latin, to employ Latin phrases in their speeches and in their writings, and to admire the achievements of the ancients. But they, along with nearly all other Americans, lost interest in building a society modeled upon ancient Sparta, Athens, or republican Rome. While Americans continued to think of themselves as republicans and continued to revere their revolutionary forebears, they proceeded to strike out into an uncharted future.

In many respects, during the antebellum era (the decades preceding the Civil War, 1861–65) America's future unfolded in unexpected directions, indeed, in directions that were the very opposite of what the revolutionary leaders had envisioned. Instead of a republic led by natural aristocrats, the United States became the world's foremost example of a democracy. Instead of a republic guided by the secular ideals of antiquity and the Enlightenment, a spectacular series of religious revivals transformed the United States into the world's most prominent example of an evangelical Protestant nation. Instead of a republic in which individuals subordinated their personal interests to those of the community, the United States became the world's most striking example of an individualistic and commercial-minded society.

Two great passions—one to fulfill the promise of equality and the other to acquire material gain—pulled Americans away from the republican vision of an organic community led by a natural aristocracy. Calling upon the principle of equality, ordinary white men everywhere insisted that they should have the same privileges and opportunities as the wellborn. At the same time, the sudden expansion of commerce and industry activated a revolution in material aspirations. Soaring material ambitions and the principle of equality fused together to shatter any possibility of implementing the classical dreams of the nation's founders.

EQUALITY AND OPPORTUNITY

Once evoked as a rallying cry of the American Revolution, the power implicit in Jefferson's assertion that "all men are created equal" ripped through

American society and culture with stunning force. It could not be stopped. Before losing its momentum, the idea of equality had energized a revolution from within. Now each and every white man claimed that he counted for just as much as any other man; while he might not have the same wealth, education, or regal bearing, he was in other respects an equal of queens, kings, nobles, and gentlemen. Equality wrapped all Americans, as novelist Herman Melville put it, in "one royal mantle of humanity." It conferred a "democratic dignity" to even "the arm that wields a pick or drives a spike." This conception of equality, that each man had equal worth as a human being, was like no other nation had ever had before.

Yet the American idea of equality did *not* include a complete leveling of society. While most Americans worried (as they had done in the Revolutionary era) that governments might be used to enrich the few, only a small minority of radical reformers called for a redistribution of existing wealth. Rather than an actual equality in wealth, most Americans sought to create a society that provided for an equality of opportunity. "Open the doors of opportunity to talent and virtue," wrote Ralph Waldo Emerson, "and . . . property rushes from the idle and the imbecile to the industrious, brave and persevering." All white men should have equal opportunities to choose their own religious affiliations, to vote in elections, to hold public office, to enter into or to sever work relationships, and to improve their material lot.

The rejection of inherited status in the late eighteenth and early nineteenth centuries fostered the fiction that everyone in fact started out equal, that, unlike anywhere else in the world, Americans competed on a level playing field. But in truth the doors of opportunity did not open equally for all. At the same time that the United States was becoming the world's most democratic and egalitarian nation, middle-class women were relegated to a separate sphere, the country's slavery system hardened, the distribution of wealth grew more unequal, class lines deepened, and the drive to exterminate or elbow aside Native Americans gained momentum.

EGALITARIAN SOCIAL WAYS

The origins of the egalitarian social ways that so impressed foreign travelers to the United States in the 1830s and 1840s could be found among some of the first settlers in British North America. In particular, the Quakers and the backcountry peoples had departed from Europe's hierarchical ways. Men should be judged by what they do rather than by their social rank, Quaker leader William Penn had held. Likewise, from the outset of settlement, backcountry people, regardless of wealth or birth, had insisted on being treated as equals.

Except in the Deep South, the egalitarian rhetoric employed in the Declaration of Independence provided an additional catalyst for a general assault on hierarchical privileges and affectations. "No man has a greater claim to special privilege for his $100,000 than I have for my $5," blurted out a legislative leader from Pennsylvania during the Revolution. Egalitarian social practices extended to New England. By 1791 geographer Jedidiah Morse described New England as a place "where every man thinks of himself at least as good as his neighbors, and believes that all mankind have, or ought to possess equal rights."

In the years following the Revolution, titles and forms of address that had previously structured exchanges between people and aided them in understanding their places in the social hierarchy increasingly gave way to the most egalitarian social relationships in the Western world. In the United States, "everybody talks to you," growled English novelist Charles Dickens. Even upon first acquaintance, Charles Murray, yet another astonished English traveler, exclaimed, "farm assistants and laborers, called me '*Charlie.*'"

Titles came to mean almost nothing in America. "Mister" was now a common greeting extended to all adult white males, not just to those who claimed to be gentlemen. When a rag picker can call himself a *"gentleman"* and a prostitute can describe herself as a *"lady,"* complained Mary Lundie Duncan, society "has suffered [an] inversion [of] the old [hierarchical] ordering of language."

Indeed, it had. Traveling Europeans reported that in the United States every white man felt free to shake any other white man's hand. Americans even initiated conversations with total strangers "on terms of perfect equality." Stagecoaches and rail cars offered only one class of seats; everyone, regardless of rank or dress, scrambled on board according to the rule of first come, first served. Whether in the stately dining room of an elegant hotel or at a country inn, everyone (except unescorted females and those with dark skins) sat at the same table to eat. There, they shared the same plates and ordered off of the same menu. Foreign travelers frequently complained that even the host sat and ate with them.

Except in the South, where blacks continued to serve their owners in slavery, no permanent class of domestic servants existed in egalitarian America. Indeed, until the first large wave of immigration began to arrive in the mid-1840s, even the wealthiest Americans had difficulty in hiring servants at any price and those employed in domestic service insisted on being called "help" rather than "servants" and on being treated as part of the family. The help objected to wearing uniforms, which they saw as badges of their inferior status. An American "will not wear a livery," reported a foreign visitor, "any more than he will wear a halter around his neck." To European travelers, such egalitarian social relationships threatened to destroy the ties essential to a well-ordered society.

EGALITARIAN WORK WAYS

The idea of equality and expanding opportunities for material advancement helped to create a new set of American work ways. Humans had long dreamed of escaping work; they imagined a golden age in which rivers flowed with wine and honey and people lived as effortlessly as the gods. But whether in the Bible's Edenic terms or the fantasies of classical poets, the idyllic life of ease had existed only in the imagination or perhaps as a brief moment in history. In either case, a work-free utopia had given way to the realities of a world in which most humans were saddled with want, pain, and interminable labor. Under such circumstances, those who had escaped the tyranny of toil enjoyed society's highest esteem.

In colonial America, only the Puritans and Quakers had regarded labor in entirely positive terms. While acknowledging the burdensome nature of work, these Protestant groups insisted that God had assigned to all humans spiritual and worldly duties. Working diligently at one's "calling" won God's blessing while not doing so brought down his wrath. Never, however, should secular work be directed toward the acquisition of personal wealth. Instead, according to Puritan and Quaker dogma, work should always have as its ultimate goal the glorification of God and the welfare of the community.

In easing the transition away from a religious to a more secular work ethic, no single person was more important than Benjamin Franklin. Consistent with Puritan and Quaker ideals, Franklin condemned a life of toil merely for personal gain. The fruits of labor should ultimately benefit the community. After accumulating a modest fortune at the age of forty-two, Franklin himself never again worked in a conventional sense. He devoted himself thereafter to leading the life of a gentleman, which in his case included a busy career in public service.

Yet there was another side of Franklin, a far more important one in terms of the emerging work ethic. Franklin dropped entirely the religious compulsion for work and reveled in offering aphorisms to the multitudes on behalf of the merits of hard work. He soon became the champion of industrious artisans and merchants alike, of all those who were seeking to advance their individual economic well-being.

During the Revolutionary era the defense of the dignity of work took the form of an assault on aristocratic leisure. Fired by republican principles of equality, merchants and artisans began to dispute the long-held patrician notion that free time and exemption from the corruptions of the marketplace allowed the gentry to act in a more disinterested and intelligent fashion than ordinary people. Merchants and artisans insisted on the contrary. The upper classes (like everyone else) may have had a personal stake in government decisions, but the work experience of ordinary people frequently provided a preparation for public service superior to that of aristocratic leisure.

Neither did the gambling, drinking, whoring, and sporting practices associated with the "idle aristocracy" escape scathing censure. To ardent republicans, such dissolute behavior threatened to destroy the very virtues essential to the young nation's survival. Though a member of the gentry himself, nothing haunted Thomas Jefferson's imagination more than the possibility of European upper class indulgences spreading like a cancer to the United States. Once introduced on American shores, he feared that aristocratic debauchery would then gnaw away at the virtue and simplicity of the nation's citizenry.

By the early nineteenth century Americans no longer viewed work negatively; indeed, they now reserved their highest praise for talented, hardworking workmen, inventors, and merchants. Writers even set about revising the lives of the nation's Revolutionary heroes; in the hands of biographers, they now became industrious workers rather than members of the leisured gentry. Parson Weems even transformed the aristocratic George Washington into a model of the work ethic. "Of all the virtues that adorned the life of this great man," wrote Weems, "there is none more worthy of our imitation than his admirable INDUSTRY." Up at the crack of dawn, toiling till dark, never tolerant of idleness in himself or in others—these traits, according to Weems, accounted for Washington's greatness.

In the nineteenth century, Americans (at least those in the northern part of the country) became known throughout the Western world for the high value and dignity they attached to work. Only in America, wrote Francis Grund in a testimony echoed countless times by other foreign visitors, was "industry . . . an honor, and idleness a disgrace." Lady Stuart Wortley employed the felicitous metaphor of the beehive to describe the self-starting nature of American workers. "No drones are admitted into the great Transatlantic hive," she wrote. "There is no time to spare; [boys] must be ready, as soon as possible, to take their places and run in the great race." In America everyone, including even the rich, was expected to work.

THE RAGE FOR SELF-IMPROVEMENT

Opening the doors of opportunity for ordinary white men and the principle of equality encouraged a rage for self-improvement. In particular, education seemed to offer possibilities for enhancing one's prospects for getting ahead materially. Thus ambitious workers became enthusiastic proponents of tax-supported education. Horace Mann, the "father" of compulsory public education in the United States, hailed the schools as "the great equalizer of the conditions of men" and as an agency for ending poverty. Mann also urged business leaders, in need of more skilled workers, to support public education. Propelled by visions of education as a means of making equality of opportunity a reality, of preparing common men for their duties as citizens, and of inculcating a common ethic of self-restraint, Americans became the world's most enthusiastic proponents of public schooling.

The rage for self-improvement extended to adults as well. Adult Americans not only sought to gain practical knowledge that would aid them in making money but also personal refinement. Cities responded to their enthusiasm by establishing public libraries. In the major industrial cities, "mechanics" (workingmen) formed dozens of libraries of their own. Equally reflective of the passion for adult education was the Lyceum movement. By the 1830s adults had organized more than a thousand Lyceums. The Lyceums scheduled discussion groups, formed libraries, and sponsored lectures. Self-improvement books and pamphlets, which came off the nation's presses in a virtual flood by mid-century, also revealed the widespread faith in the power of individuals to transform themselves.

EGALITARIAN POLITICAL WAYS

The ideas of equality and opportunity were likewise powerful forces in creating the nation's new democratic political culture. As we have seen in the previous chapter, even in the midst of the American Revolution ordinary artisans and merchants began to seize upon the principle of equality to attack the office-holding monopoly of the gentry. Not only did they reject the argument that free time and exemption from daily involvement in the marketplace or the workplace made the gentry ideal public servants, but they even challenged the very essence of classical republicanism, the belief that a common good could arise out of a single corporate, organic community. Implicitly, the opponents of gentry leadership suggested that no such common good existed. Instead, they said, everyone, including the gentry itself, had personal, sometimes conflicting stakes in government decisions. Therefore, in order to protect their specific interests, everyone should be represented in government.

By the 1820s other preconditions for a more democratic political culture had been established as well. Believing that voting should be a privilege rather than a right, the creators of the first state governments had limited suffrage to those who had a "stake in society," in other words, to those who at least owned some property. But, as Francis Lieber wrote in 1859, there were "thousands of men without property who have quite as great a stake in the public's welfare as those who may possess a house or enjoy a certain amount of revenue." By 1824, only four states retained significant property qualifications for voting. By then, nearly all states had dropped or reduced their property requirements for holding public office as well. By 1832, in all the states (except in South Carolina) the voters rather than state legislatures were choosing presidential electors. Responding to the rising democratic tide, the process of choosing political candidates also changed. Rather than using caucuses, which critics smeared as monarchial ("King Caucus") to nominate candidates for public office, by 1832 parties were using conventions to select state, local, and national tickets, write party platforms, and celebrate their common partisanship.

By the 1830s, the main outlines of the nation's new democratic political ways were taking shape. No longer did voters automatically defer to the opinions and decisions of elected officials. Instead of independent judgments, politicians were increasingly expected to acquiesce to the will of the majority. No longer were voters as suspicious as they once had been of political parties. Earlier perceived as a threat to republicanism, citizens increasingly regarded them as necessary for mobilizing the will of the people. No longer did qualified voters stay at home on election day. Voter turnouts soared so that by the 1840s more than 75 percent of the electorate regularly went to the polls.

No longer did the nation's political leadership portray themselves as superior men nor refer to the ordinary people in unflattering terms. Instead, the politicians found it expedient to claim that they themselves came from lowly origins. They praised the wisdom of the "common man." "The people in every part of the United States," declared President Andrew Jackson in 1837, "are too enlightened not to understand their own rights and interests and to detect and defeat every effort to gain undue advantages over them. . . ."

George Bancroft, a prominent historian and an ardent Jacksonian, took Jackson's position a step further. Influenced by European romanticism, Bancroft posited the existence of a transcendental spirit that expressed itself through the combined wisdom of ordinary men. "The munificent Author of our being," wrote Bancroft, "has conferred the gifts of mind upon every member of the human race without distinction to outward circumstance."

Nineteenth-century democratic politics included mass entertainment. At colorful rallies, complete with parades, bands, banners, floats, and picnics, politicians mixed with the common people. They shook hands, joked, gossiped, discussed the voter's family, and kissed babies. Such gala gatherings doubtlessly helped to meet deeply felt needs for fraternal comradery in a society in which such opportunities were rarer than in Europe. In a restless, rootless society in which traditional affiliations and social adhesives had been weakened or destroyed, political parties offered men (and a large number of women as well) a personal identity and a sense of belonging.

No longer were politics limited to the wealthy, who served part-time and sometimes only out of a sense of duty. Instead, democratic politics gave rise to a new kind of politician, one whose life revolved around his party and who depended on the success of his party for his livelihood. He might profit from

President-elect Andrew Jackson on His Way to Washington, 1828. Never before had a president been so closely identified with the ordinary white people. Jackson's election symbolized the end of gentry rule and the triumph of "democratic" politics.

the salary provided to officeholders (initially republicanism called for office-holders to serve without compensation) or from an appointment to a government position. In either case, politics offered an avenue of upward social mobility for ordinary white men. Martin Van Buren was a graphic case in point. The son of a New York tavern keeper, as a professional politician Van Buren rose through the party ranks to eventually reach the White House itself.

As voters increasingly associated their economic well-being with the actions of governments, they looked to political parties to protect and promote equality and opportunity while resisting the twin threats of privilege and aristocracy. Such concerns provoked the formation of the Anti-Masonic party in the 1820s. When ardent Masons in upstate New York allegedly murdered a disgruntled member who was threatening to reveal the fraternity's secrets and when local officials failed to bring the perpetrators to justice, angry citizens charged that the Masons were undemocratic (because of their secrecy and social exclusivity), that the order enjoyed special privileges, and that the Masons were promoting a false religion of free thinkers. The first party to arise from the ranks of the ordinary people, the Anti-Masonic party, among other things, tried to bar Masons from public office.

During the 1830s, the issue of banking soon replaced anti-Masonry in raising concerns about equality and special privileges. The Democratic Party of Andrew Jackson and the Whig Party, which derived its name from the antimonarchal party in England, took distinctive positions on banking. To Jackson and his party, banks, with their power to issue paper money, constituted a special privilege granted by governments. Banks cheated the ordinary people and helped to create an artificial aristocracy, Jackson said. The Whigs, on the other hand, insisted that, by chartering banks and subsidizing important construction projects, governments could stimulate more-rapid economic development. Economic growth would open up additional opportunities, the Whigs claimed. In this sense, the expanded role of government in the economy was consistent with the nation's ideals of equality and opportunity.

Equality and opportunity shaped much of the political discourse of the 1850s as well. The new Republican party, which grew out of the ashes of the earlier Whigs and the Know Nothing (anti-Catholic, anti-immigrant) movement, adopted as its slogan: "Free Soil, Free Labor, and Free Men." Northern farmers and workers who supported the party equated republicanism with an absence of slavery; they urged the application of a free labor ideology to the settlement of the nation's western territories. The Democratic party in the South, on the other hand, insisted that white men enjoyed equality and opportunity because blacks were enslaved. They also argued that slavery corresponded more closely than did northern individualism to classical republican principles of an organic community.

The new democratic ways were manifestly restricted to white males. They excluded women, African Americans, and Indians. If anything, blacks and Indians fared worse in the white man's democratic culture than they had in the more hierarchical, gentry-controlled society of earlier times. The rejection of the assumption of reciprocal obligations between superiors and inferiors accompanied the destruction of the traditional hierarchy. President Andrew Jackson, while acting on his belief that Indian tribes could survive only by isolating them from white society, placated popular white opinion in the West and the South by forcibly removing the Indian tribes east of the Mississippi River. The empowerment of ordinary white men also seemed to encourage the expression of deeper racial prejudice in both the North and the South and to trigger in the North increasing mob violence against blacks as well as more circumscription of black rights and opportunities. In the white man's democracy of the antebellum era, blacks no longer experienced even the modicum of protection once offered by hierarchical customs and elite authority.

IN PURSUIT OF MATERIAL GAIN

"I know of no country, indeed, where the love of money has taken a stronger hold on the affections of men" than in the United States, so concluded Alexis de Tocqueville along with nearly every other European traveler to America as well as many Americans themselves. Before the Revolution, ordinary Americans had had little reason to believe that the future would be very different from the past, but in the early nineteenth century tens of thousands of them began to experience for the first time the exhilarating possibilities of "getting ahead." "We are most certainly in another world here," exclaimed de Tocqueville. "Political passions are only on the surface. The profound passion, the only one which profoundly stirs the human heart, the passion of all days, is the acquisition of riches."

OPENING THE DOORS OF OPPORTUNITY

Contributing to the unprecedented burst of enthusiasm for seeking personal gain was the removal of traditional obstacles to opportunity. Ordinary white men now employed the idea of equality to demand an expansion in opportunities for improving their material welfare. "While we do not propose any war upon capital," Abraham Lincoln told a New Haven, Connecticut, audience in the midst of a shoemakers' strike in 1860, "we do wish to allow the humblest man an equal chance to get rich with everybody else." His listeners responded with deafening applause.

Ordinary white men insisted that the professions, once reserved to the gentry, be opened up to all. During the first third of the nineteenth century, new state laws permitted almost any enterprising individual to become a doctor or a lawyer. "The bar is now crowded with bustling and restless men," wrote attorney David Dudley Field in 1844. "The quiet, decorous manners, the gravity, and the solid learning, so often conjoined in a former generation,

Broadway, New York City, 1836. This lively scene from downtown Manhattan lends support to Alexis de Tocqueville's observation that "I know of no country, indeed, where the love of money has taken a stronger hold on the affections of men" than in the United States. In the nineteenth century, the soaring material aspirations of ordinary white men helped to break up the nation's traditional hierarchy.

are now rarely seen together. A new race has sprung up and supplanted the old." In local courts, Abraham Lincoln was only one of many men of modest social origins who began to serve as prosecutors, lawyers, and judges. The removal of barriers to entering the professions even extended to the clergy. While the more conservative Congregationalists, Presbyterians, and Episcopalians continued to insist on an educated ministry, the faster-growing evangelical denominations welcomed into their flocks untutored preachers from the ranks of the ordinary people.

Obstacles to opportunity arising from older patterns of work dependency collapsed as well. While slavery did not end until the Civil War, the practice of tying people together in the workplace through white indentured servitude gradually dwindled away in the antebellum era. Traditional forms of apprenticeship in which masters exercised nearly unbridled authority over younger men learning a trade also declined. Like other white workers, by the 1840s apprentices were free to negotiate their wages and working conditions. By then, the long-held assumption of worker dependency on landowners, masters, and employers had given way to a new norm of self-directed, "free" labor. The freer labor market weakened traditional patriarchy as well. "Boys are men at 16," complained Thomas D'Arcy McGee. "They all work for themselves."

More important to the creation of a heady atmosphere of material aspirations than the opening of the professions and the collapse of older work dependencies, however, was the removal of earlier geographic limits to opportunity. The treaty with Britain ending the Revolutionary War in 1783 presented the United States with the vast area between the Appalachian Mountains and the Mississippi River. With a single stroke of the pen, the purchase of Louisiana from France in 1803 doubled the nation's size. The acquisition in the 1840s of Texas, the Southwest, and the Oregon country nearly doubled the nation's area yet again.

The exceptionally favorable ratio of arable land to people broke open all efforts to limit landholding to the few. Even in the late colonial era, two-thirds of the white families in America owned the farms that they tilled. In the post-Revolutionary era, government policy responded even more favorably to the relentless land seekers, first by lowering the price per acre, then by decreasing the minimum plot for sale from 640 acres in 1796 to a mere 40 in 1832, and finally in 1862 by offering 80 acres of land to homesteaders for free. While reality never matched the myth of a farm for every white settler, ownership by European standards was extraordinarily widespread. At mid-century, even in the slaveholding South, more than 80 percent of the white farmers worked their own land.

Widespread land ownership by rural Americans meant far more than simply white families gaining personal security or opportunities to improve their personal fortunes. To Jefferson, America's sprawling "unoccupied" lands represented an essential precondition for the success of the nation's republican experiment. The vast expanses of "free" land shielded America from the development of the vast inequities in wealth that characterized Europe's aristocratic societies. Free land guaranteed that far into the future the great majority of Americans would avoid the economic "dependence [that] begets subservience and venality." Since the Creator had made "his peculiar deposit for substantial and genuine virtue" in the yeoman farmer, wrote Jefferson, large quantities of free land ensured that the United States would long remain a nation of God's "chosen people." Of course such a view tended to ignore the property claims of Native Americans. Hence, the expansion of the property-holding opportunities of white men nearly always entailed the extirpation of other people's property rights.

In time—indeed even during Jefferson's lifetime—the gap between the ideal of a largely self-sufficient, yeoman farmer and the realities of agricultural America grew more pronounced. Although sometimes grudgingly, farmers too became buyers and sellers. Their fate, like that of the urban merchants, was increasingly dependent on the vicissitudes of the marketplace. Yet few

American myths have been more resilient than that of the independent, yeoman farmer. It allowed Americans to think of themselves as an exceptionally moral people and encouraged the belief that the distribution of the nation's wealth was far more equitable than the facts actually warranted.

To seize the new opportunities for getting ahead, Americans migrated as never before. Between the settlement at Jamestown in 1607 and the Declaration of Independence in 1776, settlers had inched their way inland only about 150 miles from the Atlantic Coast, but during the next hundred years they poured over and through the Appalachian Mountains (previously visualized as virtually an unscalable wall to Westward migration) into the Mississippi River Valley, across the Great Plains and Rocky Mountains, and on to the Pacific Coast. That a new state entered the Union on the average of every two and a half years between 1815 and 1850 reflected the astonishing rapidity with which Euro-Americans dispersed into the great interior of North America. Seeking new opportunities, young adults forsook their kin and their neighbors. They moved to-and-fro—from country to town, from town to country, from East to West, and then not infrequently they backtracked to a place where they had lived before.

Despite the damage that ceaseless mobility inflicted upon social stability, the settlers were remarkably successful in transplanting their traditional ways to the West. For example, characteristically New England ways predominated in upstate New York and along the southern rim of the Great Lakes. Between this band of settlement in the North and the hill country of the Ohio River Valley, New England ways merged with the more diverse ways of the Scots, Scots-Irish, Germans, and Quakers from Pennsylvania and western Virginia. Disorderly backcountry ways prevailed in the hill country on both sides of the Ohio Valley (including Kentucky), in the Southern uplands (of Tennessee, Georgia, Alabama, and Mississippi), and westward (into Missouri, Arkansas, and Texas). In the Deep South (of Alabama, Mississippi, Louisiana, and eastern Texas), the settlers brought with them the more hierarchical ways of the eastern Tidewater. That the migrants moved mostly as families and to familiar climates, soils, and landscapes aided them in preserving cultural traditions.

NINETEENTH-CENTURY ECONOMIC REVOLUTIONS

Unleashing older geographic hurdles to opportunity was only one spur, albeit an important one, to the pursuit of material gain. As late as 1820, nearly 80 percent of the nation's population was still employed in agriculture. But these figures disguised seething changes. Beneath a surface that exhibited an illusion of agricultural self-sufficiency, America was becoming a busy nation of buyers and sellers.

No simple hypothesis adequately explains the coming of "the market revolution." Abroad, the intermittent French Revolutionary and Napoleonic wars (1791–1815) created a vigorous demand for American products. In particular, a soaring international demand for cotton in the first half of the nineteenth century triggered a general economic expansion in the United States. At home, a growing literacy rate not only enabled common men to read the Scriptures but opened up new opportunities for them to engage in buying and selling. Unlike Europe, the United States had no complex web of internal barriers to trade; in a single stroke the Constitution of 1787 had created a vast free trade area. No internal tariffs or duties prevented individuals from buying and selling throughout the entire nation.

Rather than inhibiting commerce, American governments abetted the market revolution. Though the subject of heated and exhausting debates in state legislatures and in Congress, the final results were clear: Local, state, and national governments extended large subsidies to what has been aptly described as a "transportation revolution." New roads, new canals, new ferries, new bridges, new shipping docks, and finally new railroads (by 1860, the nation had more railroad mileage than the rest of the world combined) sharply reduced the costs of shipping goods and stimulated regional specialization.

Older obstacles to the formation of corporations came tumbling down as well. In earlier times, the privileges of incorporation had been extended to only the few by special acts of colonial assemblies or later by state legislatures, but beginning in the 1830s the states adopted general incorporation laws that allowed anyone who met minimum qualifications to receive a corporate charter. Such charters permitted small investors to pool their resources without risking personal bankruptcy (limited liability). Banks, railroads, and manufacturing firms—any business that required large amounts of capital—increasingly turned to the corporate form. In addition, the incorporation of private banks, which greatly expanded the nation's supply of credit, unleashed entrepreneurial energies among those who otherwise could never have entered the marketplace.

In the end, no banks, corporations, or governments could account for the economic miracle of these years. The sudden emergence of the United States as an unusually prosperous and enterprising society sprang in large part from the appetites of the ordinary people; they were increasingly consumed with the spirit of moneymaking and getting ahead. "The voice of the people and their government is loud and unanimous for commerce," complained a puzzled Columbia professor as early as 1800. "Their inclination and habits are adapted to trade and traffic. From one end of the continent to the other, the universal roar is Commerce! Commerce! at all events, Commerce!"

The antebellum era also witnessed the beginnings of "the industrial revolution." Before about 1815 nearly all goods had been fabricated in the home for personal use or in the small shops of skilled artisans. Customers would simply ask an artisan to fashion a pair of shoes or a chair according to his or her wishes. Using skills passed down through many generations, the typical artisan was simultaneously both a small manufacturer and a tradesman. Completely responsible for the making of the product from start to finish, artisans frequently took a fierce pride in the quality of their work.

During the nineteenth century, the artisan or handicraft mode of production gradually gave way to the factory or industrial system of production. In order to maximize production and offer customers goods at cheaper prices, merchants, master artisans, or others with foresight and surplus capital, enlarged their work forces, broke down the work into a series of simpler tasks, and employed more or new machinery. While many of the earliest technological innovations essential to the industrial revolution were developed in England, Americans were quicker to seize upon them. In contrast to the more traditional societies of Europe, "everything new is quickly introduced here," exclaimed a foreign visitor in 1820. "There is no clinging to old ways; the moment an American hears the word 'invention' he pricks up his ears."

THE CELEBRATION OF GAIN

Commerce not only seemed to offer immense opportunities for many to get ahead materially, but trade could, its champions argued, serve as a new and an effective social adhesive. "In Europe," wrote Alexis de Tocqueville, "we are wont to look upon a restless disposition, an unbounded desire for riches, and an excessive love of independence as propensities dangerous to society." But not necessarily so in the United States. Older dependencies, the use of coercion, and even appeals to virtue no longer seemed necessary to the celebrants of commerce. Commercial transactions, enthused Samuel Blodget, forged *"golden chains"* among people who otherwise would have had no social connections whatsoever. Buying and selling, Blodget continued, created *"the best social system that ever was formed."* It was the common pursuit of "private interest," concluded de Tocqueville, that held America together.

To many Americans, commerce also seemed to square with the egalitarian ideology of the young nation. True, we know today that the distribution of wealth between the rich and the poor worsened during the nineteenth century. Yet "the market house, like the grave is a place of perfect equality," grumbled Philip Freneau, a defender of the older world of personal dependencies and hierarchies. Commercial transactions obliterated connections based on custom, patronage, and deference. In commerce, there were no dependencies and no obligations except those arrived at in explicit exchanges. To that extent, all parties involved in trade were equals.

Even more startling to foreign visitors was the growing respect accorded to men who were engaged in buying and selling. Europeans and colonial Americans alike had always reserved their highest esteem for the landed gentry, for those who did not have to work or at the least those who gave the appearance of not working. But Americans, at least those in the northern half of the nation, openly celebrated business and businessmen. "Is not the merchant as respectable a member of the community as the luxurious planter, the time-serving politician, or the cringing office-seeker?" rhetorically queried Freeman Hunt in the 1830s. Americans increasingly accorded the doing and making of things a transcendent or religious-like value.

THE EQUATION OF SUCCESS WITH MONEYMAKING

Equally astonishing, at least from the aristocratic European perspective of Alexis de Tocqueville, was the fact that Americans worked "specifically to gain money." While politicians might visualize success in terms of power, teachers in terms of the effective cultivation of young minds, evangelists in terms of conversion of unbelievers, no definition of success came to enjoy greater favor in the United States than making money. "To get, and to have the reputation for possessing [money], is the ruling [American] passion," declared Henry W. Bellows in remarks that were echoed by scores of other antebellum observers.

Nothing, it seemed, helped to distinguish the United States from Europe more than the equation of success with money. It has endured to this day. In the 1880s, Englishman James Bryce reported that "the pursuit of wealth is nowhere so eager as in America." And in 1908 John Van Dyke proclaimed: "everyone knows that success with the great masses spells money. It is money that the new generation expects to win. . . . The boy will make it, and the girl, if she is not a goose, will marry it. They will get it in one way or another."

Equating success with the acquisition of wealth gave rise to America's most prized formula for upward mobility—the self-made man. "This is the country of *self-made* men," boasted an American as early as the 1840s, "which nothing better could be said of any state of society." Benjamin Franklin, in his *Autobiography*, published in the eighteenth century, had already explained to tens of thousands of Americans how they might, by hard work, careful time management, and the practice of frugality, rise from obscure origins to fame and fortune. According to the gospel of the self-made man, in America (again unlike Europe) birth, personal connections, and religious affiliations counted for nothing. All it took to succeed in America was personal determination. Anticipating the United States Army's recruiting slogan of the 1990s, Joel Hawes told a group of young artisans in 1826: *"You may be whatever you resolve to be."*

In the latter half of the nineteenth century, authors, especially in advice-to-boys novels, flooded the country with tales of boys climbing out of poverty to achieve great wealth. The "rags to riches" story made Horatio Alger, the most famed of these pulp-fiction writers, rich in his own right. A Philadelphia cleric, Russell H. Conwell, delivered a sermon embodying the success formula (entitled "Acres of Diamonds") no fewer than six thousand times. When asked why he told people how to get rich rather than preaching the gospel, Conwell replied: "Because to make money honestly is to preach the gospel." As proof of what the practice of hard work and personal thrift could accomplish, authors particularly liked to cite the careers of Cornelius Vanderbilt, Andrew Carnegie, and John D. Rockefeller.

The gospel of the self-made man exercised an incalculable influence on American ways. While the realities of upward mobility never matched the more extravagant claims of the success writers, dreams of getting ahead energized the lives of countless white American families. They worked harder than ever before. They became far more time conscious; the mass manufacturing of clocks in the 1830s marked the beginning of the modern obsession with punctuality. Even when engaged in grueling work with their hands (manual labor) and seemingly trapped in dead-end jobs, they were less inclined than their European counterparts to form labor unions or to support socialism.

The gospel of success encouraged a new kind of individualism, an acquisitive individualism that revolved around the idea that economic obligations applied only to one's self. The new form of individualism was put in its bluntest terms by de Tocqueville: Americans "owe nothing to any man . . . they acquire the habit of always considering themselves standing alone, and they are apt to imagine that their whole destiny is in their own hands. Thus not only does . . . every man forget his ancestors, but . . . separates his contemporaries from him[self]."

In economic matters the individual's personal welfare should be first and foremost. As Ralph Waldo Emerson rhetorically exclaimed in his popular essay "Self-Reliance": "Are they *my* poor?" Others, following the lead of such free trade economists as Adam Smith, concluded that the pursuit of individual interest could benefit the entire community. Because of the economic growth induced by the untrammeled pursuit of private interest, nearly everyone in the community would be better off than before. Regardless of rationale, the new individualism meant that, for many, earlier dreams of a biblical commonwealth or a classical republic in which self-interest would be subordinated had given way to another dream, one of a nation characterized by the spirit of personal enterprise and the right to amass wealth and power for one's self.

While moneymaking could become an end in itself, for most Americans it was primarily a means to acquiring more consumer goods, greater creature comforts, and, above all, more power and status. With the erosion of traditional deference based on birth and dependencies, money became an increasingly important source of personal power. Without the existence of traditional hierarchies, the making of money also was for many (perhaps most) Americans the most legitimate and democratic way of distinguishing one person from another.

THE COSTS OF PURSUING PERSONAL GAIN

Neither personal satisfaction nor happiness necessarily accompanied the preoccupation with moneymaking. At least this was the conclusion of a legion of foreign observers and a substantial number of Americans themselves. Anxieties seemed to arise precisely from the fact that there were no limits to individual aspirations in antebellum America. With the future wide open, no man—no matter how much success he had enjoyed in the past—could any longer take satisfaction from his present condition. He always worried about whether his success would continue into the future or that someone else might overtake him. Worries arising from the "bootless chase" of gain made Americans an especially glum people, reported de Tocqueville. "A cloud habitually hung upon [their] brows."

The psychic costs of failure in such a society could be particularly poignant. The career of Chauncy Jerome, who earned a fortune from selling clocks, was a case in point. Upon making a series of unwise investments, Jerome lost everything. In bankruptcy, his friends no longer had any respect for him. "I never was any better when I owned [my fortune] than I am now, and never behaved any better," he reported bitterly. "But how different the feeling towards you, when your neighbors can make nothing more out of you." Shunned by former friends and forced to return to the ranks of the common laborers, Chauncy Jerome died in poverty.

The land of opportunity left behind countless Chauncy Jeromes. Many failed to succeed. By mid-century half or more of all adult white men held no landed property. Given the widespread presumption that white men in America were the architects of their own destiny, who could the propertyless blame for their failure except themselves? By this logic, they were led to the conclusion that they were morally unfit, that they lacked the ambition, thrift, and inner strength to succeed. Rather than embracing such a damning indictment to their self-esteem, propertyless whites frequently took refuge in the existence of even more impoverished and degraded groups such as Irish immigrants, Native Americans, and African Americans. By depicting African Americans as lazy, stupid, comically ridiculous, and incapable of upward mobility, the enormously popular blackface minstrel shows of the nineteenth and early twentieth centuries reassured poor white people that, no matter how bad off they were, black people were worse off. Such a presumption gave even the most miserable whites a stake in preserving the nation's system of white racial supremacy.

Squaring Christian morality with the values of the marketplace also disturbed some Americans. "The general system of our trade . . . is a system of selfishness," flatly declared Ralph Waldo Emerson in 1841. It "is a system of distrust, of concealment, of superior keenness, not of giving but of taking. . . ." The "sins" of trade, he said, extended far beyond the merchant and the manufacturer. "The trail of the serpent reaches into all the lucrative professions and practices of men." Regardless of occupation, a tender conscience disqualified one for success. Success in trade and the professions required a "certain shutting of the eyes," compromises, and a denial of "the sentiments of love and generosity," Emerson concluded.

With moneymaking the nation's "only enthusiasm," there was little time or room in the United States for play, celebrations, or the carnivalesque. "In no country that I know is there so much hard, toilsome, unremitting labor," reported one foreign visitor, "in none so little recreation and enjoyment of life." A host of foreign travelers to America agreed. "From the time we landed in New England," Englishman Sir Charles Lyell reported, "we seemed to have been in a country where all, whether rich or poor, were laboring from morning till night, without ever indulging in a holiday." While these reports exaggerated American antipathy to play, they correctly captured the prevailing spirit of those who were most bent on getting ahead. Of all people, even Adam Smith, the Scottish political economist who championed free trade and hard work as a means of enhancing a nation's wealth, complained that Americans engaged in "unnecessary and excessive enterprise."

By the middle of the nineteenth century, a growing number of the nation's poets, writers, and painters found a life devoted to the pursuit of one's own material welfare too cramped. It seemed to leave too little room for love, human feelings, and for deeper expressions of the self. In opposition to the dominant spirit of acquisitive individualism, they developed what Robert Bellah and his associates have recently described as an "expressive individualism." No one represented this new form of individualism more clearly than the poet Walt Whitman. For Whitman, success was to be found in a life that was rich in experience—in strong emotions and in the sensual—rather than in material acquisition. Expressive individualism meant to Whitman above all else the freedom from the trammels imposed on the self by the pursuit of wealth:

> Afoot and light-hearted I take to the open road,
> Healthy, free, the world before me,
> The long brown path before me, leading wherever I choose.

European visitors frequently claimed that the unrelenting pursuit of gain, when combined with republican egalitarianism, had caused America to revert to a state of barbarism. In America, every man was for himself; he cut all ties with family, with a particular place, with the past, indeed, with everything external to himself. Enjoying no feelings nor time for anything more profound or refined than those provoked by wheeling and dealing, Americans could never, many agreed, support nor produce great works in literature and the fine arts. A large outpouring of literature by American authors in the 1840s and 1850s reflects the obvious exaggeration of such conclusions.

The reversion to barbarism, if so it was, included a special proclivity for violence, especially in the fast-growing cities and in the South and the West. Public violence, concluded one foreign traveler, is "the greatest evil in North America—worse than slavery." While very few went that far, many commented on the seemingly universal presence of weapons and the regularity with which they were employed—even "against brothers, cousins, and neighbors!" as one traveler put it. Just as ordinary white men had obtained the right to vote, they were more likely than Europeans to use force in resolving problems. In particular, the newly empowered white men, who were no longer as constrained by tradition nor by elite authority, perpetrated acts of violence against the weak and the marginal, such as free blacks, black slaves, Indians, Mexicans, Mormons, and Catholics. Once comparative statistics became available, they revealed (as today) a far higher rate of violent acts in the United States than in Western Europe.

THE SOUTHERN EXCEPTION

In many respects southern history in the decades before the Civil War followed a path similar to that of the North's. In both sections, the doors of opportunity for ordinary white men widened; white men in both regions scrambled to get ahead and to rise in society. In both sections, the presence of independent white farmers who owned their own land and cultivated it with their own hands were especially conspicuous. These farmers jealously guarded their personal independence and the principle of social egalitarianism. Finally, in the South as in the North, large numbers endorsed the view that all white males ought to have the right to vote and that public-office holders ought to be responsive to the electorate.

Nonetheless, in important respects southern history followed a distinctive trajectory. Unlike the North, the South remained an overwhelmingly agricultural region. While the rapid expansion of cotton production in the antebellum era tied the region's economy to an international market, society in the Deep South continued to be dominated by the large holders of land and slaves. Rather than merchants and manufacturers, the large planters set the tone of southern life. As in the past, they continued to be the primary shapers of southern ways. The existence of a large African American slave population in the South also distinguished the two regions. Opportunities for the economic exploitation of blacks and concern for the maintenance of white supremacy reinforced the white South's determination to retain and perpetuate the region's traditional ways.

THE HIERARCHICAL WAYS OF THE OLD SOUTH

Rather than to northern merchants or manufacturers, the southern planters looked to the English aristocracy as their models for the good life. As we have seen in Chapter 2, long before the nineteenth century, the tobacco and rice planters along the Atlantic Tidewater saw themselves as descendants of the English Cavaliers. Here, they constructed the legendary "Old South." It included white-pillared mansions in the Greek revival style, which, according to an Irish visitor, were "exactly similar to the old manor houses of England." The planters lived, he added, in "a style which approaches nearer to that of the English country gentleman than what is to be met with anywhere else on the continent." Although frequently cruder, rawer, and more volatile, the newer cotton nabobs of the Southwest also tried to imitate the graceful ways of the Atlantic Tidewater planters.

While the typical large southern landholders lusted after wealth and pursued it with an ardor that resembled no one more than northern businessmen, allegiance to the aristocratic ideal required them to conspicuously display contempt for northern ways of work and leisure. Regardless of social class, white southerners rarely infused work with the high moral purpose that it was given by northerners. To southerners, work was what it had always been, something that had to be done in order to have time to enjoy one's leisure time. Unlike northerners, southerners saw no need to rationalize their pursuit of leisure. Leisure could and should be enjoyed for its own sake.

Styles of leisure differed according to class. Planters threw lavish parties, extended a warm hospitality to visitors of their own class, and kept stables of thoroughbred racing horses. Imagining themselves as descendants of the medieval knights and lords portrayed in Sir Walter Scott's enormously popular novels, the planters even reenacted fantasies of feudal chivalry and splendor. They revived the medieval dueling code and held jousting tournaments precisely in the manner described by Scott. The plain white folk took their pleasures in simpler forms. Above all, they hunted and fished. Gambling, drinking, and fighting were almost equally popular. "Sober restraint," as historian William Barney has cryptically observed, "was not high on the list of Southern virtues."

From the perspective of northerners, southern males were obsessively concerned with protecting their sense of manhood. In the North, a middle-class male won the esteem of his fellows by achieving a reputation for hard work, attention to religious duty, and self-control, but in the South male status flowed from the possession of honor. Honor could never be taken for granted; it had to be publicly displayed and asserted in face-to-face encounters. Even the slightest challenge to one's honor represented a personal affront and, unless countered, carried with it the shame of being no better than the lowest slave. Gentlemen responded to challenges to their honor by fighting duels while the more ordinary white men resorted to knife-wielding brawls. Concern for the preservation of honor contributed to the South's exceptionally high homicide rate, a rate that typically exceeded that of the North by four times.

Patriarchy remained more central to southern than to northern ways. While in the more egalitarian North, the word "master," which had been long associated with hierarchy and superiority in rank, fell into disuse, it remained a key word in the South's lexicon. Not only was "master" the proper way of addressing the owner of a large plantation but it implied the complete subordination of all others—of wives, children, and slaves. Everyone on the plantation deferred to the master's every whim. Plantation "mistresses" were also accorded an exaggerated deference, but for their alleged delicacy and innocence rather than for their real power.

While rarely openly challenging the roles assigned to them, sometimes plantation mistresses bridled at male presumptions of superiority. "How men can go blustering around, making everybody uncomfortable, simply to show that they are the masters and we are only women and children at their mercy!" exclaimed Mary Chesnut in her diary. In particular, miscegenation strained relations between husbands and wives. "Like the patriarchs of old," sneered Chesnut, "our men live all in one house with their wives and concubines; and the mulattoes one sees in every family partly resemble the white children. Any lady is ready to tell you who is the father of all the mulattoes one sees in everybody's household but her own. Those, she seems to think, drop from the clouds."

Gamble Plantation House, Ellenton, Florida, Juxtaposed with Slave Quarters. These illustrations reflect the persistence in the South of more traditional ways and a hierarchical social order.

African Americans and the Doors of Opportunity

Neither, of course, did or could African Americans duplicate northern white ways. The doors of opportunity for political participation and material advancement remained closed for both slaves *and* free blacks. Pervasive racial prejudice severely circumscribed the lives of free blacks everywhere. With few exceptions, even in the North they could neither vote, attend public schools, nor sit next to whites in churches. Yet, in the wake of the American Revolution, free African Americans created an impressive set of institutions. Pooling their own talents and meager resources, they founded schools, antislavery organizations, and, above all, churches. Despite the ravages that white discrimination inflicted upon them, these institutions gave free blacks a stronger sense of self-worth, community, and cultural autonomy.

As we observed in Chapter 2, well before the nineteenth century a distinctive set of African American ways developed within the institution of slavery. These included ways of family and religion. Southern law did not recognize the legality of slave marriages, but, since slave marriages promised to improve the morale of his workforce and increase its value through the birth of additional children, slaveholders usually permitted or even encouraged slave unions. Slaves likewise valued marriage. Although forced separations split many black marriages, roughly two-thirds of slave families included the presence of both parents. That slave families characteristically occupied separate cabins rather than living in barracks or dormitories strengthened family life and helped to nurture a separate African American culture.

Religion also continued to play a large role in the lives of enslaved African Americans. Slaves typically blended African religious practices with evangelical Protestantism. While white masters sought to indoctrinate slaves in a kind of Christianity that celebrated passive submission, black Christians tended to deemphasize original sin and the church as a symbol of authority while stressing the biblical story of Moses leading the Children of Israel out of Egyptian bondage. Spirituals, work songs, and folktales—all central to African American slave culture as well—frequently contained subtly subversive messages. For example, slaves identified with the folk tales of Brer Rabbit, who, while physically vulnerable, used cunning and wit to outsmart his more powerful enemies. Despite the odds arrayed against them, such cultural expressions indicated that the slaves were by no means acquiescent to their plight.

Legal disabilities, including bans against owning property and making contracts, as well as the ever-present threat of physical punishment, were major determinants of slave work ways. Overseers and drivers carried whips and were prepared to use them. Fear of the whip on a bare back frequently set the pace of work. The absence of positive incentives encouraged a passive resistance to work. If unobserved by superiors, slaves might shirk their tasks, misuse or break valuable tools, or steal food. In some places, however, masters and slaves reached an understanding about work duties that involved a combination of the carrot and the stick. By working diligently, slaves in the rice-growing South Carolina lowlands finished their tasks "by one or two o'clock in the afternoon," reported a Methodist preacher, and had "the rest of the day for themselves, which they spend in working their own private fields . . . planting rice, corn, potatoes, tobacco &c. for their own use and profit." Hardworking slaves might also be rewarded with an opportunity to work at less exhausting and more psychologically fulfilling jobs than as field hands. At least 10 percent of the slaves were employed in such capacities as drivers (of other slaves), carpenters, blacksmiths, coachmen, stewards, and house servants.

While there were some opportunities for ambitious slaves to "get ahead," they could advance only so far. In the antebellum era, legal barriers made it increasingly difficult for them to purchase their own freedom. Neither was running away a viable option for most slaves. Likewise, given the white monopoly on guns and their superior numbers, slave revolts never succeeded. Of the several attempted, all were brutally crushed. The absence of educational opportunities represented yet another barrier to self-advancement. No more than 2 percent of the slaves could read and write on the eve of the Civil War.

CONCLUSION

For tens of thousands of ordinary white families in the nineteenth century, the United States became a land of unprecedented opportunities. Opportunities for political choices multiplied with the extension of suffrage to all white men and the development of a system of competitive politics. Opportunities to choose religious affiliations proliferated with the weakening of formal connections between church and state and the competition between revivalistic denominations for new members. Opportunities for material advancement by ordinary white families increased with the unleashing of older restraints on personal gain, the opening of vast new territories in the West, the construction of a national system of transportation, and the rapid growth of the economy.

The explosive expansion of opportunities for ordinary white families redirected and reshaped American ways of politics, religion, commerce, work, and success. It encouraged a new kind of political culture, one in which the political system was more responsive to the ordinary white voter. It encouraged a new kind of individualism, one that celebrated the right of each person to amass wealth and power for themselves. What remains to be seen is how the revolution in choices would affect American ways of ordering society.

5

IN SEARCH OF A NEW MORAL ORDER

"**P**ray for me," wrote John Fisher from Michigan to his English kin in 1837, "that the acquiring of the things of this life may not engage the whole of my attention." Fisher yearned for something more in his life than the relentless pursuit of personal wealth. In the spring of 1838, he found an answer. At a Methodist prayer meeting, feelings of guilt suddenly overwhelmed him. He was now convinced that he "had sinned against God all my life long & that I deserved to be sent to hell." He repented of his sins, and three weeks later he reported that God had forgiven him. "My load of guilt was gone," he wrote. Fisher now knew "such rejoicing as I never saw or felt before."

Like John Fisher, millions of other Americans in the nineteenth century looked beyond the marketplace for moral approval, a validation of their self-worth, and a larger meaning for their day-to-day existence. Their search led in a variety of sometimes strange and unpredictable directions. Spiritualism, phrenology, transcendentalism, vegetarianism, and a score of other religious or cultlike causes had their enthusiasts. Yet none of these movements approximated the popularity or the significance of evangelical Protestantism. To the utter astonishment of the Revolutionary era's nineteenth-century surviving leaders, who had expected the republic to take a mainly secular course, millions of Americans flocked to evangelical churches. Not only did evangelicalism offer spiritual succor and fulfillment to individuals but its influence reached everywhere—into families, voluntary societies, political parties, newspapers and magazines, and the public schoolrooms of America.

Evangelicalism was at the center of a widespread nineteenth-century search for a new moral order. Gardiner Spring, an evangelist, explained in 1820 that "liberty without godliness is but another name for anarchism or despotism." With the traditional external restraints on the individual weakened or shattered, evangelicals urged upon all Americans a strict, biblically based, personal morality. By mid-nineteenth century, an ethic of self-control had become the hallmark of the rapidly growing middle class of ambitious farmers, artisans, merchants, and manufacturers. While not rejecting republican principles, many evangelicals also dreamed of nothing less than the creation of God's kingdom on earth. This led them to seek the reformation of individual sinners. Others, who usually shared the New England idea of community and a new, heightened moral sensibility, sought to remake society at large. They even went so far as to challenge America's traditional ways of gender, race, and private property.

THE RISE OF POPULAR CHRISTIANITY

A great popular religious uprising was at the center of the quest for a new moral order. Unlike the first Great Awakening of the eighteenth century, the revivals that repeatedly seared their way across the land between 1795 and 1865 arose from the bottom up rather than the top down. As never before, the people themselves seized control of their religious lives. "If all men are 'BORN EQUAL,'" exclaimed evangelist Lorenzo Dow, "then there can be no just reason . . . why [man] may or should not think, and judge, and act for himself in matters of religion, opinion, and private judgment." In a culture that increasingly balked at the more obvious symbols of hierarchy, a remarkable number of Americans interpreted Luther's "priesthood of all believers" to mean precisely that—that religion ought to be of, by, and for the people.

AMERICA AS A RELIGIOUS MARKETPLACE

The separation of church and state encouraged the democratization of American religion. In nineteenth-century Europe, religious unorthodoxy could still bring down the wrath of the state; dissenters could be charged with treason, fined, and even imprisoned. But in America the once-important concept of a "dissenter" became virtually meaningless. In the new republic, each religious group was on an equal footing and any religious idea (except open blasphemy) could receive a public hearing. Neither did Americans pay taxes to support churches. The Constitution's First Amendment explicitly prohibited the national government from making any laws regarding the establishment of religion, and in 1833 the last state (Massachusetts) ended its tax support of churches.

With the separation of church and state, the new nation became in effect a huge, sprawling religiously free marketplace. Competition to retain the allegiance of existing church members, to recruit new members, and to raise money unleashed a spectacular sales campaign—one whose stunning successes would make even modern Madison Avenue hucksters turn green with envy.

To seize upon the opportunities opened up by America's religious marketplace, a large army of mostly untutored but dedicated preachers took to the field. Their sheer numbers exploded, from eighteen hundred in all of America in 1775 to nearly forty thousand in 1845. In egalitarian America, anyone could become a preacher. A minister no longer needed to have a classical education nor come from the ranks of the gentry. The divine call could even descend on ordinary "plowmen, tailors, carpenters, or shoemakers," explained Bishop Francis Asbury, head of the American Methodist Church.

In their quest for souls, the preachers no longer restricted their efforts within established churches. Many had no regularized denominational affiliation at all. They scoured the countryside and the cities, everywhere preaching the gospel to whomever would listen. They sometimes even formed their own churches. Two of these churches, the Mormons and the Disciples of Christ, grew into major American denominations.

Farmer-preachers, men who tilled the soil during the week and preached on Sunday, became the mainstay of the Baptist ministry, while the Methodists sent out dozens of young circuit riders. The circuit riders made their way by horseback through the miseries of winter's cold and summer's heat. Admiration for their fortitude in the face of bad weather led to a saying among the country people: "There is nothing out today but crows and Methodist preachers." An envious Reverend Horace Bushnell concluded that a military metaphor was particularly appropriate for describing the intrepid circuit riders. They were, he said, "a kind of light artillery that God has organized to pursue and overtake the fugitives that flee into the wilderness from his presence."

THE SECOND GREAT AWAKENING

A spectacular camp meeting in the small backcountry community of Cane Ridge, Kentucky, in 1801 unofficially launched what is sometimes called the Second Great Awakening. Led by Baptist and Methodist exhorters (whose numbers included at least one black) as many as twenty-five thousand people may have gathered to listen to sermons, to pray, to repent, and to experience conversion. Women, men, children, rich and poor, even the state's governor—every kind of person came. In follow-up camp meetings over the next six months, more than a hundred thousand Kentuckians, nearly half the state's entire population, experienced a spiritual rebirth.

The next year the revivals spread like wildfire west through the hill country on both sides of the Ohio River, to the Deep South, and then eastward to the more settled areas along the Atlantic Coast. Every year, boasted Methodist Bishop Francis Asbury in 1811, camp meetings brought together three to four million people. This figure represented nearly one-third of the nation's entire population! For millions of Americans, camp meetings became in effect a summer holiday at which they not only escaped normal routines but experienced a religious rebirth or a spiritual revitalization.

At the same time that the Methodists, Baptists, and a host of lesser religious groups were bringing in thousands of the unchurched, a new kind of evangelical Calvinism also began to take shape in New England. New England's evangelicalism arose in part as a reaction against the growing influence of religious liberalism. As early as the middle decades of the eighteenth century, liberal ministers within the Congregationalist establishment began moving away from a rigid Calvinism and belief in the intrinsically sinful nature of all humans. Rejecting the trinity in favor of a single godhead, in the early nineteenth century some of the Congregational churches officially declared

A Methodist Circuit Rider.
Despite the adversities of travel,
in the nineteenth century, the
intrepid Methodist circuit riders
converted millions to evangelical forms of Christianity.

A Camp Meeting. In 1811, Methodist Bishop Francis Asbury boasted that nearly one-
third of Americans attended a camp meeting each summer.

themselves Unitarian. Though small in numbers, the Unitarians appealed to better-educated and more affluent New Englanders. In time, they even won control of the Harvard Divinity School. While never organized into a formal church, the Transcendentalists likewise promoted a liberal form of religion. Ralph Waldo Emerson, whose first occupation had been that of a Unitarian minister, believed that God, or the Oversoul, resided everywhere and that all men possessed a spark of divinity.

In 1801, the same year as Kentucky's Cane Ridge camp meetings, the Reverend Timothy Dwight, the president of Congregationalist Yale College and a grandson of Jonathan Edwards, countered religious liberalism by provoking a series of campus revivals. These revivals incited a whole generation of campus converts to carry the gospel to the western (now midwestern) states. Revival flames also repeatedly blazed forth in the areas settled by New Englanders—upstate New York and around the southern rim of the Great Lakes. Indeed, because of the sustained intensity of religious life in upstate New York, the region became known as the "burned-over district." Not only did the revivals in the burned-over district invigorate older denominations, but the area gave birth to such exotic new religious movements as Mormonism, Adventism, Shakerism, and Spiritualism.

To the horror of Old School Calvinists, a band of upstart Congregationalist and Presbyterian preachers in the burned-over district adopted methods similar to the Methodists and the Baptists. Charles Grandison Finney, a Presbyterian, vaulted into national prominence by leading a revival in Rochester, New York, in 1830–31. Theologically self-taught, Finney, a former school teacher and lawyer, preached in the vernacular; he advised preachers to throw away their notes and use the *"language of common life."* He set up an "anxious bench" in front of his pulpit where sinners concerned about the fate of their souls awaited his special prayers and admonishments. No one could escape Finney and his followers; they relentlessly pursued "the damned" into the streets, their homes, and their places of work. As Finney himself put it, he had brought the methods of the "ignorant Methodist and Baptist exhorters" to the conversion of the "highest classes of society."

Finney's stunning successes at Rochester were only a beginning. Finney himself led highly successful revivals in Philadelphia, New York, and Boston. The Second Great Awakening witnessed the mass conversion of blacks; led mostly by black revivalists, free blacks and slaves alike turned in droves to evangelical Christianity. In 1857–58, businessmen fomented revivals in the nation's largest cities; there, thousands gathered for daily noonday prayer meetings. During the Civil War (1861–65), revivals repeatedly swept through both Union and Confederate Army camps.

Successful revivals radically reconfigured denominational strengths, as Table 5.1 reveals. In 1776, when the Americans declared their independence from Britain, the Methodist church hardly existed at all and the Baptists ranked third behind the Congregationalists and Anglicans in membership. By 1850 two-thirds of all Protestants were Methodists or Baptists. (The Roman

| TABLE 5.1 | DENOMINATIONAL SHARES OF RELIGIOUS ADHERENTS IN THE UNITED STATES, 1776 AND 1850 |

1776		1850	
1. Congregationalists	20.4%	1. Methodists	34.2%
2. Presbyterians	19.0	2. Baptists	20.5
3. Baptists	16.9	3. Roman Catholics	13.9
4. Episcopalians	15.7	4. Presbyterians	11.6
5. Methodists	2.5	5. Congregationalists	4.0
6. Roman Catholics	1.8	6. Episcopalians	3.5

SOURCE: Mark A. Noll, *A History of Christianity in the United States and Canada* (Grand Rapids, Mich.: Wm. B. Eerdmans, 1992), p. 153.

Catholic Church, the beneficiary of thousands of immigrants in the 1830s and 1840s, leaped from tenth to third place among American churches.)

EVANGELICALISM AS A DEMOCRATIC MOVEMENT

The stunning successes of the revivals reflected their congruency with larger nineteenth-century American beliefs and practices. The evangelical emphasis upon each person's capacity to receive or reject salvation accorded with American individualism. By appealing to high and low alike, the revivals were in harmony with American egalitarianism and democracy. Finally, in their reliance upon intuition and their scorn for complex theological arguments, evangelicals reflected popular suspicions of the intellect.

Everywhere the evangelicals retreated from a strict Calvinism. In the first Great Awakening, evangelists had for the most part insisted on the Calvinistic idea that salvation ultimately rested with God alone rather than with mere mortals. Nineteenth-century evangelicals, on the other hand, devised ways of affirming God's sovereignty while allowing room for potential converts to choose for themselves between eternal salvation and damnation. In addition, securing salvation no longer required lengthy study, prayer, self-reflection, or a prolonged struggle with one's inner emotions. Evangelicals telescoped the process of conversion into a single, dramatic moment. To a hurrying, time-conscious population, the evangelical exhorter promised the possibility of instant salvation achieved mostly if not entirely by personal effort.

Religious democratization included more emotionally expressive forms of religious experience. No one could be quite sure what to expect at evangelical services. While evangelists usually sought to tame the more extreme forms of religious feeling, crying out in anguish, barking like dogs, jerking, and rolling on the ground sometimes broke out in the midst of revivals. Rather than ministers of deep learning who presented scholarly discourses as sermons, evangelical groups featured preachers who were spell-binding storytellers, men (and sometimes women) who spoke in the idiom of the common people rather than that of elites. Evangelicals introduced into church services more lively music. They favored emotionally evocative hymns that could be sung by the worshipers themselves.

A simpler theology, one that could be more easily grasped by ordinary people, reflected the democratic character of the evangelical movement. As Elias Smith, a former New England Baptist who later joined the newly formed Disciples of Christ, put it, republican Americans should be freed from sub-servience "to a catechism, creed, covenant or a superstitious priest." They should rely upon nothing except the Bible. Insistence upon a literal reading of the Bible as the ultimate source of authority encouraged a return in reli-gious practices to the first church, that founded by Jesus and his apostles. And it meant that evangelicals even questioned or ignored theological propo-sitions that had long been at the center of Protestantism. Where in the Bible, they rhetorically asked, could one find references to predestination, limited atonement, and other abstruse theological issues?

Within evangelical congregations, previously rigid hierarchies frequently gave way to more-democratic forms of church community. In nearly all evan-gelical groups, the laity gained more authority. Ministers frequently con-demned the refinement and elegance associated with the gentry and praised the honesty and simplicity of the ordinary people. Not only did the clergy, the elders, and the rich and well-born experience an erosion of deference, but the popular religious movements challenged religious patriarchy as well. A disproportionate number of the revival converts were women and young people. Emboldened by their conversions, both groups frequently insisted that—at least on spiritual matters—they were the equals of adult men.

Like no religion imposed from above could possibly do, religious de-mocratization energized the spiritual life of the ordinary people. "It is truly wonderful," marveled transplanted German theologian Philip Schaff in 1855, "what a multitude of churches, ministers, colleges, theological seminaries, and benevolent associations are . . . founded and maintained entirely by free-will offerings." Indeed, nineteenth-century diaries, letters, and ordinary con-versations breathed an everyday preoccupation with religion that never ceases to astonish modern scholars. Such was the degree of religious ardor among the people at large, explained Schaff, that nothing approximated it anywhere else in the Western world.

Yet, as revivalist constituencies grew in wealth and social standing in the nineteenth century, it became increasingly difficult for them to resist the temptations of respectability. Worship services gradually became more re-strained, the singing of spirituals less frequent, and the preaching less fer-vent. Many evangelicals eventually insisted upon a better-trained clergy; for example, in the three decades prior to the Civil War, the Methodists founded more than thirty colleges in sixteen states. In the middle of the nineteenth century, the Methodists even removed their ban on pew rentals, a move that old-time evangelist Peter Cartwright described as "a Yankee triumph." Yet such concessions to propriety and urbane congeniality came at a cost, for it opened the door to competition from new evangelical groups, to what historian Nathan Hatch has aptly described as a "recurring populist impulse in American Christianity."

THE SHAPING OF AN EVANGELICAL REPUBLIC

By the mid-nineteenth century, dreams of an America shaped in the image of ancient Athens or republican Rome had faded into the distant background. Instead of the writings of the ancients, the evangelicals drew upon the Bible. They dreamed of an America that conformed to God's laws. By mid-century, Abraham Lincoln seemed like a far more appropriate spokesman for the new republic than Thomas Jefferson. While Lincoln was not a member of a church, his mindset was religious and he regularly employed biblical imagery in his speeches and his writings. And, unlike Jefferson, Lincoln had also risen from the ranks of the ordinary people.

EVANGELICAL COMMUNITIES

The spiritual fervor generated by revivals led to the formation of a variety of evangelical communities. One kind sought to achieve greater holiness—indeed, in some cases prefect lives—by separating themselves as much as possible from secular society. Before the Civil War, these evangelicals formed more than 150 utopian communities. Sometimes they broke radically with traditional ways of property ownership, marriage, and the family. For example, the Shakers, who built handsome, productive colonies in New England, upstate New York, and northern Ohio, renounced entirely sexual intercourse and private property.

While sharing property, another perfectionist-inspired colony, Oneida in New York, developed a quite different set of sexual practices. Concluding that monogamous marriages encouraged selfishness, John Humphrey Noyes, the founder of the community, advocated what he called "complex marriages." In Oneida, every adult was married to all other adults in the colony. To control births, males practiced intercourse without ejaculation, and the community decided who would have children and when. In the end, the colony was unable to resist external pressures aimed at its unorthodox marital and sexual practices. In 1879, Oneida abandoned complex marriages and became (and remains today) a prosperous joint-stock corporation.

While many of the religious-centered colonies were small in numbers and survived only a few years, the Church of Jesus Christ of Latter-day Saints (Mormons) became an enduring community that shaped millions of lives. The founder, Joseph Smith, who grew up in the burned-over district of upstate New York, claimed that a heavenly emissary guided him to the location of the *Book of Mormon,* a set of golden plates which contained a revelation from God in addition to that of the Bible. Translated by Smith, the *Book of*

Mormon disclosed that the lost tribes of Israel had come to the Americas centuries earlier. One group had founded a Christian colony, but it had been wiped out by heathen tribes who survived as American Indians. Smith and his followers tried to restore the perfect colony that they believed had once existed in America. Victimized by mobs, who were particularly offended by the Mormon advocacy of polygamy, the main body of Mormons eventually established a prosperous colony in the Great Salt Lake Valley.

Unlike Mormons, Shakers, and the Oneidas, the millions of Methodist, Baptist, and Presbyterian converts sought to conform to God's commands while continuing to live among "the damned." Religious life for them usually began in the home. Evangelicals tried to transform the home into a sacred institution, a place shielded from the corrupting influences of the outside world. Families worshiped in their homes; they scheduled regular prayers and Bible readings. "In the rural homes in the little Scotch-Irish communities where we grew up," recalled Caroline Coleman from western South Carolina, "the big Family Bible was at the center around which family life revolved."

The local Baptist, Methodist, or Presbyterian churches served as centers for the formation of tightly-knit religious communities. The communities modeled themselves upon an idealized version of the family; church members were expected to behave toward one another and to address one another as "Brother" and "Sister" in Christ. Insisting that outward behavior should always conform with inward conversion, these evangelical communities exercised a close vigilance over the moral lives of their members. "When one joined the Methodist church," recalled Elizabeth Hawks of the 1860s, "he was expected to give up all such things as cards, dancing, theatres, in fact all so called worldly amusements." In particular, the evangelicals sought to restrain such traditional patriarchal and male vices as swearing, drinking, and fighting.

Evangelical communities received a steady transfusion of new strength from annually scheduled revivals. Revivals held in local churches usually lasted about a week while camp meetings typically continued for two weeks or more. In one sense, the revivals were social occasions; nearly everyone—both church members and nonmembers—attended. "One would think that Ringling Brothers Circus was in town, not so, just [a] protracted meeting," wrote one North Carolinian in 1881. Young people seized upon the revivals as a respectable setting for courtship. More important, the annual revivals provided opportunities for the conversion of lost souls and the spiritual renewal of longtime Christians. Public conversion experiences, public prayers for forgiveness, and the act of formally joining a church greatly strengthened the bonds of evangelical communities.

EVANGELICALISM AND THE FORMATION OF THE MIDDLE CLASS

Evangelicalism contributed to the formation of the nineteenth century's fast-growing middle class. The new class defined itself in part by wealth and occupation. By 1850 nearly 60 percent of the adult males in the United States owned no landed property while the top 5 percent of the population owned about 60 percent of all property. In between was a group of farmers, merchants, professionals, independent artisans, and small manufacturers. Frequently comprised of self-made men and located mostly in the northern half of the nation, this middle group exercised an exceptionally large influence on the nation's businesses, churches, schools, and media.

A special moral discipline supplemented wealth and occupation as a foundation for the new class. The breakup of the old order and the weakening of traditional boundaries to the pursuit of self-interest intensified personal anxieties and concerns for social stability. Responding to these apprehensions and seeking a new source of order, many turned from outward to inward restraints. Evangelical faith assisted them in their efforts to instill in themselves and others an ethic of self-restraint. The ideal American, wrote Philip Schaff, "holds his passion in check; is master of his sensual nature; obeys natural laws, not under pressure from without, but from inward impulse, cheerfully and joyfully." Ideally, an interior moral gyroscope safely guided each person through the bewildering changes that were transforming American society.

Self-restraint not only promised to promote social order but also offered a possible rationalization for success in moneymaking. While evangelicals rarely vindicated acquisitiveness per se, their emphasis on individual choice as the key to salvation squared with the middle-class male's conviction that individual effort accounted largely for his material success. Carried a step further, such men reasoned that the secret to their success sprang from their moral superiority. Although not an evangelical, transcendentalist Ralph Waldo Emerson explicitly married moral excellence and material success when he wrote: "A dollar is not value, but representative of values, and [in the final analysis] of moral values." In other words, the marketplace automatically rewarded moral fitness while punishing those weak in moral character.

Finally, a reputation for the practice of self-restraint helped to set the middle class apart from the more "dissolute" classes, especially the working class from below and the rich from above. Indeed, revivals, such as Finney's in Rochester, tended to sort people out according to their personal behavior as much as their income levels. Converts were known for their temperance, hard work, and dedication to family and community. Nonconverts, on the other hand, shared casual attitudes toward time and work; they frequently spent their spare time drinking, gambling, and patronizing low forms of amusements.

In at least two respects, the ethos of self-restraint produced measurable results: Evangelical, middle-class families had fewer children and they drank less alcohol than other Americans. Spurred on by an abundance of cheap corn liquor, drinking had increased sharply after the Revolution. By 1830 in per capita terms (counting women and children as well as men) Americans drank more than five gallons of distilled spirits annually, a figure three times higher than today. To evangelicals, the loss of self-control and the social costs—such as broken homes, violence, poverty, and crime—associated with drinking were manifestations of the devil's work. A nationwide temperance crusade, which employed revivalist methods and was led by ministers and women, produced amazing results. By the middle of the 1840s per capita drinking in the United States had fallen below two gallons.

Likewise the birthrate, especially among middle-class families, plummeted downward in the nineteenth century. For white women it fell from an average of 7.0 in 1800 to 5.4 in 1850 and then to 3.6 by 1900. Delayed marriages, primitive birth control devices, male withdrawal, abortions, and, above all, abstinence from intercourse—all assisted middle-class families in reducing the number of their children. Abstinence required severe self-restraint and reflected the increasingly tight control that middle-class Americans imposed on their lives. For example, Harriet Beecher Stowe, ten years after her wedding, praised her husband, Calvin, for improvement in the restraint of his sexual passion, noting that he had almost achieved "the mastery of yourself in the most difficult point of all." A smaller family might not only assist the upwardly mobile in achieving material success, but it also established a family's reputation for self-restraint and social responsibility. The middle class identified large families with irresponsible immigrants and the working class.

The ideal of domesticity also became a vital component of the new middle-class order. With men increasingly working outside the home and with women in more prosperous families increasingly relieved from the tasks associated with the older household economy, the middle-class home took on a new social identity. It became a sacred place and a special female domain. There, women, presumed to be more delicate, sensitive, and moral than men, were expected to cultivate compassion, gentleness, piety, and benevolence. They assumed the main responsibility for the moral nurture of children and for restraining the impulsiveness of men. Serving as models of propriety and acting in quiet ways, women were asked to exercise a large but unobtrusive influence in the community as well.

EDUCATION AND POLITICS

To evangelicals, education was another important way of implementing God's will. Evangelicals, especially in those areas settled by New Englanders and their descendants, founded literally dozens of new denominationally affiliated colleges. Their influence extended to state-controlled colleges; Protestant clergymen served as presidents of nearly all of these institutions. State colleges typically required attendance at Protestant chapel services and taught orthodox Protestant doctrines. "A state university in this country should be religious," declared the president of the University of Michigan in 1863. "It should be Christian without being sectarian."

Whereas the public school movement made little headway in the South during the antebellum era, both the rage for self-improvement (see Chapter 4) and evangelicalism were responsible for sweeping away opposition to tax-supported education in the North. Ambitious workers in particular saw the public schools as a way of advancing the opportunities for their children to get ahead materially. Protestant reformers, on the other hand, saw in the schools an opportunity to create a common culture. All children should be subjected to a disciplined environment and inculcated in the same set of Protestant values. To the chagrin of Catholics, Protestant theology and teachers completely dominated the public school system. *McGuffey's Eclectic Readers,* first published in 1836–37 and soon to become the most popular primary school text in the nation, revolved around a biblical worldview. Students not only learned from *McGuffey* that life on earth was merely a preparation for life after death, but found in almost every sentence admonitions for obedience, sobriety, punctuality, frugality, and hard work.

Evangelicals also carried their crusading zeal into the political arena. While a minority of evangelicals stressed personal holiness and either withdrew entirely from politics or drew a firm line between the political and spiritual worlds, other evangelicals, in particular New Englanders and those with New England roots, turned to politics as a means of promoting the establishment of God's kingdom on earth. This Puritan-evangelical camp usually supported the Whig party and its successor, the Republican party. Along with supporting government promotion of economic growth, the Whigs had a strong moral agenda. Indeed, the connections between the northern evangelicals and Whigs were so strong that historian Daniel Walker Howe has characterized the party as "in many ways the evangelical united front at the polling place." Backcountry and southern evangelicals (along with Roman Catholics), on the other hand, tended to vote Democratic.

TURNING THE WORLD UPSIDE DOWN

A new moral sensibility, one that spread through much of the Western world in the nineteenth century, served as the general catalyst for America's first great age of social reform. To obtain conformity with the new sensibility, reformers launched campaigns against cruelty (even against animals), drunkenness, prostitution, and Sabbath-breaking. They supported the rehabilitation of criminals, the establishment of public school systems, education of the deaf and the blind, and the more humane treatment of the insane. By seeking to abolish slavery, extend equal rights to women, and construct utopian communities based upon the common ownership of property, tiny but vocal groups of reformers even challenged America's fundamental ways of ordering society.

SOURCES OF THE NEW SENSIBILITY

The new sensibility drew upon several sources: the traditional New England idea of community, the republican ideals of the American Revolution, romanticism, evangelical religious visions, the growing middle class's sense of propriety, and a general optimism that sprang out of material progress. Spectacular triumphs in eighteenth- and nineteenth-century science and technology reinforced faith in the capacity of humans to create a more humanitarian society. Reformers concluded that improvements in human relationships should equal the escalating progress manifest in the material world.

Nineteenth-century reformers frequently saw their own crusades in terms of fulfilling the unkept promises of the American Revolution. No single document of the Revolution was more important to them than the Declaration of Independence. The principle that "all men are created equal" became a rallying cry of the women's rights and the antislavery movements. Both the abolitionists and the feminists adopted declarations of sentiments modeled upon the Declaration of Independence.

The new moral sensibility also drew upon both the Enlightenment and Scottish common sense philosophy. The Enlightenment notion of the plasticity of human nature led to the conclusion that altering the environment or circumstances could reduce or eliminate human suffering. Scottish common sense realism, which dominated the American academic curricula between about 1820 and 1870, insisted that all people had a conscience, or an internal voice, that urged them to act morally. Nurture of the conscience could aid individuals in resisting immoral temptations.

Romanticism, an artistic and literary movement of European origins, offered its own path toward a new moral sensibility. Objecting to the Enlightenment's placement of an exclusive reliance upon reason and observation, the romantics assigned a central role to intuition and emotion as sources of truth. The human mind had the capacity to perceive directly the essence of things, especially to apprehend what was morally right or wrong. By turning inward, for example, romantics believed that they could intuitively judge the moral merits of such social institutions as slavery. Reflective of the same impulse as romanticism, a powerful wave of sentimentality swept through the middle class Anglo-American world in the early nineteenth century.

One group of romantics, the New England Transcendentalists (named after a group of writers who met informally in Boston), rejected John Locke's idea of the mind as an organ that received data through the five senses and clicked out mechanical responses based on the sensations that it received. To the Transcendentalists, each human possessed powerful intuitive capacities beyond the five senses. These capacities allowed them to perceive a larger reality, especially higher spiritual and moral truths.

The transcendentalists were nearly all strident moralists. They frequently condemned the common obsession with moneymaking. Henry David Thoreau lived alone for two years in a hut that he built on the shores of Walden Pond near Concord in order that he might escape from the daily details and corruptions of society. As a protest against a government that supported slavery, Thoreau even went to jail for a few days in the summer of 1846. In his essay, "On the Duty of Civil Disobedience," Thoreau defended civil disobedience to immoral actions by governments.

Yet as important as the Declaration of Independence, the Enlightenment, and romanticism were to the new moral sensibility, they did not equal the significance of evangelical Protestantism. In particular, evangelical converts who were the products of New England's emphasis on the importance of community saw themselves as Christian soldiers engaged in a great cosmic war, one pitting the forces of righteousness (God) against evil (Satan). The war's battleground extended beyond the heavens to include earth-bound mortals. Every person had to take sides; either they accepted Jesus Christ as their savior and thereby enlisted in the Lord's battalions or they rejected Christ and by default joined the legions of the devil. "We are either marching toward heaven or towards hell," explained a Finney convert to his sister. "How is it with you?" he rhetorically asked.

Belief in the imminent arrival of the millennium added an even stronger sense of urgency to those who sought to bring every facet of life into conformity with God's intentions. "If the church would do her duty," Finney optimistically predicted in the midst of his great Rochester revival, "the millennium may come in this country in three years." He charged his young converts to go out into the world and to completely transform it. Finney also preached perfectionism. No Christian should "rest satisfied until they are as perfect as God," Finney said.

Individual Reform

A sense of religious duty, especially among the northern Congregationalists and Presbyterians, inspired an amazing array of benevolent societies. Seeking to impose a common morality on the entire nation, voluntary societies sprang up to suppress vice, encourage temperance, combat gambling, curb profanity, punish Sabbath-breaking, establish Sunday schools, and to distribute Bibles and religious tracts to the unchurched. In attempting to reach those bereft of religion, evangelical societies spawned the nation's first efforts to assist the poor, care for the aged, redeem prostitutes, and reform juvenile delinquents. Dreaming of nothing less than spreading the evangelical message everywhere, thousands of antebellum Americans also generously supported missionary efforts in foreign countries.

While Protestant moral reformers were trying to save the nation by the establishment of a common Christian morality, other humanitarian reformers sought to reform individuals or to relieve suffering by the creation of new social institutions. Physical separation from corrupting influences, the reformers believed, was essential to the eradication of pauperism, the rehabilitation of criminals, and the effective treatment of insanity. In fortresslike penitentiaries, reformatories, orphan asylums, and mental hospitals, the reformers sought to instill self-control by imposing a rigorous regimen of moral education, discipline, work, and an orderly environment upon their charges. While a religious, humanitarian zeal to create a more perfect society fired the founders of such institutions, they also offered a place in which social deviants and dependents could be separated from the main society. Usually underfunded and overpopulated, even before the Civil War, many of the institutions became in effect human warehouses. Maintaining order in such circumstances superceded efforts at reforming or rehabilitating the inmates.

The Antislavery Crusade

Temperance, worldwide missionary efforts, penal reforms, aid to the blind, public schools, and dozens of other causes fit comfortably within New England's religious traditions. Abolitionism, feminism, and northern communal experiments were, on the other hand, decidedly another matter. These latter causes marked radical departures from traditional American ways. By challenging or rejecting basic American assumptions of white racial superiority, sexual hierarchy, and the individualistic values of the marketplace, these reform proposals threatened to turn the fundamental ordering ways of the nineteenth century upside down.

Millennial and perfectionist impulses in the 1830s revived the moribund antislavery movement of the Revolutionary era. In the immediate wake of the Revolution, most of slavery's earlier foes acquiesced to a compromise. While slavery was "not a beautiful thing, a thing to be espoused and idolized," wrote an evangelical who was representative of this view, it was "the best attainable thing, in this country, for the [N]egro." Others sought to counter southern fears of emancipation by transporting free blacks to Africa. In 1822 the colonizers managed to send a few former slaves to Liberia in West Africa. But the limits of colonization soon became obvious. The costs were enormous and it won only modest support among either blacks or slaveholders.

It was, as Abraham Lincoln later observed, "the logic and moral power of [William Lloyd] Garrison" that brought about a decisive turning point in the history of antislavery. Garrison, a New Englander with an evangelical mindset, transformed abolitionism into a militant religious crusade. Slavery was *the* nation's single, most glaring sin, Garrison concluded. Its existence more than anything else kept the republic from achieving perfection. Slavery not only violated the right to life and liberty that had been enunciated so powerfully in the Declaration of Independence, Garrison argued, but it violated "all the injunctions of the Gospel . . . subjecting its victims to every species of torture, degrading them to a level with beasts." Garrison accepted the truly radical notion (for his day) that blacks should be accepted as the full equals of whites. Winning adherents almost exclusively in New England and the regions settled by New Englanders, abolitionists claimed by 1838 to have thirteen hundred antislavery societies with 109,000 members.

Garrison quickly won support from a growing number of black abolitionists. One was an escaped slave, Frederick Douglass, who opened his speeches with these lines: "I appear before the immense assembly this evening as a thief and a robber. I stole this head, these limbs, this body from my master, and ran with them." His memoir, *The Narrative of the Life of Frederick Douglass* (1845), presented a vivid, firsthand description of slavery as well as a ringing indictment of the institution. Douglass dreamed of an America in which all racial differences would dissolve into "a composite American nationality."

Denied positions of leadership in white antislavery organizations, northern blacks formed their own societies, launched petition drives against slavery, and in particular played a pivotal role in the operation of the Underground

Narrative of the Life of Frederick Douglass, an American Slave, Written by Himself, 1845. In their campaign against slavery, the abolitionists frequently employed the narratives of runaway slaves. The most popular of these was that penned by Frederick Douglass. Shortly to become the nation's most prominent black intellectual, Douglass continued to agitate for the rights of African Americans after the Civil War.

Railroad that provided escape routes for runaway slaves through the northern states into Canada. One fugitive slave, Harriet Tubman, known as the Black Moses, risked life and limb when, on at least nineteen separate occasions, she made trips into the slave states where she assisted in freeing as many as three hundred slaves. Slaveholders posted a $40,000 reward for her capture.

In proposing to end slavery, the abolitionists encountered harsh public responses in both North and South. Everywhere they incited fears that blacks might achieve equality with whites. Perceiving potential racial equality as a threat to their power, local elites—"gentlemen of property and standing"—in the North led mobs in attacking abolitionists, destroying their printing presses, disrupting meetings, and assaulting black neighborhoods. In October of 1834, rampaging whites destroyed forty-five homes in Philadelphia's black community. On November 7, 1837, abolitionists acquired their first martyr when a mob murdered Elijah Lovejoy in Alton, Illinois. The next day Alton's residents cheered as Lovejoy's mutilated corpse was dragged through the town's streets.

Despite these violent reactions, the abolitionists played a key role in eventually mobilizing northern public opinion against southern slavery. But their success was *not* due to their moral condemnations of slavery. Instead, the idea that an aggressive slave power was threatening to seize control of the national government became the abolitionists' most persuasive argument. Many northerners who were otherwise indifferent toward slavery became convinced that a ruthless slave power threatened their own civil liberties and their rights to access to western lands. The Fugitive Slave Law of 1850 (which took away from accused runaways the right to trial by jury and the right to testify on their own behalf) and the Kansas Nebraska Act of 1854 (which allowed for the potential establishment of slavery in an area where the institution had been earlier excluded), among other measures in the 1850s, reinforced northern apprehensions.

White abolitionists themselves were not without their own racial stereotypes and prejudices. The Constitution of the American Anti-Slavery Society, observed a black abolitionist, made no mention of social equality, either of slaves or free blacks. Yet large numbers of white abolitionists courageously continued to fight racial discrimination. They took the lead in trying to make abolition the chief aim of the Civil War (1861–65) and demanded that black troops receive equal pay. They helped obtain the ratification of the Thirteenth, Fourteenth, and Fifteenth Amendments to the Constitution that abolished slavery, guaranteed full citizenship to blacks, and extended suffrage to black men. While the fervor of the original abolitionists eventually receded, they provided much of the inspiration for twentieth-century movements for greater racial justice.

The Birth of Feminism

As with other nineteenth-century reform movements, the women's rights movement owed much to evangelicalism. Never before except perhaps among the Quakers had women played such a large role in religious life. While most evangelicals took seriously biblical injunctions against women preaching, several women became powerful exhorters. Nancy Gove Cram, for example, created a sensation in frontier New York where she preached to large crowds in barns and out-of-doors. Both Anne Lee (Shakers) and Ellen White (Seventh Day Adventist) were responsible for forming new denominations. Founded by evangelicals, Oberlin College became the first institution of higher learning in the country to admit both men and women.

Even when prohibited from preaching, women frequently prayed and testified before mixed-sex audiences. In nearly all denominations, women became more active in religious instruction, benevolent associations, moral direction of the home, and in social reform. While men dominated the leadership of the reform organizations, women in large numbers circulated petitions, solicited funds, distributed pamphlets, and sometimes spoke publicly on behalf of a wide range of causes. Such participation represented a sharp departure from traditional notions of proper gender roles.

Yet most evangelical men and women shared the traditional belief that the subordinate position of women rested on biblical authority. The Bible put Eve under both the command of Adam and the shadow of original sin. In defense of gender hierarchy, the Apostle Paul had written in Ephesians 5:22–23: "Wives, submit yourselves unto your own husbands, as unto the Lord." Given that evangelical reformers were tied to a strict interpretation of the Bible, for them to question sexual hierarchy seemed to welcome spiritual and social anarchy. William Lloyd Garrison reflected the ambivalence typical of many male reformers. He encouraged women to join in reform efforts that directly affected the home, but he condemned as unwarranted "interference" their involvement in activities distant from the home.

A reconsideration of gender inequality and subordination resulted when female reformers bumped up against the boundaries of their domain. Catharine Beecher, oldest child of evangelist-reformer Lyman Beecher and sister of Harriet Beecher Stowe (author of *Uncle Tom's Cabin*), took the first major step in reworking evangelical Protestantism and broadening the definition of "woman's sphere." Beecher argued that women should be the primary agents in creating a middle-class Christian society. To accomplish this end, women needed more and better education. Angelina and Sarah Grimke, daughters of a prominent Charleston slaveholding family, who left home and became abolitionists, moved far beyond Beecher. Abolitionism, which Angelina described as "the high school of morals in our land—the school in which *human rights* are more fully investigated" than any other, led her to conclude that all humans possessed the same moral nature. Therefore they should enjoy the same rights. "My doctrine then is," she wrote, "that whatever it is morally right for man to do it is morally right for woman to do."

Discrimination encountered within the abolitionist movement led infuriated women to make women's rights a separate cause. In particular men and women abolitionists clashed over whether women ought to lecture audiences composed of both sexes. In 1848, Lucretia Mott and Elizabeth Cady Stanton proceeded to organize a women's rights convention at Seneca Falls, New York. There, they adopted a Declaration of Sentiments modeled upon the Declaration of Independence. It began with the assertion that "all men and women are created equal." While passing twelve resolutions, only one, the call for women's suffrage, failed to pass unanimously. Ironically, suffrage became the main demand of the post–Civil War women's rights advocates. By mid-century, feminist conventions had been held in every northern state.

Yet the women's rights advocates achieved limited gains. Women did obtain in several states laws that gave married women property rights, the right to sue and be sued, and the right to obtain a divorce more easily than in the past. But they did not secure the right to vote throughout the nation until 1920, seventy-two years after the Seneca Falls convention. Feminists faced a formidable obstacle in the alternative ideal of domesticity. Since the separate sphere position not only allowed women to enjoy the main responsibility for morally nurturing the family and permitted them to engage in reforms that affected the family, it blunted the demands for full equality (see chapter 6).

Susan B. Anthony and Elizabeth Cady Stanton, from a Photograph Taken in 1892. In 1848, Stanton, along with Lucretia Mott, organized the first women's rights convention at Seneca Falls, New York. Stalwart advocates of feminism in the nineteenth century, Anthony and Stanton continued to battle for women's rights (as well as for the rights of African Americans) until their deaths early in the twentieth century.

THE SOUTH: "THE ENEMY
OF INNOVATION AND CHANGE"

Unlike the tumultuous North, the South was, boasted South Carolina planter Henry W. Ravenel in 1852, the "enemy of innovation and change." It had not always been so. During the Revolutionary era, southern planters had been at the forefront of the Enlightenment; they had fervently defended equal rights, questioned the morality of slavery, and advocated the separation of church and state. But, during the antebellum decades, the southern social climate underwent a sharp reversal. Assaulted by the North for its "peculiar institution" of slavery, the white South increasingly became a citadel of cultural conservatism.

Religious orthodoxy fortified the South's resistance to change. Whereas Anglicanism had been the religion of choice among the colonial gentry, evangelical Protestantism made sweeping gains among all white social classes (as well as the slaves) in the antebellum era. As we have seen, evangelicals in both regions stressed the need for a conversion experience, for self-control, and for individual piety. Everywhere, they denounced such patriarchal vices as drinking, fighting, gambling, and swearing.

But in other respects northern and southern Protestant churches parted ways. While northern antebellum revivals spawned an amazing array of proposals for remaking the world, such responses were largely absent in southern religion. Fortunately, as one North Carolina editor wrote, the South was free from "the isms which infest Europe and the Eastern and Western states of the country." Acutely conscious of the dangers for their world lurking in any ideas that questioned existing social arrangements, southern churchmen actively resisted social reform. Only temperance received more than their lukewarm support. Even public education made little headway in the South. Divided over the issue of slavery, eventually Baptists, Methodists, and Presbyterians split into northern and southern wings. The persistence of religious orthodoxy not only helped to give the South its distinctive identity but long served to unite southerners in their opposition to "innovation and change."

As sectional tensions mounted in the 1850s, southern white thought grew more stridently conservative. Southern spokesmen even went so far as to tie their defense of traditional ways with renunciations of the nation's Revolutionary heritage. "I repudiate, as ridiculously absurd," thundered South Carolina planter, James H. Hammond, "that much lauded but nowhere accredited dogma of Mr. JEFFERSON, 'that all men are born equal.'" Observing that "conservatism in any form is scoffed at" in the North, he asked rhetorically, "where will all this end?"

Southerners like Hammond recognized that northern assaults on slavery jeopardized the region's entire culture, for African American bondage in countless ways shaped the daily lives of both blacks and whites. Given its centrality to southern culture, white southerners felt obligated to defend slavery not just on biblical grounds, as a profit-making system, or as an institution of racial control but as an integral component of the region's "superior civilization." Unlike in the North where "selfishness is almost the only motive of human conduct . . . where every man is taught that it is his duty to . . . better his pecuniary condition," observed George Fitzhugh, southern masters and their slaves subordinated their individual interest to a "*community* of interests." Exempted from worries about unemployment, food and shelter, and the trials of old age, the slaves were far better off, Fitzhugh and other southerners insisted, than were the "wage slaves" of the North.

On the eve of the Civil War, opposing regional stereotypes hardened. Southern white thinking began with the premise that sheer greed drove the lives of middle-class northerners. And, given the miserable conditions of the northern wage earners, they concluded that northern criticism of slavery represented nothing more than blatant hypocrisy. Middle-class northerners, on the other hand, started with the premise that southerners, like blacks, Indians, and immigrants, lacked self-control. By resorting to violence, drinking whisky, and having sexual liaisons with their female slaves, southern white men had regressed to a state of barbarism.

In a letter to his father, Charles C. Jones, Jr., of Savannah, Georgia, in January of 1861, summed up the regional differences. Northerners and southerners, he wrote, were "two races which . . . have been so entirely separated by the climate, by morals, by religion, and by estimates so totally opposite of all that constitutes honor, truth, and manliness, that they cannot longer coexist under the same government." Later that same year, the first shots were fired in the most deadly war that Americans have ever fought.

CONCLUSION

Like a jackhammer on a city street, opening the doors of opportunity for ordinary white people broke up the cement of the old order. Monarchy had been forcibly rejected by the Revolution itself, and, by the 1820s, the older gentry and clerical elites no longer commanded the same authority that they had once enjoyed. Common folk were now far less likely to respect their betters, connections between church and state had been (or were coming) uncoupled, and droves of people were abandoning their settled communities. Ordinary white men were now far freer than in the past to strike out on their own and determine their own loyalties and enter into them voluntarily.

Driven by anxieties arising from these startling changes and by dreams of what the new republic might become, Americans embarked upon a remarkable new age of cultural ferment and experimentation. At its center was a great popular religious uprising. Millions experienced spiritual rebirth and joined evangelical communities where they found both the potential building materials for a new moral order and a larger sense of purpose for their lives than the mere acquisition of wealth. The new age of cultural ferment also produced America's first great age of social reform. Some sought to transform individual behavior while others tried to radically transform traditional ways of governing relationships between men and women as well as between blacks and whites.

MIDDLE-CLASS WAYS, 1830–1930

6

MIDDLE-CLASS WAYS

The seventy-seven years between 1837, the year of Victoria's ascension to the throne of Great Britain, and 1914, the year that World War I broke out in Europe, were momentous ones for the United States. These were years of geographic expansion. With the annexation of Texas, the Mexican cession, the Gadsden Purchase, and the settlement of the boundary issue in the Northwest, the United States filled out its continental borders. In addition, the new republic acquired a far-flung overseas empire including Alaska, Hawaii, Puerto Rico, and the Philippines. These were years of armed conflict, including the Mexican War, the Civil War, the Spanish-American War, the suppression of the Filipino uprising, and the final phase of a four-hundred-year war with the American Indians. Abetted by massive waves of immigration, the nation's population also soared, from sixteen million people in 1837 to nearly one hundred million in 1914. The economy grew even more rapidly. Still predominately an agricultural republic in 1837, by 1914 the United States had already become the greatest industrial giant the world had ever seen.

These same years approximated the supremacy within the United States of a new middle-class culture. (This culture is also sometimes labeled *Victorian* or *bourgeois,* thereby implying that the middle classes throughout the Western world shared a common set of values, attitudes, and behaviors.) With the breakdown of the eighteenth century's hierarchical order and the opening up of new opportunities for ordinary white people in the nineteenth century, white middle-class Protestants claimed for themselves and their culture the moral leadership of the new nation. Such a claim rested on their supreme confidence that they, and they alone, represented the nation's "best" and most "respectable" people. After all, it was their undeviating attention to self-control, they concluded, that had brought them material success and had distinguished them from the nation's more "dissolute" peoples.

SELF-CONTROL AND THE FAMILY

With the authority of traditional hierarchies, churches, and local communities in retreat, no institution was more important to the middle class than the family. The family now took over tasks that earlier had been shared with others. The most important of these was the obligation to mold in each child a sturdy moral conscience. Once a set of simple moral truths had been firmly embedded in each child's personality, he or she would no longer require external restraints. Self-control would then come automatically. The middle class also looked to the family as a resource for bringing greater order, stability, and warmth into their lives. To counter the disintegrative forces arising from the rapidly changing world of business and industry, the Victorian family invented its own rich world of symbols, rituals, and myths.

Separate Spheres

In principle, the middle class promoted the idea of "separate spheres." According to this doctrine, women should occupy the private sphere of the home while men should occupy the public sphere of work. Within the home, the woman was to care for children, manage the household, and comfort her husband. Within the public sphere, the husband was to be the family's breadwinner. Contrary to the imagery conjured up by the phrase "separate spheres," the proponents of the doctrine never intended that the occupants remain exclusively within these respective spheres. For example, the mother/wife could—indeed, even should—venture into the public realm to do church and philanthropic work while the husband/father was expected to perform specific family rituals within the home.

Neither was the ideology of separate spheres entirely new. By arguing that women should assume a special responsibility for the rearing of a virtuous citizenry, the founders of the new republic had anticipated the nineteenth century's enthusiasm for the separate sphere doctrine. But the great economic upheavals of the nineteenth century were more important catalysts for drawing sharper boundaries between the lives of middle-class women and men. Furthermore, these revolutions relocated some forms of work from the home to the office building and the factory. No longer was the home a major production site; household items ranging from bread to clothing were increasingly made outside the home. Nonetheless, women did continue to perform unpaid reproductive and household chores in their own homes.

As the home was emptied of its earlier productive functions, in principle it became a place devoted more exclusively to the family and to culture. Here, the woman was expected to construct a refuge, "an elysium," as one writer put it, "to which [the husband] can flee and find rest from the stormy strife of a selfish world." Here, as in Charles Dickens's *A Christmas Carol*, one escaped from the cold, domineering office of Scrooge to the warmth of the Cratchett's family hearth. The ideal Victorian home was not only a shelter from the anxieties of modern life, as literary historian Walter Houghton has observed, but it was also "a shelter for those moral and spiritual values which the commercial spirit" was "threatening to destroy."

Proponents of the separate spheres doctrine urged mothers to take on an expanded role in parenting. Indeed, fulfilling the obligations of motherhood now became a middle-class woman's major lifework. A mother's love, her voice, and her smile became powerful Victorian symbols. It was now the

A Middle-Class Victorian Family at Home. Nothing of the trials and cares of the outside world intrude on this idyllic family scene from the 1869 publication *The American Home* by Catharine Beecher and Harriet Beecher Stowe. For the middle class, the home assumed many of the cultural and social responsibilities earlier assigned to churches, communities, and the upper classes.

mother rather than the father who was primarily responsible for a child's success or failure in life. Consistent with the new role of women in parenting, by the 1850s the courts had begun to make mothers rather than fathers the custodial parent of minor children in divorce cases.

As suggested by the changing conceptions of motherhood, the middle class sharpened gender distinctions. In the past, part of the rationale for patriarchy had rested on the assumption that men possessed superior reasoning powers and were less given to passion than women. But, in the nineteenth century, confronted by the perils and opportunities of the new economy and the specter of social disorder, attitudes toward gender differences changed. Men now became increasingly thought of as the more aggressive and impulsive sex. The most admired men were those who exercised self-control while channeling their volcanic passions into their work.

Women, on the other hand, were now thought to come by self-control and self-sacrifice more naturally than men. Innately gentler, less selfish, more pious, and more refined than men, they could, by example and instruction, influence positively the moral lives of their beaus, their husbands, and their children. Hence, while men's work was being thought of as a career or a job, women's work retained the older meaning of a "calling," an occupation defined in terms of its contribution to a larger good. Walter Houghton has compared the role of the Victorian mother to that of a priestess. "On the shoulders of its priestess, the wife and mother," he has written, "fell the burden of stemming the amoral and irreligious drift of modern industrial society." While such thinking placed women on a higher moral plane than men, it at the same time reinforced other pressures that were confining women's activities to the home. In other words, the idea of female moral superiority served to firm up the walls that excluded women from those centers of economic and political power that existed outside the home.

CHILDREN AND SELF-CONTROL

Before the great economic revolutions of the nineteenth century, land had been the basic resource of society. But with growing numbers of families detached from farms, bequeathing a legacy in land was no longer practicable. Instead of a landed inheritance, middle-class families now sought to equip their children for the future with superior moral and intellectual resources.

The most important of these was self-control. "The *child* must be *treated* as a *free, self-guiding, self-controlling being,*" wrote Bronson Alcott. "He must be allowed to feel that he is under his own guidance." Gaining a self-command of feelings and impulses required a more regimented childhood than in the past; consequently middle-class families employed more rigid schedules for feeding, toilet training, play, religious instruction, and school than their predecessors. Rather than the rod for discipline, parents resorted more frequently to the withdrawal of affection and the inculcation of guilt. Obtaining control over the self was no easy task. After having lost her temper, a nine-year-old Louisa May Alcott resolved to do better. "If I only *kept* all [of the resolutions] I make," she wrote in her diary, "I should be the best girl in the world. But, I don't, and so am very bad." In a notation beneath the entry, one she wrote much later upon reviewing the diary for use in an autobiography, Alcott wrote: "Poor little sinner! She says the same at fifty [years old]—L. M. A."

Consistent with the ideology of separate spheres, middle-class boys and girls were reared differently. Mothers urged their sons to strive for "manly independence" while daughters were told to aspire to "moral purity" and "true womanhood." Yet middle-class families encouraged intense emotional bonds between mothers and sons, hoping that sentimental attachments would help boys to internalize self-control and lead them to look to their mothers rather than to their peers for a proper standard of moral conduct. While there was less concern about the likelihood of young women achieving true womanhood than young men achieving manly independence, a large outpouring of advice literature told girls how to develop good manners, morals, and domestic skills.

The increased importance attached to the development of self-control placed heavier demands and expectations on formal education. The "primary objective" of education was not the cultivation of the intellect, explained educational reformer Henry Barnard at mid-nineteenth century, but "the regulation of feelings and dispositions [and] the extirpation of vicious propensities." Along with the family, the public schools sought through Bible readings, didactic tales, commentaries, and simplistic aphorisms to hammer into each child's personality a few general but immutable moral absolutes. Once these moral imperatives had been internalized, they would, as one educator said, "endure as long as life endures." With this legacy, each child was ready, upon achieving adulthood, to make his or her own way in the world.

In time, middle-class parents sought even more from education. To obtain training and formal certification for well-paid jobs in bureaucracies and in the professions, they sent their sons to high schools, professional schools, and colleges. Seeking to shield them from seduction, economic exploitation, and mental overstimulation and to prepare them for lives as wives and mothers, middle-class parents also prolonged the formal education of their daughters.

THE INVENTION OF THE VICTORIAN FAMILY

In countering the psychic ravages of their time and in making the home more effective as an agency promoting self-control, the middle class invented a new kind of family. It was an institution with a strong sense of its own existence. Each family constructed for itself a past, one similar to that which elite families had always possessed. To bolster claims for their families as historical entities, the middle class began as never before to invest with deeper meanings material objects that had been handed down from earlier generations. Furniture, silver, and quilts that formerly had had only economic significance now became priceless family heirlooms. As never before, families began to preserve photograph albums, diaries, letters, and other memorabilia.

Courtship, the first step in the creation of a new family, became a far more important ritual than in the past. In the more prolonged courtships of the middle class, the family's parlor was a special site. In this feminized enclave where the family took special care to exhibit its claims to respectability, the young woman might offer her beau cakes and tea and sing and play the piano for him. The couple might also recite poetry and read aloud to one another. While typical couples engaged in some touching and kissing during courtship, other physical intimacies were less likely. The plunge in the incidence of premarital pregnancies (especially within the middle class) in the nineteenth century reflected the effectiveness of prohibitions against the physical expression of sexual passion.

For the middle class, weddings likewise grew in symbolic significance. The newly invented wedding costume—a luminous white gown, veil, and bouquet—that sharply distinguished the bride from all the other women present, vividly dramatized the fact that weddings had become the foremost rite of passage for middle-class females. Weddings were increasingly familial rather than communal ceremonies; invitations were sent out only to family members and to close friends. Wedding anniversaries, once rarely celebrated, now became a special occasion for acknowledging the solemn bond that had inaugurated the formation of a new family.

Set aside at a separate time in a special "dining room," the evening meal now became far more formal and ceremonial than in the past. It "was a ritual," recalled Henry Seidel Canby of family dinners during his boyhood in Wilmington, Delaware, in the 1890s. The saying of grace before the meal and the rite of sharing food reinforced family bonds. "It was this familiar movement," Canby contended, "this routine with a certainty of repetition, that inspired confidence in a patterned universe," a confidence that he found sorely wanting in the twentieth century.

Once primarily a day for religious and public activities, Sundays became a special middle-class family holiday. With far more success than their Sabbatarian predecessors, the middle classes in both Great Britain and the United States succeeded in shutting down trade and public leisure activities on Sunday. While proper Victorians attended church services, much of the remainder of the day was spent in ritualistic family activities. It was then that the middle classes gathered for a special ceremonial feast, the Sunday family dinner.

Christmas underwent a roughly similar transformation. The traditional Christmas had been an unruly rite of communal renewal. In practices such as wassailing and mumming, the ordinary people took to the streets; they dressed in wild attire, sometimes donned masks, sang rude songs, made mocking and obscene gestures, and insisted that their superiors treat them with food and drink. Never endorsed by evangelical Protestants, who considered the traditional celebration to be both pagan and papist, the older Christmas practices nearly died out in both Britain and America.

But in the middle decades of the nineteenth century, the middle classes in the English-speaking world invented an almost entirely new way of celebrating Christmas. The popular English novelist, Charles Dickens, who wrote A Christmas Carol in 1843, seems to have almost singlehandedly transformed Christmas into a mostly family affair. Families sent out special cards to relatives and close friends; they brought a tree (once considered a pagan practice) indoors and decorated it; they invented the modern Santa Claus as a benevolent, fun-loving, avuncular figure; they gave and received gifts; and they shared a special meal on Christmas day. The ritualized nature of the holiday, with its emphasis upon doing things as they had always been done, symbolically linked present families with their predecessors.

The creation of a set of special times helped the middle class to compensate for the weakening of traditional communal and religious senses of time. The numerically standardized clock time of the office and the factory had robbed traditional time of its rich associations with the natural rhythms of night and day and the seasons as well as the traditional church calendar. Along side of clock time, middle-class families created their own special times, which, as we have seen, they sought to stock with an abundance of powerful symbolic meanings.

MIDDLE-CLASS SEX WAYS

When we think of the Victorian age today, sexual repression is the first thought that is likely to leap to our minds. This is partly because of a striking absence of candor (compared to today) that characterized both public and private discussion of sexuality in the nineteenth century. The use of sexual euphemisms abounded. Rather than speaking of a woman's arms or legs—both terms suggested an untoward familiarity—refined people spoke of her "limbs." "Bosom" was the polite name for breasts, "the secret vice" meant masturbation, "the social evil" referred to prostitution, and "fallen doves" was a polite term for prostitutes.

Our view of Victorian sexuality has been further shaped by the campaigns in the late nineteenth and early twentieth century against obscenity and birth control. The name of Anthony Comstock, a former Connecticut dry-goods salesman who made it his lifework to suppress obscenity, has become virtually synonymous with sexual repression. Comstock's crowning achievement came in 1873 when Congress passed without debate the so-called Comstock Law, a statute that barred all "obscene" materials from the mails. Supervising enforcement of the new law fell to none other than Comstock himself. In a well-financed campaign—again led by Comstock—state and local governments across the country tightened up and more strictly enforced their laws against pornography and the sale of contraceptives. Perhaps it was little wonder then that British playwright George Bernard Shaw coined the term "Comstockery" to sum up America's constrictive sexual attitudes and practices.

While most Americans were less zealous than Comstock in cracking down on obscenity and contraceptives, his campaign *did* rest on wide public support. Profoundly influenced by the chivalric notions of love popularized by the romantic poets and the sentimental novelists of the day, the middle-class Victorians saw romantic love and raw sexual lust as incompatible feelings. Love represented a far more refined and elevated attraction to another person than did lust. Indeed, love was a powerful force for sexual purity; by strengthening their resolve to resist temptation, love of an angelic woman could even save men from capitulating to their baser, carnal yearnings. Ideally, then, sex should be reserved exclusively for marriage, and even then should remain subordinated to, and thoroughly immersed in, powerful feelings of romantic love.

Apart from the popularity of romantic love, a burgeoning body of sexual advice literature tied good physical health to the practice of sexual restraint. Influenced by the theory that the body was a closed energy system, whose sexual resources were depleted with each use, the reformers insisted that sexual indulgence jeopardized one's bodily well-being. It could result in such calamities as "seminal weakness, impotence, . . . pulmonary consumption, hypochondriasis, loss of memory, . . . and death." In particular, doctors and health reformers railed against masturbation; the "solitary vice" not only could cause illness and insanity, they said, but its practice drained women's bodies of vital psychic energy and men's of a portion of their lifetime endowment of sperm.

The middle-class preoccupation with sexual restraint arose from something more than concern for good health, though indeed much of the day's conventional medical wisdom attributed frightening consequences to sexual excesses. It entailed something more than enhancing one's prospects for material success, albeit this was no insignificant consideration. Dr. John Cowan, for example, explained that "a continent life . . . surely guides to success in all business undertakings." It also entailed something more than a strategy for establishing a family's respectability and its credentials for moral leadership, although these considerations too undoubtedly influenced the sexual attitudes and behavior of countless middle-class families.

Ultimately, the driving force behind the campaign for repression arose from profound middle-class anxieties. The principle of equality and the opening up of opportunities for getting ahead materially had released sexuality from its traditional moorings, as it had removed other restraints on the individual. For example, neither parents nor clergy any longer had the authority to enforce marriage in the event of an unwanted pregnancy. A host of sexual radicals—Robert Dale Owen, Fanny Wright, John Humphrey Noyes, and Victoria Woodhull, among others—proposed daring alternatives to the confinement of sexuality within monogamous marriages. Perhaps even more disturbing to the middle class was the apparent rise in the practice of birth control, the increasing numbers of surgical abortions, the burgeoning market for pornography, and the growth of prostitution. Dammed up behind a wall of Victorian propriety and prudery was a separate world of seething sexuality, one that might at any moment burst through the floodgates and inundate the middle-class family and the entire nineteenth-century social order.

A part of middle-class erotic anxiety may have also arisen from their own changing sexual ways. As historians John D'Emilio and Estelle Freedman have shown in their history of American sexuality, middle-class families took steps, albeit frequently halting ones, that gradually unlinked the ages-old connection between reproduction and sexuality. Rather than anchoring sexual experience in reproduction, they increasingly tied it to love, intimacy, and even personal pleasure. From such surviving sources as diaries and private correspondence, we know that growing numbers of middle-class couples believed that having sexual intercourse (apart from any consideration of reproduction) strengthened their marriages. By the late Victorian era, even physicians and health reformers were beginning to endorse this position. "The sexual relationship is among the most important uses of married life," reported a medical text in 1883. "It vivifies the affection for each other, as nothing else in the world can, and is a powerful reminder of their mutual obligation to each other and to the community in which they live."

Additional wealth, more leisure time, and greater control over fertility facilitated the severance of sex from reproduction. A falling birthrate for white women—from an average of seven children in 1800 to less than four in 1900—suggested that married couples might have been exploring the possibilities of erotic experiences that were unconnected to reproduction. It is more likely, however, that this "fertility revolution" arose more from a recognition (perhaps unconsciously) by urban middle-class families that children were no longer economic assets. Having fewer children meant not only more disposable income but allowed the family to invest more of its resources in each individual child (especially in their sons). With smaller families each child could receive additional financial assistance in preparing them for jobs that required more advanced skills. Reducing the number of children may have also represented an assertion of female autonomy, for it relieved the wife of burdens associated with reproduction and allowed her to wield more control over her own sexuality.

In nineteenth century America, curtailing the incidence of unwanted pregnancies was not an easy or simple matter. Couples rarely employed condoms or diaphragms; these mechanical prophylactics were difficult to obtain and frowned upon by public opinion. Instead, they more frequently relied on mutual consent: coitus interruptus (male withdrawal before ejaculation), the rhythm method (intercourse only during a woman's infertile period), and abstinence. As many as one in four pregnancies (about the same rate as in 1990) may have also been terminated by surgical abortion.

SELF-CONTROL AND THE QUEST FOR REFINEMENT

In the middle-class effort to acquire greater control over themselves and others, no strategy proved more popular than refinement. Earlier, in the more rank-ordered, hierarchical society of the eighteenth century, refinement was for the most part reserved to the gentry. Only the great southern planters and wealthy northern merchants had the financial wherewithal to build and furnish stately mansions. They were the only people to dress and behave like the European aristocracy. Everyone else—or so it was presumed by the gentry— had inferior tastes and sensibilities.

At first glance, republican America would not seem to offer fertile ground for the growth of refinement. After all, according to America's revolutionary theorists, a successful republic required the rejection of the European aristocracy's fopperies and extravagances. Furthermore, refinement, which envisioned an existence devoted to leisure and art, seemed to run counter to the self-denial and hard work that were at the heart of middle-class Protestant life. Aristocratic idleness had to be exorcised if the individual and society were to be saved. Nonetheless, in the nineteenth century the expanding middle class of merchants, professionals, prosperous farmers, small manufacturers, and skilled artisans claimed for themselves the refinement that had formerly been monopolized by the gentry. Awash with large infusions of new purchasing power and the proliferation of mass-produced, cheaper goods, refinement spread downward from the elite to the sprawling middle class.

REFINING THE HOME

Middle-class refinement began with the home. "A man is not a whole or a complete man," wrote poet Walt Whitman, "unless he owns a house and the ground it stands on." In the eighteenth century, the "middling ranks" had frequently lived in structures of unpainted wooden planks or in log cabins, but nineteenth-century aspirants to respectability strove to acquire larger houses and to make them more attractive. Sturdy red brick or stone became the building material of choice for the upper end of the middle class while the remainder usually settled for white, balloon-framed houses with green shutters. (Still standing in many communities today are recently refurbished gingerbread houses. With turrets, cupolas, and extended verandas, they are revealing statements of their age.) Whether red, white, or another color, the new houses literally blazed to the outside world a message of middle-class respectability.

Neither did middle-class families any longer build their houses next to the streets nor in neighborhoods that included the poor. By insisting on front yards that were artfully decorated with trees, shrubs, and flowers and

A Nineteenth-Century Victorian Mansion, Rhinebeck, New York. "A man is not a whole or a complete man," wrote poet Walt Whitman, "unless he owns a house and the ground it stands on." Set off from the street, the soaring gothic houses of the middle class were both monuments to individual achievement and to family respectability. Even today, they continue to evoke images of tranquility and stability.

enclosed by a white picket fence, middle-class families created attractive barriers between themselves and the squalor of the streets.

More highly differentiated spaces within the home also reflected the
middle-class quest for respectability and refinement. While in modest homes
working, cooking, eating, and sleeping might all take place in the same room
or set of rooms, space in Victorian homes became far more specialized. Ideally, each house contained separate rooms for each major activity. With a
higher value placed on modesty and privacy than in the past, the family no
longer slept together in the same room or in the same bed. In middle-class
houses, hallways and separate bedrooms segregated the parents from the
children and the children from one another.

The tasteful decoration of rooms was an equally important marker of
refinement. Taste in decoration, according to John Ruskin, an Englishman
who was widely read on both sides of the Atlantic, reflected a family's morality. "Taste is not only a part and an index of morality," Ruskin wrote, "it is the
ONLY morality. . . . Tell me what you like, and I will tell you what you are."
A huge middle-class market developed in the nineteenth century for New
Haven clocks, Waltham watches, Lowell carpets, machine-pressed glassware,
upholstered sofas, mahogany bureaus, and dozens of other mass-produced
imitations of costly luxuries that were beyond the budgets of the typical
working-class family. None of the furnishings was more important than mirrors. Mirrors could be found nearly everywhere—on walls, on doors, over
mantles, and on chests of drawers. The proliferation of mirrors reflected a
growing concern for how one presented one's self to others.

In publicly displaying their refinement, the middle class gave special
attention to parlors. Emptied of tools and beds, it was in the parlor that the
middle-class family represented an ideal version of itself to itself and to others. In order to avoid harshness, angularity, and sharp lines, middle-class
families decorated their parlors with a profusion of soft, warm fabrics. Carpets covered the floors, thick draperies shrouded the windows, and mountains of pillows were deposited everywhere. Ideally, each parlor contained a
piano or a parlor organ and a well-stocked bookcase. In the creation of the
parlor, historian Richard Bushman has trenchantly observed, "people implicitly claimed the right to live like rulers."

Refining Manners

Refined manners and proper dress were equally important to the middle
class. With traditional hierarchies broken up or in disarray, it was increasingly difficult to identify people socially. Strange faces replaced familiar ones,
especially in the flux of the rapidly growing cities. Amidst this social confusion, manners and dress assisted the respectable people in locating and assessing one another. Exhibitions of good manners and fashionable dress
even provided strangers with passports into local circles of respectability
and extended to them additional opportunities for advancing their material
fortunes.

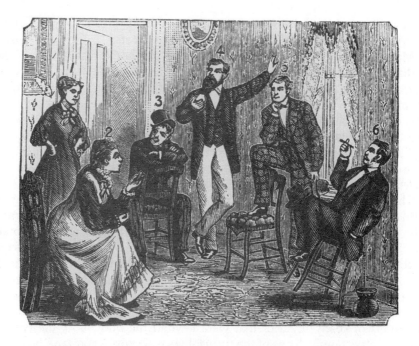

"Ungraceful Positions" versus "Gentility in the Parlor." Taken from a manual on good manners, the top drawing constitutes an inventory of improper etiquette, while all the errors are corrected in the bottom drawing. These lessons in etiquette reflect the increasing importance that the middle class attached to good manners and proper dress.

Until the nineteenth century, refined manners had been mostly a concern of the gentry. The lower social ranks of American society paid little attention to etiquette. They frequently ate with their hands and drank from a common cup. Coughing, spitting, scratching, nose blowing, farting, and urinating in public places were not uncommon. Emotions were by later standards freely expressed; loud, blunt talk and boisterous laughter frequently punctuated the social intercourse of the ordinary people.

The nineteenth century witnessed a seismic shift in manners, one in which the middle classes throughout the Western world appropriated the etiquette of the gentry. Courtesy books, many of whose rules could be traced back to the courts of the Italian Renaissance, flooded into middle-class homes. In his novel *The Rise of Silas Lapham* (1885), William Dean Howells had the self-made Lapham family from rural New Hampshire anxiously consult a book on manners before they dined with the patrician Corey family of Boston. By learning proper manners, the manual promised the Laphams, as well as countless others, that they could avoid social mortification.

Conduct manuals offered readers seeking middle-class respectability a complex set of directions for presenting themselves effectively in public places. Readers should above all else avoid picking their noses, passing gas, clearing their throats, yawning, or scratching themselves in public. Even the popular American practice of chewing and spitting tobacco came under assault. "In public," as John Kasson has perceptively observed, "the individual uneasily pretended to be in private." When confronted with strangers, maintenance of physical distance, aversion of eye contact, and sober facial expressions helped to preserve one's sense of privacy and dignity. Acquaintances, lovers, even husbands and wives, were warned never to embrace or kiss in public. "Happily," unlike in Europe, added one writer on manners, "kissing and embracing among men are never seen in this country."

Avoidance of conspicuous public display included dress. In the eighteenth century, men in the upper ranks frequently dressed as flamboyantly as women. Properly dressed gentlemen donned powdered wigs, brightly-hued jackets, silk cuffs, ruffles, tightly-fitted breeches, and knee-length, white silk stockings. In the nineteenth century men's dress underwent a fundamental shift. The dark, sober suit became the standard uniform of business and professional men throughout the Western world. Its full-cut coat, "great" overcoat, and loose-fitting pants disguised the true shape of the man's body while exaggerating the size of his shoulders and his girth. The fashion of full beards and mustaches, popular in the second half of the nineteenth century in both Europe and America, also aided men in presenting themselves as persons of substance, gravity, and maturity.

Fashionable women's dress likewise underwent important changes. During the daylight hours, no proper woman exposed to public gaze more of her skin than her face. Gloves, cuffs, long sleeves, high collars, leggings, stockings, shoes, "a sea of petticoats," and floor-length dresses ensured the sartorial modesty of women. As with men, women's street clothes steadily darkened over the nineteenth century. Yet female dress simultaneously highlighted sexual differences. A prominently protruding bustle and a corset that pushed the breasts upward and tightly constricted the waist left no doubts about a woman's sexual identity.

The act of eating provided one of the most demanding tests for assessing one's mastery of the body and the emotions. In earlier times (except among the gentry) etiquette in eating was by today's standards astonishingly crude. People not only ate with their hands but they slurped soup and sauces directly from their plates, dipped their fingers and hands into common bowls, and drank from common goblets. But as early as the eighteenth century, the middling ranks began to adopt far more refined eating ways, including for the first time the use of forks. While opponents complained that eating peas with a fork was like "eating soup with a knitting needle," skillful handling of the new eating instrument helped to verify one's proficiency in the acquisition of genteel table manners.

REFINING CHRISTIANITY

While many Catholics, Jews, and secular-oriented intellectuals embraced at least some if not all of the middle-class Victorian ways, Protestantism was at the core of the new culture. Indeed, the new culture's supremacy arose in part from the sweeping successes of the great religious revivals of the nineteenth century. Evangelical faith reinforced and fortified the middle class's quest for self-control. By equating religious duty and morality with success in moneymaking, religious faith could also offer a potential rationale for the accumulation of personal wealth. Finally, a commitment to church, family, and community and a reputation for temperance and hard work—all of these provided visible markers of middle-class respectability.

Yet the relationship between Protestantism and refinement was an uneasy one. Traditionally, many Protestant groups, especially those with Calvinistic antecedents, had condemned the refinement of the upper classes. Refinement, they insisted, represented an alluring secular alternative to Christianity. It diverted attention from God and his commandments. Lorenzo Dow, a popular antebellum evangelist, warned that the "Schools of Babylon" included the "dancing school," the "school of music," and the school for the "promotion of polite literature." Furthermore, renunciation of an earlier life devoted to imitating the behavior of the European aristocracy was a standard episode in nineteenth-century American conversion narratives.

Yet, in the end, the allure of respectability and refinement proved difficult if not impossible for middle-class Protestants to resist. At first, the Methodists and the Baptists, the two most successful evangelical denominations, held out; they stood firm against genteel refinement. But as early as the 1830s the Congregationalists, the Presbyterians, and the Unitarians began to embrace gentrification. In time, spokesmen and women for these denominations began to virtually equate good manners and proper dress with godly morality.

By mid-nineteenth century, in the more prosperous urban churches, the evangelical fires that had fed the millennial vision of the United States as a future heaven on earth had noticeably slackened. Emotionally searing revivals were less common. Ministers in these churches toned down their insistence upon a sudden, apocalyptic conversion experience. In his popular book, *Christian Nurture* (1847), Horace Bushnell even went so far as to propose a gradual, step-by-step process of conversion, one that began with the spiritual nurture of the young. Though hotly contested by traditional evangelicals, such a view won increasing favor among middle-class Protestants. Urban, middle-class church services also grew more formal and liturgical. Disregarding earlier objections to the use of musical instruments in worship services, urban Protestant churches even began to feature great organs and robed choirs.

Nothing reflected more tangibly the growing refinement of nineteenth-century Protestantism than a revolution in church architecture. Until the nineteenth century, Calvinistic Protestant groups had associated elegant church buildings with the hated Roman Catholics or with the almost equally despised Church of England (or the Protestant Episcopal Church as it was known in America after the Revolution). The lavish churches of the Catholics and the Episcopalians, according to Puritans (Congregationalists), Quakers, Presbyterians, Methodists, and Baptists, deflected attention from God and encouraged the worship of false idols. In keeping with the principle of simplicity, these Protestant denominations usually held services in unpainted, unadorned, box-shaped "meetinghouses."

Except among the Quakers and the more radical of the evangelicals, such attitudes toward church architecture completely flip-flopped during the nineteenth century. Protestant church buildings, especially those in the cities, increasingly imitated the latest styles of the Church of England. Massive gothic structures became the style of choice; as early as 1858, even the Methodists, a denomination that once took pride in its plebeian origins, built St. Paul's, a large gothic-style church in New York City. While without the financial means to duplicate the grandeur of their larger urban counterparts, the towns of New England also upgraded the appearance of their churches. Everywhere they replaced their older, unpainted meetinghouses with white rectangular buildings. A towering spire and belfry at the church entrance vividly testified to how far the nineteenth-century Congregationalists had departed from their more austere seventeenth-century Puritan ancestors.

By the latter half of the nineteenth century the rising tide toward a more refined Protestantism could not be stopped. Across the land on Sunday mornings well-dressed worshipers sat in the cushioned pews of elegant church buildings where they listened to the soaring swells of great organs, the voices of trained choirs, and the polished sermons of educated ministers. Such refinement had its costs. For it drove the working class out of the great middle-class-dominated urban Protestant churches. "The Protestant Church is too aristocratic for the clothes [the working people] are able to wear," explained a manufacturer. Working-class Protestant families either rejected formal ties to churches altogether or they embraced new evangelical groups who welcomed them as social equals and who rejected conspicuous displays of gentility.

SELF-CONTROL AND
THE EXALTATION OF CULTURE

The middle-class quest for refinement included the acquisition of what nineteenth-century Americans called "culture." Indeed, after the Civil War, as the middle class was losing some of its religious fervor, culture began to occupy a place alongside the Puritans' City on a Hill, the Revolution's virtue, and the antebellum era's Kingdom of God on Earth as expressions of the nation's highest aspirations.

THE VICTORIAN CONCEPTION OF CULTURE

The term *culture* meant something decidedly different in the nineteenth century than what it means to us today (and as the word is employed throughout this book). Today *culture* usually refers to those resources that humans call upon to aid them in coping with the world about them. Therefore, culture includes virtually all customs and institutions. As an example of this usage, we have examined in this chapter such topics as middle-class ways of work, gender, family, sex, child rearing, and religion. We have considered each of these ways as an integral component of a larger middle-class culture. Put somewhat differently, the modern definition of culture embraces the entire complex of values and practices that shape and guide human behavior.

The Victorian conception of culture, on the other hand, was less a matter of describing how people behaved than *how they ought to behave.* Culture should be didactic; it should teach people how to behave morally. Moreover, it should elevate them from the everyday world of the "trivial and the sordid" (in the words of American Ralph Waldo Emerson) into a realm of "sweetness and light" (the words of Englishman Matthew Arnold). More specifically, culture referred to a Euro-American heritage of good manners, a knowledge of great literature, and a respect for the fine arts. Sometimes labeled as genteel, high, or polite, this notion of culture, in its most restrictive and exquisite form, entailed in Arnold's oft-quoted words "the best that has been thought and said in the world."

This conception of culture rested on a set of bedrock assumptions, all of which were coming under increasing assault even as they were uttered. One of these was a belief in an orderly universe, one presided over by a benevolent God and governed by immutable natural laws. Ultimate truths existed not only in nature, the Victorians believed, but also in religion, ethics, politics, economics, and the arts. Therefore, nothing—not literature, religion, nor politics—was immune from moral judgment. Such thinking not only offered the comfort of belief in a set of transcendental certainties, but also eased the difficulties of reaching correct moral judgements. A second bedrock Victorian assumption was a deep faith in the capacity of the human mind, either through reason or intuition, to perceive these ultimate truths.

Conceptual polarities helped the middle-class Victorians to mentally order their experiences. On one side was "right," and on the other "wrong." On one side was the "human" or the "civilized" while on the other was the "animal" or the "savage." The list could be expanded indefinitely: men/women, adults/children, whites/blacks, heroes/ordinary mortals, the refined/the crude, and the worthy/the unworthy. To the Victorians, such dichotomies were *not* merely mental constructs invented by humans for simplifying reality so that it could be more easily understood. These dichotomies had a real and permanent existence apart from how humans thought about them.

THE POPULARITY OF CULTURE

To a degree that astonishes us today, millions of Americans in the nineteenth century sought not only to acquaint themselves with the best that had been thought and said but also with the best paintings and the best music the world had ever produced. The operas *"Lucretia Borgia* and *Faust, The Barber of Seville* and *Don Giovanni,* are everywhere popular," reported George Makepeace Town in 1870, "you may hear their airs in the drawing rooms and concert halls, as well as whistled by the street boys and ground out on the hand organs." In towns both small and large opera houses sprang up across the nation. By the end of the century, no parlor was complete without a piano, and nearly every middle-class woman enjoyed at least rudimentary skills in playing the instrument. Piano music promoted refined behavior, even among males. "Husbands and brothers may be made almost domestic by one cheerful note," observed an advice manual of the 1890s. Millions purchased color reproductions of original paintings in the form of lithographs and hung them on their parlors or in their hallways.

Yet all of these signs of the popularity of culture paled beside that of reading. Abetted by the public school movement and an explosion in the publication of newspapers, magazines, and books, reading became virtually a national obsession. Everyone was urged to read. Americans read alone; they read aloud to one another; they read to improve themselves morally and materially; and they read to acquire culture. "A book case filled with well selected and well bound volumes"—this was the "one luxury," according to Catharine Maria Sedgwick in her novel *Home,* "which long habit and well cultivated taste [have] rendered essential to happiness."

Authors were among the nation's most celebrated heroes. Several were imports from other parts of the English-speaking world. William Shakespeare, Charles Dickens, and Sir Walter Scott were more than household names in America; millions of Americans could quote from Shakespeare at length or summarize the plots of Scott's *Ivanhoe* or Dickens's *A Tale of Two Cities.* Almost equally revered were such American writers as Henry Wadsworth Longfellow, Ralph Waldo Emerson, and Louisa May Alcott. That, in 1887, thousands of schoolchildren across the nation sent poet John Greenleaf Whittier greetings on his eightieth birthday suggested the high value that the nation attached to its literary culture.

The principal guardians of culture, as of the middle-class home, morality, and refinement more generally, were women. No matter what other gifts a woman might have, her life was incomplete without culture. She was required,

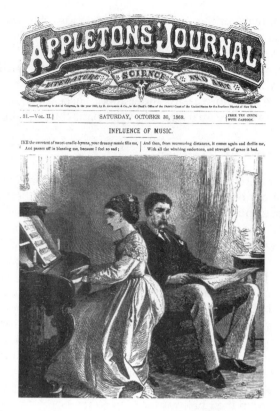

The Influence of Music. Taken from the cover of a popular nineteenth-century periodical and entitled "Influence of Music," this 1869 lithograph suggests that playing
and listening to refined music tamed the "savage" impulses of men. The beaux arts,
middle-class Victorians believed, elevated the human spirit, encouraged an inward
grace, and improved personal morality.

as part of her special obligation in domesticating men and children, to be ac-
quainted with books and be able to converse about them intelligently.
Women not only comprised the nation's largest reading group, by the 1830s
they were also authoring more books than men. Sentimental fiction by such
women authors as Harriet Beecher Stowe and Susannah Rowson—books
that frequently offered middle-class housewives directions for achieving
refinement and changing the behavior of others—poured off the nation's
presses. Much to the annoyance of men like Nathaniel Hawthorne, who
described them as "scribbling women," these women were the nineteenth-
century's best-selling writers. Since they could be paid less than men and
since they were regarded as the fitter guardians of young children, women
soon held most of the teaching positions in the nation's rapidly expanding
school system as well. Scholar Ann Douglas has summed up these varied
trends in the phrase "the feminization of American culture."

The Value and Uses of Culture

The more generous members of the nation's literary and artistic elite dreamed of creating a nation that shared refined manners, a respect for the intellect, and a reverence for the arts. Such a common culture, they believed, would encourage self-control—no mean feat in itself—and serve as a powerful, new social adhesive. In short, the elite transformed culture into a powerful ideology.

Initially, the ideology of culture rose to prominence, not as an answer to social anarchy or individual impulsiveness, but as a means of individual growth. In the antebellum era, amidst the mad scramble of millions of Americans to seize upon the expanding opportunities to acquire wealth, some ministers, orators, and essayists urged the ordinary people to enrich their lives by realizing more fully their moral and intellectual potentials. Instead of a life devoted to moneygrubbing, Emerson envisioned a life in which "the individual declares his independence, takes his life into his own hand, and sets forth in quest of Culture."

After the Civil War, the view of culture as an external force shaping an individual's aspirations and motives became increasingly popular. It was then that Chautauqua, founded in 1874 as a summer retreat for Methodist Sunday-school teachers, eventually brought culture to the nation's most remote towns and cities. It was then that the key institutions of "high" culture, the ones that remain to this day, came into being. Cities built immense central public libraries and colossal municipal museums. Magnates of industry and commerce sponsored symphony orchestras and founded a host of new private universities. Everywhere, from the white middle-class suburbs and the mansions of the rich to the inner city immigrant ghettos and the remote Indian reservations, teachers sought to inculcate their students with the Victorian version of culture. That as late as 1910 over half the high-school students in the United States were taking Latin and more than a quarter of them German suggested the strong persistence of traditional cultural ideals.

Culture had uses other than promoting self-control and a more stable social order. For, above all else, culture, along with refinement more generally, supported class authority. While only the parvenu—the new wealthy magnates of industry and finance—fully embraced the European aristocracy's excesses in consumption and leisure, the possession of culture strengthened the power of the middle class. Culture not only aided the middle class in drawing a firmer boundary between itself and the working class but its presence or absence could be employed to deny an individual or a group access to power. Not possessing good manners or the ability to converse well, showing bad taste in clothes or ignorance of the arts, could, for example, exclude unskilled working people, recently arrived immigrants, African Americans, and Native Americans from the full range of choices and opportunities that were available to white Protestant middle-class males.

Reformers sought to resolve the contradictions between the ideal of equality and refinement by making everyone cultured, by inviting everyone into the parlor. According to middle-class mythology, even ordinary workers could establish credentials for respectability; they could, if they practiced self-restraint with enough tenacity, purchase their own homes, buy carpets for their floors, and hang lace curtains on their windows. Nothing prevented them from learning good manners, reading great books, and reciting poetry.

No one provided a more forcible confirmation of the possibility of resolving the contradictions between equality and refinement than Abraham Lincoln. "This middle-class country [has] got a middle-class president, at last," exclaimed Emerson in 1865. By the practice of Victorian virtues, Lincoln moved upward—from the spare log cabin of his birth to a home with a white picket fence in Springfield, Illinois, and then finally to occupancy of the White House itself. Lincoln's ascent up the ladder of respectability bore mute testimony to the fact that in America anyone could escape the coils of poverty. Such thinking relieved the middle class of guilt and responsibility for the plight of the poor. For, ultimately, those who failed had only themselves to blame.

POLITICS AND THE MIDDLE-CLASS SOCIAL VISION

The family, the school, the park, the museum, the library, and the symphony orchestra were not the only means by which the middle class sought to achieve its vision of a nation bound together by a common culture. The middle class also turned to politics. While not exclusively a party of the middle class, the long-term successes of the Republican party accurately reflected the class's stunning power in American politics. Between the election of Abraham Lincoln in 1860 and Franklin D. Roosevelt in 1932, eleven Republicans and only two Democrats won the presidency.

Apart from favoring the use of federal power to promote economic growth, the middle class pushed a political agenda designed to promote cultural unity. Frequently inspired by an evangelical Protestant fervor and the New England idea of community, at the local level the middle class warmly embraced the public school movement, opposed public support of parochial schools, favored a strict enforcement of the Sabbath, and in particular supported laws restricting or banishing the sale of alcoholic beverages. Each of these measures encountered opposition, most frequently from southerners (or those with southern origins) and from immigrants. These groups usually identified with the Democratic party.

In the final two decades of the nineteenth and the first two decades of the twentieth century, the middle class became increasingly conscious of new threats to its hegemony over American life. One arose from immigrants and the working class (see chapter 7). The other arose from the growth of giant corporations. To the middle class, it seemed that one day the United States had been a nation of small shops, small retail outlets, small bankers, small farmers, and independent professional men. "A general equality of condition" prevailed, as one of them put it. But the next day corporate leviathans towered over the nation and a few men had acquired enormous fortunes. "A greater number of gigantic fortunes exists [in the United States] than in any other country in the world," according to widely read Englishman James Bryce.

The corporations introduced a new kind of hierarchical order, one that many middle-class observers feared might be just as dangerous to the republic's survival as the hereditary hierarchies of old. From the Revolutionary era, the middle class had learned the principle that a republic's success depended on a wide distribution of wealth and power among the ordinary citizenry. By the end of the nineteenth century, the nation had undergone a wrenching transformation; by then the richest 10 percent of the population controlled more than 65 percent of the nation's wealth. The giant corporations also challenged middle-class values. In the corporate world, upward mobility seemed to be tied more to the possession of specialized skills, self-presentation, and the ability get along with others than it did to hard work, frugality, and self-control.

To a substantial degree, the political contests of the Progressive era (approximately 1900–1917) revolved around what to do about the big corporations and the accumulation of enormous quantities of wealth in the hands of the few. Some sought to break up the corporations (the antitrust response), and others to nationalize them (the socialist response). Others argued for letting them alone (the laissez-faire response), while still others sought to regulate the corporations (the regulatory response). In the end, the political system empowered federal and state bureaucracies to alter some of the behaviors of corporations, though as frequently as not the regulators turned out to be the puppets of the very groups that they were supposed to regulate. The Progressives also obtained the ratification of the Sixteenth Amendment, which allowed for a graduated federal income tax system, and Congress passed the first federal tax on estates, both measures that could have potentially limited the accumulation of great fortunes.

UPPER-CLASS WAYS

The rise to supremacy of middle-class ways placed the nation's wealthiest citizens in an awkward position. While there had always been Americans with aristocratic pretensions, the nation had never had a hereditary upper class in the European sense. In addition, republican ideology and the opening of the doors of opportunity for ordinary white men had combined in the early nineteenth century to weaken traditional elite authority. Nevertheless, by mid-nineteenth century, wealthy families in every major city and throughout the slave-owning South sought to distinguish themselves from the middle class by aping the ways of the European aristocracy.

Fed by the spectacular transfusions of new wealth arising from the Industrial Revolution and the creation of huge corporations, by the 1880s and 1890s the efforts to create an American aristocracy had, in the words of historian Robert Wiebe, "the look of a formidable enterprise." Each city had its fashionable residential area of the super rich: In Chicago it was the Gold Coast, in Manhattan Fifth Avenue, in San Francisco Nob Hill, and in Denver Quality Hill. On the hillsides above the humid city of Cincinnati, a traveler observed in 1883, "the homes of Cincinnati's merchant princes and millionaires are found . . . elegant cottages, tasteful villas, and substantial mansions, surrounded by a paradise of grass, gardens, lawns, and tree-shaded roads." The wealthy escaped summer's heat by building lavish "cottages" in such cooler spots as Newport, Rhode Island, and Bell Harbor, Maine, and, when wintry winds began to blow, they made their way to resorts in the Carolinas, Georgia, and eventually Florida. They engaged in conspicuous consumption, sent their sons to the colleges that catered only to the nation's most affluent, formed socially exclusive clubs, and patronized expensive sports.

But neither the accumulation of great fortunes nor the adoption of aristocratic lifestyles necessarily led to high social standing. Older established elites frequently shut out the nouveau riche. In the East, the Boston Brahmin and Philadelphia Main Line families, who had acquired their wealth in the colonial and Revolutionary eras, created close-knit, virtually impenetrable, family dynasties. Even such relatively raw and open cities as San Francisco and Denver had their established elites. In New York, a flood of moneyed newcomers overwhelmed the city's older elite. Led by Ward McAllister, a southern-born lawyer who had made a fortune in the California gold rush, New York's wealthy sought to construct a distinctive upper class. They set up rules of conduct and developed a careful list of those whom they deemed as eligible for New York's high "society." McAllister's *Social Register,* first published in 1888, contained a list of the "Four Hundred"—the cream of New York's society—based on the invitation list to Mrs. William Astor's great ball on February 1, 1892. Late in the nineteenth century, numerous smaller cities claimed their own local Four Hundreds.

Yet, as hard as they tried, American plutocrats never succeeded in constructing an upper class in the European sense. Each city had its own rich, its own Four Hundred, but they rarely interacted much with the nabobs from other cities and even when they were lumped together failed to constitute a nationally coherent class. Neither did the superrich win the admiration nor the full approval of the nation's middle class. While embracing genteel refinement, most of the middle class disliked the wealthy's relaxation of self-control and their unproductive use of leisure. Both Thorstein Veblen in his *The Theory of the Leisure Class* and middle-class cartoonists mercilessly lampooned the ways of the upper class, in particular their un-aristocratic inclination to ostentatiously display their wealth or to accumulate ever more wealth, inclinations more easily resisted by Europe's landed aristocracy than by America's entrepreneurial buccaneers. While possessing "the loftiest pretensions to 'aristocracy,'" sneered British counsel Thomas Grattan, America's very rich frequently descended "to very low methods of money-making." Finally, great waves of new wealth regularly overwhelmed those who sought to build an American aristocracy. Money, as Robert Wiebe has observed, purchased luxurious goods "but not class position."

Conclusion

During the nineteenth century, the United States became the world's foremost example of a middle-class society and culture. True, the Victorian age witnessed the rising power of the bourgeoisie, or middle class, everywhere in the Western world, but in Europe aristocracies continued to exercise great cultural power. It was only in America that middle-class ways became so central and so dominant. Indeed, while conveniently ignoring workingmen, Native Americans, and African Americans, it seemed to many observers that the middle class was all there was in America. In constructing its own set of ways, the middle class even emptied other groups of some of their vitality. By appropriating from the working class the value of work, from the aristocracy the value of genteel refinement, and from evangelical Protestants the value of personal morality and high moral purpose, the middle class claimed (and to a substantial extent gained) the cultural leadership of the entire nation.

7

THE WAYS OF OTHERS

Nothing worried middle-class Victorians more than passion. "Accustomed to a decorous self-restraint, passion, even trivial passion, was salt on our tongues," recalled Henry Seidel Canby in a highly perceptive memoir of middle-class life in Wilmington, Delaware, in the 1890s. To the Canbys as well as to other middle-class families, it was the absence of self-control that more than anything else distinguished "Us" from "Them." To the white middle class, the new Americans (the immigrants), the working class (who were more often than not also immigrants), the African Americans, and the Native Americans all seemed to have a fundamental character flaw. They all took their pleasures wherever and whenever they could and let tomorrow take care of itself. "They had a better time [than we did]," confessed a palpably envious Canby, "for they let themselves go." Canby, of course, exaggerated. His stereotype revealed as much about his own class as it did about the cultural "outsiders."

Yet the cultural outsiders did share important characteristics. They all greeted the individualistic, bourgeois spirit of the nineteenth century with less enthusiasm than the white middle class did. They saw nothing manifestly superior in the single-minded pursuit of individual gain nor in other middle-class Victorian ways. Rather than fully embracing the ways of the dominant culture, Indians, blacks, immigrants, and even many white southerners found in the preservation, invention, and perpetuation of their own distinctive ways a source of identity and of strength. In addition, the ways of the outsiders frequently clashed, not only with those of the dominant northern middle class but with the ways of one another as well. Indeed, since the early nineteenth century, class, ethnicity, race, religion, and region have been the ultimate sources of many of the nation's most heated cultural conflicts.

NATIVE AMERICAN WAYS UNDER ASSAULT

No major group, except perhaps African Americans, had a more difficult time in resisting the pressures of the dominant middle class than Native Americans. In 1800, despite nearly three hundred years of almost relentless assaults from European invaders, powerful independent Indian tribes still occupied much of the interior of North America. Each of the Indian nations

had its own language, its own customs, its own government, and its own religion. Contrary to modern media images, Native Americans lived mostly in
fixed villages where they typically pursued a food-getting cycle of farming,
hunting, fishing, gathering, and sometimes raiding.

Over the next century, the situation of Native Americans changed drastically. Many lost their lives. The Indian population plunged from perhaps a
million or more people in 1800 to less than a quarter million a century later.
The Indians also lost their tribal independence, at least a portion of their culture, and nearly all their lands. By 1900 they had been militarily subdued and
pushed off their lands onto tiny, desolate reservations where most of them
lived in deplorable poverty.

"An Unspeakable Sadness"

No simple hypothesis adequately explains this "unspeakable sadness," to
employ the moving words that an Indian leader once used to describe what
had happened. In theory, the interior of North America could have been set
aside as a permanent homeland for the continent's indigenous peoples. There,
in principle, the Indians could have carried on much as they had in the past.
An indigenous homeland would have also accorded with a generous reading
of the Declaration of Independence. The Declaration asserted that all peoples
were entitled to the right of self-government. Such a proposal would have
won the warm endorsement of the Indians themselves. The Indians repeatedly expressed a willingness and a readiness to live in peaceful coexistence
with white Americans.

Unfortunately for the Indians, the idea of a homeland ran afoul of deeply
held white convictions. To one large white group, the Indians stood in the
way of white men increasing their personal fortunes. Rationalizing their ag-
grandizement in terms of their self-acclaimed racial superiority, they concluded that the Indians were simply obstacles who should be pushed aside,
or, if necessary, even killed. To them, the Indians differed little from wild ver-
min. The prospect of killing Indians appalled another white group, the humanitarians. They dreamed of a day when, by adopting white ways, Indians
would be fully integrated into white society.

Yet the humanitarians and the land-hungry whites did *agree* on one key
point: The Indians had no legitimate claims to cultures of their own. Equating
progress and civilization with individualism and private property, whites
found particularly repulsive the Indian practices of tribal (rather than individual) land ownership and the sharing of the fruits of the land among all
tribal members. Unless abandoned for white ways, it disqualified the Indians
for consideration as equals to whites.

Government Indian policy in the nineteenth century reflected these views.
Until 1871, when Congress abolished the practice of making treaties with
separate tribes, the government negotiated dozens of treaties—many of them
the product of chicanery and corruption—which called for both Indian land
cessions and for the establishment of "civilizing missions" among the tribes.

The Indian agents and the missionaries, those whites responsible for the civilizing missions, urged the Indians to renounce their ancestral ways. They visualized the reservations, those lands retained by the Indians, as protected, transitional spaces. Here, the Indians would be granted the time necessary for them to make the transition from "savagery" to "civilization."

INDIAN RESPONSES

Native Americans devised various strategies for responding to the massive white assaults on their lives, their lands, and their cultures. Sometimes they sank into hopeless despair and resigned to their fate at the hands of the advancing whites. Sometimes they fled. For example, as late as 1877, the legendary Nez Perce Chief Joseph tried to lead his people to safety by a long flight across the Pacific Northwest, into Canada, and finally back into the United States. Throughout much of the nineteenth century, a large portion of the Indian population could, by modern terms, be classified as political refugees.

When unable or unwilling to flee the rapidly advancing white invaders, Indian strategy usually oscillated between resistance and accommodation. The accommodationists cooperated with but were rarely controlled by the whites. They frequently adopted some aspects of white culture. The resisters, on the other hand, openly rejected some if not all aspects of white culture. Most Indians probably occupied positions between these two poles or, as the occasion seemed to warrant, shifted from one position to the other.

No example of the promise and tragedy of accommodation was more poignant than that of the Cherokees. During the first three decades of the nineteenth century, the Cherokees, who held lands in northern Georgia, western North Carolina, and eastern Tennessee, adopted a written constitution modeled after that of the United States, declared themselves an independent nation, developed their own alphabet, published a bilingual newspaper, and set up schools. Thousands converted (at least nominally) to evangelical Christianity. Cherokee society even paralleled white society by becoming far more socially stratified than it had been in the past. Seizing upon the skyrocketing demand for cotton, some of the tribe's leaders, particularly half-bloods who were able to deal more effectively with white society than the full-bloods, became large planters who owned hundreds of slaves and thousands of acres of prime cotton land.

To the land-hungry whites, Cherokee accommodation had worked all too well. They turned to their governments for help in ridding the region of the Indians. While the U.S. Supreme Court tried to protect Cherokee rights, President Andrew Jackson sided with the white expansionists. By harassment, intimidation, and bribery, the federal government persuaded a minority of the chiefs to sign a treaty of removal. Despite bitter protests from both Indians and white missionaries, all the Indians except a few who escaped into the mountains were removed (forcibly if necessary) to Indian Territory (what is now Oklahoma). Along the "The Trail of Tears," as the long Cherokee trek to Indian Territory in 1838 was known, approximately one-quarter of their population perished. Altogether, between 1820 and 1850 forced removal uprooted more than one hundred thousand eastern Indians, many of whom had taken up white paths of adaptation to the changing world about them.

Resistance to white assaults frequently combined sacred and military power. Military resistance was nothing new. Since the fifteenth century, when the Spaniards first encroached on the native peoples of North America, whites and Indians had been fighting in what historians sometimes describe as the "Four Hundred Years War." In the first phase of this prolonged conflict, the Indians had been able to shrewdly parlay one European power against the other, but, with the rise of the United States, the Indians could no longer count on white allies. The Indians then had to contend alone with a new republic that enjoyed vastly superior numbers and material resources. Armed resistance ended symbolically with the Wounded Knee massacre in 1890.

A group of Indian prophets extending from Handsome Lake in the eighteenth century to Tenskwatawa and Wovoka in the nineteenth century, supplied the ideological core of the Indian resistance movement. Each of the prophets had apocalyptic visions; in these visions they crossed a boundary that normally separated the temporal and the spiritual worlds. From the world of the spirits they received instructions to carry back to their peoples.

The lessons of the prophets were strikingly similar. Indian woes, they taught, stemmed from a failure of the Indian people to adhere to traditional ways. Dependency on white trade goods, conversion to Christianity, surrendering native lands to alien peoples, and negligence in performing traditional religious rituals—all of these had led to a disastrous loss of sacred power. The restoration of sacred power required a cultural revitalization. Some prophets sought to revitalize their people by blending the old and the new. For example, in 1799 Handsome Lake, an Iroquois prophet, preached a combination of Indian and white ways that included peace, temperance, land retention, and the rituals of Gaiwiio, a new religion that joined Christianity and traditional Iroquois beliefs.

Other prophets urged more radical forms of revitalization and resistance. During the first decade of the nineteenth century, the Shawnee prophet Tenskwatawa exhorted all of the Indian people to renounce alcohol and all other white goods (except guns when used in self-defense) and to return to the old ways of hunting with the bow and the arrow. "You must not dress like the White Man or wear hats like them, . . . and when the weather is not severe, you must go naked excepting the breach cloth. . . ." He condemned intertribal warfare and urged tribal unity.

In 1888, in the wake of Indian military defeat and the virtual demise of the bison, the Paiute prophet Wovoka developed a powerful new religion centered on the Ghost Dance. By conducting proper ceremonies and rituals, Wovoka prophesied that the fallen warriors and the buffalo would return and drive away the whites. While Wovoka's prophesies went unfulfilled, religious revitalization continues to this day to serve as an important means of resisting white assaults on traditional Native American ways.

THE CULMINATION OF THE WHITE ASSAULT

The Dawes Act of 1887, passed during the final military subjugation of the Plains Indians, represented the culmination of nineteenth-century Indian policy. The act allowed for the transfer of 160 acres of former tribal lands to individual Indian families. Private rather than tribal ownership, the humanitarians believed, would awaken in the Indians desires for personal gain similar to those that preoccupied middle-class whites. The government, with tribal consent, could sell the remaining lands to white settlers. The proceeds from these sales were to be set aside for Indian education and "civilization."

As an alternative to the enormous power of traditional tribal structures and the ancestral ways of the Indians, the Dawes Act proposed to create among the Indians a facsimile of middle-class Victorian culture. The Indian families were expected to move out of their tribal villages onto individual farms, to establish male-dominated nuclear families, and to adopt the acquisitive values of white society. By promising the final annihilation of tribal life and by the opening up of new lands for white settlement, the Dawes Act pleased both the white humanitarians and the land-hungry whites.

But the results were less than happy for the Indians. By the 1930s Indian-owned lands had shrunk from 138 million acres to less than 48 million acres. Left on mostly barren lands unsuited for successful farming and lacking in a plentiful supply of game, shocking numbers of the Indians sank into shattering cycles of dependency, disease, alcoholism, appalling poverty, and early death.

The whites added to Indian miseries by their continuing attacks on tribal customs. In particular, those customs that ran counter to the middle-class white concern with self-control bothered Bureau of Indian Affairs officials. For example, they banned tribal dances and they tried to stop the ingestion of peyote, which was, according to the Reverend G. A. Watermulter (1914) "a habit-forming, physically weakening, will-relaxing, imagination-exciting drug." Acting upon the admonition of Captain Richard Henry Pratt, the founder of the Carlisle Indian boarding school in Pennsylvania, that they should "Kill the Indian in him and save the man," the Bureau established a system of boarding and day schools. By removing Native American children from direct tribal and family influences and teaching them to be ashamed of their traditional cultures, the schools sought to convert the Indian children to white middle-class ways.

Despite staggering white pressures, only a small fraction of the Indian population fully assimilated into the dominant white culture. Neither education in the ways of the whites nor the Dawes Act succeeded in equalizing the conditions of opportunity between Indians and whites. Continuing white prejudice and discrimination severely circumscribed Indian opportunities to improve their material lot. The Indians themselves resisted assimilation; few of them found the acquisitive individualism of white culture intrinsically superior to their own. They continued to yearn for a less competitive culture, one in which the earth's bounty was shared by everyone.

New Government Boarding School on the Pine Ridge Indian Reservation in South Dakota, 1891. Notice the juxtaposition of traditional tribal lodgings in the foreground and the new boarding school in the background. Boarding schools, which separated Native American children from their elders and their tribal groups, were designed to convert Indian youths to the middle-class ways of white America.

In the meantime, whites apparently shielded themselves from a full recognition of the tragedies and miseries of the Indian people by weaving around them a romantic shroud of fantasy and nostalgia. Dime novels, and then later the movies, radio, and television, and finally even history textbooks pointedly avoided telling the true story of a bloody, contested Euro-American invasion of the Americas. According to this literature and iconography, it was the Indians—emphatically not the whites—who were the aggressors. In 1883 William "Buffalo Bill" Cody turned a romanticized version of relationships between Indians and whites into a successful business formula with his Wild West Show. Immensely popular in both America and in Europe, the show featured stereotypical Indians chasing buffalo, performing war dances, and attacking a white settler's cabin. At this juncture in the drama, Bill Cody came to the rescue, saving white "civilization" from "savagery." Such a process of justification for the white incursions on Indian lives and properties was so successful that by 1900 it took a leap of the imagination for most white Americans to realize that only a century earlier dozens of independent Indian cultures had once existed in the vast interior of North America.

ETHNIC/WORKING-CLASS WAYS

During Henry Seidel Canby's boyhood days in Wilmington, Delaware, in the 1890s, the United States was in the midst of two great revolutions, each of which contributed to the growth of a large class of what he and his friends saw as cultural outsiders. First was the Industrial Revolution. In the first half of the nineteenth century, probably two-thirds of the white men in the United States had owned productive property (in particular, farms) or they worked in the shops of small craftsmen. In either case, they were largely free of economic dependencies and of rigorously prescribed rhythms of work. But, as the century wore on, wealth resided less in land and in small shops and more in capital (the money to produce new goods).

Growing numbers of Americans then found themselves employed by large corporations. Such employment meant more economic dependency and a substantial loss of control over one's work experiences. Some workers became salaried professionals and self-employed entrepreneurs, but the vast majority—perhaps two-thirds of all Americans—toiled for wages rather than for salaries or profits. This army of wage earners dug the nation's canals, built its railroads, loaded and unloaded its ships and boxcars, and manned its blast furnaces. Millions of immigrants, in particular young Irish women, also toiled as household servants in middle- and upper-class homes.

The second revolution entailed the massive migration of peoples to the United States. In 1820, nearly all of the white people in the nation had origins in England, Northern Ireland, Scotland, and Germany. (African Americans comprised almost 10 percent of the population; the 1820 Census did not attempt to count Native Americans.) Some 95 percent of the population was Protestant. During the next hundred years great waves of immigrants drastically altered the nation's ethnic and religious mix. By 1920, more than half of the white population could trace their origins to places other than England, Scotland, and Northern Ireland. They came mainly from Ireland, Germany, Southern and Eastern Europe, Canada, and Mexico. By then some 30 percent of the nation's peoples were Catholics and perhaps 2 percent were Jewish.

Industrial Work Ways

While they came mostly from the European countryside, the majority of the new immigrants took up residence in the cities. There, they usually became members of the new industrial working class. "Not every foreigner is a workingman," observed a Protestant minister in the 1890s, "but in the cities, at least, it may almost be said that every workingman is a foreigner." By the first decade of the twentieth century, immigrant men and their male children made up 70 percent of the workforce in fifteen of the nation's nineteen leading industries.

In the factories, the unskilled wage earners encountered an utterly unfamiliar kind of work discipline. In the preindustrial past, daylight hours, the rhythms of the seasons, and ancient customs had dictated the pace and the nature of work. Both on the farms and in the skilled trades, work had often entailed bouts of intense labor mixed with periods of complete idleness. Depending on custom, within the workplace the men might tell stories, sing, gamble, and drink beer. But with the arrival of the Industrial Revolution, employers sought to wipe out the older ways of work. They insisted on a sober and orderly work force. Machines and clocks relentlessly dictated the pace of work. Having lost much of their control over their work experience, factory workers sometimes bitterly complained. They described themselves as "wage slaves."

By their absenteeism from work, by changing jobs with startling frequency, by forming labor unions, and by striking, the wage earners actively resisted the new work discipline. Strikes multiplied from about five hundred per year in the 1880s to more than two thousand in the 1890s. To subdue the strikers, for the first time in American history (except the Civil War) the state employed massive force against its own citizens. Fears of "the dangerous classes," as the upstart workers were described by the middle-class press, mounted. With the terrors of the Civil War still lurking in their memories, some observers feared that the "labor question" might become the "irrepressible conflict" of their generation.

Yet no civil war between labor and capital ever came. American workers never developed a full-blown "class consciousness." Neither did they ever embrace labor unions nor socialism with the same enthusiasm as Europe's industrial workers. Extraordinary ethnic and racial cleavages in America weakened the potential unity of the wage earners. No other society in the world drew so many newcomers from such diverse backgrounds. Differences in language, religion, and Old World animosities shattered the working class into mutually suspicious groups. In addition, some crafts and skilled workers such as bricklayers, typographers, and toolmakers secured for themselves privileged positions. Referred to as the "aristocracy of labor," these workers rarely identified with the unskilled workers at the bottom of the laboring pyramid. Above all, the idea of America as a special land of opportunity and the lure of middle-class respectability worked against the possibility of the working class mounting a full-scale assault on the nation's new industrial order.

Yet, wage-earning immigrants rarely became total converts to the white middle class's ideology of success. In the first place, by equating material success with moral worth, such an ideology implicitly condemned the vast majority of workers to both material and moral failure. Second, the rapid upward mobility of the self-made man, which was so dear to middle-class thinking, was simply beyond the reach of all but a tiny fraction of the working class.

Wage earners tended to define success in more realistic terms. Rather than as the fulfillment of individual ambitions, success meant a steady job and ample support of family and kin. In particular, the workers placed the welfare and preservation of family and relatives before that of personal advancement. Literally millions of workers, for instance, sent hard-earned savings back to Europe to enable relatives to pay for their transatlantic voyage to America. Unlike the middle class, blue-collar workers also had large numbers of children. More children meant more family income. Countless sons and daughters of immigrant working-class families passed up opportunities to obtain additional education or skills so they could contribute directly to the family's welfare.

Still, unlike most of their counterparts in Europe, American wage earners could realistically dream of moving up the class ladder even if it were only slightly. By toiling diligently at their jobs and slowly saving a little money, they could imagine one day buying their own homes and perhaps even owning a small business. Although such dreams frequently proved illusory, a majority of the workers eventually did make some improvements in their material lot. They frequently occupied a crowded, insecure borderland between the lower and the middle class.

In addition, within each ethnic working-class group, a sizable minority became successful entrepreneurs. Most started out by providing basic goods and services for their own communities. Exploiting the immigrants' preference for buying goods from their own countrymen, with whom they shared a common language and trust, they opened grocery stores, butcher shops, dry goods stores, and saloons. Some even turned to banking and construction.

Of all ethnic occupations, the best known were those available in politics, entertainment, and crime. Ethnicity became virtually synonymous with the rise of big city political machines and political bosses in the late nineteenth century. Denied opportunities in more respectable occupations, entrepreneurship in crime, show business, and professional sports likewise became ladders of upward mobility for the new Americans. In exchange for "protection," ethnic "mobsters" extorted money from saloon keepers, brothel operators, contractors, and small manufacturers. By the 1920s, during the age when alcohol was legally banned in America, underworld crime escalated into a substantial enterprise. Along with African Americans, immigrants and their descendants also achieved a special prominence as both performers and entrepreneurs in the rapidly growing commercial entertainment industry.

Working-Class Ways of Leisure

While employers were able to impose a large measure of order on the men, women, and sometimes children in their factories, their hegemony rarely extended to their employee's time away from work. It was outside the workplace—in their churches, neighborhoods, families, clubs, and saloons—that most wage earners succeeded in preserving and creating their own cultures. Within this infrastructure, distinctively working-class rather than middle-class ways predominated.

One of the most important of these ways was leisure. The workers, who as we have seen were increasingly comprised of immigrants and non-Protestants, tended to reject the old-stock middle-class Protestant strictures on recreation. Workers usually placed a higher value on play for its own sake, sensual gratification, spontaneity, and conviviality than on self-control or on recreation as a means of refreshing oneself for more serious duties. Unlike the middle class, many workers, especially bachelors, who comprised a far larger percentage of the population in the nineteenth century than they do today, enthusiastically embraced sports, gambling, and drinking. Outside the parameters of middle-class respectability and frequently illegal, the leisure activities patronized by the working class comprised a kind of Victorian underworld or counterculture.

Prizefighting illustrated the large disparity in views on recreation between the working and the middle class. Illegal almost everywhere, pugilism manifestly mocked Victorian values, especially the cardinal virtue of self-control. The prevailing rules of the ring permitted a battle just short of an unregulated physical brawl. Sensing that their bets were in jeopardy or that their favorite had been treated unfairly and amply fortified by copious quantities of alcohol, spectators frequently joined the frays. But while the middle class condemned the brutality and disorderliness of the prize ring, working-men, especially those of Irish origins, held prizefighting and prizefighters in the highest esteem. No one was more admired by workingmen than John L. Sullivan, the heavyweight champion from 1882 to 1892. By his own brute strength, his brawny body, and his swift fists, "the Boston Strong Boy" had conquered all comers in what workingmen considered to be the ultimate metaphor of masculine superiority.

The classes also parted ways over the celebration of holidays. In the first place, immigrants upon their arrival in America were shocked to discover the sheer paucity of official holidays; except for the Fourth of July and Christmas, Protestant America celebrated no national holidays. The calendars of immigrants, on the other hand, literally teemed with holidays. The Greek Orthodox Church alone recognized more than eighty holy days. To add to employer woes, neither Greek Orthodox, Roman Catholic, nor Jewish religious calendars coincided. Immigrants also took off from work (sometimes for several days) to celebrate weddings and funerals. In addition, the immigrant working class typically celebrated holidays (including Sundays) with far more gusto than the middle class. Workers flocked into the streets, the parks, and the saloons (if open), where they carried banners, sang, talked, held parades, played games, and drank alcoholic beverages.

Neither prizefighting nor holidays approximated the significance of saloons as centers of alternative ways that were anathema to the dominant culture. To the Protestant middle class, abstinence, or at the least temperance, provided irrefutable proof that one had achieved self-control. To the mostly immigrant working class, on the other hand, drink was a source of nutrition, relaxation, and conviviality. To escape the demanding routines of the workplace, to make and cement friendships, and to preserve ancient customs, workingmen regularly gathered at saloons. That Chicago alone in 1884 had thirty-five hundred saloons, more than existed in all fifteen southern states combined, reflected the special importance of saloons to working-class culture.

The saloons fostered an ethic totally at odds with that of middle-class Protestants. Rather than individual moneymaking and the privacy of the home, the saloons encouraged nonmaterial values, sharing, and public display. For example, "treating," a common custom in Ireland and among Irish-American working men, required that any man who happened to be in a

Little Mint Saloon on East Third Street, Davenport, Iowa, in about 1900. An important institution of those outside the dominant middle-class culture, saloons fostered spare-time activities that revolved around sharing, public display, and an all-male camaraderie.

saloon when acquaintances strolled in must offer them drinks and pay for all the drinks that they consumed. Deeply embedded in working-class lifestyles, such a ritual implied not only a resistance to individual acquisitiveness, but affirmed the reciprocity, solidarity, and equality of all working men.

By the time that the United States entered World War I in 1917, leisure had become a far less important arena of class conflict. By then the middle class itself had begun a noticeable retreat from its earlier strictures on leisure and even adopted some of the leisure practices of the ethnic working class. In the twentieth century, workers lost some of their communal control over leisure to the recreational entrepreneurs who managed the outdoor amusement parks, the dance pavilions, and especially the movie houses. Yet, according to historian Roy Rosenszweig, the increasing commercialization of working-class leisure fostered a growing solidarity of workers across ethnic lines. For example, commercialized leisure may have encouraged a growing number of intermarriages among Catholics from different ethnic backgrounds.

THE RELIGIOUS WAYS OF THE NEW AMERICANS

No aspect of culture was more important to the new Americans than their religion. Nearly all of the immigrants came from countries where Catholicism was the religion of the insiders. In Europe, they could usually take their religious affiliations and identities for granted. But in predominantly Protestant America, Catholics were clearly religious outsiders. Under such circumstances, the Church took on a vastly added importance in the lives of its adherents. The Church's familiar rituals and its authoritarian structure offered the immigrants a source of comfort, certainty, and security. In time, the Church did even more; it eventually "constructed" what historian Charles R. Morris has described as "a virtual state-within-a-state." This virtual Catholic state within the United States permitted Catholics to "live almost their entire lives within a thick cocoon of Catholic institutions." "I felt that, although I was human and capable of mistakes," explained a young woman, "God and the Catholic community would always keep me safe and free from worry." Catholic institutions shielded countless immigrants from many of the potentially disturbing influences that emanated from the dominant middle-class Protestant culture.

More than to Rome, to early Spanish missions, or to the English Catholic settlers in colonial Maryland, the modern American Catholic Church traces its origins to nineteenth-century Ireland. Shaped by their terribly harsh experiences in Ireland, including the Great Potato Famine and English exploitation, the Irish immigrants brought with them an especially militant and austere form of Catholicism. In America, a series of strong-minded Irish bishops set about rebuilding the Church according to their own understanding of Catholicism. After the Civil War, successive waves of German, Italian, and Eastern European immigrants contended with the Irish for hegemony over the American Church, but with only limited success. Until far into the twentieth century, most of the clergy and a vast majority of the hierarchy were of Irish descent.

The response of Protestants to the great Catholic "invasion" reinforced and added to the importance of the Church in the lives of countless immigrants. In the antebellum era, the arrival of great numbers of Irish immigrants sent shock waves through Protestant America. Apart from traditional animosities toward Catholics that originated in the Protestant Reformation, Protestant Americans saw the Catholic Church as antithetical to republicanism. They associated the church with monarchies, hierarchies, and tyrannies. Fed by a spate of "confessions" by former nuns—or more frequently persons claiming to be nuns—who reported that they had been held in sexual bondage by priests, anti-Catholicism turned violent in the 1830s and 1840s. Pitched battles broke out between Catholics and Protestants in Philadelphia, New York, Boston, and more than a dozen smaller cities. Adding fuel to the religious war was the issue of education. Disturbed that the public schools taught Protestant doctrine, Catholics set up separate, church-supported parochial school systems. By the late nineteenth century, parochial schools had become an integral component in the "thick cocoon of Catholic institutions" that perpetuated distinctive Catholic communities in America.

The Church's hierarchy served a similar function. At the top was the Pope, who Catholics believed was Christ's direct representative on earth. In the realms of spirituality and morality, the Pope was for Catholics nothing less than an absolute monarch. When speaking officially on spiritual manners, the Vatican Council in 1870 ruled that the Pope was infallible. With few exceptions, American Catholics embraced the motto *Roma locuta est; causa finita est* ("Rome has spoken: the case is closed"). Thus Church laws, such as those requiring attendance at mass on Sundays and on holy days, carried an authority for Catholics that equaled biblical commandments for Protestants. From the Pope, authority flowed downward through an elaborate hierarchy to the local parish priest.

By insisting that access to the sacred required a set of formal devotional exercises, the Church further bolstered its authority over the spiritual lives of its charges. Without regular confessions of sins to priests, participation in mass, and the acceptance of penances, salvation was impossible. At the center of Catholic devotion was the mass. Conducted in an atmosphere of great solemnity and amid the sights, smells, and sounds of burning candles, tinkling bells, fragrant incense, and colorful flowers, the mass contained all the ingredients of high liturgical drama. Adding to the grandeur of the occasion was the priest, who, dressed in special robes, walked about the altar while praying in Latin, a virtually unknown tongue to the laity.

The importance of ritual to Catholics extended far beyond the celebration of mass and the other sacraments. A devotion to saints also distinguished the lives of Catholics from Protestants. Parents named their children for saints, churches and schools were named for saints, and so were baseball teams. Because saints were human, they were thought to be more approachable than God; they had the power to mediate between mortals and God. To Catholics, none of the saints were closer to God than Mary, the Mother of Christ. Given Mary's special position within the network of heavenly relatives, Catholics believed that prayers to her were particularly effective. Other popular devotional exercises included the saying of the rosary, the signing of the cross, and the use of holy water.

The parish church, along with the precinct captain's house, the saloon, the funeral home, the fire station, the corner grocery store, and the parochial school—all these were keys to the creation of one of the most remarkable institutions in the American city, the Catholic-ethnic neighborhood. It was to these neighborhoods that the immigrants first flocked; there they encountered familiar sights, sounds, and smells. There the immigrants "create for themselves," observed a visitor, "distinct communities, almost as impervious to American sentiments and influences as are the inhabitants of Dublin or Hamburg. They have their own theaters, recreations, amusements, military and national organizations; to a great extent their own schools, churches, and their own newspapers and periodical literature." Gala processions, scheduled in conjunction with religious holidays, underscored the central place occupied by the parish church in Catholic neighborhoods. "As the procession filed through the streets," historian Jay Dolan has written, "Catholics were marking off their neighborhood, laying claim to it, and telling people that this was their piece of earth."

The building of close-knit Catholic-ethnic neighborhoods was not the only way that the American Catholic Church served as an agency of cultural conservatism. In the late nineteenth and early twentieth centuries, a small but

Italian-American Catholics in Chicago Celebrating the Feast of Santa Maria Incoronata Early in the Twentieth Century. Processions such as these helped immigrant Catholics to mark off and stake a claim to their own neighborhoods as well as to public spaces in their new land. The photo also suggests the effectiveness with which the new Americans were able to perpetuate their traditional ways.

influential group of Catholic leaders, including the archbishop of Baltimore, James Cardinal Gibbons, sought to make the Church more acceptable to mainstream middle-class Victorian America. While by no means departing substantively from Catholic orthodoxy, the reformers placed less stress on devotional supernaturalism and offered mild support to labor unions as well as to social reforms. In what was known as the "Americanist" controversy, the Vatican quickly squelched the incipient liberalization of the American Church. In 1899, Pope Leo XIII issued an encyclical aimed at Cardinal Gibbons that specifically denounced what he called "Americanism."

While Gibbons and his allies insisted that the Pope had condemned a "phantom heresy," the Pope's action in this matter as well as in others effectively intimidated efforts to bring the Church into closer touch with mainstream American culture and with modern intellectual developments. For the next half-century, the intellectual life of Catholic colleges and universities stood in startling contrast to that of Protestant and public-supported institutions. While non-Catholic institutions frequently offered a hearing if not always a warm welcome to the ideas of such seminal thinkers as Charles

Darwin, Karl Marx, Albert Einstein, and Sigmund Freud, Catholic schools shut out everything that smacked of what Pope Leo XIII described as "modernism." Instead of including or considering the latest intellectual speculation, their curricula continued to revolve around the classic medieval theology of Thomas Aquinas.

Catholicism was, of course, not the only faith of the new Americans. Nearly all of the English, Scots, Scots-Irish, and Scandinavians, and well over half of the German immigrants were Protestants. Their Protestantism eased their way into the dominant culture. In terms of numbers, no ethnoreligious group exercised a larger influence on shaping mainstream American culture than the Jews. Unlike most of the adherents of Catholicism and Eastern Orthodoxy, the Jews had always been a minority group in nations dominated by other religions. Rather than from the countryside of Europe, most of the impoverished Jewish immigrants came to the United States from the cities of Eastern Europe. Hence, they already had generations of experience in coping with prejudice and with living in urban ghettos. "Their devotion to education," historian Loren Baritz has written, "was virtually religious." In addition to education, a passionate commitment to hard work also contributed to their disproportionate success in their new land.

American Jews eventually divided into three main religious groups: Reform, Conservative, and Orthodox. Founded before the Civil War by Jews from Germany, Reformed Judaism vastly simplified and relaxed the traditional religious observances. Like liberal Protestants, they even allowed women to read from the Torah (the Jewish holy book) and eventually become rabbis. The Orthodox, whose main support came from the immigrants from Eastern Europe, insisted on a strict adherence to traditional observances; Orthodox worship services, for example, strictly separated men from women. Only men could lead the services. Conservatives stood between the Reform and the Orthodox versions of Judaism. While preserving more of the customary observances than the Reformers, the Conservatives permitted families to worship together. In the early twentieth century, many Jews abandoned formal religious affiliations altogether. By the 1930s fewer than one-third of the Jewish families in America belonged to a temple or a synagogue.

THE ISSUE OF ASSIMILATION RECAPITULATED

Adhering to the ideal of the United States as a special sanctuary for the oppressed and perceiving a need to fill up an empty country, government between the 1820s and the 1920s left immigration largely unfettered. But the welcoming mat was never universal. As we observed earlier, from the late 1830s to the mid-1850s, an anti-Catholic, anti-Irish movement flourished. It never totally died out. Beginning in the 1870s, Asians were the special target of a second nativist movement. Then in the 1880s, a third nativist movement, one directed at all immigrants, got underway. This movement culminated in the Immigration Act of 1924, which for the next forty years shut the doors to all except a tiny number of immigrants.

The speed and degree to which the immigrants and their descendants assimilated into the dominant culture has occasioned heated debate among scholars. While most immigrants came to the United States hoping to improve their material lot, few of them had any intention of altering their traditional ways. That, to this day, ethnicity and religious affiliation are usually better predictors of whom one will marry, invite to dinner, or vote for than is income or educational level suggests the degree to which the immigrants and their descendants were able to resist complete assimilation. "The Polish children treat their immigrant parents with contempt, . . . speak American slang, are addicted to American popular music, and popular culture, accept fully the American way of piling up money and material goods when possible," sociologist Michael Parenti found in the 1960s. "Yet they keep almost all their social contacts within the confines of the Polish-American community, and have no direct exposure to, and little interest in, middle-class American society."

Nonetheless, in the end, especially as the twentieth century wore on, the vast majority of the immigrants and their descendants became far less discernible as a distinctive cultural group. Such terms as the "steam heat" or the "lace curtain" Irish suggested the upward mobility of Irish Americans and their adoption of at least some aspects of middle-class culture. Other ethnic groups experienced a similar transition. Indeed, by the last quarter of the twentieth century the average income of Catholic and Jewish families even exceeded that of Protestant families. In addition, the ethnics eventually became citizens, voted, and increasingly thought of themselves as "Americans." In the 1930s they developed a special affection for President Franklin D. Roosevelt and his New Deal, they enthusiastically supported the United States in World War II, they became ardent anticommunists during the Cold War, and in the 1960s they reacted to student radicals with the slogan "America—love it or leave it." Conspicuously exhibiting their patriotism and their adherence to a common set of American ways, they eventually seemed in some respects to be the most archetypical "American" of all social groups.

Scholars have interpreted the relationship between the dominant and outsider cultures in a variety of ways. One is to dismiss the issue of assimilation entirely. Differences in ethnicity and religion were comparatively unimportant, these scholars argue; after all, both the new Americans and the older stock white Americans were products of a common European culture. Another position is to maintain that the immigrants and their offspring *selectively* assimilated the ways of the dominant culture; for example, the new Americans might embrace and participate in the nation's political life while simultaneously retaining in other respects separate ethnic cultures. A third is to emphasize the importance of coercion in assimilation; during World War I, for example, anti-German hysteria made it impossible for German Americans, as historian Gary Gerstle has insisted, to remain "American in politics and German in culture; they had to be American through and through." And perhaps no agency of cultural coercion was more important than the public school; until the 1980s the public schools unrelentingly taught the values of the dominant culture. Finally, scholars have speculated that, in the twentieth century, the powerful forces of the mass media and mass consumption have brought the ways of the two groups closer together. In other words, the nationalization of sights, sounds, and consumption has acted to produce new sets of ways that are shared across ethnic and religious boundaries.

Regardless of how assimilation or its absence is to be understood, it is clear that the influence of new Americans eventually extended far beyond their own ranks. Not only did they provide much of the back-breaking labor during the Industrial Revolution, but they soon began to play prominent roles in American politics, in issues of order and disorder in American cities, and in show business. In show business, they, along with African Americans, introduced millions of old-stock, Protestant, middle-class Americans to a set of alternative ways. A familiarity with these ways frequently contributed to a relaxation of the middle class's emphasis on self-control and prepared the groundwork for their adoption of the twentieth century's "modern" ways. Likewise, the new Americans, along with African Americans, helped to foment a rebellion against Victorian art and literature. In the twentieth century, both the blacks and the new Americans became major contributors to the development of the nation's "modern" high culture.

BLACKS, WHITES, AND THE PROMISE OF A NEW SOUTH

As with immigrants, when Henry Seidel Canby composed his memoirs of his boyhood in Wilmington, Delaware, in the 1890s, he easily located the position of African Americans on the nation's social and cultural spectrum. African Americans were on the fringe; they were social and cultural outsiders. Regardless of their educational attainments, wealth, religious persuasion, or place of residence, skin pigmentation automatically excluded them from becoming full-scale participants in the dominant culture.

Locating the position of white southerners posed a more difficult problem for Canby and for others. In some respects white southerners seemed even more Victorian than middle-class Protestant northerners. The South was, after all, "the habitat of the quintessential WASP [white Anglo-Saxon Protestant]," Professor George B. Tindall told the Southern Historical Convention in 1973. "Is it not, in fact," he rhetorically asked, "the biggest single WASP nest this side of the Atlantic?" The great multitude of immigrants who arrived in the nineteenth and early twentieth centuries deliberately bypassed the South. Hence, the southern white population remained overwhelmingly English, Welsh, Scots, and Scots-Irish in its ethnic origins. Neither did any other region of the country approximate the South's loyalty to and enthusiasm for evangelical Protestantism. Nothing was more central to both white and black southern ways than the "old time religion," a faith based upon a literal reading of the Bible and belief in the experience of a spiritual rebirth (the conversion experience). With respect to ethnicity and religion, then, the white South qualified for full membership in the dominant Victorian culture.

Yet southern ways were not identical with those of the Northern middle class. In the South, the ways of traditional hierarchy lingered on with far more force than they did in the North. Despite the enthusiasm and broad claims made on behalf of the achievements of a new, industrial South in the late nineteenth and early twentieth centuries, the full impact of the Industrial Revolution, with its large cities and sprawling middle class, failed to reach the region until the middle decades of the twentieth century. In the South, "there is in substance no middle class," said a Republican Congressman with only slight exaggeration in the 1850s. "Great wealth and hopeless poverty is the settled condition [of the region]." The long-term absence of a substantial middle class precluded the possibility of the South replicating northern ways. So did race. Unlike the North, the South was a manifestly biracial society. "Southern whites cannot walk, talk, sing, conceive of laws or justice, think of sex, love, the family or freedom without responding to the presence of Negroes," explained black novelist Ralph Ellison in 1964.

The Ways of the Newly Freed People

The Civil War and Reconstruction (1861–77) seemed to present unprecedented opportunities for radically altering southern ways. Initially, President Abraham Lincoln limited northern war aims to the restoration of the Union. But, as the war dragged on, pressures mounted for broadening the conflict's objectives. One pressure arose from African Americans; they refused to act like slaves and called the attention of northern whites to the war's revolutionary potential. The other pressure arose from northern whites, many of whom eventually came to see the war as a splendid opportunity for remaking the South in the image of the North.

The Radical Republicans, as the northern reformers were dubbed, embraced a set of divergent, but overlapping goals. As products of the antebellum abolitionist crusade, some Radicals wanted to create a far more egalitarian society, one in which skin color would count for nothing. Others cared little or nothing for the fate of blacks but hated the haughty southern white "aristocracy." Despite their differences, the Radicals eventually settled on one principal goal—the extension of equal political and civil rights to African Americans.

Given the racial attitudes of the day, this was no small step. The Thirteenth through the Fifteenth Amendments to the Constitution freed blacks from slavery, made them United States citizens, and extended suffrage to black males. The second clause of the Fourteenth Amendment prohibited the individual states from depriving any citizen of his or her rights and privileges without due process of law. This clause eventually served as the text for a far-reaching body of rights, such as the 1954 Supreme Court decision that ended the racial segregation of the nation's schools.

But Congress rejected the more extreme proposals of the Radicals. While blacks were in principle to enjoy all of the same rights as white citizens of the United States, in the end the national government was unable or unwilling to establish effective tools for securing this lofty ideal. In particular, the government failed to provide the newly freed people with the economic strength required to realize fully their rights as citizens. There was no large-scale confiscation and redistribution of southern lands, no massive federal financial assistance to the ex-slaves, nor were there provisions for extended federal protection of the freed people in the ex-Confederate states. In short, there was nothing comparable to a Marshall Plan (America's economic assistance program for Europe after World War II) for the South. A rumor spread across the South that every former slave family would receive forty acres and a mule, but nothing came of the idea. Even though white southerners had engaged in treason during the war, northerners were reluctant to take away their property (other than their property in slaves). They considered private property to be an inviolable right.

The congressional majority apparently agreed with the self-help philosophy of black leader Frederick Douglass, who in 1862 had said: "Let them [the freed people] alone. Our duty is done better by not hindering than by helping our fellow man." He added that "the best way to help them is just to let them help themselves." Equal legal rights and the right to compete unimpeded in the marketplace—these, the Radicals concluded, were enough aid to the newly freed slaves. With these rights, they thought, the freed people had the same opportunities as ordinary white families in the North. Applying the white middle-class formula of success to the newly freed blacks, they reasoned that by practicing hard work, individual initiative, and frugality the ex-slaves too could achieve economic self-sufficiency.

Realizing such an idyllic scenario turned out to be far more difficult than the northern Radicals had presumed. Apart from confronting pervasive racial prejudice and discrimination, the propertyless freed people possessed only one economic resource—their labor. Whites owned nearly all of the land, the draft animals, and the tools needed for survival. Despite these handicaps, about one-fifth of the freed families eventually obtained land of their own. But the overwhelming majority of the remainder became sharecroppers, a system that until the middle of the twentieth century came to dominate the southern countryside for both poor whites and blacks. While rarely able to improve their living standards above the subsistence level, by eliminating hated white overseers, detailed white supervision, and gang labor, the black families did enjoy in the sharecropping system more personal autonomy than they had had during slavery.

Blacks quickly seized upon their new opportunities for political participation. While underrepresented as elected officials (in terms of their proportion of the total population), during the last half of the nineteenth century hundreds of former slaves won election to public offices. Eighteen even obtained seats in the United States Congress. On the state level, blacks and their white allies (contemptuously referred to by their opponents as carpetbaggers and scalawags) established public school systems where none had existed before, drew up more humanitarian legal codes, and passed a body of civil rights legislation.

Blacks sought to make the most of their new freedom in other respects. They at once set about distancing themselves as much as they could from older forms of coercion and personal dependency. Insisting that their families should no longer act like slaves, they moved out of the former slave quarters and pulled their wives and children out of the fields. Anchored in the ways that had sustained them during slavery, the newly emancipated slaves quickly began rebuilding their own black communities. At the center of the new communities was the family. Once the war had ended in 1865, separated husbands, wives, parents, and children rushed to seek each other out and to restore severed relationships. Thousands of former slaves reaffirmed their commitments to their families by insisting on official wedding ceremonies. That black parents everywhere enthusiastically embraced opportunities for their children to learn how to read and write reflected an equal dedication to family welfare.

An African Methodist Episcopal Church in the South. Simple structures, such as this one built in the late nineteenth century, served as churches for the newly freed African American people. Along with families, churches were key institutions in perpetuating a distinctively African American culture.

Even more than in the past, religion provided a key pillar of black communities. Everywhere across the South newly freed blacks seceded from white churches and formed their own churches with their own ministers. While sharing with white evangelicals an emphasis on spiritual rebirth, black Methodist and Baptist ministers made Christianity into a religion of liberation. No themes for sermons and Sunday school lessons were more popular than Moses leading his oppressed people out of the land of bondage and of Jesus promising relief from earthly burdens. Congregational participation in worship services included exuberant expressions of religious feelings. Congregations shouted responses to calls by their preachers, they clapped their hands, and swayed in unison as they sang moving spirituals.

PRESERVING AND CONSTRUCTING A
SOUTHERN CULTURAL IDENTITY

Despite Reconstruction and the efforts of freed blacks to invent and perpetuate new ways, within three decades after the Civil War most blacks and perhaps many whites must have wondered if southern ways had changed very much. The much vaunted New South, which promised to bring industry, rapid economic growth, and a large middle class to the region, never achieved anything approximating full realization. True, by 1900 the South could boast of significant growth in railroad mileage, iron and steel production, timber and tobacco processing, and in textile manufacturing, but still the growth of the South's economy lagged far behind the North's. Indeed, in terms of per capita income, the region fell even further behind the North.

Neither did the destruction of slavery and plantation agriculture bring down the region's hierarchical social order. By controlling a highly disproportionate share of the South's farmlands, the families of the pre–Civil War planters retained most of their traditional economic power. In the meantime, the conditions of the yeoman white farmers deteriorated. Faced with falling cotton prices, some 80 percent of them lost their land in the postwar era.

Aiding and abetting the white South's resistance to cultural change was the invention and perpetuation of powerful myths. One was that of the Old South. In the minds of white southerners, the pre–Civil War plantation South became everything the industrial North was not. Rather than a region of smokestacks, crowded tenements, and screeching machinery, in the imaginations of both northerners and southerners the romanticized Old South evoked images of gallant gentlemen, refined ladies, contented slaves, moonlight, mint juleps, and magnolias. The Old South possessed a way of life that was less material, less hurried, and richer in the possibilities of sensual fulfillment than that of the North.

A second myth was that of the Lost Cause. It told of how brave Confederate soldiers had defended a noble way of life—the Old South—against the rapacious Yankees. Following the leadership of the United Confederate Veterans and the United Daughters of the Confederacy, between about the 1880s and the 1920s, towns across the South erected literally hundreds of monuments with statues of solitary but ever vigilant Confederate soldiers always peering northward. While southern Protestantism was sparse on iconography, the myth of the Lost Cause was another matter. It became in the words of historian Charles Reagan Wilson "a civil religion." White southerners transformed Robert E. Lee, Jefferson Davis, and other wartime heroes into saints and martyrs. For generations, Decoration Day was a special time of regional unity. Decoration Day brought out thousands of people who carried spring flowers to the graves of those who had been killed decades earlier.

Religion also bolstered the South's cultural identity. While northern Protestants were relaxing their insistence on the need for dramatic conversion experiences and on biblical literalism, southern Protestants remained loyal to their evangelical roots. "The South is by a long way the most simply and sincerely religious country that I ever was in," wrote Sir William Archer, an English visitor in 1910. For southerners, he added, "God is very real and personal." Indeed, he was. Religious faith and language extended everywhere; it permeated public discourse, courtship, child rearing, and social relationships. In the twentieth century, the South's striking degree of religiosity led to the region being dubbed America's "Bible Belt."

Likewise, sports and special forms of music promoted southern unity and identity. Having had a long tradition of physical display and aggressive competition, southerners eagerly embraced the rapid growth of organized sports in the post–Civil War era. Baseball came first. By the 1890s, every town of any consequence had one or more teams. The adoption of yet another northern game—football—by southern colleges and universities became an even more effective vehicle for the reassertion of state and regional pride. Teams adopted the colors of the Confederacy; they sought the imprimaturs of legendary figures from the region's past and symbolic regional victories through football victories over northern foes. Discontented people from both races helped to make the South what historian Edward L. Ayers has aptly described as "the crucible for the blues, jazz, and country music." Through a complex process of adaptation and invention, a set of young southern musicians, who began to come of age in the 1880s and 1890s, created a distinctive culture of regional music. In time, the influence of this culture would extend throughout the world.

THE NEW RACIAL SETTLEMENT

In the meantime, race relations worsened. Even as late as the early 1890s, blacks had continued in many places to vote and hold public office and to mingle with whites in public places, but by then the possibility of a racially integrated society was rapidly fading away. Acting on resentments arising from the South's declining rural economy, from black assertiveness, and from stories heard in childhood of the heroism and nobility of their fathers and brothers in the Civil War, a new generation of southern whites escalated the level of rhetoric and violence against blacks. Between 1892 and 1903, an orgy of violence swept across the South; during these years the lynching of African

Americans averaged more than 150 per year. In particular, any behavior interpreted as a sexual overture by black men to white women brought down the full wrath of white society. Retaliation by mutilation (including castration) and the killing of blacks not only aided white men in "keeping blacks in their places," but apparently reassured them of their "superior" status and in their own sense of manhood and honor.

During the same era, law became an important tool for ensuring white supremacy. By passing an ingenious battery of laws requiring voters to pay poll taxes, be literate, interpret state constitutions correctly, and have grandfathers who had been eligible to vote, by 1905 southern white lawmakers effectively denied blacks the right to vote throughout most of the South. Southern white lawmakers also set about legalizing segregation (the physical separation of blacks and whites in public facilities of all kinds), which the U.S. Supreme Court officially sanctioned in *Plessy* v. *Ferguson* (1896). As long as the facilities provided to each race were equal in quality, the court said, segregation did not violate the equal protection clause of the Fourteenth Amendment. While in fact facilities were rarely equal, expectations of futility, expense, and physical violence dissuaded blacks from challenging the application of segregation statutes.

The *Plessy* decision reflected the North's acceptance of the South's new racial settlement. By the turn of the century, white northerners no longer resisted the white South's imposition of open segregation, its implicit violations of the Fourteenth and Fifteenth Amendments, or to its reign of terror against African Americans. Indeed, the great majority of white northerners shared white southern beliefs in black inferiority. Everywhere in the nation the media and the entertainment industries stereotyped African Americans. The popular theater of the day, for example, featured white men in blackface poking fun at blacks for their laziness, their stupidity, and their physical appearance. Even more ominously, D. W. Griffith in his popular film *Birth of a Nation* (1915) depicted blacks as dangerous savages. The application of Darwinian ideas to the evolution of races added a supposedly scientific note to the prevailing white racism. Racists argued that peoples with the highest material cultures, namely whites, had succeeded best in the racial "struggle for survival." Such views became part of the conventional wisdom of white social scientists and lent support to the treatment of African Americans as second-class citizens until as late as the 1940s and 1950s.

Mirroring the new racism, the position of African Americans in the North slipped downward as well. While none of the northern states followed the southern example of disfranchising blacks, both silent and overt segregation and discrimination increased in the North. Antidiscrimination laws adopted by the northern states in the wake of the Civil War went unenforced. Everywhere African Americans were denied opportunities for better jobs and invariably received lower pay than whites. Even as late as 1950, the median family income for blacks was about half that of whites. Excluded by income and color from living where they pleased, most of northern and southern urban blacks increasingly squeezed into crowded ghettos.

Despite the odds arrayed against them, urban blacks were able to build some community structures. A sense of community arose in part from sports, the services provided by black professionals, newspapers, and small businesses, and, above all, from churches. Based on professions, skills, and businesses that served mainly black customers, as early as the 1880s a tiny but significant black middle class began to take shape in the major cities of both the South and the North. As with middle-class whites, the black middle class formed fraternal lodges, temperance societies, churches, and business organizations. Middle-class black women's clubs also paralleled white organizations. As with white middle-class Victorian culture, the black middle class strove to promote self-control in themselves and their children. They also saw the home as a refuge from the outside world and sought to distinguish themselves by their refinement and their support of high culture. Yet, no matter how much their ways resembled those of middle-class whites, the two groups were separated by the seemingly unbridgeable chasm of race.

CONCLUSION

During the nineteenth and early twentieth centuries, sharp social and cultural boundaries divided the American people. None was sharper nor more difficult to cross than that of race. Religious and ethnic boundaries were almost equally clear. The Irish and the Italians "meant nothing to us," recalled Henry Seidel Canby of his middle-class family in upstate Delaware, "they were only population." Besides, they were Catholics, "which put them still further outside our world." Between Canby's family and the South was yet another dividing line. "To the southward," he said, was "an alien state."

As Canby recognized, each of the outsider or minority groups sought in varying degrees to establish and perpetuate identities of their own. While family, leisure, and work ways frequently served to promote distinctive identities, no institution was more important to the outsiders than their churches. Each of the groups found in their respective religions a reservoir of strength. In addition, simply being outsiders served to bolster distinctive identities; perceptions or experiences of prejudice and discrimination drove countless Native Americans, African Americans, and immigrants to retreat into the security and warmth of their own groups. Finally, the Civil War and Reconstruction and the insecurities arising from the presence of a large black population in their midst encouraged white southerners to cling to and promote a separate regional identity.

IV

MODERN WAYS, 1890–PRESENT

8

THE ORIGINS OF MODERN WAYS

The origins of distinctively modern ways—the ways with which we are familiar today—can be traced back to the era between the 1880s and the 1930s. In this age, evidence of a general retreat from the all-important middle-class concern with self-control was unmistakable. Even earlier (as we observed in the previous chapter), Native Americans, African Americans, and a fast-growing working class had perpetuated alternative cultures that seemed from the perspective of the middle class to place too little emphasis on restraining the self. Modern ways not only borrowed from the ways of these outsiders but also from a new, more assertive class of the spectacularly rich. The families of the nouveau riche frequently took their behavioral cues from the freer ways of the European aristocracy. Still more distressing to the custodians of traditional middle-class culture was the discovery of discontent within its own ranks. Frequently less evangelical, more impatient with the demands for self-control, and increasingly dissatisfied with the tepidity of their day-to-day existence, a new generation of the middle class hungered for more personal freedom, for additional excitement, and for greater self-fulfillment.

Expressions of the new hunger took many forms. A rage for competitive athletics, for adventurism in foreign affairs, for the outdoors, for amusement parks, for the movies, for more energetic music, and for dancing—these and other forms of release and excitement swept across the nation. And who could resist the new, mass-produced consumer goods? Great department stores, chain stores, and mail-order houses offered consumers a previously unimaginable cornucopia of consumer delights. Finally, a more liberal Protestantism, new social thought, and daring departures from traditional forms in art and literature—all of these and more reflected growing fissures in the foundations of middle-class culture and morality. By the 1920s signs of the arrival of modern ways were everywhere.

FROM PRODUCTION TO CONSUMPTION

No sign of the coming of modern culture was more important than a shifting emphasis of the nation's economy from production to consumption. In the nineteenth century, the main task of the economy had been the production of more and more goods. Self-control and the middle-class ethos of hard-work, frugality, and civic responsibility had been well-suited for a production-oriented society of small entrepreneurs. But in the world of twentieth-century corporate capitalism, mass consumption became equally important to the success of the nation's economy.

Consumption raised to the fore a new dream of the good life. For count-less Americans, including the expanded middle class, the new vision sup-plemented or pushed aside earlier dreams of a Christian City on a Hill, a republic of virtue, a Kingdom of God on Earth, or a nation tied together by a common culture devoted to refinement and a shared respect for great litera-ture and great art. The new vision centered on personal pleasure, comfort, material well-being, buying and selling, and was associated with the cult of the new, with youth, and with money as the measure of all things. No longer was freedom restricted to the workplace and to the polling booth; for millions it meant the right to buy things. "Every free-born American," said advertising executive Kenneth Goode, has a "right to name his own neces-sities." Unlike opportunities in the arenas of work and politics, consumer freedom was equally available to women. The "woman of today," declared a Piggly Wiggly supermarket ad, was "free to choose" from a multitude of products. The new culture as Herbert Duce, a merchant, candidly confessed in 1912, "does not say, 'Pray, obey, sacrifice thyself, respect the King, fear thy master.'" Instead, "it whispers, 'Amuse thyself, take care of thyself.'" It was this culture, a culture revolving around consumption, that the peoples the world over came to see as the very essence of American life.

AN ECONOMY OF MASS PRODUCTION

At bottom, the new culture of consumption rested on the economy's capacity to mass-produce goods. In the eighteenth century, nearly every product found in American households was either made in the home or by skilled craftsmen outside the home. The revolution in manufacturing in the nine-teenth and twentieth centuries substituted mass-manufactured products for custom-made goods. By the end of the nineteenth century, millions of boys and men dressed in "ready-to-wear" garments rather than clothes made in the home or by high-priced tailors. Similar shifts occurred in the food that people ate and in home furnishings. The necessities of life were not the only mass-manufactured items. The number of pianos sold in the United States, for example, jumped from 32,000 in 1890 to 374,000 in 1904.

No single product epitomized the significance of mass-manufacturing more than the automobile. Initially a luxury item available only to the few or the foolish, by the end of the 1920s the car had become virtually a family ne-cessity. By then, one car existed for each five Americans; with a little crowd-ing, the entire population of the country could have been rolling down the highway at the same time. By introducing an assembly line and other efficien-cies in production, Henry Ford slashed the price of his Model T, or Tin Lizzie, as it was affectionately nicknamed by its owners, from $600 in 1912 to $290 by 1924. With the cost equaling only three months of a typical worker's wage, a new Model T was now within the financial reach of millions of ordinary Americans. "Why on earth do you need to study what's changing this country?" a Muncie, Indiana, resident asked the sociologist team of Robert and Helen Lynd in the 1920s. "I can tell you what's happening in just four letters: A-U-T-O." The car opened up new realms of experience to millions whose lives had earlier been restricted to home, neighborhood, and workplace.

The merchandising of mass-manufactured goods underwent a similar revolution. Department stores (so named because they displayed their goods in separate sections or departments) led the way in both the marketing of the nation's industrial largesse and in altering public attitudes toward consumption. In the final decades of the nineteenth century, innovative entrepreneurs such as Marshall Field in Chicago, John Wanamaker in Philadelphia, and Rowland Macey in New York City built department stores into major urban

Mannequins Displaying the Latest Parisian Fashions. Along with new strategies in advertising, lavish, brilliantly lit department stores, such as Marshall Field's in Chicago, led the way in altering public attitudes toward consumption. Consumption raised to the fore a new dream of what the nation might become. It frequently pushed aside or replaced such earlier visions as a Puritan city on a hill, a republic of virtue, a Kingdom of God on earth, or a common culture built on the cultivation of the beaux arts.

institutions. While department stores sold goods mainly to the middle and upper classes in the big cities, chain stores such as F. W. Woolworth and A & P supplied mass-produced goods to the urban working class and the residents of smaller cities. In the meantime, mail-order houses opened up the horizons of consumption to rural and small town Americans. The encyclopedic catalogs of the Sears & Roebuck company not only offered an amazing array of consumer goods, but they educated their readers on up-to-date fashions as well.

Churches, governments at all levels, and colleges—these and other institutions eventually rallied behind the new order of consumption. In earlier times, independent colleges of commerce had been mainly concerned with how to make rather than how to market goods. But by the turn of the century marketing had become central to the mission of the new business colleges that were rapidly becoming an integral component of the nation's burgeoning university system. While governments during the Progressive era sometimes sought to curb and control the growth of corporate capitalism, in the 1920s the Department of Commerce under the direction of Herbert Hoover freely used federal power to aid corporations in promoting the expansion of the consumer revolution. Except for a tiny minority, church leaders too eventually came to terms with the ethical and spiritual issues raised by consumption. Mostly they sided with America's new, more commercially oriented society.

STRATEGIES OF ENTICEMENT

The marketers of the mass-manufactured goods soon recognized that success required much more than controlling prices and costs. Potential buyers had to be persuaded that they now needed products that they had not earlier realized they needed. "Competitive commerce," wrote the Reverend Walter Rauschenbusch, a critic of the consumer revolution, "spreads things before us and beseeches and persuades us to buy what we do not want. Men try to break down [our] self-restraint . . . and reduce us to the moral habits of savages who gorge today and fast tomorrow."

The main strategy for breaking down self-restraint and enticing buyers to purchase products that they did not previously want was to associate the acquisition and consumption of goods with much more than simply utility or rational needs. The marketers sought to convince potential buyers that the ownership of their goods would bring enhanced personal pleasures, introduce greater excitement into otherwise drab lives, and provide effective therapy for a vast range of personal anxieties.

The history of advertising illustrates the new strategies of enticement. While earlier advertisements had frequently consisted of little more than an announcement in a newspaper of the availability of a product, patent medicine vendors pioneered in the creation of ads designed to grab the attention of their readers with striking visuals and sweeping claims for their products. The new ads pointed away from the presentation of sober information;

instead they addressed the nonrational fears and yearnings of potential buyers. For example, an ad in the 1920s for a new Ford depicted a couple with a
child walking through a tree-shrouded suburban neighborhood. Gesturing
toward the street filled with gleaming Fords, the wife plaintively says to her
husband: "EVERYONE OWNS A CAR BUT US." According to the ad, ownership of a new car would "add much to the happiness of your family,"
"bring more glorious pleasure into your life," and "increase your chances of
success."

In order to associate the buying of their goods with excitement, exotic
dreams, and the solution of personal problems, retailers transformed the appearance of their stores. Shoppers in the mammoth department stores found
not only artfully displayed goods but also stained-glass skylights, spiraling
marble staircases, brilliant chandeliers, rich walnut paneling, and plush carpets. The management of visual space on behalf of selling goods reached its
apogee in large glass display windows where onlookers could see vivid en-
sembles of goods drenched in color and light. By 1920 merchants even began
to display women's underwear on full-bodied mannequins, an act that would
certainly have shocked middle-class sensibilities a decade earlier. No proper
Victorian would have been surprised to learn that a character in novelist John
Dos Passos's novel 1919 became "terribly agitated" by seeing "girls' underwear in store windows."

Retailers recognized that they could increase the attractiveness of their
goods by associating them with fashion. Well before the advent of modern
advertising and the modern department store, tasteful consumption had
served as a cultural marker of the middle class, but in the new age merchants seized upon the opportunities and anxieties arising from the fluidity
of American class boundaries to present their goods as the embodiments of
the latest Parisian fashions. By the 1920s department stores staged great fashion pageants, complete with live models, orchestras, and theatrical performances. "Fashion," said a retailer in 1908, "imparts to merchandise a value
over and above its intrinsic worth." By purchasing fashionable products, the
merchants promised, one could feel special, escape the humdrum of everyday life, and at least temporarily set aside fears of being an outsider.

Strategies of enticement included other kinds of spectacle. In order to pub-
licize the introduction of electric lighting in the commercial districts and to
invite people to shop at night, in the 1920s businessmen across the country
began organizing dazzling color and light shows. Merchants also seized
upon the 1920s mania for public parades. Huge Thanksgiving Day parades
sponsored by department stores like Macy's in New York and Hudson's
in Detroit ushered in each year's frenzied Christmas retail season. Perhaps
nothing was more emblematic of the centrality of consumption to the birth of
modern ways than Times Square in downtown New York City. By 1929, the
New York City police estimated that every night nearly five hundred thousand people passed in and out of Times Square. Partly they came to patron-
ize the theaters, movie palaces, restaurants, hotels, and retail stores that were
clustered there. But they came also to see the bright lights; Times Square was,

as one observer put it, "America's Mecca of Light and Color." There, signs—signs that far surpassed the sheer size and intensity of light and color of those in Paris, Berlin, and London—blinked, jumped, and flashed their messages. They all urged Americans to buy, and then to buy some more.

A New Middle Class

No group participated with more enthusiasm in the new consumer-centered economy than a rapidly expanding middle class. The first, or original middle class, which took shape between the 1830s and the 1860s, consisted mainly of shopkeepers, artisans, professional men, successful farmers, and the owners and operators of small factories and retail establishments. Apart from occupation and income, a special moral discipline, one that stemmed mainly from a strong and unquestioning religious faith, distinguished the original middle class from the "dissolute" workingmen from below and the "profligate" rich from above. It had been this class, with its emphasis on evangelical religion, self-control, the family, refinement, and respectability, that had established the supremacy of Victorian culture.

With the rapid growth in corporate capitalism, virtually a new, or second, middle class formed alongside the older class. The new class came mostly from an explosive expansion of the white-collar workforce. Between 1870 and 1930, the number of doctors, lawyers, accountants, architects, engineers, and teachers more than quadrupled while at the same time the number of middle managers, salespeople, and secretaries grew nearly twice as fast as the workforce as a whole.

Nothing set apart the white-collar workers from their neighbors more than their possession of unique skills and specialized knowledge. In the early nineteenth century, the widespread hostility toward hierarchy and privilege, the demands for equality of opportunity, and the pell-mell economic expansion had greatly weakened the traditional entrance requirements into the professions. However, all this began to change at the end of the nineteenth and in the first decades of the twentieth century. To protect their exclusivity, their privileges, and their prestige, each of the professions set up new and far stiffer entry requirements. For instance, the American Medical Association demanded that would-be physicians obtain specialized training and pass a battery of examinations before they could legally practice medicine. Everywhere state and local governments cooperated in the process of making doctors their own professional gatekeepers. Rather than simply mastering the three R's, even teachers of the primary grades eventually had to obtain a college degree and complete a prescribed set of pedagogical courses.

Whether employed as middle managers in corporate bureaucracies, physicians, or educators, the white-collar workers shared an enthusiasm for rationality or what they frequently called "science." Rather than in terms of developing the personal "Character" so important to Victorians (as Robert Wiebe has observed), the new middle class justified itself in terms of acquiring specialized "Knowledge." In the early twentieth century, "scientific management," a movement whose very name evoked the new orientation of the corporate world, swept through the ranks of the middle managers. Rather than as a grand design or an enterprise seeking to discover the ultimate laws of nature, science in their view was nearly always synonymous with a particular method or procedure. Facts became their stock-in-trade; they irrevocably bound themselves to facts about customers, suppliers, markets, trends, timetables, interest rates, and profit margins. Facts in the form of statistics especially intrigued them. The reduction of complex data into numbers, they reasoned, increased the reliability and objectivity of their conclusions.

Their education, their training, and their occupational world—all of these tended to loosen white-collar ties to tradition and to a particular place. While rarely rejecting religion outright, the new class frequently insisted on a less evangelical and more liberal Protestantism. Rather than resting on a national consensus of religiously anchored moral values, the moral values of the new class tended to reflect a conformity with the requirements and expectations of their occupational world.

Away from their workplaces, the new class relaxed the traditional bourgeois emphasis on self-control. Especially in their free time, they were far more likely than the older class to embrace new, more expressive forms of

Bungalow, Lincoln, Nebraska, Built about 1910. The low-slung, one-story or one-and-a-half story bungalows usually featured a generous front porch and a living room but no parlor. Rather than as a statement of the owner's material success or class standing, the house was designed for the comfort of its middle-class occupants. Compare this home with the Victorian mansion on page 144.

individualism. The new individualism frequently entailed the patronization of commercial entertainment, bringing more informality and spontaneity into one's life, and opening one's self up to more intense feelings. Even middle-class housing reflected a noticeable retreat from Victorian formality and restraint. The soaring gothic houses of an earlier era, with their wide verandas, parlors, and hallways, had been built as monuments to individual achievement. But, by the outbreak of World War I, these elaborate structures had given way in popularity to far simpler houses—to bungalow and colonial revival styles—designed mainly for family comfort and enjoyment. In the place of formal parlors and grand entrance halls came the living room, a room intended for a more informal style of family life.

THE QUEST FOR EXCITEMENT

At the turn of the century, middle-class Americans, especially those living in larger cities and those employed in white-collar bureaucracies, began to undo more than their earlier self-imposed constraints on consumption. In the past, suspicion had surrounded those experiences that elicited strong feelings. Too much excitement and the release of feelings might not only jeopardize one's chances for material success, members of the middle class reasoned, but such experiences also placed in harm's way the nation's entire social order. Thus the middle class expressly condemned drinking, loud talking, extravagant gesturing, wagering, prizefighting, and exhibitions of personal affection.

While concern with self-control remained a central component of middle-class life in the late Victorian age (from the 1880s to World War I), an opposing impulse also began to push its way to the forefront with greater and greater force in all aspects of middle- and upper-class life. Frequently a close ally of the consumer revolution, this second impulse took the form of a widespread quest for more intense experiences. It found outlets or expression in support for commercial leisure and in what Theodore Roosevelt labeled as "the strenuous life." It not only began to effect a revolution in leisure ways but gender ways as well.

THE GROWTH OF COMMERCIAL ENTERTAINMENT

In the past, the middle class had approved only of "rational recreation," those leisure endeavors that remained within the parameters of respectability and that reinvigorated the mind and the body for work and civic duties. Leisure should be mostly confined to the private sphere of the family, to close friends, and to solitary activity. In the security of their homes, middle-class families enjoyed the increasing availability of inexpensive books, newspapers, periodicals, sheet music, pianos, and more exotic foods while avoiding the rowdiness of commercialized public recreation. Consistent with the idea of the home as a moral training ground and as a special emotional refuge, women were expected to be the main providers of middle-class leisure.

Outside the home, middle-class men and women created respectable semi-public or public arenas of spare-time activities. These included fraternal groups for men, church societies for women, and temperance organizations for both sexes. As early as the 1840s, middle-class reformers had also begun to endorse public parks as retreats in which urban residents could escape the ills of the cities and be rejuvenated by the powers of nature. In 1856, New York City employed Frederick Law Olmstead to design Central Park. The rage for city parks then took off. By 1920, nearly every city of any consequence in the nation sported a network of parks.

Slowly in the late nineteenth century and then far more quickly as the twentieth century advanced, middle-class restraints on participation in commercialized leisure also relaxed. Part of the relaxation stemmed from the examples furnished by those from both below and above. Below the middle class, the burgeoning working class (in particular the recent arrivals from Europe) and African Americans exhibited a more physically expressive life than did the middle class. From above, the wealthy, especially the parvenu, likewise flaunted traditional middle-class strictures on feelings and leisure. In their private clubs and summer resorts the wealthy shed lingering suspicions of play-for-play's-sake. The Grafton Country Club of Worcester, Massachusetts, for instance, even adopted as its motto "Each to His Pleasure," a direct rebuke of the middle-class work ethic.

A turning point in the history of middle-class leisure came in the 1880s and 1890s when entrepreneurs of entertainment launched a widespread campaign to woo larger audiences. Since by the standards of the day the presence of substantial numbers of women automatically made an audience respectable, the entertainment entrepreneurs made a special effort to attract middle-class women to their venues. Fortunately for them, such marketing strategies coincided with impulses by growing numbers of women at the turn of the century to free themselves from the more constrictive forms of Victorianism. In particular, dance halls and amusement parks appealed to single working women; at these places, secretaries and other female white-collar workers could experiment with new forms of propriety away from the watchful eyes of their parents.

A series of world fairs or expositions—in Chicago (1893), Atlanta (1895), Nashville (1897), Omaha (1898), Buffalo (1901), and St. Louis (1904)—introduced millions of middle-class women and men to the new world of commercial amusements for the first time. Visitors to these expositions encountered two sharply opposing districts. In one district, the fair's managers featured high culture; they built an ideal, orderly world that included monumental, usually classical, architecture as well as exhibitions of modern science and technology. In the other district, the Midway, entertainment and spectacle ruled supreme. Here, visitors could find garish signs and posters, overdecorated buildings, roller coaster rides, and stage shows of singers, dancers, comics, and acrobats. To make suspicious visitors feel more comfortable, observed historian David Nasaw, "the concessionaires cloaked their amuse-ments in educational disguise." For example, they billed the performances of gyrating belly dancers as "authentic foreign" dances and women in tights or in skin-tight bathing suits as acrobats or championship swimmers. Across the country, similar strategies employed by local fairs and traveling cir-cuses helped to break down the middle class's resistance to commercial amusements.

The entrepreneurs of entertainment won a series of smashing victories. By cleansing itself of profanity, smoking, alcohol, and prostitution, vaudeville—while continuing to feature a mix of rowdy singers, jugglers, acrobats, magi-cians, animal acts, and comics—entered a new age of prosperity and accept-ability. "Ladies and Children can [now] safely attend without an escort," claimed Tony Pastor, a former choirboy and a pioneer in courting the pa-tronage of middle-class women who had long been taught to shun the stage and its fruits as the devil's work. "No drink stronger than ice water" would be sold at the shows, boasted Pastor.

While most members of the middle class continued to avoid the tradi-tional saloon (still patronized mainly by the working class), as early as the 1890s in the larger cities restaurant owners began to open cabarets and night-clubs atop hotels and near theater districts. Because dining was the stated function of these establishments, middle-class men and women felt more comfortable about listening to live music, watching professional dancers, or dancing themselves. The cabaret, concluded Lewis Erenberg in his study of New York City nightlife, "relaxed boundaries between the sexes, between au-diences and performers, between ethnic groups and Protestants, between black culture and whites." In the 1910s, a dance hall craze swept the country. People danced in new, more provocative ways. The Turkey Trot, the Bunny Hug, the Grizzly Bear, and the more lasting Fox Trot (all animal names sug-gestive of more sensuality and less self-restraint in dancing) increasingly re-placed the more stately waltz. Lavish ballrooms, live music, and usually the absence of alcohol at least partly reassured those middle-class patrons con-cerned about the abandonment of personal control.

Near the turn of the century, every large city in the country hosted at least one outdoor amusement park, complete with band pavilions, circus acts, and mechanical contrivances such as Ferris wheels, all located in exotic settings. "Coney Island has a code of conduct which is all her own," Guy Carryl ex-plained in 1901. While at amusement parks, patrons felt more comfortable in suspending at least some of their middle-class proprieties. Unlike the gender-segregated leisure of the nineteenth century, the younger members of both sexes and all classes came together at amusement parks where they cavorted, laughed merrily, talked loudly, and embraced one another openly.

A freer spirit also invaded popular music. Until late in the nineteenth cen-tury, hymns as well as nostalgic and mournful songs that were frequently drenched in sentimentality and moral uplift characterized popular music. Then, in the so-called Gay Nineties, far more cheerful, energetic, and even sensually suggestive tunes spread through the midways and the burgeoning

Midland Beach, Staten Island, 1898. This beach scene suggests a modest retreat from the all-important middle-class concern with self-control. At the beach, as at amusement parks, vaudeville, and later at the movies, the sexes and social classes mingled together indiscriminately. In the twentieth century, leisure increasingly became something to be indulged in for its own sake.

sheet music industry. The lively marches of John Philip Sousa became a national rage. While roundly condemned by its opponents as black brothel music, the lusty exuberance of ragtime seemed to allow millions of white Americans to imagine that they too could enjoy the freedom from restraints which they attributed to African Americans. Ragtime's "primitive rhythms . . . excite the basic human instincts," concluded a critic of the new music. To the proponents of music as an instrument for promoting self-control and as a source of moral uplift, the arrival of jazz among white audiences in the 1920s was even more startling and dangerous. The emotional release triggered by jazz, according to a critic, led to a "blatant disregard of even the elementary rules of civilization."

In the end, no new form of commercial entertainment equaled the popularity of the movies. While the movies originated in unsavory all-male arcades and cheap working-class nickelodeons, they soon achieved their greatest successes in the huge neoclassical movie palaces of the 1920s. By the end of the decade one hundred million people a week went to the movies, a figure roughly equal to the nation's population. As in the amusement parks, the classes and the sexes (but not usually the races) mixed indiscriminately. Frequently treating moviegoers to a world of lavish homes, fast cars, and equally fast dance steps, films suggested several avenues of escape from Victorian restraints.

Paradoxically, the movies catered to both modern and traditional values. Reeling from criticism of the salacious contents of its films, Hollywood in 1922 set up a censorship office under Will Hays. While Hays permitted sexual suggestiveness and innuendo, he carefully monitored which portions of the female anatomy could be exposed on film and insisted that those guilty of promiscuous sex on film be properly punished. In their conclusions, if not in earlier scenes, Hays mandated that the films had to reaffirm traditional values.

THE STRENUOUS LIFE

During the 1890s and in the first three decades of the twentieth century the impulse of the urban, white-collar-centered middle class to relax its emphasis on decorum and restraint also led in the direction of a more strenuous life. In communing with untamed nature, in more rugged physical activities, and in competitive athletics, growing numbers of Americans saw opportunities not only to enjoy more intense experiences in controlled settings but to improve their health.

No single person incarnated and popularized the principles of the strenuous life more fully than Theodore Roosevelt, the nation's president from 1901 to 1909. Sickly as a youth, Roosevelt took boxing lessons and worked out regularly with dumbbells and horizontal bars for his entire life. In his twenties he left the safety of the East to take up the hazardous life of a cowboy in the Dakotas. With the outbreak of the Spanish-American War in 1898, he organized and led a cavalry unit of cowboys and college students that won national renown for their bravery in Cuba. Preaching to and bullying opponents both at home and abroad, Roosevelt as president enthralled the nation with his vigor. "In life, as in a football game," he once advised the nation's boys, "the principle to follow is: Hit the line hard, don't foul, and don't shirk, but hit the line hard."

Roosevelt's vigor and physicality reflected larger national trends. Musclemen Eugen Sandow and Bernarr MacFadden became national celebrities; MacFadden, a friend of Roosevelt's, declared in the first issue of his magazine, *Physical Culture* (1899), that "Weakness Is a Crime." In the 1890s a bicycling rage swept across the nation; astride their "wheels," men, women, and children experienced a new sense of physical freedom as they pedaled away from the confines of their homes through the city streets and into the countryside. In the summers, growing numbers of middle-class Americans fled to the seasides and to the mountain resorts. Those seeking more physically demanding vacations hiked, canoed, and camped. Nature lovers

embarked on a national campaign to preserve the last of the nation's wilder-
nesses as national parks. Bird-watching became something of a national
mania; in a six-year span Boston and New York publishers sold more than
seventy thousand books on birds. "A bird on the wing," historian John
Higham has speculated, " . . . symbolize[d] for Americans the boundless
space they wished to inhabit."

The middle class began to shed much of its suspicions of commercial
sports. Earlier, "respectable" people had frequently associated baseball with
drinking, gambling, and a loss of self-control, but during the first two decades
of the twentieth century the sport "came of age." Gaining acceptability among
nearly all social groups, baseball truly became America's "National Game."
Even the president of the nation extended his endorsement; in 1910 William
Howard Taft established the precedent of the president's opening each season
by throwing out the first ball. By then, every city, town, and village of any
consequence fielded at least one amateur, semiprofessional, or professional
team. The annual World Series (begun in 1903) between the pennant winners
of the American and National Leagues became an annual fall rite that
finished an exciting conclusion to regular season play.

The growth in the popularity of college football also reflected the larger
quest for excitement. Initially a sport organized and managed by students of
upper-class origins, college football "took off" as a commercial spectacle in
the 1890s. Locked in circulation wars, the daily newspapers devoted a staggering amount of space to the gridiron wars of the nation's colleges. "Thanksgiving day is no longer a solemn festival to God for mercies given," declared
The New York Herald in 1893. "It is a holiday granted by the State and the
Nation to see a game of football." No sport equaled the capacity of college
football in allowing middle-class spectators to express strong emotions
within socially acceptable settings.

The development of an ideology of strenuosity accompanied the growth
of the commercial sporting spectacles. Earlier, only a small band of "muscu-
lar" Christians had had the temerity to suggest that individual and national
strength required as much attention to physical fitness as it did to work and
to the cultivation of spirituality. But by the 1890s certain members of families
of old wealth and a rising corps of experts on the human body were insisting that properly regulated sports and other vigorous forms of physicality
were essential to the nation's well-being. "No amount of commercial prosperity can supply the lack of heroic virtues" that were all too prevalent in
modern America, Theodore Roosevelt said. To counter the "over-civilized"
life, Roosevelt advocated the cultivation of the virtues found in the soldier,
the cowboy, and the prizefighter.

The enthusiasm for strenuosity penetrated deeply into the American psyche. It encouraged an admiration for Civil War generals, for medieval
knights, for Napoleon, and for foreign adventurism. It shaped the contents of
a massive outpouring of boys' literature. Frank Merriwell, the hero of more
than two hundred books written by Gilbert Patten, became a shorthand way
of describing a boy who not only possessed middle-class Protestant virtues

but who could more than hold his own in physical combat and on the field of play. While downplaying class, ethnic, and racial identities, strenuous activities offered fraternal bonding experiences for men and boys.

The ideology of strenuosity was a core ingredient in a mammoth set of programs designed to manage the spare-time activities of the nation's adolescent boys. In the 1890–1920 era the Young Men's Christian Association, urban churches, public schools, city playground associations, and the Boy Scouts became major sponsors of organized physical activities for boys. Even the more fervent evangelical Protestants, who had once been highly suspicious of sports, became converts to the idea that within controlled settings competitive physical activity could be beneficial to both society and the individual.

The ideology of strenuosity suggested changing ideas about the proper roles of the sexes. Earlier, *manliness* to the middle class had meant the opposite of childlike; it signified adulthood, maturity, and self-control. But as the opportunities for the overt expressions of manliness in the workplace declined and as male social dominance seemed less secure, manliness, even within the middle class, acquired tougher, more assertive qualities. It included the negation of all that was considered soft, feminine, and sentimental. Manly men purged longings for ease and comfort; they welcomed strife, exertion, and physical risks. Near the end of the century, daring cowboys, detectives, soldiers, adventurers, and athletes began to replace industrialists, statesmen, clergymen, and literati as manly heroes.

Reflecting in part the formation of an army of female office workers, sales clerks, teachers, and social workers—a development that liberated growing numbers of younger women from the home—the boundaries of acceptable physical freedom for women also began to relax. The bicycling craze of the 1890s led the way. While critics worried that bicycling might lure young women away from the home and its duties, lead them to remote spots alone with men where they might be seduced, or stimulate the genitals resulting in equally unimaginable horrors, cycling conjured up images not only of a more autonomous woman emancipated from Victorian inhibitions but led to freer forms of female dress as well. Between about 1895 and World War I, the Gibson Girl (named after the popular drawings of Charles Dana Gibson) became a special heroine of the new urban white-collar class. Witty, sophisticated, and flirtatious, she was at ease on the dance floor, the golf course, the tennis court, or on a bicycle.

Of course there were limits on female physical freedom. Prior to the 1920s, any female activity that smacked too much of manliness or the loss of self-control was roundly condemned. Play for the Gibson Girl required discretion and moderation; for example, a proper woman did not dare place a croquet mallet between her legs to execute a more effective shot, or, if playing tennis, smash overheads or run swiftly about the court. Even in the more liberated 1920s, the public admired most of those female athletes who retained feminine qualities. While sportswriters dubbed tennis star Helen Wills "Little Miss Poker Face" because she wore a "false, unnatural front . . . like a cold

A Gibson Girl. While exhibiting impeccable posture, modestly dressed, and in complete control of her bicycle, this turn-of-the-century cycling Gibson Girl suggests the possibility of a new degree of female autonomy. Astride her bicycle, the most adventuresome of the Gibson Girls might ride away from chaperones, family, and at least some of the middle-class Victorian expectations of women.

gray veil" when she played, they reassured fans that off the court she was the epitome of femininity—a "gay, sprightly, pleasing young girl who could enjoy herself and be gracious in the process."

THE GROWING SECULARIZATION OF AMERICAN LIFE

A new expanded middle class, the quest for greater excitement, and the glittering promises of consumer ecstasies were all indicative of a growing secularization or worldliness of American life. At the end of the Victorian era, ever larger spheres of American culture were slipping away from religious influence and control. For example, religiously sanctioned marriages in Muncie, Indiana, the sociologist team of Helen and Robert Lynd found, fell from 85 percent in 1890 to 63 percent in 1923. The burgeoning cities were for the most part more secular and less morally strict than rural and small-town America. "Freed from the benevolent restraints of the small town, thousands of young men and women in every great city have received none of the lessons in self-control which even savage tribes imparted to their appetites as well as their emotions," complained social reformer Jane Addams. Likewise, the giant corporations were more immune to religious influence than were small businesses.

In ever larger realms of human experience, religious explanations gave way to the secular authority of science. Even the more religiously inclined frequently acquiesced to or even welcomed scientific explanations of the physical world. They recognized that keeping certain kinds of inquiry free of religious ideas and influences had practical advantages. For example, most religious people at the turn-of-the century would have viewed with skepticism a claim that a train had jumped the tracks because of God or the devil. "So in modern America," as historian George Marsden has observed, " . . . scientists and technicians of all sorts, no matter how religious, are expected to check their religious beliefs at the door when they enter the laboratory."

SHAKING THE RELIGIOUS FOUNDATIONS

On the surface, Protestant churches, which had always been at the heart of middle-class ways, never seemed stronger than at the beginning of the twentieth century. Membership, attendance, and revenues were growing at least as fast as the population. In the larger cities, affluent Protestants were building massive gothic churches and promoting a social gospel to ease some of the ravages that the Industrial Revolution had inflicted on the less fortunate. In the early twentieth century, the Protestant churches were at the forefront of the Progressive reform movement. The churches led efforts to cleanse government of corruption, curb the power of big business, and prohibit the consumption of alcoholic beverages.

Yet during these same years new ideas directly challenged the very foundations of religious orthodoxy. In the second half of the nineteenth century, "higher criticism," a movement launched earlier by German scholars to subject the Bible to the scrutiny and criticism commonly employed in examining other historical texts, gained momentum in the United States. The higher critics no longer began their inquiries based on the premise that the Bible was supernatural in origin. In 1896, Andrew Dickson White, a founder of Cornell University, described the authority of Scripture as "the tyranny of sacred books imperfectly transcribed, [and] viewed through distorting superstitions." The higher critics saw the Bible as simply a literary text, one composed by ancient Israelites and Christians to preserve a record of their religious experiences. Furthermore, scholars increasingly considered Christianity as among the world's major religions, but not a religion especially ordained by God.

The theory of evolution presented an equally serious challenge to religious orthodoxy. Whereas the Bible asserted that all species were God's immutable creations, Englishman Charles Darwin in his *Origin of Species* (1859) argued instead that all plants and animals had evolved over eons of time through a process he called "natural selection." Not only did such a theory seem to eliminate the need to call upon a supernatural power to explain the existence of flora and fauna, but it reduced the elevated position within the universe that humans had long claimed for themselves. Now rather than special creations of God, humans were said to have evolved from lower life forms. In this crucial sense, humans were no different than other plants and animals.

Contrary to much that has been written on the subject, evolution did *not* become a major subject of popular debate until the 1920s. Before that, many Protestant theologians had reached a compromise with Darwinism. They simply asserted that evolution was God's way of creating and directing natural forces. Interpreting evolution as an engine of material and moral progress also increased its acceptability among Americans. But while these compromises seemingly answered the charges that Darwinism required an abandonment of religious belief, they failed to halt the general trend toward a growing reliance on a worldview grounded in nature and science rather than in the supernatural.

By the 1910s the united front that Protestant churches had presented throughout much of the nineteenth century could no longer be taken for granted. Not only were growing numbers of Roman Catholics and Jews confuting the notion that the United States was a distinctively Protestant nation, but a major cleavage was beginning to develop within the larger Protestant consensus. Responding to the transformation of the middle class resulting from the massive infusions of new white-collar workers, to the allure of refinement, to the problems of industrialism, and to the challenges presented by Darwinism and higher criticism of the Bible, one group of Protestants— variously labeled as "liberal"or "modern"—retreated from evangelical orthodoxy. Theologically, these Protestants emphasized the ethical rather than the supernatural or miraculous aspects of the biblical narrative. Not surprisingly, their retreat from orthodoxy provoked a vigorous response. The orthodox, who would become known as "fundamentalists," continued to insist that the Bible was the Word of God and inerrant in all its teachings. In the 1920s, the split between fundamentalist and modernist Protestants widened. It remains to this day an important division within American Protestantism.

SECULARIZATION AND EDUCATION

Since schools were major transmitters of society's values and beliefs, they played a key role in the broader process of secularizing American life. During the public school movement of the antebellum era, the schools had been virtual extensions of the nation's Protestant churches. Teachers not only required students to recite the Protestant version of the Lord's Prayer and to read the King James (Protestant) version of the Bible in the classroom, but they taught Protestant theological doctrines as well. Seeking to avoid controversy in the face of Catholic protests, the public schools began in the middle decades of the nineteenth century to retreat to a more secular stance. While retaining an emphasis on traditional morality, the later editions of McGuffey's *Eclectic Readers,* the most popular textbook of the day, dropped their explicitly religious messages. By the early twentieth century, John Dewey, who was to exercise an incalculable influence on American education for more than a half-century, was even proposing that teachers no longer indoctrinate their charges with fixed truths and absolute moral principles. Instead, Dewey urged teachers to impress on students the tentative, pragmatic nature of all knowledge.

A similar trend occurred in higher education. Prior to the Civil War, ministerial training had been the main purpose of the nation's colleges; nearly all of them had clerics as presidents, required chapel attendance, and taught Protestant theological principles. Even as late as 1915, it was still "customary in state universities, no less than denominational colleges, to question a candidate for appointment concerning his church connections. Any church connection will do," claimed an article in *The Nation.* Nonetheless, by World War I, religion and religious points of view no longer occupied a central place in the curriculum of most colleges. By then, students could take dozens of courses without hearing any reference whatsoever to religion.

Neither the faculties nor the administrators deliberately set out to secularize the nation's fast-growing system of higher education. Quite the contrary. The educators in the universities, like their pre–Civil War predecessors, sought to impress on the minds of their students the unity of all knowledge. "For them," as Julie A. Reuben has argued, "the term *truth* encompassed all 'correct knowledge.'" Whether derived from common sense, science, or religion, all truths were of the same family; they emanated from the same God. Hence, no inherent conflict existed between the truths of science, morality, or religion.

Despite strenuous efforts by turn-of-the-century educators to preserve and promote the unity of all knowledge, their task became increasingly difficult. Darwinism in particular presented a formidable challenge. How could belief in the harmony of truths be sustained when evolution offered an account of the origin of the species completely at odds with Scripture? Furthermore, Darwin's theory called into question the contention that the order observed in the universe was proof of God's existence ("the argument from design"). Not only did Darwinism seem to contradict the fundamental premises necessary for belief in the unity of truths, but it encouraged scientists to reject efforts to adjust their conclusions to fit popular religious or moral beliefs. Indeed, scientists increasingly sought to separate their work from religious and moral dogma. They insisted on a model of science that began with the open questioning of received truths and required the experimental verification of hypotheses.

Neither did the faculties nor the administrators of the universities intend to foment a revolt against the Victorian ideology of culture. Indeed, they continued to urge their students to subordinate material pursuits to the cultivation of the mind and to value the fine arts over the practical arts. Properly trained to appreciate the finer things in life, they envisioned such young men and women evolving into a disinterested, cultivated elite that would take over and ennoble newspaper editorships, political offices, the professions, business firms, and the other seats of power and influence in America. On the campuses themselves, dozens of eloquent professors of English, history, philosophy, and the classics introduced thousands of students to "great" novels, poems, philosophical treatises, and histories.

Yet the proponents of steeping students in the ideology of culture won no smashing victories. Undergraduates typically devoted far more of their energy to their social lives than to Shakespeare or Goethe. Rather than entering college to become connoisseurs of high culture, the students came mostly to obtain degrees that would enhance their prospects for acceptance into high society or allow them to enter occupations that qualified them for admission into the upper ranks of the new white-collar class. At best, students majoring in engineering, agriculture, or business took only a few courses in the arts and the humanities.

SHAKING THE INTELLECTUAL FOUNDATIONS

New ideas in philosophy and the social sciences also inflicted damage on the intellectual foundations of Victorian culture. Social scientists increasingly sought to understand the "laws" or "principles" that governed society without resorting to supernatural authority or assumptions that a superintending purpose (for example, God's) guided the universe. Influenced by Darwinism, they sometimes reached startling conclusions. For example, William Graham Sumner, a minister turned Yale professor, once declared that "man had no more right to life than a rattlesnake; he has no more right to liberty than any wild beast; his right to pursue happiness is nothing but a license to maintain the struggle for existence. . . ." Others, such as Lester Ward, sought to soften the implications for humans of a world devoid of ultimate purpose. Since (unlike other animals) humans had minds capable of invention and control, Ward reasoned, they could to some degree escape the rigors of the struggle for existence.

Perhaps no two intellectuals were more responsible for preparing the way for modernism in America than William James and John Dewey. A product of a New England literary family, early in his career James rejected the typical Victorian dichotomy between humans and animals. He became a convert to the Darwinian premise that humans existed on a continuum with other animals. As with the brains of other animals, the human brain was simply a biological organ that had evolved capacities for selecting and employing perceptions that were useful for the specie's survival.

While the human mind could formulate abstract concepts based upon these perceptions, these concepts were necessarily selective and distortions of "truth" or the reality presumed to exist outside the senses. "No theory is absolutely a transcript of reality," wrote James. To conclude that truths were proximate or relative was, to say the least, unsettling to many of James's contemporaries. But, to James himself and those influenced by him, it opened up an infinitely exciting new way of looking at the world. Ultimately, it completely annihilated the possibility of assuming that such Victorian conceptual polarities as human/animal, man/woman, and civilized/savage had a "real" existence apart from how humans thought about them.

Dewey, who described ideas as instruments to be tried out in the real world, had a similar outlook. Without predetermining the ultimate shape of society, Dewey proposed to employ the methods of science to reach judgments about whether human institutions and traditional practices improved the odds for survival and/or enhanced the quality of life. If alternatives (including some variant of socialism) proved superior by these twin tests, then society should consider their adoption. A broadened meaning of democracy followed from Dewey's reasoning. Rather than consisting only of the principles of individual liberty and equality of opportunity, Dewey argued that democracy should also include the principle of "fraternity" or "community." Only through a rich communal life, Dewey said, could individuals fully realize their potentialities.

Although by no means fully recognized at the time, "the culture of inquiry" that Dewey and James among others were helping to create contributed to growing fissures in the very footings of Victorian culture. In history, Frederick Jackson Turner ascribed American democracy to the existence of a frontier (a naturalistic explanation) and Charles A. Beard argued that the nation's founders, when drawing up the Constitution, were guided as much by their personal as by the public interest. Oliver Wendell Holmes, Jr., and Roscoe Pound concluded that law arose not from eternal verities but from day-to-day human experience. And Thorstein Veblen insisted that modern institutions, such as marriage, were simply survivals from earlier historical eras (and hence frequently archaic) rather than the products of immutable natural laws or institutions ordained by God.

SHAKING THE LITERARY AND ARTISTIC FOUNDATIONS

New developments in literature and the arts also foreshadowed the arrival of modern ways. In the latter half of the nineteenth century, a group of writers, magazine editors, book publishers, Protestant ministers, art gallery directors, and college professors constituted the guardians of the Victorian or genteel conception of culture. Located mostly in New England, they saw the best in literature and the fine arts, and refined tastes and good manners as major pillars of morality and as sources of noble ideals. A shared culture, they believed, could serve as a powerful social adhesive. It could help to tie together an otherwise divided people.

As powerful as these guardians of culture were, their ideology of culture had never held complete sway over American life. Neither vaudeville, minstrel shows, dime novels, nor comic books ever met their moral or esthetic standards. From the standpoint of genteel culture, the popular cultural forms too often placed considerations of entertainment and amusement before the value of edification. In addition, several of the nation's distinguished writers bridled at the arrogance and pretentiousness of the New England literati and their followers. "I have never tried . . . to help cultivate the cultivated classes," sneered Mark Twain, the Missouri-born novelist and humorist. With "the word Culture," added poet Walt Whitman, "we find ourselves abruptly in close quarters with the enemy."

Without breaking completely with the prevailing conventions of their age, first European and then American novelists and poets in the 1880–1920 era began exploring new subject matter that frequently shocked Victorian sensibilities. One region of exploration was the depths of the mind that lay below and frequently hidden from rational thought. For example, in a moving short story, "The Yellow Wallpaper," Charlotte Perkins Gilman described the mental breakdown of a Victorian woman imprisoned in the domestic sphere. Novelists also began to explore the underside of Victorian life—the world of crime, prostitution, brutality, depravity, and poverty. Sometimes labeled as literary naturalists and frequently influenced by Darwinism, these writers told stories of people whose lives were governed by natural forces beyond their control. The premise of such stories ran counter to the Victorian faith in the capacities of humans to determine their own destinies.

A similar trend occurred in the visual arts. At the turn of the century a group of New York painters, known as the "Ashcan School," breached the Victorian dichotomy between "life" and "art" and departed from Victorian subject matter by depicting gritty street scenes and the vibrancy of working-class life. "A child of the slums will make a better painting than a drawing room lady gone over by a beauty salon," exclaimed George Luks, one of the Ashcan painters. Even more shocking to Victorian sensibilities were the paintings exhibited at the Armory Show in New York City in 1913. At the Armory Show, Americans saw for the first time European avant-garde or abstract paintings, paintings that made no pretenses of representing likenesses to objects that could be seen with the eyes or captured on camera. Neither did the "modern" painters accept the Victorian notion that art should be morally uplifting or inspiring; instead, they frequently endorsed as a rationale for their work the aphorism "art for art's sake." In the years just before World War I the Armory Show was just one indication of the beginnings of a far larger literary and artistic uprising. Another was the development of Greenwich Village in New York City as the gathering place for a group of young men and women who openly flaunted their rejection of middle-class ways. They adopted experimental, bohemian lifestyles. The women bobbed their hair and smoked and drank in public; women and men lived openly together outside of marriage; and whites fraternized with blacks and Jews with gentiles. The Village not only became the center of avant-garde painting, music, literature, and drama, but also served as the major entrepot for the latest European ideas.

Several currents of thought influenced these "modernist" rebels. As we have seen, Darwinism unleashed a profound rethinking of the nature of mind, religion, and morality. Many of the young rebels owed large debts to such American thinkers as James, Dewey, and Veblen. In the immediate prewar years, radicalism, especially that of the homegrown Industrial Workers of the World, inspired the Greenwich Village rebels. They also seized upon such daring European writers as Karl Marx, Friederich Nietzsche, Oscar Wilde, George Bernard Shaw, and Henrik Ibsen and such painters as Paul Cezanne and Vincent van Gogh.

Above all, Sigmund Freud, the Viennese doctor who invented psycho-analysis, provided them with ammunition for casting aside the strictures of middle-class ways. Unlike the Victorians who viewed the mind as a conscious, rational, lightening-quick, almost error-free, calculating machine, Freud emphasized the unconscious, that portion of the mind often inaccessible to conscious comprehension or control. Within the unconscious dwelled powerful primitive instincts (in the id). Of these, the sexual drive was by far the most potent. These desires or drives, said Freud, were locked in a never-ending struggle with the conscious (the ego), which determined what a person could do, and the moral values (the superego), which prescribed what a person should do. Although Freud offered no easy resolution of the warring impulses within the psyche, his popularizers frequently suggested or implied that the freeing of instinctual drives (especially the sexual) could result in greater individual happiness.

World War I (1914–18) hastened the arrival of the modern literary and artistic rebellion. The war irreparably damaged the Victorian faith in moral progress and in the unity of Euro-American culture. "The plunge of civilization into the abyss of blood and horror," wrote the aging novelist, Henry James, "so gives away the whole long age during which we have supposed the world to be gradually bettering and [the] meaning is too tragic for words." Stripping life and death of dignity and eroding confidence, the war encouraged the young intellectuals to turn inward, to the self rather than to society, for inspiration and fulfillment. With the war, "the bohemian tendency triumphed in the Village," Malcolm Cowley later wrote, "and talk about revolution gave way to talk about psychoanalysis."

The rebellion reached a kind of fruition in the 1920s. Not since the 1840s and 1850s had the nation witnessed such a flowering of literary and artistic works that were destined to become classics. They included the poetry of T. S. Eliot and Ezra Pound, novels by F. Scott Fitzgerald, Ernest Hemingway, Willa Cather, and William Faulkner, and the paintings of Edward Hopper, Charles Sheeler, and Georgia O'Keefe. Frank Lloyd Wright led an idiosyncratic but ultimately modernist movement in architecture. And finally there was jazz, America's most original contribution to the world's music.

The rebels universally attacked what they usually called Puritanism, by which they meant Victorian America rather than the historical Puritanism about which they knew little. Puritanism, as Charles A. Beard wrote, became an epithet for "anything that interfere[d] with the new freedom, free verse, psychoanalysis, or even the double entendre." It had overvalued respectability, propriety, and material things while restricting the pursuit of pleasure and choking off creativity. Prizing novelty and originality, the rebels valued art for its own sake and its capacity to provide personal liberation from conventions rather than for its capacity to instruct or provide moral uplift. The rebels frequently turned upside down or merged the polarities that were so precious to the Victorians. They gloried in the presumed innocence of childhood, in the primitive, and in the impulsive.

In the end, the rebellion nearly destroyed the Victorian ideology of culture. No longer did England, the slavish admirers of English high culture, nor the Northeastern white Protestant intellectuals exercise such a commanding influence over the nation's high culture. The center of the nation's intellectual life shifted from Boston and its environs to New York City and to Chicago. Several of the most prominent of the young writers and artists became expatriates; they fled the country for the friendlier confines of the Left Bank in Paris. Freer of racial, ethnic, and gender prejudice than most Americans, the rebels experimented with greater sexual equality and praised the artistic works of the black Harlem Renaissance. Even before World War I, Jewish intellectuals began to achieve a special prominence. In the 1930s, the diaspora of Jews from fascist Europe added to the heterogeneous and cosmopolitan character of the nation's literary and artistic leadership.

Not only did the rebels consciously break with earlier standards of art and literature, but they also experienced a profound alienation from the mainstream of American society. Victorian intellectuals had shared the major assumptions of their age and had believed that they had a large responsibility in instructing and uplifting the masses. Although several of the most creative intellectuals had long been critical of mass tastes (consider for example Henry David Thoreau), the intensity of their estrangement had never been as great as that experienced by the artists and literati of the 1920s. Their rebellion fostered a widening chasm between the artistic and literary community on the one side and society on the other.

Conclusion

Between the 1880s and the 1930s, the preconditions were established for a fundamental transformation in American ways. The development of a new middle class, the growth of large business organizations, the rise of a mass-manufacturing economy, and new forms of advertising and entertainment encouraged the adoption of values and behaviors conducive to consumption. For growing numbers of Americans, self-control—at least in one's leisure time—increasingly gave way to self-indulgence and a quest for greater excitement. Simultaneously, the edifice supporting traditional religious beliefs and the Victorian conception of high culture weakened. By the 1920s, the nation was in the midst of a new cultural era, one that for the lack of a better name scholars have labeled as "modern."

9

Modern Ways

No one knows for certain when the term *modern* was first used to describe a set of ways associated with the twentieth century. Perhaps English novelist Virginia Woolf was responsible. At least nearly all subsequent writers on modern ways seem to feel obligated to quote her statement that "on or about December 1910, human character changed." Or perhaps it was Nebraska-reared novelist Willa Cather who wrote: "The world broke in two in 1922 or thereabouts." While scholars quarrel about an exact date for the arrival of modern ways, they have increasingly come to agree that sometime early in the twentieth century there was a profound shift in sensibility. In its vanguard stood a group of rebellious artists and intellectuals. These modernist rebels embarked on a remarkable explosion of creativity—in painting, music, and sculpture, in architecture, in the novel, and in poetry.

But the intelligentsia was not the only group to engage in new modes of thinking, seeing, hearing, and behaving. Eventually modern ways would come to encompass much of American life in the twentieth century. The adherents of modern ways counted more on expertise than on personal character, more on the accumulation of information than on folk wisdom, more on moral relativism than absolute notions of right and wrong, and more on a secular-scientific outlook than on a religiously orthodox worldview. Above all else, they placed less emphasis on self-control and more on self-fulfillment than their nineteenth-century predecessors.

Yet, while few Americans were willing to deny themselves all of the pleasures and the advantages offered by modern ways, many—indeed perhaps most—continued to build their lives around traditional ways. Even those who embraced modern ways most fully and enthusiastically frequently experienced agonizing doubts. In their personal if not in their public lives, they tried the difficult if not impossible task of accommodating the older with the newer ways.

THE TWENTIES: A PIVOTAL DECADE

"A vast dissolution of ancient habits"—this was how columnist Walter Lippmann characterized the modern ways of the 1920s. While Lippmann surely exaggerated, the decade has struck observers then and since as a pivotal one in the history of American culture. It was in the 1920s that the trends we observed in the previous two chapters—the growing ethnic and religious pluralism of the United States, the development of a mass-consumption economy, the quest for greater excitement, and the increasing secularization of American life—all came into sharper focus. In that "decade of prosperity," millions of Americans joined in an unprecedented orgy of individual consumption. In the same decade, many Americans seemed to seize every opportunity they could to "have fun;" novelist F. Scott Fitzgerald called it "the jazz age," a label that conjured up images of primitive rhythms, of "flaming youth," and of unrestrained sexual behavior. In the 1920s, many Americans continued to retreat from a religiously based life. The "irreligion in the modern world [is] radical to a degree for which there is, I think, no counterpart," concluded Lippmann in 1929.

THE CITY AS THE HOME OF MODERN WAYS

Modern ways enjoyed their greatest support in the cities. Not only did the majority of the American people now live in cities for the first time in the nation's history, but city residents also began to insist that the urban style of life was superior to that of the small town and the countryside. Life in the city, claimed its enthusiasts, was far more exciting, glamorous, fulfilling, and receptive to new ideas than in the countryside. To the delight of his big-city audiences in the 1920s, essayist H. L. Mencken characterized rural Americans as the "anthropoid rabble" who were determined to shield themselves "from whatever knowledge violated their superstitions."

The city also furnished the home for most of the nation's ethnic and religious minorities. In the 1920s, these "outsiders" began to articulate more boldly defenses of their own ways. To the advocates of the "new pluralism," one could be a loyal American without abandoning his or her ethnic or religious distinctiveness. A march on Washington by one hundred thousand Catholic men on September 21, 1924, vividly suggested the possibilities of the new pluralism. As representatives of the Catholic Holy Name Society, the men carried both papal banners *and* tiny U.S. flags. When they were addressed by Boston's William Cardinal O'Connell, who "flung the challenge to those who would question the loyalty of Catholics to America," the "entire assemblage . . . rose to its feet spontaneously and cheered so enthusiastically that it temporarily halted the address. . . ."

Such exhibitions of loyalty to the nation hardly implied an enthusiasm for complete cultural assimilation. If anything, ethnic and racial minorities stepped up their efforts to preserve their ways from the influence of the dominant culture; they sought to strengthen their kinship networks, their churches, and their voluntary associations. To a substantial degree, as historian Lizabeth Cohen has shown, ethnic stores, mutual-aid societies, and banks succeeded in resisting chain stores and other nationalizing institutions.

Even intercollegiate football rallied Catholics around their shared religious identity. Beginning in the 1920s Catholics everywhere, regardless of ethnic origins and even those who had never gone to college (dubbed by sports-writers as the "subway alumni" if they were from the cities or as the "coalfield alums" if they were from the Catholic communities in western Pennsylvania or eastern Ohio), became rabid fans of Notre Dame football. "The custom be-gan in primary and secondary parochial schools, each Friday in the fall, to have students pray for a Notre Dame victory the next day," recalled Mary Jo Weaver, a professor of religion at Indiana University. "It was an important part of our 'Holy War' against the Protestant majority in America."

Supplemented by the arrival from the southern countryside of two million blacks in the 1910s and another million in the 1920s, the visibility of African Americans in the northern cities increased. In 1917 and in 1919, the presence of more blacks, competition for jobs, pressures on housing and public services, and racial prejudices spawned bloody race riots in more than a half-dozen northern cities, giving the lie to any thoughts that the cities were uniquely free of racism. In the 1920s, the Harlem Renaissance, a great outpouring of black literature, painting, and music, called national and even international attention to the nation's submerged black population. "Negro life is seiz-ing its first chances for group expression and self-determination," asserted Alain Locke in an anthology revealingly entitled *The New Negro* (1926). The black role in popular entertainment, though as often as not confirming white stereotypes of African Americans, became more conspicuous than ever be-fore. Those white Americans seeking freedom from Victorian constraints of-ten found in the black jazz of Louis Armstrong and Duke Ellington and in the blues songs of Bessie Smith sources of personal liberation.

The northern urban experience encouraged a stronger racial conscious-ness and more aggressive efforts by blacks to assert rights. Rather than di-verting their energies into futile opposition to racial segregation and disfran-chisement, Booker T. Washington had told blacks in the era preceding World War I that they should develop the skills and the self-discipline that would secure their self-respect and prove their economic worth to potential em-ployers. But, in the same era, W. E. B. DuBois countered Washington by arguing that African Americans should insist on the restoration of their civil and political rights. Taking a similar position was the National Associa-tion for the Advancement of Colored People (NAACP), an organization co-founded by DuBois in 1910 that experienced rapid growth in membership among urban blacks in the 1920s. Receiving far more attention in the media of the 1920s was Marcus Garvey's Back to Africa movement. With a half-million followers, Garvey's movement promised racial glory in an Empire of Africa and sought to instill among the urban black poor a sense of racial pride and courage.

Representatives of minorities were not the only advocates of a new cul-tural pluralism. During the World War I era and afterwards, the artistic and literary rebels also welcomed ethnic and racial diversity; they conspicuously rejected both the value of a single, unitary culture as well as the Victorian ide-ology of culture. In place of the ideal of a single culture, Randolph Bourne argued as early as 1916 that the United States ought to adopt as its goal a cosmopolitan, "federation of cultures." A member of the Greenwich Village circle, John Collier, who would later be appointed Commissioner of Indian Affairs by President Franklin D. Roosevelt, saw in the collectivism of Navajo Indian culture a healthy antidote to white individualism.

Even more "responsible for demolishing Victorian certainties about culture," contends Lewis Perry, were the anthropologists. Beginning with their teacher, Franz Boas, Margaret Mead in *Coming of Age in Samoa* (1928) and Ruth Benedict in *Patterns of Culture* (1934), introduced literally thousands of readers to the decidedly modern value of cultural pluralism. Mead even audaciously suggested that the adolescent girls suffered from fewer tensions and frustrations in supposedly primitive cultures than they did in the more repressive industrial cultures of Western societies.

THE "NEW" WOMAN AS A SYMBOL OF MODERN WAYS

Nothing was more central to the modern spirit of the 1920s than the arrival of the much-ballyhooed "new" woman. Well before the 1920s, urban middle- and upper-class women had begun to bump up against the perimeters of their "separate sphere." The bicycling craze, the Gibson Girl, and freer forms of dance all suggested an expanding realm of physical freedom for women. By 1920 women were attending coeducational high schools and colleges in record numbers; young women were pouring into the job market as secretaries and sales clerks; and a few more women were entering the professions (especially teaching) than formerly. In 1920, with the ratification of the Nineteenth Amendment, women finally realized the long-deferred dream of nationwide suffrage.

But there was far more involved in the idea of the new woman than sports, education, jobs, and the right to vote. No longer a clone of her mother, according to a *Chicago Tribune* advertisement of the 1920s, the new woman relaxed her self-imposed restraints. "Today's woman gets what she wants," flatly declared the ad. Rather than buying particular goods to establish her family's middle-class identity, fashionable consumption was important to the new woman's sense of personal well-being. She bought "glassware in sapphire blue or glowing amber," read the ad, and "soap to match her bathroom's color scheme." She was a more erotic creature than her mother. In dress, she replaced "voluminous petticoats" with "slim sheaths of silk."

As the *Tribune* ad hinted, it was the young, unmarried, urban, middle-class woman, the flapper, who became the ultimate and perhaps most enduring symbol of the Jazz Age. In just about every respect imaginable, the flapper flaunted her rejection of the Victorian code of proper female behavior. Rather than a model of propriety and self-restraint, the flapper talked freely, laughed gaily, gestured extravagantly, and, in the eyes of her Victorian predecessors, dressed immodestly. Blithely, she smoked and drank illegal alcoholic beverages. Indeed, she sometimes drank enough that it visibly affected her behavior. She bobbed her hair, flattened her breasts, threw away her corsets and petticoats, and shortened her skirts. Rather than pinching her cheeks to make them rosier, as her mother had done, she painted her cheeks with rouge—not so much to enhance her sexual appeal but as to make another gesture of defiance against older ways. The flappers also relaxed the traditional constraints on courtship. "None of the Victorian mothers—and most of the mothers were Victorian," wrote novelist F. Scott Fitzgerald, "had any idea of how casually their daughters were accustomed to being kissed."

The flapper danced with abandon. No longer did young people in the big cities dance the stately waltz at arm's length to the romantic notes of the violin. Instead, they now danced cheek-to-cheek in "a syncopated embrace" to the "barbaric" notes of the saxophone. There were, of course, pockets of resistance, even on college campuses. In 1921, the *Daily Nebraskan* described its campus as safely immunized against the "Eastern dances," and reported that University of Nebraska students had rallied behind "simple dress" as a means of returning the nation to "normalcy."

The flapper was not alone in helping to usher in modern sexuality. In the late Victorian age (1880s to World War I), some doctors, health reformers, and middle-class couples had already begun to dissolve the ages-old associations

Flappers. Precariously but confidently dancing atop a skyscraper in the 1920s, these flappers openly defy the Victorian ways of their mothers. Representatives of the "modern" woman, the flappers took chances, used makeup, wore short skirts, and publicly exhibited their feelings.

of sexual intercourse with sin and reproduction. By the turn of the century, according to historian Kathy Peiss, it was not unusual for working-class girls in the larger cities to exchange sexual favors for "treats" from men. In the meantime, influenced by Sigmund Freud, Havelock Ellis, and Ellen Key, the literary and artistic rebels in Greenwich Village and elsewhere advocated and practiced freer forms of sexuality. The sexual radicals insisted that women, like men, possessed erotic capacities and that sexual gratification was essential to emotional health. The career of Margaret Sanger, the leading exponent of birth control, illustrated the growing acceptance of a more liberated and positive sexual ideology. Before World War I, Sanger had been something of a social pariah; she had been arrested and jailed for distributing birth control information. After the war, she became a heroine of modern Americans. She published birth control manuals, gave public lectures on birth control, and opened family planning clinics.

The mass media and the advertising industry contributed even more to the creation of modern sexual ideology. The glamorous woman with undisguised sexual appeal became a favorite trope of advertisers. For example, a 1924 Palmolive soap ad depicted a scantily clad woman in an exotic setting and promised the "beauty secret of Cleopatra hidden in every cake." A bumper crop of new magazines offered readers who had never heard of Freud or the libido stories with such alluring titles as "Indolent Kisses," "Confessions of a Chorus Girl," and "What I Told My Daughter the Night Before Her Marriage." The movies were equally provocative. Clara Bow became the "It" girl of the 1920s, and movie ads promised kisses "where heart, soul and sense in concert move, and the blood is lava, and the pulse is ablaze."

The prevalence of sexual suggestiveness and the growing acceptance of a positive sexual ideology fed the impression then and since that the 1920s experienced a "sexual revolution." When compared with the sex ways of the middle-class Victorians of the nineteenth century, perhaps there was a revolution. The prevalence of intercourse, particularly between married couples in the urban white-collar class, may have increased. And, according to the studies of Alfred Kinsey, middle-class women born after 1900 were more likely to engage in premarital intercourse than those born in the nineteenth century.

Yet there were clearly limits on the sexual revolution of the 1920s. Although the widely publicized form of sexual play known as "petting" shocked contemporaries, Paula Fass has found that petting entailed conventions of physical intimacy that usually fell short of intercourse. While modern women were expected to be sexually alluring, almost no one endorsed promiscuity. Modern women were supposed to arouse male desire but not to initiate sexual relations. Any woman transgressing these boundaries jeopardized her reputation. For other Americans, particularly those living in the countryside, in small towns, and in the ethnic enclaves of the larger cities, sexual behavior may have changed little if at all in the twenties.

Both the new woman and the acceptance of a modern sexual ideology may be interpreted as victories of male over traditionally middle-class female values. The popular media and the advertisers encouraged women to engage in

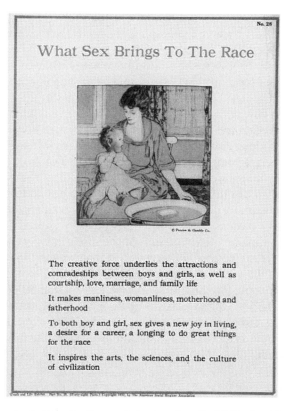

"What Sex Brings to the Race," a Poster of the American Social Hygiene Association, 1922.
Part of a campaign to prevent the spread of venereal disease, this poster represents a
step away from the restrictiveness of the middle-class Victorian ideology of sexuality.
While not endorsing sex as a pleasure to be enjoyed for its own sake, the poster does
suggest that when sexuality is channeled into marriage and reproduction it can bring
enormous benefits to the lives of both sexes.

such stereotypically boyish and manly acts as smoking, drinking, betting,
freer forms of dance and music, prankishness, and other traditionally anti-
feminine and antibourgeois behaviors. For example, advertising pioneer
Edward Bernays sold cigarettes to women as "torches of freedom." (He noted
at the same time that smoking cigarettes stimulated the erogenous zone
of the lips.) A similar trend toward more boylike or manlike behavior by
women was evident in literature and the arts. In short, the "new" or "modern" woman aided and abetted what Ann Douglas has described as the "mas-
culinization" of American culture. These new, more expressive forms of individualism may have contained largely hidden costs for women. For they
seemed to unleash earlier restraints that men had imposed on themselves in
their relationships with women. Ultimately, men may have felt even freer
than in the past to mistreat women both emotionally and physically.

Built into the adventurous autonomy of the modern woman was a new set of expectations. Instead of a complete release from the "tyrannies" of the home, the modern wife and mother was told that she needed to do even more. To feed her family properly, she should have a scientific knowledge of calories, vitamins, and food groups. To promote her husband's career, she should become a skilled hostess. To rear happy children, she should acquire a knowledge of modern psychology. For guidance in performing her enlarged range of duties, the modern housewife was expected to turn away from the folk wisdom handed down by family, friends, or ministers. Instead, in a characteristically modern admonition, she was advised to look to outside expertise.

In particular, no modern woman could escape the commandment that she remain forever youthful. Hence, the arrival of the modern woman coincided with the growth of the modern cosmetics industry and the proliferation of beauty parlors. Perpetual youthfulness required slimness. Thus, dieting became a major preoccupation of the modern woman. In the face of the new cultural requirements of womanhood, older feminist causes slid into the background. In 1921, for example, feminists unveiled the Equal Rights Amendment, a proposed constitutional amendment that called for the end of sexual discrimination. But it was never adopted. That same year, Atlantic City, New Jersey, crowned the first Miss America. Miss America was soon to become a powerful symbol of the coercion imposed on women by the modern beauty culture.

WAYS AT WAR

Not surprisingly, the widespread outburst of shockingly new behaviors in the 1920s provoked a cultural war, a war whose issues continue to reverberate into our own times. According to observers then and since, the opposition to modern ways came primarily from the countryside and from small towns. Peoples from these places tended to see themselves under siege by the big city's ethnic and religious pluralism, its commercial amusements, and its moral relativism. They yearned for the restoration of a golden past of middle-class families and communities. In these idealized communities, independent farmers, public-spirited businessmen, and industrious workingmen lived side by side in complete harmony. Everyone practiced self-control and agreed that religion provided the ultimate source of moral authority.

Yet the opposition to modern ways did not come exclusively from non-urban areas. Regardless of where they lived, the majority of Americans probably found some or most of the modern values and behaviors to one degree or another objectionable. While urban Catholic ethnics usually disagreed sharply with Protestant traditionalists regarding prohibition and the desirability of pluralism, they too objected to the new woman and to modern sexual ideology. The older middle class of small businessmen, locally-oriented professionals, prosperous farmers, and skilled or semiskilled working people also approached the expressive individualism of modern culture with caution and feelings of unease. Unlike the new urban white-collar class, these traditionalists more often than not continued to find their identities and their values in the familiar ways handed down from the past and in their families, their churches, and in their local communities or neighborhoods rather than in their occupations or in what was currently fashionable. As the older middle class sensed that it was losing cultural authority to the newer white-collar urban-centered middle class, it became more defensive and suspicious.

Above all else, traditionalists and modernists divided on the ultimate source of moral authority. For moral direction, both Protestant and Catholic traditionalists relied upon revealed religion—for Protestants, the Bible, and for Catholics, the institutional church. On the other hand, modernists were just as likely, or perhaps more likely, to look elsewhere. They turned to scientific and professional expertise, to the cultures of their workplaces, to the opinions of others, and to media models for guidance on how they should behave.

While traditionalists were never in full agreement on how to respond to the modernist challenges, they launched two major counteroffensives. One took aim at the modern notion of a pluralistic order that recognized the intrinsic value of minority cultures. This counteroffensive had direct origins in the anxieties spawned by World War I. "Once lead this people into war," President Woodrow Wilson had warned before America's entry into the conflict, "and they'll forget there ever was such a thing as tolerance." Wilson's prediction proved to be chillingly accurate. Everywhere, the war fanned the flames of cultural conformity. Acutely aware of the absence of enthusiasm on the part of many Americans for entering the war in the first place as well as of the ties that bound American ethnic groups to their homelands in Europe, national, state, and local governments as well as private groups launched a massive propaganda campaign on behalf of the war effort.

Ironically, ethnic Germans, the immigrant group frequently praised as the most assimilable before the war, now became the special targets of nativist bigotry. Regardless of protests to the contrary, German Americans found themselves treated as enemy agents. Cloaking themselves in wartime patriotism, opponents of radicalism likewise employed both legal and extralegal weapons against the Industrial Workers of the World and the Socialist party. Wartime anxieties and the Russian Revolution of 1917 contributed to a nationwide "Red Scare" in 1919.

Fears that ethnic and religious pluralism and alien ideologies jeopardized the nation's cultural homogeneity continued after the war. Under the battle cry of restoring "one-hundred percent Americanism" and frequently under the umbrella of their local churches and/or the revived Ku Klux Klan, the more militant of the traditionalist Protestants made Catholics, Jews, African Americans, and foreigners their special targets. They resurrected ages-old charges of an international Jewish conspiracy to take over the world, exposed "papal plots" against traditional liberties, tried to close parochial schools, and sought to reduce Catholic and Jewish influence in politics. They led the campaign to obtain the passage of the Immigration Act of 1924, an act that not only brought a halt to massive immigration to America but also blatantly discriminated against Asians and immigrants from Southern and Eastern Europe. However, to attribute anti-Jewish, anti-Catholic, and antiblack attitudes only to the more extreme traditionalists of the 1920s would be a serious mistake. When non-Protestants tried to enter the nation's elite colleges, clubs, and boardrooms, they frequently encountered there too unscalable ethnoreligious barriers—but in these instances the barriers were usually disguised as character tests or as merit systems.

The noisy, organized, and sometimes violent campaigns against non-Protestants and blacks echoed themes similar to the fascist movements of the same era on the European continent. Both movements, as George Mowry has observed, idealized a preindustrial world, were intensely nationalistic, insisted on racial purity, attacked minorities, and condemned modern ways (especially the personal behavior of those living in the large cities). But the revived Ku Klux Klan, the major organizational form of America's variant of fascism, was never as successful as the fascist movements in Germany or Italy. In the United States, Klan supporters confronted a stronger tradition of respect for individual liberties and for political accommodation than in Italy or Germany. And, unlike the European fascist movements, the Klan won almost no support among intellectuals or those employed in managerial bureaucracies. But, even as the Klan faded in the late 1920s, large numbers of Americans continued to blame non-Protestants and modern ways for what they considered America's fall from a golden age.

Traditionalist or fundamentalist Protestants aimed a second major counteroffensive at modern science and modern Protestantism. While World War I had temporarily brought Protestants together, once the conflict ended the smoldering divisions of the prewar era resurfaced. In the 1920s the trend within urban white-collar congregations toward modernism or liberalism gained additional momentum. Pastors of these congregations downgraded the importance of a religious conversion experience and theological orthodoxy; they preached more soothing sermons that accommodated religion with biblical criticism, Darwinism, and modern ways more generally. Rather than emphasizing salvation or personal sin, these ministers were more likely to stress amiable human relationships, personal fulfillment, and greater tolerance of non-Protestants.

The highly publicized Scopes trial in Dayton, Tennessee, in 1925 brought the conflict between modernist and fundamentalist Protestants to a dramatic climax. Consistent with their belief in the inerrancy of the Bible, fundamentalists had obtained the passage of several state laws banning the teaching of "atheistic" evolution in the public schools. Supported by the American Civil Liberties Union, John T. Scopes, a high school biology teacher, challenged the constitutionality of Tennessee's statute. The subsequent trial attracted the attention of the entire world. William Jennings Bryan, thrice the Democratic presidential nominee and the nation's leading crusader against evolution, joined the prosecution. Bryan was not completely amiss when he charged that a "scientific soviet is attempting to dictate what shall be taught in our schools and, in so doing, is attempting to mold the religion of the nation." Clarence Darrow, a famous trial lawyer and a publicly confessed agnostic, joined the defense team. Darrow mercilessly ridiculed Bryan's "fool ideas" about the Bible. The court found Scopes guilty, though his sentence was later reversed on a technicality.

Contrary to impressions cultivated by the urban press and subsequently by historians, the Scopes trial did *not* signal a defeat nor the end of traditional ways. Despite the negative conclusions of the big-city press, it is quite likely that a majority of the American people continued after the trial to oppose the teaching of evolution in the public schools. Neither did the modernists rout the traditionalists politically in the 1920s. The traditionalists won nearly all of the decade's political frays, including the election of three presidents and, more important in symbolic terms, succeeded in retaining the prohibition of alcoholic beverages as the law of the land.

LOOKING BACKWARD AND FORWARD

Like a mighty earthquake, the Great Depression of the 1930s rocked the nation to its very foundations. At the bottom of the Depression in 1933, nearly a quarter of the labor force was out of work. For those who did have jobs, their wages plunged downward. In the major cities, hungry women and men lined up in front of soup kitchens; thousands more lived in shanty towns known as "Hoovervilles," a derisive reference to President Herbert Hoover. Confronted with an uncertain future, the birth rate fell to the lowest point in the nation's history and the marriage rate dropped 20 percent. Only in the early 1940s, in the midst of World War II, did the nation finally recover the prosperity that it had enjoyed in the 1920s.

Responding to the Great Depression pulled Americans in opposing directions. In one direction, there was the powerful appeal of the past. It seemed to many that recovery from the economic disaster could be achieved only by renouncing the excesses of the 1920s. Americans must return to the virtues of yesteryear—to the self-control and hard work that had served them so well in the nineteenth century. In another direction, there was the allure of the future. The Great Depression, proponents of this view said, had discredited the idea that the economy could be left on its own. The state must in the future play a far greater role in guiding the nation's destiny.

LOOKING BACKWARD OR FORWARD

The exigencies of the Great Depression quickly pushed aside or into the background the major cultural conflicts of the 1920s. In the immediate wake of the stock market crash of 1929, large numbers of Americans believed that they had gone too far, that they were now paying the price for their free spending, their frivolity, and their pursuit of personal pleasure. Skirt lengths dropped to well below the knees and, along with the price of common stocks, public support for modern architecture, music, painting, and literature plummeted.

Governor's Mansion, Colonial Williamsburg. Along with Baseball's Hall of Fame and Museum, hundreds of murals produced by the Federal Arts Project, historical novels, and biographies of national heroes, the reconstructed colonial village of Williamsburg, Virginia, offered vivid reminders of a presumably more purposeful and coherent past to many Americans during the Great Depression of the 1930s.

Amidst the confusion and the futility of the present, many Americans resurrected visions of a more purposeful and coherent past. The reconstructed colonial village of Williamsburg, Virginia, opened in 1935, served well this longing for an idyllic past. Cleansed of nearly all evidence of squalor and slavery, Colonial Williamsburg, according to its sponsors, depicted the "moral and spiritual values" that were of "lasting importance to all men everywhere." Baseball's Hall of Fame and Museum, opened in Cooperstown, New York, in 1938, evoked a similar nostalgia for a simpler, supposedly superior past. "Turning back to the past when men presumably did things right," to quote historian Francis O'Connor, was the favorite theme of more than twenty-five hundred murals produced through the relief efforts of the Federal Arts Project in the 1930s. Historical novels were in vogue; no novel of the depression decade approximated the popularity of Margaret Mitchell's *Gone with the Wind* (1936), an epic that recalled the glory of the Old South. Americans responded warmly to majestic biographies. Their favorite subject for biography was Abraham Lincoln, the president who had guided the nation through an earlier crisis.

In their enthusiasm for "streamlining," a popular industrial design concept in the 1930s, other Americans seemed to be looking forward to the possibilities of technology and science as means of escaping the Great Depression. Inspired by the airplane and the imagery of flight, industrial designers assaulted sharp corners and abrupt protrusions in favor of extended lines and fluid curves. To create feelings of aerodynamic smoothness, they employed such newer materials as aluminum, chrome, and plastics. Finding its most compelling form in the bullet-shaped railroad locomotive, which were introduced with great fanfare in the 1930s, designers applied the concept of streamlining to nearly everything. Perhaps the smooth-formed aluminum diner served as the most enduring symbol of the streamlining fad. Within the home, streamlined products found their way into kitchens and bathrooms.

A reconciliation of the old and the new may be detected in Walt Disney's tremendously popular cartoon *The Three Little Pigs*, which first appeared in 1933. On its face, the cartoon seemed to be simply an endorsement of such old-fashioned virtues as hard work and self-constraint. In the cartoon, as well as in the folktale versions of the story, two of the three porkers quickly assemble a fragile house of straw and sticks so that they may "play around all day." Righteously asserting that "work and play don't mix," the third porker laboriously built himself a sturdy house of brick and stone. In the folktale version, the arrival of the wolf spells disaster for the pigs who had neglected the practice of old-fashioned virtues. But in Disney's cartoon, the third pig elects to save his fun-loving cohorts from the jaws of the wolf (read Depression) by inviting them to stay at his house. We also learn that the third pig, despite his admonitions on behalf of the virtues of hard work, is ultimately no enemy of play. He owns a piano, and, presumably to the mounting annoyance of the wolf, plays it with great gusto. At the end of the story, to a honky-tonk pianistic rendition, the three little pigs sing merrily together "Who's Afraid of the Big Bad Wolf." Echoing Franklin D. Roosevelt's plea in his inaugural address in 1933 that the "only thing we have to fear is fear itself," the song became an instant hit. As Terry Cooney has observed, Disney's cartoon offered at least a tentative resolution of the conflict between traditional work and modern leisure. It may also be understood as endorsing the idea of mutual sharing in a time of crisis.

Even before the advent of the Great Depression, popular culture began a process of revising the traditional formula for success. As if unconsciously recognizing that success had to be won increasingly in the bureaucratic maze of corporations or through salesmanship, the need for heroes who leaped to fame and fortune outside the world of ordinary work seemed to grow more pronounced. No longer were the heroes lone businessmen, statesmen, or philanthropists but the stars of sports, the movies, and popular music. From the movies in the 1920s came Rudolph Valentino, Clara Bow, Charlie Chaplin, and Douglas Fairbanks and from the world of sports came Babe Ruth, Jack Dempsey, and Red Grange. These heroes from the world of entertainment rather than production assisted the public in compensating for feelings of individual powerlessness, concern for the erosion of Victorian values, and gnawing doubts about the efficacy of the traditional formulas for achieving individual success.

No hero of the day equaled the capacity of Babe Ruth in projecting multiple images of the quick, decisive problem solver, the quintessential consumer, and the embodiment of the American success dream. Ruth was dramatic proof that men could still rise from lowly beginnings to fame and fortune. The simple, direct solutions represented in Ruth's mighty home run blasts reassured and inspired millions of Americans who were frustrated by the absence of potency that they felt in their jobs and in their personal relationships. At the same time, Ruth's ethnicity and religion (of German and Catholic origins) and his hedonistic lifestyle were powerful symbols of modern ways.

Contrary to what might have been expected, the Great Depression produced few instances of a complete renunciation of the older ideas of success and opportunity. Rather than disavowals, popular magazines of the day as well as ordinary citizens (including the jobless) were more likely to reassert with renewed vigor their faith in America as a special land of opportunity. Indeed, rather than seeing widespread joblessness as a failure of the economic system, many if not most of those out of work saw their unemployment as evidence of personal moral failure. They frequently refused to accept relief.

Nonetheless, the most popular success manual of the decade, one that continues to have a wide sale to this day, Dale Carnegie's *How to Win Friends and Influence People* (1936), indicated by its very title that those striving for success needed to develop character traits beyond the older formula of industry, thrift, dependability, and self-control. To Carnegie, the key to success lay not so much in the cultivation of traits that were conducive to ever greater productivity but in the management of the impressions that one made on others. To be successful, the ambitious should avoid conflict, develop good manners, and, above all else, strive to make others feel important. The cultivation of a hollow or false sense of self as suggested by Carnegie became the subject for Arthur Miller's tragic drama, *Death of a Salesman* (1949).

INDIVIDUALISM (OR LIBERALISM) REFORMULATED

While reaffirmations of the old were commonplace in the 1930s, the exigencies of the Great Depression virtually forced Americans to reexamine their adherence to individualism (sometimes also described as liberalism or classical liberalism). From the struggle against monarchal and hierarchical authority during the Revolutionary era and from the opening of the doors of opportunity for ordinary white men in the nineteenth century, individualism had emerged as a powerful if not carefully articulated American ideology. To its proponents, the rights and interests of the individual came ultimately before those of the society or the community. They tended to see the state (and not the economic system for example) as the individual's primary oppressor. Individuals and society prospered most, the proponents of acquisitive (but not necessarily expressive) individualism said, when the economic laws

Unless SomeTHING!

of supply and demand were allowed to operate free of state control. This laissez-faire (hands-off by the state) policy ensured that individuals got what they deserved, for economic success or failure was the individual's responsibility, and his or hers alone.

During the Great Depression, the most comprehensive indictment of individualism came not from Franklin D. Roosevelt's New Deal but from the left—from Marxism, socialism, communism, and variants thereof. Confidently predicting that capitalism was on the verge of collapse, leftists renounced traditional, or more precisely, acquisitive individualism (leftists were far less likely to criticize the expressive individualism found in a modern or bohemian lifestyle). Many of them looked to the newly founded communist state of the Soviet Union. The USSR offered a concrete model of a possible alternative to American individualism. With the Great Depression, the apparent Soviet success with a centrally planned society stood in stark contrast to the helplessness of the Western capitalistic nations. While the United States permitted the "anarchy" of the marketplace to determine its destiny, the Soviet Union appeared to harness its economy to the satisfaction of the needs of all. The USSR's militant antifascism added to its appeal.

The influence of the left extended well beyond its critique of acquisitive individualism. Before many leftists suffered a profound disillusionment with Stalinism in the late 1930s, some hundred thousand men and women joined the American Communist Party or cooperated with it in an effort not only to defend the USSR as the world's first "worker's state" but to organize industrial workers into labor unions and to do battle with racial injustice. In particular, artists and writers, acting in concert with the Popular Front, a broad alliance of leftist groups between 1935 and 1939, rediscovered the ordinary people. In dozens of novels, museum exhibitions, murals, Hollywood films, and theater productions, they celebrated the virtues and the strengths of "the common man." Their subject matter and style became known as socialist (or sometimes Marxist) realism.

Many, perhaps most, intellectuals did not go so far as the communists in repudiating individualism. Especially influential among the meliorists was philosopher John Dewey. In *Liberalism and Social Action* (1935), Dewey indicted both acquisitive individualism and Franklin D. Roosevelt's New Deal. Dewey called for a "renascent liberalism." The older liberalism in which society rested upon individual contracts and a maximum degree of individual freedom was no longer adequate, Dewey wrote. Industrialization, the formation of giant corporations, and more particularly the Depression required a new liberalism committed to bold social experimentation. Rather than starting from the preset dogma represented in either socialism or capitalism, Dewey said that the vision and the authority for such experimentation should flow from the bottom up (democratically) and be guided by the principles of systematic scientific inquiry.

In the end, the more ad hoc, piecemeal measures of the New Deal received far more public support than did the more radical departures from individualism suggested by Dewey or by the Communist Party. Without a guiding social philosophy or a comprehensive vision of an alternative to individualism, Roosevelt invoked traditional values while supporting a wide-ranging set of new initiatives by the state. In so doing, FDR transformed the meaning of the word "liberalism." With Roosevelt, liberalism no longer meant a hands-off role for government but instead an activist state that provided at the least a minimal safety net for all its citizens. As early as 1934, FDR juxtaposed his idea of "liberty" as the "greater security for the average man" against the older idea of the freedom of contract which he said served "the privileged few." To be truly free, FDR said, each citizen must have a modicum of economic security.

The New Deal's redefinition of liberalism established the expectation that in the future the national government would not hesitate to use some of its powers to counter the worst aspects of economic depressions. Borrowing from the theory of English economist John Maynard Keynes, future (but not New Deal) policymakers sought to maintain high levels of employment through the use of government taxing and spending powers. Otherwise, Keynesian principles left most of the economic decision making in private hands. In this sense, Keynesian economics accorded with traditional American individualism.

Consistent with the principle that a roughly equal distribution of wealth was vital to the health of a republic, the New Deal also sought to do something about what FDR called the "unjust concentration of wealth and economic power" in the hands of the few. The Revenue Act of 1935 (called the "Wealth Tax Act") threatened, according to its critics, to "soak the rich," but in fact loopholes resulted in a bill that only moderately raised taxes on high incomes and inheritances. New revenue measures during World War II and the early Cold War that imposed heavier taxes on the upper income brackets and on estates contributed more than the 1935 act to a minor redistribution of wealth in America. Between the 1940s and the 1980s, the portion of the nation's total wealth owned by the top 10 percent dropped slightly—to about 65 percent.

The New Deal's limited and tentative expansion of the state's role in American life was not the only significant departure from traditional individualism during the Depression. In the past, workers and employers alike had frequently perceived the collectivism of labor unions to be at odds with individualism. But in the 1930s the effects of the Depression and support by FDR's New Deal led millions of workers to join labor unions. Comprised of skilled workers, the older American Federation of Labor had for the most part ignored workers in the mass-production industries, but the Congress of Industrial Organizations (CIO), founded in 1935, spread the message that the "political liberty for which our forefathers fought" had been "made meaningless by economic inequality" and "industrial despotism." "Can you really be free if [your rights in the workplace] are not recognized and respected?" queried one union newspaper. Acting collectively, the unions sought in effect to redefine individualism so that it included the right to a living wage, to some control over the conditions of work, and to greater job security.

Of course not all Americans embraced either the CIO's or the New Deal's reformulation of individualism into what was increasingly called "liberalism." Opponents, who were now usually labeled as "conservatives," harked back to the earlier, more restricted meaning of individualism. Rallying around the slogan "freedom of enterprise," they insisted that the formation of unions and the New Deal's welfare state restricted economic freedom. The growing dependency on the state, ex-President Herbert Hoover said, was turning Americans into "lazy parasites." Conservatives frequently saw the retreat from laissez-faire as a slippery slope, one that could ultimately lead to a totalitarian state. Austrian economist Frederich A. Hayek, in a surprise bestseller entitled *The Road to Serfdom* (1944), even equated FDR's New Deal with Hitler's Germany and Stalin's Soviet Union. In the postwar era, such an equation—as exaggerated as it surely was—became virtually a truism for the opponents of the New Deal's version of liberalism.

"THE AMERICAN WAY OF LIFE"

Few if any events impinged on American ways more deeply or broadly than World War II and the early Cold War (from the 1940s through the 1950s). World War II brought with it economic recovery, and, while many Americans worried about the return of a depression, the economy continued to bound forward with a few minor setbacks until the 1970s. With the explosion of nuclear bombs over Japan in 1945, the "antibiotic revolution," and the development of the marvelous new medium of television, American scientific and technological know-how once again astonished the world. As in the past, Americans moved and then moved again—from the countryside to the cities, from the inner cities to the suburbs, and from the "rust belt" (Northeast) to the Sunbelt (the South and Southwest). In the meantime, threats, both real and perceived, from abroad provided a justification for the United States taking on a permanent (even a dominant) role in world affairs. To fight both hot and cold wars, the size and scope of the national government expanded far beyond anything previously imaginable.

In complex ways not easily understood, these events came together to encourage an ideology that called for the homogenization of American culture. In all aspects of the culture, it seemed, the urge was to unite, to include, to blend, in short, to create a single, unitary "American way of life." Once the ingredients of this way of life had been formulated and agreed upon, they were juxtaposed against the nation's ideological enemies: first the Axis Powers in World War II and then the Russian and Chinese communists during the Cold War. But the ideology of an American way of life became far more than simply a rhetorical weapon to be employed against foreign foes. It soon evolved into an ideal standard by which countless Americans measured themselves.

"Freedom"

During both World War II and the Cold War, the elusive but highly evocative word *freedom* became the centerpiece of the American way of life ideology. In 1941, in the face of the threatening Axis Powers, President Franklin D. Roosevelt announced the Four Freedoms—freedom of speech, freedom of worship, freedom from want, and freedom from fear. The Four Freedoms became the nation's rallying cry for fighting World War II. But it was left to a popular illustrator, Norman Rockwell, to flesh out and relate the Four Freedoms to the American way of life.

For the cover of the *Saturday Evening Post* in 1943, Rockwell translated FDR's Four Freedom into terms that vividly conveyed the distinctive ideological posture of the United States. In the first panel, representing freedom of speech, Rockwell depicted a workingman speaking at a town meeting. In the second panel, which represented freedom of worship, he pictured members of distinctive religious groups worshiping peacefully together. These

Four Freedoms. This popular Office of War Information poster, which was reproduced from Norman Rockwell's painting *The Four Freedoms,* sought to juxtapose American ideals with those of the Axis Powers of Germany and Japan.

two panels not only served as statements of traditional American freedoms, but they also indicated the value placed on inclusiveness and presumably tolerance of peoples of diverse class, ethnic, and religious backgrounds. (African Americans, however, were conspicuously absent from all four panels).

While freedom of religion and of speech certainly predated the Great Depression, the other two panels representing freedom from want and the freedom from fear were essentially new freedoms. Implicitly if not explicitly they had been among the primary objectives of the New Deal. In the freedom from want panel, Rockwell presented a family enjoying a sumptuous Thanksgiving dinner. It suggested that all Americans could unite behind the promise of consumption and material abundance. In the freedom from fear panel, Rockwell drew a mother and father standing over a sleeping child. It not only reflected the need for personal security but suggested that the nuclear family was the bedrock of the American way of life.

When contrasted with Nazi Germany's blatant racism, the establishment of the Four Freedoms as the essence of the American way of life encouraged the nation to embrace the modern value of social inclusiveness. In sharp contrast to the Nazis, who endorsed Aryan superiority, Americans now officially claimed to stand for the enjoyment of freedom by all racial, ethnic, and religious groups. Many Americans saw a shared belief in pluralism as a great unifying force. Writing for the Office of War Information, novelist Pearl Buck put it succinctly: "persons of many lands can live together . . . and if they believe in freedom they can become a united people." Throughout both World War II and the Cold War, the popularity of inclusiveness in government propaganda and the popular media made many ethnics, Catholics, and Jews, in the words of historian Eric Foner, "feel fully American for the first time."

While elevating freedom and tolerance to a new prominence encouraged the acceptance of ethnic and religious minorities, their consequences were far more problematic for racial minorities. During the war, government propaganda and war films depicted the Japanese as bestial and subhuman rats, dogs, snakes, and gorillas. Even after learning about the horrors of the Holocaust, eight out of ten Americans believed that the Japanese were more "cruel at heart" than the Germans. Apart from Japanese Americans themselves, almost no one protested the most blatant violation of freedom since slavery—the forced relocation and incarceration of Japanese Americans during World War II.

The glaring discrepancy between the rhetorical enthusiasm for freedom on the one hand and racial discrimination on the other was not lost upon African Americans. In the face of Nazi racism and threats of a march on Washington by blacks, FDR in 1941 issued an executive order banning discrimination in hiring based on "race, color, or national origins" by the national government or its contractors. But severe labor shortages in World War II did far more to expand work opportunities for blacks than the poorly enforced executive order. During the war, black newspapers also launched the "Double V" campaign for victory over fascism abroad and racism at home. Despite the second-class citizenship of blacks, the wartime proliferation of

official and unofficial propaganda on behalf of tolerance and social inclusiveness portended the possibility of a better future for African Americans.

Neither was the ideal of an American way of life free of ambiguity for
women. During World War II, millions of women flocked into factories to
fill industrial jobs vacated by men. The celebrated emblem of the female factory worker was Rosie the Riveter. But few Americans seemed to think that
Rosie's work might emancipate her from traditional female roles. Instead,
Rosie was, according to the popular view of the day, making temporary sacri-
fices on behalf of the war effort so that she could one day become a full-time
housewife with "a little house of [her] own, and a husband to meet every
night at the door."

Neither did all Americans agree with Roosevelt's and Rockwell's rendition
of the Four Freedoms or, at the least, Rockwell's interpretation of them. Even
during World War II, conservatives observed that freedom from want implied a dependence on government, indeed, a backhanded endorsement of
the New Deal. By implication, the conservatives suggested that the freedom
to starve might be a more accurate statement of traditional American principles. Any creed seeking to sum up the American way of life, they insisted,
should include "freedom of enterprise." In their campaign on behalf of making "free enterprise" the centerpiece of the American way of life, the conservatives achieved striking successes. Not only did freedom of enterprise frequently supercede or envelop the other Four Freedoms in the post–World
War II ideological confrontations with the Soviet Union, but it became a powerful rhetorical weapon in the conservative postwar defense of the status quo.

ANTICOMMUNISM

In the post–World War II era, anticommunism joined "freedom" as an integral component of the American way of life ideology. In 1947, President
Harry S Truman announced what became known as the policy of contain-
ment when he asserted that in the future the United States would support
"freedom-loving peoples" everywhere against threats from international
communism. Soon American policymakers and the media conceptualized
the Cold War as a conflict between the free and the enslaved worlds. Apart
from the debasement of the language entailed in classifying Franco's Spain
and dozens of other tyrannical regimes as part of the "free world," this simplistic bipolar conception of the world encouraged Americans to confuse the
rising power of revolutionary nationalism with a monolithic communism directed from within the walls of the Kremlin. In other words, in the postwar
era Americans tended to see the Soviet Union behind every social upheaval
in Asia, Africa, and Latin America.

Even art became a weapon in the Cold War. Unlike the USSR, which insisted on a socialist realism in its arts, Americans, according to the popular
media, championed complete artistic freedom. Abstract expressionism, a
postwar style of painting in New York City, satisfied perfectly the need for
positioning the United States vis-à-vis the USSR. Swirling and splattering

paint on giant canvasses in unrecognizable forms, the paintings of Jackson Pollock seemed the complete antithesis of social-realist paintings. The abstract expressionists demonstrated, in the words of one cold warrior, the virtues of "freedom of expression" in an "open and free society." Cooperating publicly with the United States Information Agency and clandestinely with the Central Intelligence Agency, the Museum of Modern Art in New York City displayed abstract expressionist paintings at art shows around the world.

The anticommunist crusade was not restricted to foreign policy. Setbacks in the Cold War and sensational revelations of spying by public officials encouraged the belief that any person, organization, or idea that could be linked in any way with communism was an enemy of the American way of life. In the late 1940s and in the 1950s, such a linkage touched off a nationwide anticommunist witch hunt, a mass hysteria that frequently made a mockery of the nation's much-vaunted freedoms. As one historian has noted, "a pervasive kind of democracy was practiced: all accusations, no matter from whom, were taken seriously."

Elbowing his way to the front of the crusade was the junior senator from Wisconsin, Joseph McCarthy. McCarthy capitalized on a multiplicity of fears and anxieties: anger by ethnics from Eastern Europe arising from the Soviet domination of their homelands, fears that the American government was "riddled" with communists or communist sympathizers, and anxieties arising from the triumphs of modern ways. Traditionalist-oriented Americans frequently identified communism with secularism (more specifically atheism), greater sexual freedom, social novelty, and intellectualism. To the more extreme of the traditionalists, modern ways and communism were virtually one and the same.

The anticommunist crusade narrowed sharply the range of political and social discourse. It helped to bring to a screeching halt proposals to extend New Deal programs. Invoking the specter of "socialized medicine" and hinting at its similarities to the Soviet system of medicine, the American Medical Association successfully blocked Truman's proposal for a national health insurance plan. And campaigns to identify the Democratic party with communism helped to elect a popular World War II general, Dwight D. Eisenhower, as president in 1952. Eisenhower considered FDR's New Deal and Truman's Fair Deal as examples of "creeping socialism." The anticommunist crusade limited the range of choices by labor unions and social organizations. Either they had to come to terms with the anticommunist movement or face extermination. Both the CIO and the NAACP renounced all former associations with the American Communist Party and expelled leaders and members considered too far to the political left.

The anticommunist crusade deeply affected the nation's intellectual life. Some artists and intellectuals stood firm; before congressional committees, they refused to name former associates in communist or other left-wing organizations. Such individuals paid a heavy price. Apart from jail sentences for contempt of Congress, they frequently found themselves occupationally blackballed.

Others who had been Marxists or had been on the far left of the political spectrum during the 1930s, openly repudiated their former allegiances. They took a hard stand against both communism and the Soviet Union. Some turned their backs on politics altogether while others called for the extension of New Deal social reforms. Of those who remained socially and politically engaged, their thought frequently took a decidedly conservative turn. With knowledge of the Holocaust, the horrors of the Allied bombings of civilian populations in World War II, and the savagery of Soviet purges looming in the background, they rediscovered the human propensity for evil and the importance of power. Joining an informal group dubbed by philosopher Morton White as the "atheists for Niebuhr," many of them endorsed theologian Reinhold Niebuhr's dim view of human nature.

The title of a much-discussed Daniel Bell essay, "The End of Ideology" (1960), captured much of the postwar intellectual mood. No longer committed to ideas or prescriptions that called for social revolution, the intellectuals accepted America's basic institutions and an economy that included a mixture of private enterprise and government involvement. Social problems remained, they agreed, but their solution required technical, piecemeal adjustments rather than wholesale changes. "Functionalism" became the theoretical rage of the day. Rather than focusing on what society should be, functionalists gave attention to how existing relationships "functioned" or worked to preserve the status quo. Sometimes labeled as the "consensus" school, historians of this period downplayed the significance of ideology and conflict in American history. They contributed to the homogenization of the larger culture by attributing conflict in the past as well as the present to psychic inadequacies rather than to region, ideology, ethnicity, race, religion, or social class. For example, the abolitionists, the populists, and the contemporary "far rightists" were said to have had "paranoid personalities."

Even the long-standing adversarial relationship between the modern artists and the general public relaxed. Not only did authorities employ abstract expressionist paintings as a weapon against the Soviet Union in the Cold War, but by the 1950s the avant-garde literature and arts of the early twentieth century now found general acceptance in university curricula and lecterns. The former avant-garde no longer gave "offense," wrote critic Leslie Fiedler, except to "a diminishing minority of ever more comical bigots." Public acceptance of modernism, several writers concluded, signaled the arrival of a new age of artistic sensibility that some described as "postmodernism." (However, a renewed outbreak of adversarial relationships and "wild" experimentation in the 1960s suggested that such a conclusion may have been premature.)

Public-school history texts uncritically proclaimed the wonders of the American way of life. "Inside their covers," Frances FitzGerald concludes on the basis of her study of postwar history texts, "America was perfect: the greatest nation in the world, the embodiment of democracy, freedom, and technological progress." Unlike earlier texts that had taken account of change and conflict in American history, the postwar texts extolled a seamless American past of stability and tranquility. They particularly praised the "free enterprise system," though, perhaps fearing that such an activity might imply to students the existence of an alternative system, they rarely made much of an effort to delineate its characteristics. The state legislature of Texas not only required that all writers of school texts sign a loyalty oath but passed a resolution urging that the "American history courses in the public schools emphasize in the textbooks our glowing and throbbing history of hearts and souls inspired by wonderful American principles and traditions."

Religion became yet another way of distinguishing the United States from the USSR. To the surprise of many, the postwar era witnessed a widespread turning to religion. As families sought to establish identities in the rootless suburbs and come to grips with a possible nuclear holocaust, church membership jumped from 50 to nearly 70 percent and weekly attendance at religious services nearly doubled between 1940 and 1958. Public opinion polls revealed a degree of religious orthodoxy in the United States that was far higher than anywhere else in the industrial world. For example nineteen out of twenty Americans believed in the existence of God and three out of four believed in life after death. Billy Graham, who started his revivalist career under the sponsorship of Protestant fundamentalists, became the icon of the nation's renewed religiosity. Immensely popular, Graham met and prayed with a succession of American presidents from Dwight Eisenhower to Bill Clinton.

For many, perhaps most, Americans, the postwar religious revival seemed to have been more about the appearance than the substance of faith. For example, less than half of those who claimed to be practicing Christians could name a single one of the four Gospels. Instead of requiring belief in a set of orthodox religious principles, more and more Americans seemed, in the words of religious historian Martin Marty, to "have faith in faith itself." As President Eisenhower said, religion was a "good thing." "Our government makes no sense, unless it is founded in a deeply felt religious faith—*and I don't care what it is.*" Postwar political leaders quickly sought to incorporate the renewal of religiosity into their formulation of the American way of life. In 1954, Congress added "under God" to the hitherto secular Pledge of Allegiance and declared in 1956 "In God We Trust" as the nation's official motto.

Yet at the same time that there was a flowering of religious "piety along the Potomac" and elsewhere, American faith in expertise and secular ways of thinking continued unabated. Indeed, public respect for scientists, social scientists, engineers, doctors, and the other professions soared to new heights. Even in the most sensitive areas of their personal lives, Americans increasingly turned to experts. While Americans had long valued education, in the postwar era more and more of them associated education with material progress, personal advancement, and success or failure in the Cold War. By providing for living allowances and tuition payments to veterans, the GI Bill of Rights Act (1944), along with the expansion of scholarships and loans, triggered a revolution in higher education. For the first time in American history, literally millions of men and women from lower-middle-class families obtained college degrees.

LIFE IN THE SUBURBS

Americans in the postwar era saw consumption and suburban living as the most important components of their way of life. No incident in the postwar era made this point more dramatically or concretely than the famed "kitchen debate" between Vice President Richard M. Nixon and Soviet Premier Nikita Khrushchev in 1959. Before flying to the Moscow trade exhibit, Nixon had been urged by a former ambassador to the USSR to emphasize how American values differed from the Soviets: "We are idealists; they are materialists," he said. But Nixon ignored the ex-ambassador's advice. In the kitchen exhibit of a suburban ranch-style house—allegedly a house that could be owned by the average American steelworker—Nixon responded to each of Khruschev's claims for the superiority of the Soviet system, *not* by reminding the premier of America's commitment to democracy, freedom, or philanthropy, but by pointing to the vast array of wonderful consumer goods that he claimed were available to the typical American family. As *Time* magazine observed, the entire nation applauded Nixon's logic in equating life in the suburbs and consumer abundance with the American way of life.

By 1959, a large range of facts supported the importance of suburbia to American life. While there was nothing new about suburbs, in the postwar era soaring automobile sales, growing family incomes, subdividers with a knack for mass-producing houses, the construction of miles and miles of multilane freeways, and federal subsidies to new homeowners transformed cornfields and cow pastures into acres and acres of suburbs. "Most of the people that I worked with [during World War II] lived in rented houses and close to slum conditions," explained Robert Montgomery, a factory worker in Elyria, Ohio. "By the fifties almost everybody in that kind of social world expected that they would live in a suburban house—one that they owned themselves. The war integrated into the mainstream a whole chunk of society that had been living on the edge." But not all urbanites had the financial wherewithal or the right skin color to move to the suburbs. Blacks, Hispanics, and the impoverished remained behind—in the rapidly decaying inner cities.

With the emergence of the suburb as the chief site for fulfilling the American way of life, pressures mounted for women to quit industrial workplaces and retreat to the home. Symptomatic of the pressure was Marynia Farnham and Ferdinand Lunberg's best-seller, *Modern Woman: The Lost Sex* (1947). Women who preferred to work outside the home, the psychologist-sociologist team wrote, were "neurotically disturbed" and afflicted with the much-dreaded "penis envy." Those women who did continue working outside the home—and in fact some 40 percent remained in the workforce—now toiled for the most part in low-paid clerical, sales, and service jobs. Frequently employed part-time, they no longer worked so much to escape poverty or to pursue a career as to ensure the existence of their family's middle-class suburban lifestyle.

According to the suburban dream, the father was the family breadwinner while the mother devoted her life to children, husband, and home. Ironically, it was in the suburbs of the 1950s, and not the Victorian age of the 1890s, that the United States came the closest to realizing on a massive scale the ideals of domesticity and a "separate sphere" for women. Inevitably, the luxury of having women stay at home became a weapon in the Cold War. Unlike the Soviet Union, where mothers toiled away from home while their children were being taught to become "good little comrades" at state-run child-care centers, American mothers, by staying home, ensured that the nation would remain forever the "land of the free." The stay-at-home mother was one of those things "that separates us from the Communist world," concluded James O'Connell, undersecretary of labor in the Kennedy Administration.

Life in the suburbs contained a mixture of the traditional and the modern. The reaffirmation of the virtues of domesticity, the renewal of religiosity, and the clear-cut separation of gender roles harked back to the Victorian era. Marriage returned to favor. To the utter surprise of demographers, who had associated a falling fertility rate with the Industrial Revolution, Americans began having babies again. According to a 1953 poll nearly three-fourths of the American people believed that an ideal family consisted of three or more children. They did not quite reach that lofty goal—the average increased from two to three—but the "baby boom" was in full swing. It ended only when the birth control pill became publicly available in 1960.

After women had taken on man-sized jobs and more "masculine" ways of dressing and behaving during World War II, the popular media and the fashion industry set out after the war to "refeminize" the American woman. The "New Look," in the words of French fashion designer, Christian Dior, emphasized "full feminine busts, and willowy waists above enormous spreading skirts." The "current ideal," explained no less an authority than *Good Housekeeping* magazine, was "firm, full, cone-shaped breasts, standing up and out without visible means of support." However understood in other respects, the obsession with breast size in the postwar era seemed to reflect an impulse to draw a firmer boundary between cultural conceptions of femininity and masculinity. In this respect, it echoed the Victorian age.

On the other hand, the daily lives of suburban families reflected less patriarchal dominance, frugality, and self-restraint than in earlier times. Even women's roles were less constricted than is commonly perceived. Popular periodicals of the day, as Joanne Meyerowitz has shown, frequently celebrated the feats of women in both the domestic and the public realm. Modern marriage, popular singer Pat Boone crooned in 1958, was a "fifty-fifty deal." In the modern suburban family, at least according to the popular media, husbands/fathers no longer ruled with an iron fist; indeed, like Dagwood Bumstead in a popular comic strip revealingly entitled *Life with Blondie,* husbands were often depicted as rather good-natured but bumbling incompetents. Also contrary to popular interpretations of the 1950s, both wives and husbands expected to enjoy marital sexual pleasures. Neither did

The Stay-at-Home Mother. Dad is nowhere in sight in this Johnson & Johnson ad that appeared in a 1947 issue of *Life.* Perhaps unconsciously, the ad suggested a downside to motherhood in the postwar era. Historian Susan Douglas has suggested that the ad may have terrorized mothers into "concentrating all their energies on baby sputum and talcum powder."

middle-class families any longer deny themselves consumer delights. As never before, they bought cars, home appliances, carpets, barbecue grills, television sets, and dozens of other consumer items. No longer did women monopolize family buying. Youth too, especially teenagers, joined the consumer binge.

Like the English gentry of the eighteenth century, each suburban family had its own rural estate (albeit miniaturized), complete with a private yard, shrubs, a tiny garden, and an unattached single-family dwelling. Rooted in architectural features pioneered by Frank Lloyd Wright at the turn of the century, the suburban house of choice was the one-story ranch style. With its picture window, built-in conveniences, open interiors, air-conditioning, central heating, and outdoor patios, the ranch-style house presumably allowed families to re-create anywhere in the nation the relaxed, fun-loving lifestyle popularly associated with sunny southern California. As with other aspects of postwar life, the ranch-style house helped to level out regional differences and leave in its wake a national suburban culture.

Leisure activities increasingly shifted from public places to the privacy of the home. In the first half of the century, city dwellers had patronized a burgeoning commercial entertainment industry, but by 1960 the movies, sports venues, big dance bands, and amusement parks had witnessed a free fall in public support. Do-it-yourself projects, home repairs, conquering the crabgrass frontier, and watching television occupied much of the suburbanite's spare time. "No man who owns his own home and lot can be a Communist," observed William J. Levitt, one of the mass-builders of suburban housing. "He has too much to do." For many, the home was a self-sufficient recreation center, or a "family playpen," to use anthropologist Margaret Mead's apt phrase. The enjoyment of children and "family togetherness," according to the popular media of the day, became virtually a moral obligation.

Television reinforced the homogenization of the culture. At first, in its early days following World War II, the new medium had offered glimpses into the nation's social and cultural heterogeneity; a series of working-class situation comedies presented families in inner-city neighborhoods and explored value conflicts that revolved around class, ethnicity, gender, and consumer spending. But in the 1950s, television programming bleached out differences. Introduced in 1953, a family sitcom, *Father Knows Best*, exemplified the shift toward a world of suburban uniformity. Insulated completely from ethnic, racial, and class conflict, the Anderson family lived an idyllic existence in a large house; the father was a benevolent despot, the mother always perfectly coiffured, and the children never given to outright rebellion.

Everything about suburban living seemed to encourage conformity. With their lives no longer anchored in small towns, rural communities, or big-city ethnic enclaves, and with the husband's job tied increasingly to the impressions that he made on others, suburban families actively sought approval from their peers. The "inner-directed" personality of the nineteenth century had given way, according to sociologist David Riesman in 1950, to an "other-directed" personality. Suburbanites not only bought similar cars and houses, but they watched the same programs on television, shared similar opinions on social issues, and behaved the same. They dressed alike: blue jeans became the teenager's uniform of choice while women began wearing slacks or shorts. No group served as more compelling examples of Riesman's other-directed personality than suburban teenagers. Radio's archetype of the other-directed teenager was Henry Aldrich, who made it his "chief endeavor [in life] to find out what are the mores [of his peers] and to obey them."

Conclusion

In the decades between World War I (1914–18) and the turbulent 1960s, modern ways "came of age." Intellectually, the dichotomies that were so precious and so central to the conception of the world held by Victorian Americans collapsed. To modern Americans, such categories as "good" and "bad," "civilized" and "savage," "right" and "wrong," "godly" and "ungodly," and "animal" and "human" were no longer set in concrete. To them such terms seemed far less certain and more ambiguous than they had to earlier generations. To modern Americans, values were never fixed; they were always in flux. Whereas middle-class Victorians had sought to suppress volcanic passions, modern Americans tried to get in touch with and explore their feelings. They were far more likely than their ancestors to embrace and savor all varieties of raw experience. Hence, they frequently elevated the values of consumption, leisure, spontaneity, and immediate gratification above those of production, hard work, frugality, and self-control.

Yet modern ways never achieved a complete triumph. Far from it. In the 1920s, traditionalists mounted a full-scale counterattack—one that enjoyed some striking successes—against modern ways. Confronted with the crisis of the Great Depression, modern Americans themselves were torn between visions of the future and impulses that led them back to the ways of the past. Confronted with powerful ideological enemies during World War II and the Cold War, Americans sought to define and conform to an American way of life that consisted of a combination of both the modern and the traditional. What few Americans could foresee in the 1950s were the seething changes bubbling below the surface. In the next decade, these exploded into a great cultural paroxysm.

THE CULMINATION OF MODERN WAYS

In the tumultuous 1960s and early 1970s, pent-up modernist impulses—some of which had been restrained since the 1920s—again surged onto the national scene. Employing sit-ins and marching in the streets, African Americans and their supporters demanded the fulfillment of the promises implicit in cultural pluralism. Hippies, as the most advanced agents of a youthful rebellion were known, openly flaunted all forms of authority. All artistic and literary barriers came tumbling down. Annihilating the ages-old dichotomy between art and life, the Living Theater in its *Paradise Now* invited the audience to come on stage, take off their clothes, and join the cast in sexual merrymaking. Millions of girls went from singing "I want to be Bobby's girl" to chanting "I Am Woman (Hear Me Roar)." In a banner headline on its cover, *Time* magazine even posed the ominous question: "IS GOD DEAD?"

Whether viewed as the culmination of modern ways or as the beginning of postmodern ways, the sixties' "counterculture" merged in the late twentieth century with an expanding consumer capitalism to usher in a new cultural era. At its center was a *new individualism*. In its demands for individual rights and individual autonomy, the new individualism moved far beyond anything imaginable to earlier generations. Not only did it entail a "rights revolution," but, equally important, a view of life as an endless array of unfettered and ever-changing individual choices. Accordingly, individuals were (or implicitly should be) free to buy consumer goods of their own choosing, to earn as much money as they possibly could, to do what they wished in their private lives, and to make or break personal ties freely. In its ultimate formulation, the new individualism commanded each person to "do your own thing."

During the final four decades of the twentieth century and extending into the twenty-first century, coming to terms with the new individualism occupied much of the nation's attention. Few Americans sought a complete restoration of such traditional inequalities as those that had earlier existed between blacks and whites or women and men. Neither did they wish a complete return to earlier strictures on personal behavior. Most welcomed the greater opportunities for personal fulfillment, the broader tolerance, and what seemed in some respects a freer and a more joyous society. Yet, at the same time, even the new individualism's staunchest exponents frequently worried about the implications of an ever-expanding set of rights, of loosening standards of personal conduct, of weakening attachments to others, and a growing estrangement from public life. Indeed, they began to ask a momentous question: In a society that seemed increasingly bereft of enduring ties and obligations beyond the self, was meaningful self-fulfillment even possible?

THE RIGHTS REVOLUTION

Of its many complex and frequently opposing departures from the past, nothing was more central to the arrival of the new individualism than a revolution in rights. Prior to the sixties, rights had consisted of a finite body of entitlements enjoyed mainly by white men. But, beginning in the fifties with the civil rights movement and continuing into the sixties and long thereafter, the modernist urge for individual fulfillment encouraged one aggrieved group after another—African Americans, women, Native Americans, Hispanics, gays, welfare recipients, the handicapped, the elderly, and even consumers (among others)—to press forward claims for equality, relief from discrimination, and additional opportunities. Not only did these groups obtain greater recognition and a growing body of legal protections, but the rights revolution also brought with it far-reaching rearrangements in American race, ethnic, and family relationships.

A convergence of circumstances helped to set the stage for the rights revolution. One was a declining concern by the mid-1950s with domestic anticommunism. Few Americans objected when the U.S. Senate censured Senator Joseph McCarthy in 1954 or when in the late fifties the U.S. Supreme Court began to strike down the Cold War legal restrictions on "subversive" speech and associations. Even more corrosive to the postwar restraints on demands for an expansion of individual rights was economic abundance. As it had not done since the 1920s, the economy's performance opened up for millions previously unimaginable vistas of greater self-fulfillment; it made possible an exceptionally large, affluent youth culture; and it encouraged rising expectations among the less privileged. In short, general prosperity underwrote the innovation and daring that marked the new individualism while at the same time minimizing its risks.

African Americans and the Rights Revolution

No cause was more central to the rights revolution than that of African Americans. The black civil rights movement not only swept aside a long-established system of *legal* segregation and discrimination, but it affirmed in a spectacular fashion the modernist values of tolerance and pluralism. Sensitizing and heightening consciousness of repression, it also furnished a model for the organized movements of other discontented groups.

By the end of World War II, not much had changed since the turn of the twentieth century in the nation's system of race relations. As had been the case in 1900, law everywhere in the South still mandated the physical separation of blacks and whites in nearly all public situations. Segregation ranged from baseball parks and telephone booths to buses and classrooms. Neither could most African Americans vote in the South. And everywhere in the nation, housing segregation, either legal or de facto, was the rule. As late as 1960, of the fifty-two thousand people living in the model suburb of Levittown, Long Island, not one was known to be black. Job discrimination also existed everywhere. No matter where they lived in America, African Americans at mid-twentieth century could daily feel the awful sting and humiliation of being treated as inferior human beings.

In retrospect, the precipitants of a massive assault on the nation's traditional ways of race are clear. They include the "Double V" campaign—victory over the Axis Powers abroad and victory over racism at home—sponsored by black newspapers during World War II. They include the massive migration of African Americans from the southern countryside to the cities. The new urban dwellers helped to make possible the important symbolic breakthrough of the integration of major league baseball by Jackie Robinson in 1947, and they became a major component of the Democratic party coalition sympathetic to black rights. The precipitants of the civil rights revolt include the rise of new African states and the demand for ethnic and racial inclusiveness during and after World War II. They included a decided shift in educated white opinion. By the 1940s few white intellectuals any longer subscribed to theories of racial inferiority. In principle if not always in practice, modernist whites endorsed the ideal of success based on talents rather than skin color. A poll taken in 1956 revealed that 75 percent of white college graduates outside the South favored the racial integration of the schools.

Initiatives for the postwar assault on traditional racism came from several quarters. One was from the urban-centered National Association for the Advancement of Colored People. Responding to a suit brought by the NAACP, in 1954 a unanimous U.S. Supreme Court reversed its *Plessy* v. *Ferguson* decision of 1896. In *Brown* v. *Board of Education,* the court ruled that school segregation violated the equal protection of the law guaranteed to each citizen by the Fourteenth Amendment. Reflecting a characteristically modernist mindset, the court cited in support of its ruling a body of social science research. According to the findings of scholars, African-American children suffered irreparable psychological damage from the experience of school segregation. Hence, separate schools prevented African Americans from fully realizing their individual potentialities. Americans with modern values (including many in the urban South) applauded the *Brown* decision while traditionalists everywhere saw it as jeopardizing the American way of life.

Another major initiative for change came from African Americans living in the urban South. They found a leader in Martin Luther King, Jr., an eloquent young black minister. A product of both southern black Christianity and a northern modernist education, King brilliantly blended the old with the new. He repeatedly called upon an ages-old trope of black Christianity, the story of a divinely inspired Moses leading the children of Israel out of Egyptian bondage and into the promised land of Canaan. Echoing the abolitionists of the antebellum era, he called on higher law. Whenever man-made law, such as segregation statutes, contradicted higher law, he wrote in his *Letter from Birmingham Jail* (1963), then it should be resisted by nonviolent means. He drew upon the existentialist theology of Martin Buber. Segregation, King argued, diminished human individuality. By substituting an "I-it" relationship for an "I-thou" relationship between peoples, segregation allowed whites to perceive of and to treat blacks as things or objects rather than as human beings. By taking the movement into the streets, the new medium of television aided King's cause. On nightly television news shows, King's peaceful resistance and moderation stood in sharp contrast to the violence of local police, the inflammatory rhetoric of segregation's supporters, and the partiality of southern courts.

Comprised of blacks and whites, civil rights demonstrations reached a massive crescendo in the summer of 1963. During one week in June, police arrested more that fifteen thousand demonstrators in 186 cities. Demanding both an expansion of freedom and more black jobs, that summer a quarter of a million people (including a substantial white minority) marched on Washington. There, on the steps of the Lincoln Memorial, Martin Luther King, Jr., announced his "dream that one day . . . the sons of former slaves and the sons of former slave-owners will be able to sit together at the table of brotherhood."

One vital ingredient was still missing from the movement. This was political leadership. Lyndon Johnson, a Texan who became president by virtue of Kennedy's assassination in 1963, filled that vacuum. The Civil Rights Act of 1964 and the Voting Rights Act of 1965, both unthinkable at the beginning of the decade, struck heavy blows at the legal bases of segregation. A far less noticed but an almost equally striking example of the startling advances of modern pluralism was the Immigration Act of 1965. The new act ended the national quota system that had long stigmatized Southern and Eastern Europeans as well as Asians. When combined, these acts represented gigantic steps in realizing more fully the egalitarian principle found in Thomas Jefferson's assertion in 1776 that "all men are created equal."

Lyndon Johnson not only presided over these momentous triumphs of egalitarian principle, but he contributed to the rights revolution in other ways. Building upon the ideas of freedom from want and freedom from fear that FDR had enunciated in his famed Four Freedoms speech in 1941, Johnson implicitly urged the impoverished and the elderly, among others, to see economic and medical security as a right or an entitlement. It was no longer enough, said Johnson in 1965, to think of equality of opportunity only in terms of eliminating discrimination that barred upward mobility. In "the next and more profound stage of the battle for civil rights . . . we seek . . . not just equality as a right and a theory, but equality as a fact and as a result." In

Martin Luther King, Jr., at the March on Washington in 1963. Such a massive demonstration on behalf of civil rights and jobs for African Americans would hardly have been conceivable a decade earlier. Other groups seeking liberation from traditional constraints drew upon the civil rights movement for inspiration and tactics.

an effort to move the country in this direction, the national government enacted the largest domestic agenda since the New Deal. It included a "war on poverty" program, medicare, medicaid, and increased federal expenditures on education.

In the meantime, the civil rights movement had polarized the nation. From the outset, traditionalist opponents had believed that racial differences were embedded in biology, the Bible, and in custom; hence, they thought that it was sheer folly for humans to think they could or should alter existing racial relationships. Throughout the South massive resistance greeted the *Brown* decision, and the peaceful marches, sit-ins, and mass arrests that King and his followers had used so successfully earlier in the South utterly failed to dismantle the North's black ghettos. A year before his death by an assassin's bullet in 1968, an incredulous King said he had never "seen as much hatred" as he encountered when he tried to integrate the white ethnic enclaves of Chicago. He confessed that open housing and equal employment opportunities for blacks remained "a distant dream."

Other blacks gave up on King's modernist goal of a racially integrated society. Drawing on the nationalist tradition of Marcus Garvey, Malcolm X, a leader of the Nation of Islam, rejected alliances with sympathetic whites or federal assistance; he insisted that blacks must rely on their own resources. The slogan of "Black Power" struck an especially responsive chord among young black activists. While never winning many victories nor carefully articulated, Black Power encouraged racial separatism. A similar separatist impulse would lead Native Americans, Chicanos, and third-generation ethnics to retreat from modern pluralism's inclusionist goal.

In the heady atmosphere of the mid-1960s few anticipated the degree to which racial separation would long afterward characterize American life. With the passage of the civil rights acts, administrative initiatives, affirmative action, and favorable court decisions, most modernists assumed that blacks would experience a rapid improvement in income, education, and integration into the larger society. But, while a significant minority of African Americans did achieve striking gains, many others remained far behind the national average in all indicators of equality with whites. At the end of the twentieth century, race seemed to remain the nation's most salient and persistent social and cultural division.

WOMEN AND THE RIGHTS REVOLUTION

As with African Americans, women at mid-twentieth century also lived with major obstacles to their self-fulfillment. These included their intimate relations with men, where they frequently experienced a world of constrained choices and belittling remarks. Having taken jobs outside the home so that they and their families could enjoy more of the fruits of the consumer society, many women found their hands simultaneously full of shopping lists, stenographic pads, dinner dishes, and diaper pails. At work, they usually held lower-paying jobs and found upward job mobility blocked.

There were other precipitants of the women's rights movement. The number of female college students doubled in the 1960s, creating a vastly larger pool of those who were more likely to become discontented with the gender status quo. The downward plunge of the birthrate in the 1960s left more women with more years of their lives free of child-care responsibilities. Finally, in the 1960s the divorce rate, which had been creeping upward throughout the twentieth century, suddenly shot upward. The upshot of all of this was that the typical woman's life included work, marriage, child-rearing, a span of her life free of child-care, and, if divorced, supporting and bringing up children alone—a far cry from the fifties' ideal of domesticity.

The arrival of a new set of female icons anticipated and contributed to the revival of feminism. A hint surfaced in 1961 that neither the cheerful housewives of television sitcoms nor the blank-faced, big-breasted, blue-eyed blondes of Hollywood would any longer suffice as models of womanhood. To many women, Jacqueline Kennedy, the new president's wife, seemed to keep in perfect suspension an older femininity and a new, more modern womanhood. Slim, stylish, rich, a dutiful wife, a mother, and formerly a career woman, she read voraciously, spoke French fluently, and loved horseback riding. Even the heroines of sixties' television sitcoms changed; on *Bewitched*, *I Dream of Jeannie*, and *The Flying Nun*, the female leads all possessed magical powers. Suggestive of yet another impulse toward greater female freedom and empowerment was the popularity of a revolutionary style of dancing.

Beginning in 1960 with "The Twist," a hit by Chubby Checker, teenagers began to dance without touching or the man leading.

Yet neither dancing apart, Jackie Kennedy, nor magical women were free of traditional feminine stereotypes. They sent women mixed, even schizoid messages. Nothing illustrated this point more forcefully or grotesquely than the go-go girl dancing in a cage. Autonomous as she danced alone, the go-go girl was literally entrapped in a cage and objectified before the voyeuristic gaze of her audience.

In 1963, away from the popular culture's confusing cross-currents, came a bombshell—Betty Friedan's *The Feminine Mystique*. Friedan stood the idealized postwar American way of life on its head. Just four years after Richard Nixon had made the suburban home, with its stay-at-home mother and its abundance of consumer goods, the emblem of the American way of life, Friedan described it as nothing less than "a comfortable concentration camp." Rather than being "gaily content in a world of bedroom, kitchen, sex, babies and home," wrote Friedan, the camp's inmates (the suburban housewives) felt "empty" and "incomplete." Despite more than a hundred years of agitation for equal access to opportunities, she continued, "our culture does not permit women to accept or gratify their basic need to grow and fulfill their potentialities as human beings." Those who sought careers, according to Friedan, were deemed neurotic and unwomanly. Influenced by Freidan's book, almost overnight—or so it seemed—women seeking career opportunities won a series of smashing victories.

Yet new federal mandates expanding possibilities for women in the job market failed to alter other forms of gender tyranny. Traditional stereotypes continued to pervade the popular media and, while an accompanying sexual revolution freed women of some of the double standard's restraints, it simultaneously seemed to reinforce the prevailing notion of women as objects for the sexual pleasure of men. Influenced by participation in the civil rights and the antiwar movements, where pleas for gender equality were usually ignored by the male leadership, a new, more radical feminism burst onto the national scene in 1968. At the Miss America beauty pageant (the only television show that Richard Nixon let his daughters stay up late at night to watch), protestors sought to call attention to how the culture placed a higher value on the way a woman looks than on her achievements by filling a "freedom trash can" with bras, girdles, hairpins, and false eyelashes.

The momentum for women's liberation continued into the 1970s. Membership in the National Organization of Women, founded in 1964 by Betty Friedan, multiplied rapidly and hundreds of thousands of women joined "consciousness-raising groups" where they discussed with other women job discrimination and relationships with their boyfriends and husbands. Frustrated by feelings of entrapment in traditional housewife roles and angry over unfair divisions of household labor, many confronted their husbands or partners. They demanded new arrangements. Initially viewed as a radical idea (or even as a communist-inspired one in the fifties), feminists successfully fought for the creation of child-care centers across the country. Symbolic of

Women Demonstrating on Behalf of the Equal Rights Amendment, Washington, D.C., 1970.
While the Equal Rights Amendment fell short of ratification, perhaps no change in
American ways during the last half of the twentieth century was more profound than
that revolving around the expectations, roles, and behaviors of women.

feminist successes was the sudden proliferation of women in sports and
eventually in the armed forces, arenas long considered special bastions of
"masculinity" and "manliness." Within five years after the passage of Title IX
of the Educational Amendments Act of 1972, nearly every high school and
college in the country rushed to form varsity programs for women. In startling
contrast with the 1950s, by the early 1970s the revived feminist movement
had opened up a far larger world of choices and opportunities for women.

THE SUPREME COURT AND THE RIGHTS REVOLUTION

From an unexpected and historically conservative branch of the national
government came yet another major contributor to the rights revolution. In
a series of landmark decisions, the "Warren Court," so named for its chief
justice, Earl Warren, who served from 1953 to 1969, vastly expanded the
constitutional protections of individual rights. Apart from the 1954 school

desegregation decision, in the late 1950s the court began to strike down the Cold War strictures on freedom of speech. Reflecting the nation's growing religious pluralism and in effect disestablishing Protestantism as the nation's unofficial religion, in the 1960s, the court extended the rights of religious minorities by prohibiting prayer and Bible readings in the public schools. Defending the rights of the less privileged and the powerless, the court required that the state provide indigent defendants in felony cases with attorneys at public expense and that the police advise suspects of their constitutional rights as well as the right to have counsel present during questioning. Dismantling a longstanding system of state and local censorship, the court extended constitutional protections to all sexually explicit materials that had any "literary or scientific, or artistic value."

Not only did the court provide an immense transfusion of additional substance into traditional civil liberties, but it also created or invented essentially new rights that would have far-reaching consequences for the history of American ways. One was the right to privacy. "The right to be let alone is the beginning of all freedom," wrote Supreme Court Justice William O. Douglas. Conceding in effect that the decade's sexual revolution could not be reversed, the court extended access to birth control not only to married couples but also eventually to unmarried adults and to minors. Although Earl Warren was no longer on the bench, these decisions led directly to *Roe* v. *Wade* (1973), which gave women the constitutional right to terminate a pregnancy. Furthermore, a bundle of court rulings and legislative actions essentially redefined the family as a collection of sovereign individuals rather than as a single unit headed by a husband/father. Consequently, within the domestic sphere, women (and to a growing extent children as well) experienced a vastly expanded set of legal protections.

Rather than subsiding during the final decades of the twentieth century, issues revolving around rights continued to occupy a central place in the national dialogue. More and more Americans demanded the removal of all obstacles to their individual fulfillment. Gays and lesbians, for example, sought guarantees of a life free of violence and discrimination. The Disabilities Act of 1990 expanded the possibilities for the handicapped to realize fuller lives. Children, the mentally ill, and the imprisoned also claimed as rights opportunities for greater self-gratification and contentment. Claims were even made on behalf of the rights of endangered species and unborn fetuses. In addition, "rights" became a favorite rhetorical weapon in the campaigns for clean air, safe water, and healthy foods.

EXPRESSIVE INDIVIDUALISM UNLEASHED

As with other modernist impulses, an extraordinary series of crises—the Great Depression, World War II, and the early Cold War—had served to set back or to contain the more expressive forms of individualism. But, alongside and frequently interacting with the revolution in rights during the 1960s was a remarkably widespread tendency to unleash restraints on individual intuitions and feelings. Pushing the earlier twentieth-century revolt against Victorian self-control to its outer limits, the cultural rebels of the day (most of whom were youth), embraced aphorisms such as: "If it feels good, do it," "Let it all hang out," and "Do your own thing." True, there was a pull in the sixties toward the creation of smaller, more intimate, face-to-face communities, but in the end this urge gave way to a far more powerful appetite for self-fulfillment and self-expression. Nearly all of the decade's cultural rebels believed that each individual possessed a unique inner core or self, one that could be released only by rejecting artificiality and external authority.

CONCERN FOR THE FATE OF THE INDIVIDUAL

Well before the 1960s, even in the midst of the enthusiasm for the idealized, fifties way of life, there was evidence in the culture of a growing concern for the fate of the individual. Artists, intellectuals, and even those employed in the world of white-collar bureaucracies began to ask with increasing frequency: "In a society of giant bureaucracies, mass media, and suburban conformity, where is there room for the individual?" Despite the creation in the sixties and afterward of a culture that seemed far more attuned to the unrestrained individual, Americans continued long afterward to voice this and related questions.

The answers proffered by social critics in the 1940s and 1950s to the place of the individual in contemporary society were far from reassuring. More than a few saw authentic individuality swamped in a flood of consumer goods. "People no longer have opinions," complained one writer, "they have refrigerators. Instead of illusions, we have television." Others worried about the effects of the media on individualism. According to a brilliant group of refugees from Nazi Germany, the mass media left modern societies dangerously susceptible to totalitarianism. The media "automatized reactions and . . . weaken[ed] forces of individual resistance," charged Theodor Adorno. Another critic, Dwight Macdonald, sarcastically described American middle-class suburban literary and artistic pretensions, because of their banality and conformity with media-provided mediocrity, as "midcult." Even fifties suburbanites themselves worried about the effects of movies, comic books, advertising, television, and rock-and-roll music on the nation's youth.

Still others complained about the sacrifice of individuality required for achieving personal success in a world of institutional behemoths. Sociologist David Riesman in *The Lonely Crowd* (1950) set the tone for a large body of social criticism in the fifties when he juxtaposed the "inner-directed man" of the nineteenth century against the "outer-directed man" of the twentieth century. *The Man in the Gray Flannel Suit* (Sloan Wilson), *The Organization Man* (William Whyte), and *White Collar Class* (C. Wright Mills)—the very titles of these popular books evoked similar images of a stifling conformity to outside pressures. To describe those whose lives were caught up in the labyrinth of organizational leviathans, beginning in the 1950s the term "rat race" became something of a cliché in newspaper stories and in everyday conversations.

Fiction and movies too reflected a concern for the individual. While fiction in the Great Depression had characteristically emphasized society and social problems, that of the forties and fifties focused on the self. Some of the most popular novels and movies championed the defiant individual. Such individuals overcame insuperable dangers by resorting exclusively to their own internal resources. "I do not recognize anyone's right to one minute of my time," announced the contumacious hero of Ayn Rand's best-selling novel, *The Fountainhead* (1943). The public responded with equal fervor to less selfish Western heroes whom they encountered in countless postwar movies and later in television shows. Acting alone and against overwhelming odds, the Western heroes invariably restored justice and order in a cleansing rite of violence. Mickey Spillane's private detective, Mike Hammer, offered yet another formulation of the defiant individual. While frequently breaking society's rules, Hammer single-handedly dispatched drug dealers, mobsters, and communists.

Other depictions of the individual were far less sanguine. Ultimately no personal choice nor inner resource made any difference, according to the novelists of World War II; one soldier was just as likely as the next to fall victim from a stray bullet. The most compelling examples of this kind of fiction came from writers outside the mainstream culture. Unlike the Western hero, individuals in the South, according to a group of regional writers, found themselves shackled in an invisible prison from the past while Jewish writers explored the anguishing inner turmoil faced by the offspring of immigrants in contemporary America. In his powerful novel, *Invisible Man* (1952), Ralph Ellison cried out against the loss of individuality and the depersonalization suffered by African Americans in white society.

Yet none of these writers anticipated or influenced the rebellious cultural styles of the sixties as much as the "beats." Echoing Walt Whitman, whom they admired, the beats renounced suburban conformity and consumerism. "Robot apartments! invisible suburbs! skeleton treasures! blind capitals! demonic industries!" shouted Allen Ginsberg in his poem *Howl* (1955). While conspicuously rejecting acquisitive individualism, they warmly embraced all of the expressive forms of individualism. Hence, they experimented with drugs, celebrated uninhibited sexuality, took to the open road, and, believing that African Americans were less culturally repressed than whites, incorporated into their argot such words from black ghetto culture as "dig," "hip," "man," "split," and "cool." Not only in the sixties but long afterwards the beats continued to serve one generation after another with heroic prototypes of cultural rebellion.

THE YOUTH CULTURE

The development of a new, more powerful, and ultimately more autonomous youth culture in the post–World War II era also foreshadowed the expressive

individualism of the turbulent sixties. In the postwar era, the return of prosperity, the sheer number of youth who were becoming teenagers, and the
mass media all contributed to the shaping of the new youth culture. Seeking
to make life for their children easier and happier than their lives had been,
parents with modern values tended to relinquish authority and influence
over their children's lives to others. As in the past, modernist parents turned
to outside experts. No authority for child rearing was more influential than
Dr. Benjamin Spock. In his *Baby and Child Care* (1946), a book second in sales
in the postwar era only to the Bible, Spock told parents to "be flexible and adjust to the baby's needs and happiness." Spock urged less old-fashioned discipline and more indulgence. "Don't be afraid to love him [your child] and
enjoy him. Every baby needs to be smiled at, talked to, played with, fondled—
gently and lovingly—just as much as he needs vitamins and calories."

From the mid-fifties onward, the new media of television probably exceeded the influence of advice from experts in shaping the lives of youth. The
baby boomers—as the exploding population born in the 1940s and 1950s
came to be known—literally grew up with television. Both the media and advertising moguls knew that if they were to succeed in the fast-growing youth
market they had to produce movies, television shows, songs, and commer-
cials that spoke to a new generation of teenagers. The special attention lav-
ished upon teenagers by advertisers and the media encouraged the young to
feel a special sense of entitlement and generational power. Having frequently
left behind extended families and older forms of community and having
abandoned moral absolutes or perhaps any standards at all, suburban parents were left in a vulnerable position. No longer did they have at their dis-
posal the same resources as their parents had had in shielding their children
against the influences of peer groups, the media, or the advertisers.

While for the most part youth values and behaviors conformed to those of
the adult world—after all, they were said to be "the silent generation"—
there were in retrospect manifest signs in the postwar era of a potential youth
rebellion. In the late 1940s a nationwide debate erupted over the "problem
of juvenile delinquency," though in fact there was no significant increase in
youth criminality. In the next decade, "hot-rodding," rock-and-roll music,
"going steady," peculiar hair styles, and a special teenage argot aroused fears
that growing numbers of middle-class suburban teenagers were adopting the
cultural values of the black ghetto and/or of the urban working class. Hollywood quickly discovered the rebellious youth. Films such as *The Wild One,
Rebel Without A Cause,* and *The Blackboard Jungle* and young stars such as
Marlon Brando and James Dean offered sympathetic portrayals of teenagers
allegedly trapped in an alienating world of suburban, middle-class adults.

But nothing disturbed suburban parents, ministers, and educators more
than the arrival in the mid-1950s of rock-and-roll music. Adapted from black
rhythm and blues, rock and roll's heavy beat and frenetic energy were far
more expressive than the decade's mainstream music. At the center of the
revolution in teenage music swaggered Elvis Presley. Exuding raw sexual
power by suggestively swaying his hips, Presley shocked white middle-class

adults. The more parents condemned Presley and other rock stars, the more their teenage children seemed to love them. By the end of the fifties, nothing separated the generations more sharply than their respective musical tastes.

THE YOUTH REVOLT

Rather than emerging from the opposing cultural styles of the adults and their offspring, however, the youth revolt got its initial impetus primarily from visions of a more humane society. For a brief but significant moment, John F. Kennedy, the newly elected president in 1960, stimulated the as yet vague urge for change. Unlike his fatherly predecessor, Dwight D. Eisenhower, the youthful president, novelist Norman Mailer predicted, would shake up suburbia with its "spirit of the supermarket, [its] homogeneous extension of stainless surfaces and psychoanalyzed people, packaged commodities and ranch houses." The expectation of change arose in part from Kennedy's image; his and his family's stunning good looks and their sheer vigor suggested change. "All at once you had something exciting," one young political campaign worker explained. Expectation of change partly arose from Kennedy's bold rhetoric. In contrast to the allegedly purposeless drift of the 1950s, he called for a renewal of national purpose. "Ask not what your country can do for you—ask what you can do for your country" were stirring words from his inaugural address that struck a responsive chord with many Americans. While timid in conceptualization and in execution, Kennedy's brief presidency (he was assassinated in 1963) helped to trigger the decade's great cultural paroxysms.

In the meantime, a tiny group of radical college students began to formulate a more explicit alternative vision of what America might become. In its Port Huron Statement, adopted by the Students for a Democratic Society in 1962, the "New Left" saw the main problem of contemporary life in terms of *alienation* rather than class conflict. In place of the alienating ways of fifties' suburbia, the New Left proposed a restoration of craft modes of work, the construction of small face-to-face communities, and participatory democracy in all aspects of group life. Influenced by such thinking, inspired by the civil rights movement, and increasingly opposed to American involvement in Vietnam, in 1964 large numbers of students protested the University of California at Berkeley's strictures on speech and assemblage. As the United States' troop commitments in Vietnam ballooned after 1964, protests spread like wildfire.

In 1968, the climactic year of the student uprising, more than two hundred major demonstrations involving more than forty thousand students rocked the nation. In dorms and crash pads, walls that had once been adorned with Beatles posters were now sporting Viet Cong flags and portraits of Ho Chi Minh, the leader of North Vietnam, and Che Guevera, the Cuban revolutionary. In utter astonishment, a writer for *Fortune* magazine warned that "these youngsters are acting out a revolution—not a protest, and not a rebellion, but an honest-to-God revolution." The protests took on worldwide dimensions.

In every major city in the noncommunist industrial world during 1968, students demonstrated and marched in the streets.

The sixties witnessed a rekindling of interest in ideology. Intellectuals reexamined sympathetically the ideas of Karl Marx, more his early writings which were concerned with alienation than his later work which emphasized class conflict. Several sought to incorporate one or another form of expressive individualism into their visions. Passionately convinced that humanity possessed immense reservoirs of untapped spiritual and emotional powers, they explored the potentialities of drugs, Eastern mysticism, and the release of behavioral restraints. Even one of the more dispassionate spokespersons of the cultural rebellion, Herbert Marcuse, argued that human unhappiness arose mostly from repression by industrial capitalism of the fundamental human drives for sensual fulfillment.

The uprising extended far beyond politics. Though the civil rights and antiwar movements were crucial catalysts to the sixties counterculture, many of the rebels had no or little interest in social causes. While some youth remained clean-shaven and immaculately dressed as they campaigned for the election of antiwar candidate Senator Eugene McCarthy for the presidency in 1968, others embraced a lifestyle that in gesture if not in substance completely repudiated the ways of their parents. Labeled as "hippies," they let their hair grow long, donned bizarre clothing, and took mind-bending drugs. Disgusted with all forms of artifice, they insisted on the importance of absolute candor in all personal and social relationships. Frequently rejecting the competitive and acquisitive individualism that they attributed to their parents, they established little worlds of their own in New York's East Village, San Francisco's Haight-Asbury district, and in some two thousand communes across the nation.

Drugs, music, and sex emerged as the rebellion's most powerful symbols. Illegal hallucinogens had long been associated with literary and artistic rebels and with "hip" African Americans, but among the rebellious young, marijuana, more commonly called "pot," replaced tobacco and alcohol as the drug of choice. The youth supported two kinds of music: folk ballads and rock and roll. The folk songs frequently protested racism, the bomb, and the Vietnam War. While initially neatly groomed and nonthreateningly boyish, the Beatles, an enormously popular English rock group, soon grew straggly beards and donned bright clothing; they became promoters of drugs ("I'd love to turn you on") and sex ("Why don't we do it in the road") while rejecting revolution ("You know, it's going to be alright"). The cultural side of the youth revolt exploded into an ecstatic and orgiastic climax in 1969 when some four hundred thousand youth gathered at the Woodstock festival in upstate New York. Heralding the festival as the dawn of a new age of love and peace (the Age of Aquarius), for three days and nights the youth reveled in drugs, sex, and rock music.

While the expressive individualism of the rebellious youth pressed well beyond the mainstream culture, it was fundamentally an extension of the modern values and behaviors of their parents. Scholars studying the youth

Hippies in a Park, New Orleans, 1971. No group in the late twentieth century reflected the key impulse of expressive individualism more dramatically than the hippies. Notice the hippies' free-flowing body movements and loose-fitting clothes. In addition, notice that, to the rebellious youth, hair and clothing no longer serve as unambiguous signs of gender differences.

revolt quickly discovered that its participants came almost exclusively from modern families, that is, suburban families who were better educated than the average, who were better-off financially than most Americans, and whose fathers worked in management or in the professions. Rather than complete opposition, the differences between children and parents were largely ones of degree. In child rearing, their parents had been guided by the gentle admonitions of Benjamin Spock; in rearing their own children the rebellious young planned to be even more permissive than their parents had been. Neither were parents and their offspring totally at odds over divorce, open sexuality, marijuana use, and relaxed lifestyles. Rather than standing in complete opposition to their parents, the youth carried the values and behaviors of their parents to their ultimate and sometimes absurd conclusions. Both modern parents and their offspring called for greater self-fulfillment.

THE SEXUAL REVOLUTION

Nothing more concretely illustrated the unleashing of expressive forms of individualism in the sixties than the sexual revolution. As early as the 1920s modernist Americans had begun to embrace a positive sexual ideology. When confined to heterosexuality and marriage, modernists had seen sexual intercourse as essential to emotional health, an important source of mutual pleasure, and a valuable means of psychic self-expression. Apparently, however, the actual sexual behavior of many Americans extended far beyond the marital bed. According to surveys of middle-class sexual behavior published by Alfred Kinsey in 1948 and in 1953, 90 percent of the males and 50 percent of the females had engaged in premarital coitus, half of the men and a quarter of the women had had extramarital sex, and more than a third of the men had participated in adult homosexual activity. Given the weakening or dissolution of traditional sources of moral authority, anthropologist Margaret Mead warned that Kinsey's findings might themselves serve as standards of sexual conduct.

Yet, despite Mead's worries, Kinsey's studies ushered in no immediate or drastic changes in the nation's sex ways. Until the 1960s, formal censorship or self-imposed restraints governed the sexual contents of much of the popular media. As late as 1953, the movie industry denied its seal of approval to *The Moon Is Blue* because the film's dialogue included the words *seduction* and *virgin*. Novels of the 1940s and 1950s continued to employ euphemisms for sexual acts. The infamous "double standard" remained largely intact. While high school and college males could gain status within their peer groups for their sexual exploits, their female counterparts did not enjoy the same freedom. Females continued to be told that "nice girls don't."

But then, as the 1950s gave way to the 1960s, the walls that had kept sexuality within certain bounds seemed suddenly to give way. Behind the collapse was the staggering fact that 46 million baby boomers (of 150 million total population) entered their teens in the early 1960s. At the same time, the courts began to relax the standards for censorship (a turning point came when the judiciary permitted the sale of D. H. Lawrence's long-suppressed novel, *Lady Chatterly's Lover*, in 1959), the Federal Drug Administration approved the distribution of the birth control pill (in 1960), and the movie theaters (with three-quarters of their audience now comprised of teenagers) began to show far more sexually risqué films. Proclaiming the message that the single woman could enjoy all the same joys of the bedroom as the single man, Helen Gurley Brown's *Sex and the Single Girl* (1963) became an instant best-seller.

Long aware that sex sells products and given to sweeping conclusions, the mass media announced in the early sixties that the nation was in the midst of a "sexual revolution." Sex-starved coeds, they suggested, were shedding their virginity en masse. Margaret Mead, who was by now a senior sage of modern ways, abandoned all semblance of careful judgement when she declared that "we have jumped from puritanism to lust." "The Puritan ethic, so long dominant in the U.S., is widely considered to be dying, if not dead," pontificated *Time* magazine in 1965, "and there are few mourners."

While change in actual sexual behavior never approximated the wild claims of the media, historian Susan Douglas has made the more important point that "imposing one's own sexual standards on others was now as anachronistic as a Jonathan Edwards sermon; sophisticated tolerance was in." By the early 1970s few restraints were left on the media. Frontal nudity, simulated or actual sexual intercourse, and sexual acts previously considered unnatural could now be seen in front-line movie houses, and what was once considered to be illegal pornography could be found in corner drugstores or in public libraries. That many more couples began living with one another outside of marriage occasioned far less public criticism than in the past. Perhaps nothing reflected the growing sexual tolerance more than the American Psychiatric Association's decision in 1973 to no longer classify homosexuality as a disease. Like the youth revolt, the sea change in sexual tolerance was not limited to the United States. It swept through the entire Western world.

Unleashing Art

Dramatists, literati, painters, architects, and musicians—all explored in the 1960s the outermost reaches of their respective genres. Long before the sixties, modernist doubts about the existence of a superintending God, an orderly universe, the human capacity for reason, and a set of absolute truths had opened up a seemingly limitless realm of possibilities for individual creativity and artistic expression. No longer obligated to elevate the spirit, to educate, or to promote morality, modern artists had been cast free of all external references and restraints. Art no longer needed to imitate life; art could be done merely for its own sake. Such an unshackling encouraged radical experimentation in form, the bridging of traditional polarities, the heightening and savoring of all varieties of experience, in short, it encouraged what George Roeder, Jr., has described as the "modernist urge to see, experience, and express everything."

Nonetheless, until the 1960s modernist artists had accepted some restraints on their work. Much of it was self-imposed. For they carried in their heads, as Robert Hughes has observed, "an invisible tribunal" of their predecessors who sat "in judgment" of the quality and style of their work. Artists also saw themselves as engaged in something—though they would be hard-pressed to define precisely what this something was—far more important than gratifying the tastes of the masses or in making money. Indeed, the modernist artistic commitment can be likened to that of a religious calling. An overt hostility to what was variously described as "puritanism," "Victorianism," "bourgeois," and/or "mass" culture frequently served as a defining characteristic of the modernist artist. While ostentatiously renouncing materialism and condemning hypocrisy, conformity, and sexual repression, they sought truth in the medium itself or the elements (in painting, for example, color, composition, dimensions) that defined their medium. As testimonials to the seriousness that they attributed to their work, they consciously exiled themselves from mainstream society, cultivated a bohemian lifestyle, and frequently took pride in living a hand-to-mouth daily existence.

By the 1960s artists (sometimes labeled in hindsight as postmodernists) came to openly reject, or at the least to compromise, even these modernist constraints. For one thing, their pose of alienation and a bohemian self-exile became far more difficult to sustain when the artists found their lifestyles and attitudes embraced by the nation's rebellious youth. Imitating the artists, literally millions of youth also took drugs, engaged in sexual experimentation, rejected materialism, and condemned conformity. In effect, co-option by the young, as David Steigerwald has written, "enlarged bohemia, commercialized it, and destroyed its artistic soul." Eventually a bohemianlike lifestyle extended far beyond the rebellious young; by the early 1970s, even Wall Street brokers were sporting long hair and sideburns and were wearing brightly colored clothes.

For another thing, many artists sought to reestablish connections of their work to society. Art, they said, could be employed to usher in the new Age of Aquarius. In order for art to become "an instrument for modifying consciousness and organizing new realms of sensibility," essayist Susan Sontag even urged the suspension of criticism. Artistic and literary criticism, she said, stifled creativity and repressed the passions. Without criticism, no one could claim that one piece of art was superior to another and no longer could formal art be separated from popular culture.

By collapsing ages-old distinctions between art and life, feelings and expressions, and high culture and popular culture, artists in the sixties further eroded the last of the modernist constraints. Perhaps no "work of art" succeeded quite so well in this regard as John Cage's 1952 recording of 4'33" which consisted of four minutes and thirty-three seconds of total silence. While regaling in the sounds around them, listeners to Cage's recording completely escaped the "tyranny" that composers traditionally imposed on their audiences. Since art no longer had to be "something," it could be anything. As depicted in Andy Warhol's silk screens of Campbell Soup cans and pictures of Marilyn Monroe, art could even be the objects of consumer society. With alienation now "in," or fashionable, and with all standards in shambles, art as traditionally understood seemed indeed to be in the throes of its final demise.

On the other hand, the unleashing of art may have also opened up new realms of art and artistic understanding. Defenders of the "artistic revolution" observed that art was no longer restricted to museums and no longer was it a limited preserve of elites. Art could be anything and everything. It could be psychedelic T-shirts, a hydroelectric dam, an atomic explosion, or "Carhenge" (a piece of "art" in Nebraska that consisted of used cars with their noses buried in the ground in a configuration resembling England's ancient Stonehenge).

TURNING INWARD

While there were abundant signs of a hungering for community in the late twentieth century, the dominant impulse of the American people everywhere and in all aspects of their lives was to turn inward, to turn away from formal and enduring associations with others, with the past, with everything outside the self. Extending and expanding on urges that had been present in modern ways from the outset, Americans looked to the self for personal fulfillment and for the resources to cope with contemporary life. Turning inward brought with it a new, far more radical form of individualism, one that esteemed a view of life comprised of an unending and unrestricted array of individual choices.

DISENGAGEMENT

"My wife is safe, my children are safe, so screw you and your Metro," read an ominous bumper sticker on a sports utility vehicle in 1999. At every level of American society and in every significant group, temptations and pressures mounted for individuals to disengage from one another and from the larger society.

Reflective of the inclination to turn inward was a startling decline in the nation's associational life. Americans voted less frequently than in the past; beginning in 1968 rarely more than half of the qualified voters went to the polls, one-third less than the figures in the 1940s and 1950s. Likewise, identification with, and membership in, political parties declined. Participation in voluntary associations, especially those that served primarily their local communities, fell. Between the 1960s and the 1990s, membership in Parent Teacher's Associations and the League of Women Voters dropped more than 40 percent. So did membership in such traditionally male civic groups as the Lions, the Masons, and the Elks. In 1999, Welcome Wagon, a symbol of 1950s suburban neighborliness and congeniality, officially announced its demise.

No imagery more vividly captured the tendency to disengage than the title of sociologist Robert Putnam's influential 1993 essay, "Bowling Alone: America's Declining Social Capital." While the total number of bowlers increased nearly 10 percent between 1980 and 1993, Putnam found that league bowling decreased by 40 percent. Lest this be considered a trivial example of the decline in the nation's associational life, Putnam observed that almost eighty million Americans went bowling at least once in 1993, almost a third more than voted in the 1994 congressional election and about the same number that claimed to attend church regularly. Neither was marriage as binding as before. By the 1980s more than half of all marriages ended in divorce (compared to one in ten in the 1890s). Far more people than in the past substituted tentative and short-term living arrangements for more enduring ones.

Work no longer linked people to one another or to their communities as firmly as it had in the past. The reconfiguration of white-collar work spaces reflected a growing isolation of the individual at work. To encourage employee unity, the Miesian model of the 1950s and 1960s had called for the elimination of interior barriers in employee workplaces, but in the 1980s and 1990s corporations replaced open spaces with individual cubicles or offices. Increasingly driven by the "bottom line," corporations were less loyal to employees than in the past. Even capable and conscientious workers could no longer be assured of lifetime employment with the same firm.

White-collar professionals also saw work more exclusively in personal rather than in social or familial terms. Corporate volatility encouraged placelessness among white-collar employees, particularly among those at the top of the corporate pyramid. In their lives away from the job, the new, more peripatetic wealthy retreated behind the walls of alarm-protected condominiums or into gated and guarded neighborhoods where they were likely to build large "trophy" houses. Except for issues that directly affected their personal welfare, they less frequently involved themselves in local civic affairs than the upper-class elites of the past.

Even the signs of apparent engagement with others were often deceptive. "Being alone together" was the way that Robert Bellah and his associates described those individuals who were involved in some of the fastest growing organizations of the late twentieth century. For instance, membership in the AARP (American Association of Retired Persons) grew spectacularly, but, while its members had common interests, they had no genuine interactions with one another. Neither did the Internet, a much-ballyhooed technological means of building "virtual" communities, live up to its promise. A 1998 study sponsored by the computer industry itself found that people who spent even a few hours a week on-line experienced higher levels of depression and loneliness than they would have had they used the computer network less frequently.

OPPOSITION TO GOVERNMENT

Congruent with the decline in associational life was a sharp fall in trust. In 1964, 77 percent of the public said that they "always" or "most of the time" trusted the decisions of the national government; by 1980 the figure had plummeted downward to less than 25 percent. Polls revealed a similar collapse of trust in lawyers, doctors, teachers, ministers, journalists, and business leaders. To the question "can people be trusted generally?" the percentage fell in a descending curve from 58 percent in 1960 to less than 40 percent in the 1990s.

Accompanying the declining trust in government was a resurgence of political conservatism. With the Great Society programs of the sixties, "liberals" (those who endorsed an expanded social safety net provided by government and the use of the state to expand individual rights) achieved their greatest triumphs since the New Deal. But during the balance of the twentieth century, "conservatives" (those favoring a reduction in government regulation, either limiting or abolishing the safety net, and general opposition to using the state to expand individual rights) returned to prominence. On the national level, conservatives won their greatest symbolic and perhaps substantive victory by electing Ronald Reagan to the presidency in 1980. Although a product of the world of commercial entertainment (Hollywood), divorced, and not religiously active, the president championed traditional values and institutions. He condemned explicit sexuality in the media and permissive child rearing and sought to restore respect for the family, the flag, and religion.

While achieving limited gains for his conservative cultural agenda, Reagan enjoyed far more success in his campaign against big government. "Government is not the solution to our problem; government *is* the problem," he announced in his first inaugural address. He denounced affirmative action on behalf of women and minorities. While not successful in decreasing the over-all growth of government (indeed, the defense budget and the national debt expanded enormously), he obtained from Congress large tax cuts and a sharp reduction in welfare expenditures. The combined effects of these measures helped to bring about a massive shift of wealth to the rich; by the mid-1990s the top 1 percent of American families owned 40 percent of the nation's wealth, a figure twice as high as twenty years earlier. Fewer Americans seemed as concerned as they had in the past about this huge step away from a major premise of the nation's founders—that the success of a republican society required a roughly equal distribution of wealth among its citizenry.

While continuing to make demands on government for benefits on behalf of their specific constituencies, by the 1990s virtually all politicians adopted a rhetorical stance of opposition to "big government." Nearly everyone, it seemed, accepted the premise that government, especially the federal government, was inherently evil. Even President Bill Clinton, a Democrat, renounced his party's long-time association with an expanded role of government. "The era of big government is over," he announced. At the local level, the zeal for cutting back on government was equally strong. Many states imposed lids on taxation—measures that particularly adversely affected education and hence the future of the nation's youth—while simultaneously rushing to privatize what in the past had been considered public services. At its most radical fringes, hostility to the state spawned a host of groups— militias, freedom fighters, and other self-proclaimed patriots—who armed themselves to fend off governmental authority. "All authority belongs to the people," read a bumper sticker on a pickup truck that prominently displayed a 30-30 rifle on a rack behind the front seat. Antistatism seemed to reach its ultimate and certainly its ugliest expression in the bombing of the federal building in Oklahoma City in 1995.

The almost reflexive antistatism of the eighties and nineties reflected a growing veneration of "free enterprise" or what was increasingly abbreviated as simply "the market." Reinforced by the collapse of the USSR in 1989 and an upwardly spiraling stock market in the 1990s, enthusiasm for the market as an all-solving mechanism knew few bounds. Echoing the acquisitive individualism of the nineteenth century, the more extreme of the market fundamentalists even argued that nothing needed or should be done by the state to counter poverty, inner-city ghettos, violence, racial or gender discrimination, declining educational performance, and pollution. Nothing was so efficacious in solving these problems, they said, as a free and unfettered market. Any efforts to inhibit it or control its vagaries were artificial, detrimental to the general welfare, and undemocratic.

THE NEW INDIVIDUALISM

Enthusiasm for an unrestrained market, along with hostility to government and disengagement from the nation's civic life, were integral components of a new individualism. While individualism had long been at the very core of American culture, in the past it had always been caged in by widely agreed-upon constraints. For example, the founders of the republic loudly proclaimed the principles of individual freedom, but at the same time they insisted that a virtuous citizenry—a citizenry that exercised self-restraint— was essential to the new republic's survival. Similarly, all the nation's major religious communities defended individual freedom, but they invariably justified such freedom only within the limits imposed by obligations to God, the community, and a divinely ordained system of personal morality. Consequently, the pursuit of material welfare, for example, never exempted the individual from obeying the Ten Commandments. In addition, the unequal rights and obligations embedded in the nation's social ways had long limited the individual freedom of women, African Americans, Native Americans, and working-class people.

As we have seen, the growing acceptance of modern ways weakened each of these traditional constraints on the individual. Cultural pluralism challenged the inequalities built into the nation's social ways, secularization eroded support for transcendental moral authority, and a consumer-centered economy encouraged Americans to abandon the middle-class Victorian emphasis on self-control. The sixties' revolution in rights and the dismissal of all forms of cultural authority, when combined with the continuing imperatives of consumer capitalism, gave even freer reign to the individual. Americans increasingly came to identify individualism with individuality, or what was said to be the expression of one's authentic inner self.

In the decade of the 1970s, the waning of public confidence in government, the economy, and expertise furnished an additional impetus for the new individualism. In particular, the trials of the times encouraged Americans to turn away from society or the community and to seek greater sufficiency in the self. Labeled by commentator Tom Wolfe as the "Me" decade and by Christopher Lasch as an age of "narcissism," millions of Americans (but especially those in the white-collar classes) sought greater control over their lives and greater personal fulfillment in arenas other than their jobs or in social involvement. They became converts to charismatic religions, experimented with vegetarianism, hallucinatory drugs, psychotherapy, or became apostles of a new physical fitness cult. The popular culture also furnished them with forceful images of individual potency. For instance in sports, by reducing the size of the strike zone, baseball increased its offensive output; television glamorized the bone-crunching game of professional football; and spectators were even introduced to what was described as "power" golf and "power" tennis.

Perhaps nothing so revealed the dynamics of the seventies' quest for greater self-sufficiency than what may be described as the new strenuosity. "I am a nervous, shy noncombatant who has no feeling for people," Dr. George A. Sheehan, the self-appointed chief philosopher of the nation's running cult said in a remarkable confession. "I do not hunger or thirst after justice. I find no happiness in carnival, no joy in community." In exceptionally demanding individual physical activities, Sheehan, like millions of others in the white-collar classes, sought and claimed to find greater self-sufficiency. Physical fitness, its advocates asserted, not only served to counter the ravages of cardiovascular disease and cancer—two ailments against which modern medicine had made little headway—but offered the individual feelings of satisfaction and greater personal potency.

In the midst of a soaring stock market, in the 1980s and the 1990s individual moneymaking moved to the forefront of the quest for greater self-fulfillment. With an enthusiasm never before equaled in American history, the mainstream culture lent its approval to individual avarice. "Greed is not a bad thing," declared junk bond dealer Ivan Boesky in 1988. "You shouldn't feel guilty." Rather than those who were responsible for making things or even those selling them, it was the young money managers on Wall Street who became the heroes of the popular culture. Madonna's "Material Girl" climbed to the top of the pop music charts. The Yuppies, as young urban professionals whose lives were absorbed in moneymaking were dubbed by the media, flaunted their wealth in a manner reminiscent of no group so much as the nouveau riche of the late nineteenth century. They embodied perfectly the equation of individual fulfillment with money and conspicuous consumption.

By the end of the twentieth century, consumer capitalism and the sixties' rebel culture were inseparable. Advertisers had co-opted the iconography of the sixties' counterculture; they tied their products to immediate gratification, individualistic lifestyles, youthfulness, uninhibited instinct, and liberation of the libido. "We consume not to fit in, but to prove, on the surface at least, that we are rock 'n' roll rebels, each of us as rule-breaking and hierarchy-defying as our heroes of the 60s, who now pitch cars, shoes, and beer," observed Thomas Frank in 1995. "Kotex was at Woodstock," declared a television ad in 2000. A rule-defying individualism even swept into the once-staid corridors of corporate power. *First Break All the Rules*—this was the title of a best-selling book in 1999 based on in-depth interviews by the Gallup organization of over eighty thousand managers in over four hundred companies. According to the new management mavens, corporate bosses needed to forget the wisdom of the past, ignore rules, and encourage "thinking outside the box."

In the end, there was reason to doubt that the new individualism's fervor for self-expression, self-actualization, self-acceptance, and any number of other *self* compounds led back to an authentic self. For each of us is, no matter how much energy we devote to the quest for a true inner self, to one degree or another a product of culture. What may have distinguished the "new individualists," then, was not so much their special propensity for expressing and realizing their inner selves, but that they rejected or gave little weight to such traditional sources of cultural authority as the family, religion, ethnicity, and the past. Instead of these, the new individualists tended to conform to directions for living their lives found in the closely intertwined worlds of commerce and entertainment. More than ever before images and messages from advertising, the movies, popular music, the Internet, sports, and above all else television furnished millions of Americans with a map for daily living. Studies repeatedly found that late-twentieth-century Americans frequently "knew" personalities on television better than they did their neighbors, their workmates, or sometimes even members of their own families.

THE QUEST FOR TIES BEYOND THE SELF

Not all evidence in late-twentieth-century American life pointed to a turning to the self. There was a substantial minority—indeed sometimes a majority—of Americans who continued to vote, to belong to civic groups, and to join in activities designed to promote the common welfare of their local communities. Large numbers of Americans attended religious services. They kept abreast of major sporting events and sought "to go with the flow" by participating in current popular fads. Without giving up the excitement and satisfactions found in the pursuit of personal fulfillment, nearly all Americans seemed to yearn for a larger sense of purpose in their lives and, at least for some, ties that extended beyond the self.

No tie was more important to them than the family or familylike arrangements. When asked what they valued most in life, Americans continued to place the family at the top of the list. Many sought to establish linkages with their ancestors. In quest of family roots, *The Financial Times* reported in 1999, fifty million people sought within a single hour to enter the genealogical Web site of the Mormon Church. The institution of marriage remained popular, albeit far less so than in the past. The number of marriages per thousand women age fifteen and older dropped 43 percent between 1960 and 1996. As in other aspects of their lives, Americans came to expect more individual fulfillment from marriage and their participation in the family. Hence, couples divorced more frequently and experimented with a variety of unorthodox family relationships. In 1996 nearly half of the people ages twenty-five to forty reported that at some point in their lives they had set up a joint household with a member of the opposite sex outside of marriage.

Television sitcoms reflected the changing nature of the family. While the popular sitcom *Roseanne* frequently mocked the idealized family of the fifties, family ties remained central to the lives of each member of Roseanne's working-class family. Viewers in the late twentieth century also watched several series based on "mismatched families"; in *Full House* a widower, his three daughters, his deceased wife's brother, and his best friend live in the same house, and in *Different Strokes* an equally if not more improbable family consisted of a white widower, his daughter, and two adopted black sons. Apparently unable to find individual fulfillment in traditional families, in *Cheers* even a neighborhood bar served as a surrogate family for an astonishingly diverse array of people.

To a degree unequaled elsewhere in the Western world, religion continued to offer Americans connections beyond the self. After a sharp drop in the sixties from the fifties' boom, overall religious membership and attendance at

"Need a Friend?" This sign on a church building in Lincoln, Nebraska, reflects both the new individualism and the quest for ties beyond the self. Religious affiliation, the sign suggests, may provide the basis for a stronger community while simultaneously offering the individual the possibility of greater self-fulfillment.

church services remained constant. But some religious groups fared far better than others. While not dwindling in total numbers, the mainstream Protestant denominations (such as the Methodists, Presbyterians, Congregationalists, Lutherans, and Episcopalians) suffered the most. According to critics, efforts beginning in the 1960s by these groups to make themselves more amenable to modern ways had for the most part backfired. Critics explained the decline in regular church attendance among Catholics in similar terms. By permitting the saying of mass and prayers in the vernacular and emphasizing the sermon, they charged, the Second Vatican Council (1962–65), which had been called by Pope John XXIII, demystified the church's ages-old liturgy. Still, nearly half of all Catholics reported regular attendance at mass, a figure far higher than anywhere in Europe (except in Portugal).

The so-called "new age" religions, the resurgence of evangelicalism, and conservative uprisings within the mainline churches—these were the most dynamic movements in late-twentieth-century American religion. A bewildering assortment of new religions—Zen, Hare Krishna, Transcendental Meditation, Scientology, and dozens of cults associated with charismatic leaders—sprang into existence. But in terms of sheer numbers and influence the new age religions paled beside a remarkable renascence of evangelicalism and a more broadly-based religious conservatism. The impulse toward religious conservatism cut across older ethnic and religious lines.

It brought to the forefront a new kind of religious conflict, one reminiscent of the 1920s. The new war revolved around the ultimate source of moral authority rather than traditional denominational or ethnic strife. Conservatives, whether Protestant, Catholic, or Jewish, relied upon an external, definable, and transcendental source of moral authority. Though no less moral, their opponents, whom we may label as "modernists," found their moral authority largely in secular sources. While most Americans occupied the vast ground between the two poles, in the 1980s and 1990s the conservatives and the modernists engaged in bitter public combat on a wide range of fronts. On the one side were the modernists who favored women's rights, gay rights, "pro-choice" stance on abortion, public funding of the arts, and the public school system; and on the other were the conservatives or traditionalists who stood against abortions, supported traditional roles for women, abhorred homosexuality, opposed public funding for the arts, and saw the schools as hotbeds of "secular humanism."

Regardless of the divisions arising over these public issues, American religion in the late twentieth century, like the larger culture, was on the whole, in the words of religious historian George Marsden, "highly individualistic." Whereas in the past Americans had turned to religion for understanding the mysteries of the universe, for solace, and for assistance in coping with the adversities of life, modern Americans tended, as they did in other aspects of their lives, to look for self-fulfillment in their religious experiences. "Need a Friend?" read a sign on the Southview Christian Church building in Lincoln, Nebraska. Rather than generating feelings of anguish, finitude, or sorrow, worship services were designed to make their congregants feel positive emotions.

Neither did ties based on ethnicity and race disappear in the late twentieth century. Indeed, the rights revolution, the persistence of divisions revolving around race, and a sudden flood of new immigrants (mainly from Latin America and Asia) heightened ethnic and racial self-awareness. Colleges across the country organized programs in ethnic studies, Native American studies, Chicano studies, African American studies, women's studies, and even "white studies." In 1999, the University of Michigan student union bulletin board listed no fewer than forty-nine campus ethnic organizations. "American culture in the late twentieth century is a very stewpot of separate identities," wrote Todd Gitlin with only slight exaggeration in 1995. "Not only blacks and feminists and gays declare that their dignity rests on their distinctiveness, but so in various ways do white Southern Baptists, Florida Jews, Oregon skinheads, Louisiana Cajuns, Brooklyn Lubavicthers, California Sikhs, Wyoming ranchers."

The nation's educational system contributed to the inclination by Americans to nurture ties and identities based on group self-awareness. In the past, the schools had been committed to the task of molding Americans of all backgrounds into a single people, but in the 1980s and 1990s "multiculturalism" emerged as the educational establishment's reigning orthodoxy. Whatever else it taught or meant, the advocates of multiculturalism insisted that far more attention than in the past ought to be given to the roles and contributions of women, blacks, and Hispanics to American history. Only through a greater knowledge of their own group and its contributions, the advocates of multiculturalism reasoned, could women and minorities fully realize their individual potentialities. At its most extreme, the multiculturalists even doubted the existence of a shared or common culture. Few found it remarkable when a Lake County, Florida, teacher said, "We regard American culture as very diverse, and we're not sure what values they [the opponents of multiculturalism] see as American values." Such a stance could and sometimes did lead to conclusions that the writings of men, such as Thomas Jefferson or the authors of *The Federalist Papers,* had nothing important to say to women or to minority groups.

Another tie beyond the self took the form of lifestyle enclaves. Unlike communities that shared a history, acted together politically, or featured strong interdependencies, the lifestyle enclaves grew out of leisure activities. They brought together people who sought to express their individuality in similar ways. Without giving up the rewards of expressive individualism, lifestyle enclaves, in the apt words of Robert Bellah and his associates, celebrated "the narcissism of similarity." For example, individuals otherwise divided by ethnicity, religion, gender, and age might join one another in an enthusiasm for golf, taste for exotic foods, jazz, foreign travel, and any number of other spare-time activities.

An enthusiasm for history also suggested a yearning for associations beyond the self. Interest in Victorian culture soared. Across the country, Americans refurbished Victorian homes, watched the dramatizations on television or in the movies of Jane Austen's nineteenth-century novels that featured the manners and morals of the early English Victorians, and Victoria's Secret, a lingerie store, successfully transformed the idea of repressed Victorian sexuality into salable commodities. Visiting historical sites, whether in the United States or in Europe, became a popular vacation rite. A renewed enthusiasm for baseball seemed to reflect a nostalgia for an earlier, presumably simpler past; recognizing this, the major league club owners began to replace their modernistic, multipurpose stadiums with facsimiles of earlier ballparks. But nothing reflected the yearning for ties with the past and for a larger, nobler way of life more than a mammoth outpouring of enthusiasm for the fiftieth anniversary of World War II. Each of the major television networks prepared huge, expensive, sprawling documentaries, and Steven Spielberg's movie *Saving Private Ryan* (1998) drew record-breaking crowds.

CONCLUSION

No one can yet confidently say whether the predominant trends of the late twentieth century were part of an older cultural paradigm or the constituents of a new one. As events unfold, scholars may decide that the late twentieth century was, like the late nineteenth and early twentieth centuries, a transitional age, one that heralded both the final stage of modern ways and the beginnings of a new cultural era. Regardless, it is clear that Americans in the late twentieth century carried modernist impulses about as far as they could possibly be taken. While the pressures of popular opinion could in their own way be, as Alexis de Tocqueville observed long ago, as inimical to individual freedom as those imposed by hierarchical societies headed by monarchs, no earlier age in American history prized more fully the idea that individuals should be given nearly unlimited discretion in fulfilling their own distinctive needs. What remained to be seen, however, was whether the new individualism would continue to occupy a central position in the American ways of the twenty-first century.

A SELECTIVE BIBLIOGRAPHY

GENERAL

While there are literally hundreds of works that treat aspects of the history of American ways, useful reference books include Mary Kupiec Cayton, Elliot J. Gorn, and Peter W. Williams, eds., *Encyclopedia of American Social History*, 3 vols. (1993); Charles Wilson and William Ferris, eds., *Encyclopedia of Southern Culture*, 3 vols. (1989); Richard W. Fox and James T. Kloppenberg, eds., *A Companion to American Thought* (1995); Charles Lippy and Peter W. Williams, eds., *Encyclopedia of the American Religious Experiences*, 3 vols. (1988); and Stephan Thernstrom, ed., *Harvard Encyclopedia of American Ethnic Groups* (1980). For the place of cultural history within the discipline of history, see Joyce Appleby, Lynn Hunt, and Margaret Jacob, *Telling the Truth about History* (1994). For more in-depth treatments of specific topics, examine such books as Thomas Bender, *Community and Social Change in America* (1978); Jon Butler and Harry S. Stout, eds., *Religion in American History: A Reader* (1998); Clifford Clark, Jr., *The American Family Home, 1800–1960* (1986); Paul Conkin, *Puritans and Pragmatists: Eight Eminent American Thinkers* (1968); Eric Foner, *The Story of American Freedom* (1998); John d'Emilio and Estelle Freedman, *Intimate Matters: A History of Sexuality in America* (1988); Carl Degler, *At Odds: Women and the Family in America from the Revolution to the Present* (1980); David Hollinger and Charles Capper, eds., *The American Intellectual Tradition*, 2 vols. (3d. ed., 1997); Robert Hughes, *American Visions: The Epic History of Art in America* (1997); James L. Huston, *Securing the Fruits of Labor: The American Concept of Wealth Distribution, 1765–1900* (1988); Joseph Kett, *Rites of Passage: Adolescence in America, 1790 to the Present* (1977); Lawrence Levine, *Black Culture and Black Consciousness: Afro-American Folk Thought from Slavery to Freedom* (1977); Lewis Perry, *Intellectual Life in America* (1984); George Marsden, *Religion and American Culture* (1990); Benjamin Rader, *American Sports* (4th ed., 1999); Daniel Rodgers, *The Work Ethic in Industrial America* (1978); Robert H. Wiebe, *Self-Rule: A Cultural History of American Democracy* (1995); and Gwendolyn Wright, *Building the Dream: A Social History of Housing in America* (1981).

THE REGIONAL WAYS OF EARLY AMERICA, 1600–1800

For Native American ways in the 1600–1800 era, consult John Bierhost, *The Mythology of North America* (1985); William Cronon, *Changes in the Land:*

Indians, Colonists, and the Ecology of New England (1983); Brian Fagan, *Ancient North America: The Archaeology of a Continent* (1991); Francis Jennings, *The Founders of America* (1993); Alvin Josephy, Jr., ed., *America in 1492* (1992); and James H. Merrell, *The Indians' New World: Catawabas and Their Neighbors from European Contact through the Era of Removal* (1989); and Helen Hornbeck Tanner, *Atlas of Great Lakes Indian History* (1987). Gary B. Nash, *Red, White, and Black: The Peoples of Early America* (3d. ed., 1991), treats the complex interactions in America of peoples from three different continents.

For general examinations of British ways in colonial North America, see David H. Fischer's provocative *Albion's Seed: Four British Folkways in America* (1989) and a remarkable synthesis, Jack P. Greene, *Pursuits of Happiness: The Social Development of Early British Colonies and the Formation of American Culture* (1988).

For the northern ways of the British North American colonies, consider Virginia DeJohn Anderson, *New England's Generation: The Great Migration and the Formation of Society and Culture in the Seventeenth Century* (1991); Richard Bushman, *From Puritan to Yankee: Character and the Social Order of Connecticut, 1760–1765* (1967); Stephen Foster, *The Long Argument: English Puritanism and the Shaping of New England Culture, 1570–1700* (1991); Carol F. Karlsen, *The Devil in the Shape of a Woman: Witchcraft in Colonial New England* (1987); Barry Levy, *Quakers and the American Family: British Settlement in the Delaware Valley* (1988); Perry Miller's most accessible book, *Errand into the Wilderness* (1956); primary sources in Perry Miller and Thomas Johnson, eds., *The Puritans*, 2 vols. (1963); Edmund S. Morgan, *The Puritan Dilemma: The Story of John Winthrop* (1958); Alan Simpson, *Puritanism in Old and New England* (1955); and Laurel Thatcher Ulrich, *A Midwife's Tale: The Life of Martha Ballard, Based on Her Diary, 1785–1812* (1991).

For the ways of the southern colonies and the backcountry, see for example John B. Boles, *Black Southerners, 1619–1869* (1982); Rhys Isaac, *The Transformation of Virginia: Community, Religion, and Authority, 1740-1790* (1982); Peter Kolchin, *American Slavery 1619–1877* (1993); Allan Kulikoff, *Tobacco and Slaves: The Development of Southern Cultures in the Chesapeake, 1680–1800* (1986); James Leyburn, *The Scotch-Irish: A Social History* (1989); Kenneth Lockridge, *The Diary and Life of William Byrd II of Virginia* (1988); Edmund S. Morgan, *American Slavery, American Freedom: The Ordeal of Colonial Virginia* (1975); John Thorton, *Africa and Africans in the Making of the Atlantic World, 1400–1680* (1992); and Peter Wood, *Black Majority: Negroes in Colonial South Carolina from 1670 through the Stono Rebellion* (1974).

THE WAYS OF THE NEW REPUBLIC, 1760–1860

Primary sources are a good place to start an examination of the early republic. Important examples include Hector St. John de Crèvecoeur, *Letters from an American Farmer* (multiple editions); David B. Davis, ed., *Antebellum Culture* (1979); Frederick Douglas, *The Life of Frederick Douglas* (multiple editions); Ralph Waldo Emerson (numerous editions and anthologies); Benjamin Franklin, *Autobiography of Benjamin Franklin* (multiple editions); *The Federalist*

Papers (multiple editions); Thomas Jefferson, *Notes on the State of Virginia* (several editions); Alexis de Tocqueville, *Democracy in America* (several editions); and Gordon S. Wood, ed., *The Rising Glory of America, 1760–1820* (1971, 1990). Wood's introduction to *The Rising Glory of America* provides an insightful overview of the era's cultural history.

For the ways of the Revolutionary era, also consider Joyce Appleby, *Capitalism and a New Social Order: The Republican Vision of the 1790s* (1984), Appleby's, *Liberalism and Republicanism in the Historical Imagination* (1992), and Appleby, ed., "Republicanism in the History and Historiography of the United States," *American Quarterly,* 37 (Fall 1985), 461–598; Bernard Bailyn, *The Ideological Origins of the American Revolution* (1967); David B. Davis, *The Problem of Slavery in the Age of Revolution, 1770–1823* (1975); Joseph Ellis, *American Sphinx: The Character of Thomas Jefferson* (1997); Robert A. Ferguson, *The American Enlightenment, 1750–1820* (1997); Jack P. Greene, ed., *The American Revolution: Its Character and Limits* (1987); Linda Kerber, *Women of the Republic* (1980); Mary Beth Norton, *Liberty's Daughters: The Revolutionary Experience of American Women, 1750–1800* (1980); Merrill Peterson, *Thomas Jefferson and the New Nation* (1980); Jack N. Rakove, *Original Meanings: Politics and Ideas in the Making of the Constitution;* Robert Shalhope, *The Roots of American Democracy: American Thought and Culture, 1760–1800* (1990); and Gordon Wood, *The Radicalism of the American Revolution* (1991).

For the antebellum era, see Robert H. Abzug, *Cosmos Crumbling: American Reform and the Religious Imagination* (1994); John W. Blasingame, *The Slave Community: Plantation Life in the Antebellum South* (1972); Jeanne Boydston, *Home and Work: Housework, Wages, and the Ideology of Labor in the Early Republic* (1990); Richard L. Bushman, *The Refinement of America: Persons, Houses, Cities* (1992); Bruce Collins, *White Society in the Antebellum South* (1985); Nancy F. Cott, *The Bonds of Womanhood: "Woman's Sphere" in New England, 1780–1835* (1977); Whitney R. Cross, *The Burned-Over District: The Social and Intellectual History of Enthusiastic Religion in Western New York, 1800–1850* (1950); Eric Foner, *Free Soil, Free Labor, Free Men: The Ideology of the Republican Party before the Civil War* (1970, 1995); Eugene Genovese, *Roll, Jordan, Roll: The World the Slaves Made* (1976); Nathan O. Hatch, *The Democratization of American Christianity* (1989); Karen Halttunen, *Confidence Men and Painted Women: A Study of Middle-Class Culture, 1800–1850* (1982); Paul Johnson, *A Shopkeeper's Millennium: Society and Revivals in Rochester, New York, 1815–1837* (1978); Marvin Meyers, *The Jacksonian Persuasion* (1957); Anne C. Rose, *Voices in the Marketplace: American Thought and Culture, 1830–1860* (1995); Charles Sellers, *The Market Revolution: Jacksonian America, 1815–1846* (1991); Robert H. Wiebe, *The Opening of American Society* (1984); Wiebe, *Self-Rule: A Cultural History of American Democracy* (1995); and Bertram Wyatt-Brown, *Southern Honor: Ethics and Behavior in the Old South* (1982).

MIDDLE-CLASS WAYS, 1830–1930

The quantity of the literature treating middle-class Victorian ways is enormous. To obtain an overview of middle-class culture, read David W. Howe's remarkable essay, "Victorian Culture in America," *American Quarterly,* Special Issue, 27 (Dec. 1975), 507–32. While dated and focused on England, Walter E. Houghton, *The Victorian Frame of Mind* (1957), is rich in detail and remains insightful. An invaluable memoir is Henry Seidel Canby, *The Age of Confidence* (1934). William L. Barney, *The Passage of the Republic* (1987), offers a useful synthesis of research in nineteenth-century social history.

Works of a more specific nature include Gunther Barth, *City People: The Rise of the Modern City Culture in Nineteenth Century America* (1980); Gail Bederman, *Manliness and Civilization: A Cultural History of Gender and Race in the United States, 1880–1917* (1995); Paul Boyer, *Urban Masses and Moral Order in America, 1820–1920* (1978); Stuart M. Blumin, *The Emergence of the Middle Class* (1989); Ann Douglas, *The Feminization of American Culture* (1977); John Gillis, *A World of Their Own Making: Myth, Ritual, and the Quest for Family Values* (1996); John Kasson, *Rudeness and Civility: Manners in Nineteenth-Century Urban America* (1990); Lawrence W. Levine, *Highbrow/Lowbrow: The Emergence of Cultural Hierarchy in America* (1988); Karen Lystra, *Searching the Heart: Women, Men, and Romantic Love in Nineteenth-Century America* (1989); Timothy R. Mahoney, *Provincial Lives: Middle-Class Experience in the Antebellum Middle West* (1999); Carroll Smith-Rosenberg, *Disorderly Conduct: Visions of Gender in Victorian America* (1985); Shelia M. Rothman, *Women's Proper Place: A History of Changing Ideals and Practices, 1870 to the Present* (1978); Mary Ryan, *Women in Public: Between Banners and Ballots, 1825–1880* (1990); Louise Stevenson, *The Victorian Homefront: American Thought and Culture, 1860–1880* (1991); and a book of sources edited by Alan Trachtenberg, *Democratic Vistas: 1860–1880* (1970), and Trachtenberg's *The Incorporation of America: Culture and Society in the Gilded Age* (1982).

For the ways of the "outsiders"—those outside the dominant northern middle-class culture—during the 1830–1930 era, see among other books Edward L. Ayers, *The Promise of the New South: Life after Reconstruction* (1992); Robert F. Berkhofer, Jr., *The White Man's Indian* (1978); John Bodnar, *The Transplanted: The History of Immigrants in Urban America* (1985); John C. Burnham, *Bad Habits* (1993); W. J. Cash, *The Mind of the South* (1941); Howard Chudacoff, *The Age of the Bachelor* (1999); Angie Debo, *And Still the Waters Run: The Betrayal of the Five Civilized Tribes* (1991); Vine Deloria, Jr., *Custer Died for Your Sins: An Indian Manifesto* (1988); Jay Dolan, *The American Catholic Experience* (1985); Gary Gerstle, "Liberty, Coercion, and the Making of Americans," and the responses to this essay in *Journal of American History,* 84, No. 2 (Sept. 1997), 524–80. Eric Foner, *Politics and Ideology in the Age of the Civil War* (1980); Elliot J. Gorn, *The Manly Art: Bare-Knuckle Prize Fighting in America* (1986); Herbert Gutman, *Work, Culture & Society in Industrializing America* (1977); Kenji Kawano, *Warriors: Navajo Code Talkers* (1990); Jacqueline Jones, *Labor of Love, Labor of Sorrow: Black Women, Work, and the Family from Slavery to the Present* (1985); Bruce Laurie, *Artisans into Workers: Labor in Nineteenth-Century America* (1989); Lawrence Levine, *Black Culture and Black Consciousness: Afro-American Folk Thought from Slavery to Freedom* (1977); Patricia Nelson Limerick, *The Legacy of Conquest: The Unbroken Past of the American West* (1987); Alessandra Lorini, *Rituals of Race: American Public Culture and the Search for Racial Democracy* (1999); J. Carroll Moody and Alice Kessler-Harris, eds., *Perspectives on American Labor History: The Problems of Synthesis* (1989); Charles R. Morris, *American Catholic* (1997); John G. Neihardt, *Black Elk Speaks* (1996); Kathy Piess, *Cheap Amusements: Working Women and Leisure in Turn-of-the-Century New York* (1986); Roy Rosenzweig, *Eight Hours for What We Will: Workers and Leisure in an Industrial City* (1983); Ted Ownby, *Subduing Satan: Religion, Recreation, and Manhood in the Rural South, 1865–1920* (1999); Richard White, *"It's Your Misfortune and None of My Own": A New History of the American West* (1991); and David Wishart, *An Unspeakable Sadness: The Dispossession of the Nebraska Indians* (1994).

Modern Ways, 1890–Present

There are no satisfactory overviews, but see David J. Singal, ed., *Modernist Culture in America* (1988), especially Singal's essay "Towards a Definition of American Modernism"; Warren Susman, *Culture as History: The Transformation of American Society in the Twentieth Century* (1984); Michael G. Kammen, *American Culture, American Tastes: Social Change and the 20th Century* (1990) and *The Tastes of Leisure: Popular Culture and Social Change in America* (1999); and Norman F. Cantor with Mindy Cantor, *The American Century: Varieties of Culture in Modern Times* (1998). Opinionated and provocative, the latter looks at high culture throughout the Western world. Eric Foner's *The Story of American Freedom* (1998), while examining the concept for the entirety of American history, is especially insightful for the modern era.

For the origins of modern ways, consider George Cotkin, *Reluctant Modernism: American Thought and Culture, 1880–1900* (1992); Nancy Cott, *The Grounding of Modern Feminism* (1987); Carl N. Degler, *In Search of Human Nature: The Decline and Revival of Darwinism in American Social Thought* (1991); Lewis Erenberg, *Steppin' Out: New York Nightlife and the Transformation of American Cluture* (1981); John Higham, "The Reorientation of American Culture in the 1890s," in Higham, ed., *Writing American History* (1970); John Kasson, *Amusing the Millions: Coney Island at the Turn of the Century* (1978); James T. Kloppenberg, *Uncertain Victory: Social Democracy and Progressivism in European and American Thought, 1870–1920* (1986); William Leach, *Land of Desire: Merchants, Power, and the Rise of a New American Culture* (1993); T. Jackson Lears, *No Place of Grace: Antimodernism and the Transformation of American Culture, 1880–1920* (1981); Henry F. May, *The End of American Innocence* (1959); Lary May, *Screening Out the Past: The Birth of Mass Culture and the Motion Picture Industry* (1980); David Nasaw, *Going Out: The Rise and Fall of Public Amusements* (1993); Dorothy Ross, *The Origin of American Social Science* (1991); Julie A. Reubin, *The Making of the Modern University* (1996); Cynthia Russett, *Darwin in America: The Intellectual Response, 1865–1912* (1976); Robert B. Westbrook, *John Dewey and American Democracy* (1991); Robert Wiebe, *The Search for Order, 1877–1920* (1967); and Oliver Zunz, *Why the American Century?* (1998) and *Making America Corporate, 1870–1920* (1990). Also examine the writings of such influential people of the day as Henry Adams, Jane Addams, Randolph Bourne, Charles Darwin, John Dewey, Charlotte Perkins Gilman, William James, Elizabeth Cady Stanton, and Thorstein Veblen.

Primary sources are an equally good way to look at modern culture from the 1920s to the 1960s. See for example the writings of Ruth Benedict, Malcolm Cowley, John Dewey, W. E. B. DuBois, Sigmund Freud, Joseph Wood Krutch, Walter Lippmann, Margaret Mead, Reinhold Niebuhr, George Santayana, and Edmund Wilson. Also see Charles Alexander, *Here the Country Lies: Nationalism and the Arts in the Twentieth Century* (1980); Beth Bailey, *From Front Porch to Back Seat: Courtship in Twentieth Century America* (1988); Christopher Brookeman, *American Culture and Society since the 1930s* (1984); Paul Carter, *The Twenties in America* (1968) and *Another Part of the Twenties* (1977), Lizabeth Cohen, *Making a New Deal: Industrial Workers in Chicago, 1919–1939* (1990); Paul Conkin, *The New Deal*, 2d. ed. (1975); Terry A. Cooney, *Balancing Acts: American Thought and Culture in the 1930s* (1995); Robert Crunden, *From Self to Society, 1919–1941* (1972); Ann Douglas, *Terrible Honesty: Mongrel Manhattan in the 1920s* (1995); Lynn Dumenil, *The Modern Temper: America in the 1920s* (1995); Lewis Erenberg, *Swingin' the Dream: Big Band Jazz and the Rebirth of American Culture* (1998); Conal Furay, *The Grass-Roots Mind in America: The American Sense of Absolutes* (1977); William Graebner, *The Age of Doubt: American Thought and Culture in the 1940s* (1990); Anthony Heilbut, *Exiled in Paradise: German Refugee Artists and Intellectuals in America from the 1930s to the Present* (1983); David Hollinger, "Ethnic Diversity, Cosmopolitanism, and the Emergence of the American Liberal Intelligentsia," in Hollinger, *In the American Province: Studies in the History and Historiography of Ideas* (1985); Nathan Huggins, *Harlem Renaissance* (1971); Joanne Meyerowitz, ed., *Not June Cleaver: Women and Gender in Postwar America, 1945–1960* (1994); Warren Susman, ed., *Culture and Commitment, 1929–1945* (1973), a source book; and Stephen J. Whitfield, *The Culture of the Cold War* (1991).

For modern ways since about the mid-twentieth century, consult the influential writings of Daniel Bell, Robert Bellah, Betty Friedan, Clifford Geertz, Will Herberg, Richard Hofstadter, Martin Luther King, Jr., Alfred Kinsey, Christopher Lasch, Russell Kirk, Margaret Mead, David Riesman, Richard Rorty, Susan Sontag, Benjamin Spock, Lionel Trilling, George Will, and Tom Wolfe. European writers who have particularly influenced the history of American ideas in recent times include Simone de Beauvoir, Michel Foucault, Claude Levi Strauss, Jean Paul Sartre, C. P. Snow, and E. P. Thompson. In addition, see James L. Baughman, *The Republic of Mass Culture: Journalism, Filmmaking, and Broadcasting in America since 1941* (1992); Paul S. Boyer, *By the Bomb's Early Light: American Thought and Culture at the Dawn of the Atomic Age* (1986, 1994); Taylor Branch, *Parting the Waters: America in the King Years* (1988); Howard Brick, *The Age of Contradiction: American Thought and Culture in the 1960s* (1998); David Brooks, *Bobos in Paradise: The New Upper Class and How They Got There* (2000); Joan Jacobs Brumberg, *The Body Project: An Intimate History of American Girls* (1997); Peter Clecak, *America's Quest for the Ideal Self: Dissent and Fulfillment in the 60s and 70s* (1983); Susan J. Douglas, *Where the Girls*

Are: Growing Up Female with the Mass Media (1994); Sara Evans, *Personal Politics: The Roots of Women's Liberation in the Civil Rights Movement and the New Left* (1979); David Farber, *The Age of Great Dreams: America in the 1960s* (1994); Thomas Frank and Matt Weiland, eds., *Commodify Your Dissent: The Business of Culture in the New Gilded Age* (1997); Mark Gerson, *The Neoconservative Vision: From the Cold War to the Culture Wars* (1996); David A. Hollinger, *Postethnic America: Beyond Multiculturalism* (1995); Robert D. Hunter, *Culture Wars: The Struggle to Define America* (1991); Andreas Huyssen, *After the Great Divide: Modernism, Mass Culture, Postmodernism* (1986); Arthur Marwick, *The Sixties: Cultural Revolution in Britain, France, Italy, and the United States* (1998); Elaine Tyler May, *Homeward Bound: American Families in the Cold War Era* (1988); Ruth Rosen, *The World Split Open: How the Modern Women's Movement Changed America* (2000); David Steigerwald, "The End of Culture," in his *The Sixties and the End of Modern America* (1975); Juan Williams, *Eyes on the Prize: America's Civil Rights Years, 1954–1965* (1988); and Robert Wuthnow, *The Restructuring of American Religion: Society and Faith since World War II* (1988).

PHOTO CREDITS

Chapter 1 P. 8, Interior of 1790 Congregational meetinghouse, Townshend, VT, Lee Snider/The Image Works; p. 10, 1830s woodcut of central Concord, MA, North Wind Picture Archives; p. 26, Quaker couple, Archive Photos.

Chapter 2 P. 34, An old Maryland manor house, North Wind Picture Archives; p. 42, African city of Benin in the seventeenth century, Corbis; p. 49, Pioneer log cabin, Virginia, Jenny Hager/The Image Works.

Chapter 3 P. 63, "Paying the Excise Man," P. Dawe, 1774, Metropolitan Museum of Art, NY; p. 71, Charles Willson Peale, "The Artist in His Museum," The Joseph Harrison, Jr., Collection, Pennsylvania Academy of the Fine Arts, Philadelphia; p. 77, Engraving of "Rights of Women" petition from *The Lady's Magazine & Repository of Entertaining Knowledge,* Library Company of Philadelphia; p. 84, Thomas Jefferson Rotunda, University of Virginia, Art Resource.

Chapter 4 P. 93, President-elect Jackson on His Way to Washington, D.C., North Wind Picture Archives; p. 96, A view of Broadway and Canal Street, 1836, collection of the New York Historical Society; p. 107, top, Gamble Plantation, Ellenton, FL, courtesy of the Florida Park Service; bottom, Slave quarters, Georgia, North Wind Picture Archives.

Chapter 5 P. 114, top, The Circuit Rider, courtesy of the Billy Graham Center Museum; bottom, Camp Meeting, courtesy of the Billy Graham Center Museum; p. 126, Frederick Douglass narrative title page, Bettmann/Corbis; p. 129, Susan B. Anthony and Elizabeth Cady Stanton, courtesy of Susan B. Anthony House.

Chapter 6 P. 137, From *The American Home,* 1869, Catherine Beecher and Harriet Beecher Stowe, General Research Division, New York Public Library; p. 144, Rhinebeck, NY, Victorian house, D. Chidester/The Image Works; p. 146, top, "Ungraceful Positions," an inventory of errors from "Hill's Manual of Social and Business Forms," courtesy of Strong Museum, Rochester, NY; bottom, "Gentility in the Parlor," an inventory of mended errors from "Hill's Manual of Social and Business Forms," courtesy of Strong Museum, Rochester, NY; p. 152, "Appleton's Journal," October 30, 1869, courtesy of the Making of America Project, www.moa.umdl.umich.edu.

Chapter 7 P. 164, Government boarding school, Pine Ridge Reservation, SD, 1891, Corbis; p. 169, Immigrant working-class saloon, courtesy of the author; p. 172, Italian feast day, Chicago, Italian American Collection, University Library, University of Illinois at Chicago; p. 178, African Methodist Episcopal Church, courtesy of the Billy Graham Center Museum.

Chapter 8 P. 187, 1899–1900 fashion models, Marshall Field's, courtesy of the Marshall Field's Archive; p. 191, 1899–1900 Bungalow House, Nebraska State Historical Society; p. 195, Midland Beach, Staten Island, NY, 1898, New York/Archive Photos; p. 199, Gibson Girl riding a bicycle, North Wind Picture Archives.

Chapter 9 P. 213, 1920s flappers, Underwood & Underwood/Corbis; p. 215, "What Sex Brings to the Race" poster,

1922, courtesy of the University of Minnesota Archives; p. 220, Governor's Mansion, Colonial Williamsburg, David Muench/Corbis; p. 226, Norman Rockwell's "Four Freedoms," War of Information poster, The Norman Rockwell Museum; p. 234, Johnson & Johnson "Giant Baby" ad, 1947, courtesy of Johnson & Johnson.

Chapter 10 P. 241, Dr. Martin Luther King, Jr., and the 1963 March on Washington, Hulton-Deutsch/Corbis; p. 244, Equal Rights Amendment demonstration, Oct. 7, 1970, Bettmann/Corbis; p. 251, Hippies in a New Orleans park, 1971, Vince Streano/Corbis; p. 261, Church sign, courtesy of Heather Furnas.

INDEX